Parker
march 1990

Interdisciplinary perspectives on modern history

Editors
Robert Fogel and Stephan Thernstrom

Ethnic Differences

Ethnic Differences

Schooling and Social Structure among the Irish, Italians, Jews, and Blacks in an American City, 1880–1935

JOEL PERLMANN

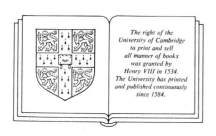

The right of the
University of Cambridge
to print and sell
all manner of books
was granted by
Henry VIII in 1534.
The University has printed
and published continuously
since 1584.

CAMBRIDGE UNIVERSITY PRESS

Cambridge

New York   Port Chester   Melbourne   Sydney

Published by the Press Syndicate of the University of Cambridge
The Pitt Building, Trumpington Street, Cambridge CB2 1RP
40 West 20th Street, New York, NY 10011, USA
10 Stamford Road, Oakleigh, Melbourne 3166, Australia

First published 1988
First paperback edition 1989

Printed in the United States of America

Library of Congress Cataloging-in-Publication Data
Perlmann, Joel.
Ethnic differences : schooling and social structure among the
Irish, Italians, Jews, and Blacks in an American city, 1880–1935
Joel Perlmann.
p.   cm. – (Interdisciplinary perspectives on modern history)
Bibliography: p.
ISBN 0-521-35093-X hard covers   ISBN 0-521-38975-5 (pbk)
1. Minorities – Education – Rhode Island – Providence – History – 19th
century.   2. Minorities – Education – Rhode Island – Providence –
History – 20th century.   3. Education, Urban – Rhode Island –
Providence – History – 19th century.   4. Education, Urban – Rhode
Island – Providence – History – 20th century.   5. Providence (R.I.) –
Social conditions.   I. Title.   II. Series.
LC3733.P76P47   1988
371.97′009745′2–dc19   87-34207   CIP

British Library Cataloguing in Publication Data
Perlmann, Joel
Ethnic differences: schooling and social structure among
the Irish, Italians, Jews, and Blacks in an American city,
1880–1935. – (Interdisciplinary perspectives
on modern history).
1. Rhode Island. Providence. Ethnic
minorities. Socioeconomic status. Role,
1880–1935 of schools
I. Title
305.8′009745′2

ISBN 0-521-35093-X hard covers
ISBN 0-521-38975-5 paperback

To my father and mother,
Moshe and Ida Perlmann

Contents

vii

Acknowledgments

This book is the latest and most sustained product of a project I began in 1974. The project quite simply could never have been undertaken without considerable financial support to collect data. That support was provided in a succession of grants by the National Institute of Education and the Center for the Study of Metropolitan Problems of the National Institute of Mental Health. I am particularly grateful to Lana Muraskin, then at N.I.E., and to Eliot Liebow and Richard Wakefield, then at N.I.M.H. After the data were prepared, the analysis was supported by a series of junior faculty grants awarded by the Harvard Graduate School of Education from funds made available by the Spencer Foundation, and finally by a National Endowment for the Humanities Research Fellowship. I am also indebted to the Harvard Graduate School of Education for a sabbatical and for virtually unlimited computer time, not to mention less tangible benefits.

In the earliest stages of my research the Joint Center for Urban Studies of M.I.T. and Harvard provided me with a Samuel Stouffer Fellowship and served for a half-dozen years as the institutional and physical base from which the project operated. Since then, I have enjoyed the complete privacy and convenience of a study at Radcliffe's Hilles Library, as well as the help of its staff.

The major library collections on Rhode Island history – the Brown University Library, the Providence Public Library, and the incomparable Rhode Island Historical Society Library – were mined endlessly. However, the project rested most heavily on manuscript records – particularly the schedules of the Rhode Island State Censuses at the Rhode Island State Record Center and the school records of Providence kept at the Central Record Office of the Providence School Department, the Classical High School, the Rhode Island College Archives, LaSalle Academy, St. Xavier's Academy, and the School Office of the Roman Catholic Diocese of Providence. In most of these institutions several research assistants and I worked daily for months, and in some for years. The public and Catholic school authorities deserve enormous credit for deciding, once proper guarantees of confidentiality had been provided, that the use of the records was to be allowed. May they serve as a model to others! The staffs of these school offices deserve special thanks; it was not their job to facilitate my work, but they did so consistently. I am particularly grateful to Ethel Borkowski, then Chief Clerk of the Central Record Office at the Providence School Committee.

Research assistants, students or recent graduates of local universities, spent thousands of hours meticulously collecting a staggering amount of material. Although too many contributed time, energy and goodwill to thank them individually here, I must single out Elizabeth Ryan, who worked with the project throughout her four years at Harvard, collecting data and programming computers. Mary Hyde carried out the initial stages of the computer programming alone – the many runs required to prepare the raw data before any analysis was possible – and then kindly helped students to take over much of that work.

Many scholars discussed my work with me and read part or all of the entire manuscript. It is a great pleasure to thank at last Theodore Brown, who offered encouragement and advice at the earliest stages of the project, as well as David Cohen, whose enthusiasm for this work, and good sense over many years, made a great difference. Others who offered counsel and encouragement, particularly in the early years of the project, include James Davis, Oscar Handlin, Christopher Jencks, Carl Kaestle, Michael Katz, Lee Rainwater, Peter Temin, and Charles Tilly. Later, Gary Gerstle, Noel Ignatiev, Jerome Karabel, Joseph Maxwell, James Sanders, and Roger Waldinger commented thoughtfully on what came to be chapters of this book. Stanley Engerman, Michael Katz, Stephen Lehmann, Robert Margo, Daniel Rodgers, Stephan Thernstrom, and Maris Vinovskis read the entire manuscript and offered a great many helpful suggestions. John Bound taught me the subtleties of statistical techniques exploited throughout the analysis (OLS and logit multiple regression analyses), answering hundreds of incessant questions with patience and discernment; he also commented on each chapter of the text. At Cambridge University Press, Frank Smith and Louise Calabro Gruendel expertly and efficiently supervised the editing and production of the book. My debt to Stephan Thernstrom, who earlier served as the chairman of my doctoral committee at Harvard, is unique. He has helped me selflessly and enthusiastically from the earliest formulation of a dissertation topic to the last draft of this book. The extent of my debt to his scholarship will be clear in some measure from the text and the notes; those, however, do not record his many acts of kind assistance during each of the past fourteen years. The efforts of all these individuals have made the book better than it would otherwise have been; needless to say, I alone bear the responsibility for the product.

My son Noam, now five years old, has lived with this book since his birth; and he surely made it better too, sometimes protesting the time it stole from him with a freshness that restored my spirit, sometimes accepting its demands with an understanding I found mystifying. Finally, throughout the years I have been engaged in this work, discussions about innumerable points with my wife Rivka, and her careful readings, have improved the intellectual quality of the entire endeavor; but that's the least of it.

Cambridge, Massachusetts, 1988   Joel Perlmann

Introduction

This book is about ethnic differences in American history – differences in schooling and in economic attainments. Dramatic differences in the school achievements of ethnic groups regularly strike observers. The current fascination with the educational achievements of Asian-Americans is typical. The *New York Times* recently pointed out that "although Asian-Americans make up only 2.1 percent of the population of the United States, they are surging into the nation's best colleges like a tidal wave," constituting, in 1985, 11% of the freshmen at Harvard, 21% at M.I.T., and a quarter or more at several of the campuses of the University of California.[1] Jews are almost as greatly overrepresented at the higher levels of education, as they have been for many decades.[2] Blacks and Hispanics, on the other hand, continue to be seriously underrepresented in higher education. The proportion of college graduates among blacks twenty-five to thirty-four years of age is about half that among whites (12.6% vs. 24.9% in 1982). It is lower still (9.7%) among Hispanics. Italians, until recently, were also considerably underrepresented.[3] Ethnic differences in schooling were equally pronounced in the years of massive immigration to the United States. In Providence, Rhode Island, in 1880, one Yankee boy in four attended high school. No more than one Irish boy in fourteen did so. In 1915, the children of immigrant Jews were more likely to reach high school than were the children of Yankees – and more than four times as likely to do so as the children of Italian immigrants.

Patterns of economic attainment also differed dramatically.[4] Blacks were disastrously less likely to improve their lot than were whites. Moreover, in 1880, the Irish advance was rapid only by comparison with the progress of blacks. During 1915–25, Jewish upward mobility was distinctly more rapid than that of other immigrants.

Ethnic differences in American social life have fascinated observers for centuries: differences in uses of leisure, family size and structure, crime, residence, religious life, labor organization, political affiliation, bigotry toward others – differences in every aspect of life. Ethnic differences in regard to schooling and economic attainment have held an especially important place. The process of economic attainment has been crucial to the absorption of immigrants, and of blacks after

1

bondage, into American life; and schooling has been perceived to be an important determinant of economic attainment, as well as an important agent of immigrant and black cultural change. Moreover, most schooling is public and is therefore an important subject of public policy. The public, indeed, supports schooling because it is meant to contribute to social equality. Large ethnic differences in school achievements, then, have often led to public anxiety about the effectiveness of schools and about the characteristics of the ethnic groups involved.[5]

How, then, did the patterns of schooling differ among immigrant groups? How did their patterns of economic attainment vary? What role did schooling play in the economic attainments of different ethnic groups? How different were the patterns of schooling and economic attainment among blacks as compared with those of various immigrant groups? How did particular ethnic patterns of schooling differ for boys and girls? How, finally, are we to explain these ethnic differences? This book addresses these questions, drawing on rich new evidence from historical records, whereas little or no direct evidence had existed before.

These questions take on special interest not merely because ethnic differences have been important in American history, but because they continue to be important today – in policy discussions about schools and about social welfare generally. Substitute the blacks or Hispanics for the Irish in the preceding examples, or the Asians for the Russian Jews in other examples, and the debates that these competing explanations generate – for all the transformations in American life – reverberate through popular culture, public policy, and the social sciences. Consider, too, differences between the blacks and the nineteenth-century Irish. If the Irish, notwithstanding the pain of their initial absorption, moved ahead more easily, what explains the difference? The historical record provides no sure guide to contemporary issues; the most important social conditions – as well as our views of legitimate social intervention – may have changed. But that record does provide a context, a sense of perspective with depth, in which to view these contemporary discussions. Thus, whereas that record provides an understanding of how groups came to be where they are, the sense that it has vital contemporary meaning as well is not illusory. Nearly all Americans have confronted the challenge of explaining ethnic differences. The challenge fascinates not only because of the importance of American ethnicity in the past and present but also because it involves interpreting the sources of motivations and behavior, an effort at the heart of historical study and of the social sciences.

Our focus is on the years 1880–1935. These particular dates are somewhat arbitrary; a change of a decade on either end would matter little. That era, however, encompassed the tremendous growth of urban industrial America, fueled by a massive influx of immigrants – larger than any before or since. It was also a period in which schooling became far more important in the life of most Americans, in which the high school developed from an elite institution to one enrolling the majority of children. At least partly for this reason, the socioeconomic attainments of individuals became more dependent on extended schooling.

Providence, Rhode Island, from which our special evidence comes, was one of America's important cities in 1880. By 1925 it had been outstripped in size by many others, but it remained a relatively large urban center. Its population included a great number of Irish immigrants. Beginning in the 1890s, large numbers of people from southern and eastern Europe also settled in the city, Italians in particular, but also many Russian Jews. Blacks had long lived in Providence, but there, as elsewhere in the northern cities of the era, they constituted only a small proportion of the entire population. Still, blacks were sufficiently numerous for us to be confident that they displayed behavior patterns similar to those that emerged in many other communities and to study these patterns intensively. These four groups – the Irish, Italians, Russian Jews, and blacks – constitute the special subjects of this study. The Irish were one of the two largest immigrant groups in nineteenth-century America (the other being the Germans, who settled mainly in other regions). The Irish posed the first great challenge to urban America's powers of absorption. They constituted a massive impoverished population, and they seemed to act in glaringly different ways from those of the native-born Americans, many of whose families had already lived in the United States for generations. Not least striking were the high rates at which they dropped out of school at early ages. The Italians, who followed the Irish, constituted a second such population and were the largest group in the later immigration. The Jews presented a vivid contrast, obtaining more schooling and advancing more rapidly into middle-class positions. The patterns of schooling among northern blacks differed from those for whites in subtle and complex ways. Black economic attainment, on the other hand, differed in a very simple way: Far greater proportions of blacks remained impoverished. These groups, then, cover a range of important patterns of schooling and advancement: an earlier example and a later example of low scholastic achievement by an immigrant group whose absorption constituted a major social problem; the classic example of high achievement in schooling and in economic pursuits; and the case of America's most abused ethnic minority, whose adjustment to life in northern cities would become a central feature of American history in the twentieth century. The period covered is one for which adequate data on the issues had been unavailable until recently. Nevertheless, interpretations concerning the later histories of these groups, as well as the relationships among ethnicity, schooling, and economic attainment, often have turned on the patterns of adjustment that occurred precisely in these years.

In the course of considering these relationships, this book touches on other issues of ethnic distinctiveness as well. It considers, for example, sharp Irish and Italian differences in reliance on Catholic schools, as well as differences among the Irish in regard to academic performance in public and Catholic schools. In the case of the Jews, an extended discussion of the immigrant generation's special position in the economic structure of the city is crucial for comprehending patterns of schooling and work among their children. Finally, in the case of the blacks, the discussion intensively explores aspects of family structure, family economy, and child labor.

Any consideration of ethnic behavior quickly leads from description to explanation: Why did groups differ? Efforts at such description and explanation have had a long and ugly history in American intellectual life, in popular notions, and in the social sciences: Ethnic stereotypes were cavalierly advanced, and the sources of presumed differences were stated or assumed to be somehow inherent in the nature of the group, perhaps in its biological makeup. These sorts of explanations continue to haunt policy debates about race differences, dark corners of social science, and surely much popular opinion as well. This study ignores them.

The range of other efforts to explain these ethnic differences – efforts that are worthy of more careful consideration here – is not terribly large. Yet these explanations imply such different ways of thinking about sources of behavior in general, and about sources of differences among ethnic groups in particular, that they have led to intense engagement and exploration. For example, it makes a great deal of difference whether the Irish enrolled in school less often than Yankees because they were poorer (and all poor people enrolled less often), because their children were treated with contempt in the schools, because they knew that regardless of their schooling the jobs open to the well-educated among the Yankees were not open to them, because their cultural past did not include familiarity with universal schooling, or because their cultural past led them to be fatalistic, compared with the Yankees, and to take less stock in efforts to improve their lot. Variations on these explanations are easy to elaborate: Perhaps, even at comparable levels of family wealth, the Irish enrolled less often in school, for they had larger families than the Yankees, and so the same amount of wealth did not go as far. Perhaps, too, Yankee schoolteachers treated Irish children with contempt and maligned their religion, thereby discouraging attendance.

As this comparison of the Irish and Yankees suggests, several factors might explain these ethnic differences. Moreover, the adequate explanation surely varies from case to case; after all, Italians differed from Irish for different reasons than Irish differed from Yankees. Nevertheless, the kinds of explanations advanced are generally familiar and relatively few in number. When, and to where, migrants came could matter a great deal. It would, for example, be foolish to compare the Irish of mid-nineteenth-century Boston and the Japanese of twentieth-century California without attention to the two social contexts. Yet even during one time period and in one place, ethnic differences in behavior often were substantial. These are the sorts of ethnic differences considered in this book.

Typically, arguments advanced to explain ethnic differences in one time and place have focused on (1) the pre-migration history of an ethnic group and the conditions of migration, (2) the extent of discrimination the group faced in the new environment, and (3) the group's position in the economy and class structure there.[6]

The pre-migration history of each group may involve many factors relevant to later adjustment – factors as varied as the level of literacy, the exposure to European socialism, the sex ratio among the migrants, and the extent of return migration. Nevertheless, two characteristics of the pre-migration background have figured especially prominently in explanations of ethnic behavior. The occupational skills of migrants, which resulted from their positions in the social structure of the country of origin, surely affected the later history of each group in America. On the other hand, various sorts of cultural attributes may have mattered too – differences in beliefs, attitudes, habits, and values.[7] The most common examples concern the nature of each group's work ethic and its attitude toward learning and schools. But other examples of presumed cultural attributes can be cited. Many pertain to family, children, or gender roles: attitudes toward employment of women, especially of wives, attitudes toward the education of girls, the notion that children should work and contribute their wages to the family economy, the strength and character of family ties of all sorts. Others concern community and market relationships: the concept of a just price for basic foods and notions of acceptable forms of popular protest to ensure the preservation of that price, the legitimacy of traditional organizations regulating business activity. Still others involve a world-view, or an attitude toward life, such as a fatalistic view of the world. These cultural attributes usually are thought to have had their source, in turn, in the economic and social structures of the countries of origin and in the positions that migrants had formerly occupied in those structures. The source of such cultural attributes might also lie in religion or other cultural heritages less directly tied to the pre-migration economy and social structure. At one extreme, these cultural attributes seem to be the stuff of ethnic stereotypes, at the other, the findings of anthropologists, social psychologists, and historians. In any case, a great deal of ink has been used in the argument over how much these groups differed in the cultural attributes they brought to America, and over how the differences in such attributes actually influenced their behavior.

The extent of discrimination and the ways in which it mattered surely varied from group to group as well. The issue is not the existence of discrimination, but whether or not it was leveled especially strongly against particular groups, and with what effects. This topic, of course, is crucial to an understanding of the black experience.

The class position of an ethnic group in the American social structure was itself a function of the pre-migration and migration history of the group and of the extent of discrimination against it, as well as of employment opportunities in the particular local economy. Nevertheless, once the migrant group had been situated in the new class structure, that class position itself surely explains much of the group's behavior.

With the help of such explanations, ethnic differences are understood to be the results of social processes that have had long histories. These explanations therefore tend to "demystify" ethnicity, to avoid treating it as a primordial, *sui generis* source of social divisions.[8] Nevertheless, that demystification is but the first step toward understanding. The second involves determining the specific manner in which these general factors – the pre-migration heritage, discrimination, and the place of the migrants in the new class structure – operated, and interacted, in the history of a given ethnic group. It also involves determining the relative importance of each factor.

This last point is especially crucial. Observers have disagreed sharply over the relative importance of factors creating particular ethnic patterns. Recent work on ethnicity in America provides an especially vivid example. In 1981, two books appeared, both seeking to explain the sources of ethnic differences in behavior and both intended as general syntheses for the intelligent lay reader: Stephen Steinberg's *The Ethnic Myth* and Thomas Sowell's *Ethnic America*. Both were widely, prominently, and often angrily reviewed. Both have been in print continuously since. Sowell argued that pre-migration cultural attributes, far more than class background or discrimination (even in the case of blacks), determined ethnic group experiences in the United States. By contrast, Steinberg argued that the social-class position of the migrants was by far the most important influence on their behavior, that pre-migration cultural attributes have been drastically overrated as sources of ethnic differences and that they rarely are necessary to explain the truly basic patterns of group behavior. Actual jobrelated skills, on the other hand, may indeed have mattered greatly, because these helped determine the class position of the migrants in the American social structure.[9]

These disagreements concerning the importance of the premigration cultural heritage generate especially strong feelings. One reason they do concerns the perceived implications for social action, particularly by the state, on behalf of ethnic groups whose members are mostly poor. If cultural factors explain poverty, the rationale for public intervention appears weaker to many people than if that poverty is attributed to discrimination or to the class structure. A second reason that discussions of cultural attributes generate strong feelings concerns self-congratulation, patronizing of others, self-righteousness, and apparent or real judgments of value that creep into the discussions – in the popular culture and quite frequently among social scientists. Those who stress that the cultures of some groups were conducive to advancement in the American milieu sometimes seem to rank those cultures high on some absolute scale of value – blurring the distinction between values conducive to upward mobility and "better" values.

Uncertainty about the relative importance of factors that produce ethnic differences is as central among American historians as it is among social scientists – even when the terminology and concerns at first seem quite removed from those of contemporary social science.[10] The issue, after all, bears directly on the relationship between class and ethnicity – which John Higham has called "one of the three or four key problems in American social history."[11]

A striking, and crucial, example of how these themes pervade the writing of American social history is found in an immensely influential essay by Herbert Gutman: "Work, Culture, and Society in Industrializing America, 1815–1919." There the concern with the factors explaining ethnic distinctiveness lies just beneath the surface.[12] Gutman's essay was not merely influential as a source of ideas; it was also paradigmatic: Many others have tried to analyze the connections between pre-migration culture and social structure in particular communities. Gutman was concerned with the recurrent clash between the needs of industrial society and the presumed preindustrial cultures of immigrants. His central theme was the influence of preindustrial (and hence generally pre-migration) culture on the work habits, family patterns, and community organization of workers and how that preindustrial culture inevitably shaped the nature of their conflicts with industrial capital as well. He tended to emphasize, it is true, traits that all preindustrial workers shared, rather than differences among pre-migration cultures. Nevertheless, his approach certainly could encourage an evaluation of the influences of specific ethnic cultures. Not surprisingly, part of the criticism of Gutman's work, raised by other historians such as Daniel Rodgers, David Montgomery, and Lawrence T. McDonnell, has concerned the importance he attributed to preindustrial culture – in contrast to the structural locations of American workers.[13]

Clearly, American ethnicity must be understood in the context of European and American capitalism and the respective class structures. Economic development in Europe – industrialization, commercial agriculture, improved transportation, and population increase – impelled millions (peasant groups, in particular, but others as well) to migrate. At the same time, American economic growth created jobs that could attract migrants. The nature of the American opportunities and the migrants' work skills ensured that most migrants, especially those in the cities, would become industrial workers, and their class position, in turn, strongly influenced their subsequent experience.

Much of the behavior of immigrant workers, then, can be understood as working-class behavior.[14] But can immigrant behavior be fully explained by the position of the immigrants in the American class structure? Can the immigrant industrial workers or immigrant shopkeepers be adequately understood simply as industrial workers or shopkeepers, their ethnic pasts being of little consequence? Obviously, some sorts of behaviors differed from group to group: patterns of language loyalty, aspects of religious observance, some leisure patterns, and choices of cuisine, for example. But what of behaviors that are more intimately related to the class position of the workers? Did such behaviors also differ in important ways between native workers and immigrant workers, and among immigrant groups? How and how much did pre-migration cultural attributes affect the behavior of the migrants?

The simplest response, and a sensible one, is that cultural attributes and the structural situation in which migrants find themselves interact, that it is foolish to think that either exists in a vacuum.[15] This formulation, however, does not resolve what has mattered so much to observers, namely, the relative power of the interacting forces. Just how much did groups differ in cultural outlook, and just how strongly did differences in outlook show themselves in social behavior relevant to class position? Although culture obviously must have interacted with social structure, just how quickly did the process of cultural change really occur? The interaction of culture and social structure allows for a range of answers to such questions, answers that might well differ from group to group and in different situations.

Thus far, I have focused on the relationship between social-class position and pre-migration cultural heritage, because that issue pervades the study of ethnicity. It also runs through the chapters that follow. No single, simple answer – for example, that such pre-migration cultural attributes were paramount or were trivial – will be found, however. The advantage of an intensive look, based on rich data, is that the conclusions are more modulated and more specific to the histories of the particular groups. The exploration of cultural influences, rather than a single conclusion concerning their influence, is one common theme in the following chapters. In exploring that theme, this book, though it deals with behavior (with school and job patterns), is also concerned with cultural history, with the history of popular ideas, attitudes, and values. However, it does not deal with cultural constructs for their own sake; it examines their strength in affecting behavior.

There are other sources of ethnic behavior besides class and pre-migration culture, and the chapters that follow consider these as well. Indeed, the distinction between class and culture as sources of behavior is similar to a second distinction, between class and discrimination, crucial to the history of blacks. Behavior that can be adequately understood as a result of black poverty (for whites in the same economic position would have behaved the same way) can be distinguished from behavior that is directly shaped by discrimination.[16] Finally, still other differences among groups that cannot simply be subsumed under the heading of class, pre-migration culture, or discrimination (family size, or the prevalence of illiteracy, for example) may have influenced American ethnic behavior as well.

Finally, of course, this study is concerned throughout with social class itself as an explanation for ethnic behavior. Assessing other explanations of ethnic patterns – discrimination, loyalty to Irish Catholicism, the rate of remigration to Italy, or pre-migration cultural heritage, for example – necessitates an awareness of the extent to which the class locations of families constrained and shaped their behaviors. Moreover, the simplest, most common, and often most forceful explanation of ethnic differences in behavior is that groups occupied different social-class positions (as a result of the processes of immigration mentioned earlier) and acted as others in comparable class positions did. To what extent, then, did ethnic differences in schooling and economic attainment reduce to social-class differences between groups? This study explores that question intensively.

Much of the uncertainty about the extent of ethnic distinctiveness, as well as disagreement about its sources, stems from the paucity of adequate evidence. Published records dating from the period rarely address questions in the way one would like, so that establishing basic patterns of schooling or economic attainment is difficult, and determining the factors responsible for those patterns is impossible. The relevant unpublished information on the social origins, school experiences, and later social destinations of individuals has remained untapped. Consequently, historians of American education typically have described programs to Americanize the immigrant, or policies leveled against blacks in the schools, or community reactions to these. Most, however, have been able to explore the relationship between patterns of school achievement and the social origins of children to only a very limited extent. Similarly, historians of the past two decades have studied the social-mobility patterns of Americans, including those of immigrants and blacks, and have studied numerous other features of daily life. However, they typically have lacked the data that would allow them to study in any depth the interconnections among social origins, schooling, and social destinations – the interconnections at the heart of all studies of contemporary social-mobility patterns.[17]

It became possible to undertake this study when several kinds of unpublished records, all pertaining to Providence, Rhode Island, were linked together for the first time. Census records provided a wealth of information on each child's origins: race, place of birth for the child as well as for both parents and grandparents, parents' occupations, number of siblings, whether or not both parents were present, address, and so forth. School records provided comparable detailed information on each child's education: schools and programs in which enrolled, grades received in courses, and years of school completed. Finally, city directories indicated the occupations of males in later life. These sources provided information on some 12,000 sampled individuals. The research design is described briefly in Chapter 1 and in more detail in the Appendix. These citywide samples reflect the experiences of the young people in Providence over the course of half a century. Social historians are now familiar with the census records and city directories; they have been mined repeatedly during the past two decades. However, the school records have never before been used so extensively. The combination of the school records with the other sources justifies the hope of breaking new ground, for the Providence data allow us to explore many possible connections among family background, schooling, and later social destinations of individuals. The information is extraordinary not only in comparison with previously available historical records but also in comparison with material on contemporary life available to sociologists or economists.

The uniqueness of this new evidence and its direct relevance to questions of ethnic differences in behavior have had a good deal to do with the nature of the presentation. This book is centrally concerned with aspects of the history of education in America; yet, in order to focus squarely on the questions formulated earlier and on the new evidence, I have skirted many topics that historians of education would typically explore, touching on them only in a few pages of the first chapter. These topics, which bear tangentially or directly on the way immigrants or blacks were treated, include the changing administrative structure of urban schools; legislation regulating schools, truancy, and child labor; the plethora of new theories of instruction and new programs; the textbooks; the strengthening of teacher preparation; and so forth. Also, they include the intellectual, social, and political context in which these institutional developments occurred – for example, struggles among social groups for political control of schools and calls for more schooling to preserve social order in the lower classes, to foster social mobility, to assimilate the immigrant, to provide mental discipline or manual training, to make the city proud of its schools, or to attract new residents. Similarly, I have reviewed only briefly the broad contours of the migration history of the individual groups – why they left, how they came, and so forth.

Focusing squarely on the sample data also means relying on quantitative evidence. The material available does not lend itself to a full description of a particular individual's experiences. Too little is known about each person to reward such an approach – quite apart from the questionable representativeness of isolated examples. Rather, the power of the evidence comes from our ability to see trends common among large numbers of individuals – trends that stand out despite the relatively small amount known about each person. Some readers are impatient with quantitative analysis. I hope they will nonetheless find the results of this analysis intriguing. For example, the children of Irish immigrants initially entered high school much more rarely than did Yankees from the same social class, but they entered at comparable rates in later decades. The sons and daughters of Italian immigrants performed equally well in their grammar school course work (as judged by their grades), but the sons were nearly twice as likely as the daughters to reach high school. Among the household heads of the city, one in five was self-employed; among the Russian Jewish household heads, seven in ten were. In the nineteenth century, the ability to read and write was far less prevalent among black adults who had come to Providence from the South than among other city residents – but far more prevalent among these blacks than among others the same age who had remained in the South. Such findings cry out for interpretation, of course, but they can be found in the first place only in the quantitative record.

A few paragraphs of the text explain briefly the logic of the quantitative techniques I have used. But the text can be read without these brief descriptions. Indeed, it can even be read without its many tables. The substance of the discussion will still stand out clearly. At the same time, I hope the descriptions and the tables are clear, so that the reader with no particular interest in quantitative materials and no training in quantitative methods can easily comprehend them (those desiring more detail about data and methods will find it in the notes and Appendix).

The Providence data set, for all its richness, will not permit us to explore all possible sources of ethnic distinctiveness with equal confidence. The data sometimes permit us to proceed further than one might have thought possible at first glance. But in the end, some hypotheses about ethnic differences can be addressed more firmly than others. I have tried to be as explicit as possible about alternative explanations of ethnic differences and about just how far they can be assessed with empirical data of any kind. Indeed, I hope that marking the limits of what I believe can be resolved will help to make discussions of American ethnicity more meaningful. Perhaps, too, others will find ways to press beyond those limits.

1 Background: The City, Schooling, and Social Structure

1.1. Providence and its schools

Providence had been one of colonial America's earliest settlements; by the time of the Revolution it had also become one of the larger settlements. The town functioned then as a commercial center for the surrounding agricultural region and as a relatively important port. However, the real growth of Providence came with the industrialization of Rhode Island in the early nineteenth century. The city evolved into the commercial and financial center for the textile-mill towns of northern Rhode Island. Moreover, the city's own industries played an important part of the region's transformation.[1]

Providence's industries were varied. Textiles never dominated there to the extent that they did in the nearby mill towns. Cotton mills and especially woolen mills were indeed numerous in the city and, by the late nineteenth century, large. However, by that time Providence was also the national center for the production of inexpensive jewelry. A jewelry firm could be started with a relatively small investment, and scores were. A related industry, the manufacture of silver and gold products, also involved some small firms, but these were overshadowed by one giant, the nationally known Gorham plant. The manufacture of base-metal products also captured major shares of industrial capital and labor. Several giant firms dominated the foundries and machine shops: the Nicholson File Company, the American Screw Company, Browne and Sharpe's machine-tool factory, and the Corliss steam-engine works. Finally, a wide range of other industries, though much less important than those already mentioned, together accounted for a substantial share of manufacturing activity: rubber products, soap, chemicals, textile dyes, and a host of others.[2]

The population growth that accompanied industrialization was dramatic. At the time of the Revolution, the inhabitants of the city numbered some 5,300. By 1830 the population stood at nearly 17,000, by 1860 at 50,000, by 1880 at 104,000. The city's population continued to grow almost as rapidly until the second decade of the twentieth century: In 1900 it included 175,000 individuals, and in 1910 there were 224,000. Thereafter, the rate of growth was much slower. There

13

were 237,000 people in Providence in 1920 and 253,000 in 1930, but no further increase at all between 1930 and 1940. In part, the deceleration and eventual cessation of population growth was due to expansion of the suburbs at the expense of the central city. But the increasing vulnerability of Rhode Island industries to competition, in particular the vulnerability of the textile industries, the cessation of free immigration, and the catastrophic impact of the Great Depression eventually halted a century of industrial expansion. In so doing, they also played an important part in halting population growth.[3]

Providence never became one of the country's giant cities; there were few such places. In 1900, only six American cities had a population of over half a million. Rather, Providence was one of the relatively large urban centers. It was the twentieth largest city in 1880 and in 1900, and it was still the twenty-seventh largest in 1920.[4]

From a few blocks on the eastern bank of the Providence River, the city had spread out in all directions, but especially westward. The downtown business center, the industrial areas, and the working-class and immigrant neighborhoods (composed, typically, of two-, three-, and four-story buildings) dominated the physical character of the city. But in addition, the city always included a substantial concentration of prosperous and well-known families on the old east-side streets near Brown University, and at the outskirts of some of the built-up areas, residences resembled suburban dwellings. On the other hand, some of the contiguous towns, especially Pawtucket, resembled extensions of the central city, rather than suburbs in any real sense.[5]

The population growth came mostly from migration – and from immigration. By 1880, some 27% of the residents had been born abroad. A majority of these immigrants were from Ireland, and nearly all the rest had come from England or Scotland or from French or English Canada. By 1900, Italians, eastern European Jews, and other immigrants from southern and eastern Europe were also numerous. Finally, the city included a black community that numbered 5,700 in 1920; it accounted for roughly 2% of the city's population throughout the years 1880–1925.[6]

The evolution of the Providence schools was, of course, closely linked to the city's changing character. During the colonial era, schooling had been primarily a private endeavor. Many small primary schools had been founded, as well as academies of quite varied stature and duration, and a college (which was to become Brown University). After 1800, some schools were supported primarily at public expense, but even these required that students pay for their textbooks and for some other expenses, such as heating the buildings. These public schools, to judge by their stagnant enrollment and by the numbers that continued to attend private institutions, were not particularly popular. The state made provision for the support of truly free schools in 1828, and a series of reforms between then and the mid-1840s culminated in what can be clearly identified as a public school system. A School Committee and a Superintendent of Schools presided over schools differentiated into primary, intermediate, and grammar levels, and in 1843 the first public high school was opened.[7]

The school system established by the 1840s still existed in its essentials four decades later, although the grades were more precisely demarcated, and expanding enrollments had required many more school buildings. Indeed, by 1880, Providence supported a well-established urban school system of considerable dimensions. Some 417 students were enrolled in the single public high school, 3,552 in eleven grammar schools, and 8,207 in seventy-two primary and intermediate schools.[8]

Most parents were sending their children to school for at least a few years by then. Thus, in 1880, 93% of all ten-year-old children attended school, but only 42% of the fifteen-year-olds did so.[9] These patterns of school attendance were not the product of legal compulsion. Halfhearted efforts to regulate the employment of children had begun decades earlier, and the first of many legislative efforts requiring children of certain ages to attend school were enacted in the early 1880s, but, as the School Committee's truant officer would later recall, enforcement had been "difficult and lax" before the mid-1890s. Even then the law covered only children under age ten and allowed these to work, too, so long as they attended school eighty days each year. Although the provisions were amended almost annually, more aggressive legislation came mostly after the turn of the century. In any case, the city's single truant officer could hardly have compelled attendance in a city of well over 100,000.[10]

The Providence High School of 1880 included Classical, English and Science, and Girls Departments. The first concentrated on Greek and Latin. The second, restricted to boys, offered English, mathematics, science, modern history, and American government. It also offered a very few courses we might today call vocational, such as commercial arithmetic. Nearly all girls enrolled in the Girls Department, which included courses similar to those in the English and Science Department, but also placed some emphasis on languages. During the last two decades of the nineteenth century, enrollment pressures at the high school forced consideration of new public secondary-level institutions. At the same time, beliefs about the purposes of high schools were changing. The result was experimentation with a range of programs, particularly of a vocational nature.

By the early years of the twentieth century, the single public high school of the nineteenth century had been replaced by four institutions. The Classical Department was one; the old English and Science and Girls Departments were combined into a second. Classical was always identified with preparatory work for college. However, as college admission requirements were transformed, especially in the second decade of the new century, Classical High came to offer more and more courses other than the classical languages. The English High School, in turn, came to specialize in commercial programs. A third institution, the Technical High School, prepared students for the industries of the city – with extensive shop offerings and later with math and science courses as well. By 1920, Classical High was offering all the math and science one might want. Technical High came to be thought of, like English High, as a school for the average child in an era when the average child needed secondary schooling, but its special feature remained the shop courses. By 1905, Tech enrolled the largest number of boys, and English High, especially its commercial programs, the largest number of girls. Because Classical, English, and Tech were all located in one part of town, a fourth public high school, Hope High, was established across town, on the east side. It offered the programs found in the Classical and English High Schools.[11]

The expansion of the high schools had raised the total number of students enrolled at the turn of the century to 1,930. Another 5,396 pupils were enrolled in eleven grammar schools, and 16,548 in sixty-eight primary schools (the old distinction between primary and intermediate schools had been dropped in 1890). Kindergartens, begun under private initiative, had been operated by the city throughout the 1890s. By 1900, they enrolled 1,281 children. Over 600 teachers were employed in the public school system; in the central administration, several Assistant Superintendents, as well as aides in charge of special programs, now joined the Superintendent.[12]

During the first decade of the present century, the Providence public school system, already large and diversified, sought to confront the challenge of urban education with a range of new activities. At the state level, legislation regulating the ages of compulsory attendance and of permissible employment in various settings was modified repeatedly, most notably when the age for legal employment was raised to thirteen years in 1902 and to fourteen years in 1907 (it was raised again to fifteen years in the mid-1920s).[13]

The legal requirement that children start school by a given age and the legal restrictions on truancy improved somewhat the poor fit between the ages of pupils and the grades in which they were enrolled. But school administrators, who had been concerned about the poor age–grade fit since at least the mid-1880s, also attacked the problem directly by focusing attention on the need for regular promotions. Moreover, in 1904, they made the system more efficient in moving pupils through by reducing the length of the primary and grammar school courses to a total of eight rather than nine years. Nevertheless, "retardation" (pupils overage for their grade) remained a continuous source of concern to educators even after World War I. Another concern was "elimination," the high dropout rates at what then seemed a young age.[14] Compulsory education was one approach to the problem; making the school curriculum more practical, more relevant to the jobs children would eventually take, was another. The school authorities introduced industrial education in the grammar school grades, and in 1918 they opened a trade school for grammar school dropouts. Similarly, the size and scope of the evening schools were also expanded in the hope of enabling some children to complete grammar school, or even high school, while working, and in order to enable others to take some additional courses.[15]

The sheer numbers as well as the range of pupils who enrolled for at least a few years also stimulated the creation of other special schools, or special classrooms for special populations. Thus, the system included "disciplinary schools" (an institution midway between the regular classroom and a reform school), "schools for backward children," "fresh-air schools" (for tuberculous children), and a school for crippled children. Similarly, school authorities hailed IQ tests, particularly in the 1920s, as a means of classifying students and channeling them in different directions. Guidance counseling, introduced with a special staff in the same years, helped in directing each pupil to what seemed the most appropriate academic program, and eventually to a job. Finally, the presence of massive numbers of immigrants and their children led to the creation of special "foreign" classes, in which new arrivals learned English, and also "Americanization" classes for adults in the evening schools.[16]

The annual reports of the Providence School Committee also provide poignant evidence that another kind of change was occurring in educational circles: an increasing concern with the economic efficiency of the schools. It soon came to be required that this large and expensive endeavor justify itself in the same terms as a solid business establishment. Throughout the nineteenth century, these reports had been concerned with educational issues, devoting a few pages to finances. By the late 1920s, each report consisted principally of financial statements. The same concern surfaced in an attempt to import "the Gary Plan," a way of regimenting pupils more completely in order to save on personnel costs.[17]

A related development was a new emphasis on expertise, on the professional nature of educational administration. An indication of that new emphasis was a number of later innovations that came in the wake of a survey of the Providence public schools made in the mid-1920s by a team from Teacher's College, Columbia University. At least one of these innovations had repeatedly failed to win legislative approval before the authority of these experts was invoked: the reduction of the large, unwieldy Providence School Committee to a small committee, no longer elected ward by ward, but partly from larger districts and partly on a citywide basis. The change probably did make the committee more efficient, as reformers argued it would. However, perhaps that efficiency was gained at the cost of distancing the committee from local leaders and thereby from local concerns.[18]

Another recommendation by these experts concerned the restructuring of the educational system to include junior high schools and more regional high schools – a restructuring that began in the late 1920s and was completed in the 1930s. The restructuring required new buildings.

Part of the justification offered in 1924 to convince the city to support the expense of constructing these buildings was that new buildings would in any case be needed shortly to house increasing enrollments. Indeed, enrollments had increased, virtually uninterrupted, for as long as anyone cared to remember. Total enrollment in the public schools in 1920, for example, stood at 36,457; in 1900 it had been 25,155, and in 1880, 12,176. But the rising curves on the graphs that the experts presented failed to predict the decline of the economy and the slower growth in population that would occur in the 1930s. These led first to a deceleration in the rate at which school enrollments had been rising, and eventually to some absolute decline.[19]

Well before 1880, public schools enrolled many more pupils than privately operated schools, but non-public institutions remained important, particularly the Catholic schools. The Catholic parishes of Providence had begun supporting some schools as early as the 1850s. These were principally primary schools; few pupils reached the higher elementary grades in these institutions before the late nineteenth century. Nevertheless, small diocesan secondary schools did exist – one for boys and another for girls – throughout the second half of the nineteenth century. After the turn of the century, these Catholic secondary schools increased in size and importance. Throughout the 1880–

1925 period, roughly one-fifth of all pupils five to fifteen years old were enrolled in Catholic schools.

A small number of other private schools, primarily for a well-to-do clientele, were also to be found in the city, but their students composed only a tiny fraction of the total city enrollment in the years 1880–1925. Their share of secondary school students was somewhat larger, at least in 1880, but that, too, had dropped sharply by the turn of the century.[20]

Providence was thus a reasonably large urban center with a heterogeneous economy based on commerce and finance as well as on a variety of major industries. It was a city in which important ethnic groups were present in substantial numbers. Finally, its school system was reasonably similar to those that have been studied in other urban centers.[21] Within these parameters, the magnificent state of its historical records, which permitted the research design described in the next section, made Providence a compelling site for a study.

1.2. The evidence

The data that permit an intensive investigation of social origins, schooling, and social destinations are described in detail in the Appendix. However, their essential characteristics can be easily and briefly described. Manuscript census schedules, the actual notations of the census-takers, provided the source from which samples of young people were drawn. These census schedules record the name, age, address, occupation, race, place of birth, sex, relation to head of household, and other critical information on every individual in every household. Large samples of adolescent boys were selected from the U.S. Census manuscript schedules for 1880 and 1900 and from Rhode Island State Census manuscript schedules for 1915 and 1925. Large samples of girls were also drawn from 1880 and 1915. Each of these six samples contained between 900 and 1,200 individuals. In order to ensure that ample numbers of children would be selected from the ethnic groups on which the study focuses, special supplemental samples of blacks were gathered for each period, and supplemental samples of Italian, Irish, and Russian Jewish children were selected for 1915 (supplemental samples for 1880 and 1915 included girls as well as boys). All samples were taken from across the entire city of Providence, rather than from a single neighborhood or group of neighborhoods.

These census records provide very little information on the kind or amount of schooling a child received. The U.S. Censuses of 1880 and

1900 did ask whether or not a child had attended school during the year preceding the census date, but this question elicited only a single, imprecise indicator of schooling; in particular, it did not tell how much schooling the child had eventually received or in what schools. In order to obtain detailed information about schooling, each child in the sample was traced in all the city's surviving school records: public, Catholic, and other private school records. The most important of these records were the actual academic records for each student. Some records had, of course, been destroyed. The Appendix discusses the state of these records in detail. But the records of secondary school enrollment, which provide the principal basis for the present study, are as nearly complete as one could ever hope to find in a major urban center, and so very nearly complete that the impact of those that have been destroyed (though noted in the few relevant contexts later) has been utterly trivial.

In order to permit intensive study of enrollment patterns within high schools, supplemental samples were drawn from the school records. These samples included the entering classes of several high school programs in 1880, 1900, and 1915. They were drawn because the proportions of high school entrants in the population, and hence their numbers in the random samples, were not large in those years. The high school entrant sample was traced back to the census manuscript schedules in order to obtain family background information on these individuals.

Information on the socioeconomic positions that male sample members occupied as young adults was found in city directories. The directories, published annually, list the names, addresses, and occupations of the city's adult male residents.

The effort required to gather this information was considerable. Indeed, it was accomplished only with the help of research assistants contributing many thousands of hours over the course of several years. That effort – because of the combination of sources, their detail, and the size and scope of the samples – has made this data set a unique source for the social history of schooling in the late nineteenth and early twentieth centuries in America.

1.3. Ethnic groups of the city: a closer look

The majority of the children of Providence throughout this period had immigrant parents: Only about 40% of the fathers were native-born in 1880 and 1900, and less than 35% in 1915 and 1925 (Table 1.1). In 1880, nine-tenths of the immigrants came from the British Isles, primarily from Ireland. At the turn of the century, such immigrants

Table 1.1. *Race and place of birth of sample members' fathers, 1880–1925*

Father's race and place of birth	Proportion of all children in sampled age range, by year (%) [subtotals in brackets]			
	1880	1900	1915	1925
U.S.: whites (all)	[38.4]	[41.8]	[33.4]	[32.3]
Yankees (native whites, native parentage)	[31.9]	[22.1]	[15.5]	[a]
R.I.-born to R.I.-born father	14.4	9.2	[a]	
Other R.I.-born	2.3	2.3		
Massachusetts-born	7.7	4.5		
Other New England-born	5.1	3.6		
Other native whites, native parentage	2.4	2.5		
Native whites, Irish parentage	3.1	12.0	10.8	
Native whites, other foreign parentage	3.4	7.7	7.1	
Blacks[b]	2.0	1.3	2.3	1.8
Ireland	41.1	20.7	13.1	7.3
England, Scotland, or Wales	12.4	12.0	7.8	4.5
Italy	0.3	6.7	15.8	28.6
Russia	0	2.5	7.3	7.2
Other countries	[6.1]	[15.1]	[20.3]	[18.4]
Canada, French	0.1	4.9	4.5	5.8[c]
Canada, other	2.5	2.8	2.0	
Scandinavia	0.2	2.6	3.0	1.6
Germany	1.9	2.5	1.7	0.9
Austria	0.1	0.5	1.2	0.8
Poland	0	0	2.8	3.8
Portugal	0.2	0.2	2.0	1.2
All others	1.0	1.5	2.9	4.3
Total (100%) N	2,039	879	1,776	1,065
Children of immigrants: proportion foreign-born Father born in:				
Ireland	12.3	8.8	3.6	1.4
England, Scotland, or Wales	44.4	24.8	20.0	10.0
Italy		83.1	37.0	8.0
Russia		81.8	39.9	11.0
All others	34.5	40.9	21.1	8.5
All children of immigrants (% foreign-born)	20.9	30.8	23.5	7.9
All children (% foreign-born)	12.3	17.6	15.3	5.4

[a]The 1915 and 1925 Rhode Island state censuses did not provide information on state of birth. The latter also did not provide sample members' grandparents' places of birth.
[b]Virtually all native-born.
[c]Not distinguished from "Canada, other" in 1925 census.

accounted for half of the foreign-born fathers, but by 1915 for only a third, and by 1925 for a sixth. The number of immigrants from southern and eastern Europe rose at a comparable rate. Especially important were the Italians: one-eighth of the foreign-born fathers in 1900, one-quarter in 1915, and over two-fifths in 1925. The other "new immigrant" groups were much smaller, although together they outnumbered the Italians until 1925. The second largest of the new European groups were the Russian Jews. Scandinavians, Germans, Austrians, Poles, Armenians, and Portuguese made up the remainder of the Europeans. Finally, 6–8% of all fathers in the later samples were Canadian immigrants, mostly French Canadian.

The children were much less likely than their parents to have been born abroad: Only 21–31% of the immigrants' children were themselves foreign-born in the first three samples, and a mere 8% in 1925. The immigrant families of 1925 included far fewer recent arrivals than families had in earlier years because of the immigration restrictions imposed by the United States in the preceding few years. The fluctuations in other years reflect mostly the shifting proportions of immigrants from different countries and different patterns of migration. Notwithstanding the fluctuations, the basic pattern was clear: A majority of the parents were foreign-born, and a majority of their children native-born.

Although two-fifths of the fathers were native-born, many of these natives were themselves sons of immigrants, especially after 1880. In that year, the second generation constituted only one-sixth of all native-born fathers. However, by 1900, nearly one-half of the native fathers were sons of immigrants, mostly from Ireland.

The native whites of native parentage generally are referred to in the discussion that follows as Yankees. Those sample members who were the children of Yankees were at least the third generation in their families to be born in the United States; many must have traced their American ancestry much further back in time. It would, however, be a mistake to assume that they all had deep roots in Providence. Only about half the Yankee fathers were born in Rhode Island (and among these, no less than four-fifths of their fathers had also been born there).[22] Many of these Rhode Island families probably migrated to Providence from rural parts of the state. Among these old Rhode Island families, some were wealthy and respected; others had simply elected to stay in one place for several generations. Nearly all of the remaining Yankee fathers came from New England, mostly from Massachusetts.[23]

All in all, it is striking how few of the children came from Yankee homes (how few were the children of native whites of native parentage); fewer still came from old Rhode Island families. In 1880, a third had been born to Yankee fathers, but by 1900 only 22%, and in 1915 only 16%. Fewer still had two Yankee parents (not shown in the table): only 11% in 1915. Similarly, only a relative handful had parents and grandparents born in Rhode Island: 9% in 1880, and 4% in 1900. Only a minute proportion of families had not experienced some form of migration in recent memory.[24]

1.4. Schooling, social class, and ethnicity

By 1880, and probably much earlier, virtually all children spent at least a few years in school – roughly between the ages of seven and eleven.[25] That some schooling was beneficial must have been very widely, probably universally, accepted. Moreover, alternative uses for children's time in the city were minimal; there was relatively little a very young child could do to bring in wages, and at home their nuisance value probably outweighed any help they might have provided. In any case, it is clear that most children, even from the poorest groups, were in school at these ages.[26] At age eleven, for example, 89% of the children of laborers were still in school, as were 88% of blacks and 91% of the children of the Irish. Dropout rates increased very rapidly with each succeeding age, so that by age thirteen 73% of Providence children were still enrolled, by age fifteen only 42%, and by age seventeen a mere 19%.

Among the boys, nearly all who left school went to work. Among the girls, higher proportions (as high as a quarter of all girls at some ages) were not at school or in gainful employment, but helping at home. The jobs of children varied by age, of course. Typically, however, early dropouts took low-skill jobs in textile mills or worked as errand boys, cash boys, and newspaper boys (or girls). Young adolescents were much less likely to get apprenticeships or jobs as clerks or sales clerks.[27]

The rates of school leaving indicate that a substantial majority of children entered school by age six or seven and remained at least through age thirteen. Thus, they must have received some six or seven years of schooling in all. Indeed, the median length of time a child spent in school in Providence in 1880 was probably about nine years.[28] Clearly, however, the experiences of the poor, and the Irish, were somewhat different. Among them, for example, dropout rates were already substantial by age thirteen. For example, whereas 80% of all children remained in school at that age, only 68% of the Irish did so.

In any case, these rates surely suggest that most children must have reached the upper primary school grades (third, fourth or fifth grade) before leaving school, and many must have reached the grammar school grades as well. That 73% were enrolled at age thirteen and 43% at age fifteen might also seem to imply that reasonably large proportions of the children were entering high school. They were not. In 1880, only 10% of the boys and 15% of the girls were enrolled in high school. Indeed, most of the teenagers who were enrolled in school (especially those fifteen or younger) were still in the primary or grammar grades. The contrast between the high proportion of teenagers in school and the low proportion reaching high school highlights the age–grade disparity, a reality of the school experience that historians have yet to explore in depth. But turn-of-the-century schoolmen who were troubled by "grade retardation" had a point. In later years, the loose age–grade fit tightened only slowly.[29]

In the following decades, school attendance generally was encouraged, and special efforts were made to raise the age at which children left school: Compulsory school legislation was repeatedly modified, the length of the primary and grammar school course was reduced by a year shortly after 1900, and secondary school programs were created with an eye to attracting students.

How much this kind of legislation, or the bureaucratic and curricular changes, mattered is difficult to judge. Jobs for children may also have become less readily available as a result of technological changes. The perception of a basic education may also have changed; more and more families may have chosen to keep their children in school an extra year or two. Finally, rising real wages for working-class families through much of this period may have contributed to the same result. We need not sort out the reasons for the growth in school enrollments during those decades. What is clear is that there was indeed substantial change.

From the point of view of school officials, the critical issue was the staggering rise in the number of students, a rise that drove them constantly to beseech the City Council to erect new buildings. The crush at the high schools was especially dramatic. Enrollment in public secondary schools stood at 417 in 1880; it reached 1,930 in 1900, 3,526 in 1915, and 5,941 in 1925. These were, of course, "live bodies" that had to be accommodated. In part, the enrollment increases were due simply to the growth of the city's population between 1880 and 1925. The proportion of children who reached high school was not rising at the same rate as these total enrollment figures. Nevertheless, that proportion was also rising rapidly. Whereas in 1880, 10% of the boys enrolled in high school, 17% did so in 1900, 34% in 1915, and 49% in 1925.

Many factors helped determine who would receive extended schooling: social class and ethnic origin, gender, the number of sib-

lings a child had, distance from a school, the child's intellectual apti-
tude and, quite simply, how much the child liked school. As with
most social behavior, we cannot fully understand the factors determining school attendance. When we take account of as many of these
social and intellectual characteristics as we can, there are still many
exceptions – children who would have been expected to leave early,
but instead stayed many years, or the reverse. Their behavior is a
reminder, first, that our measures of social characteristics are imperfect and, second, that countless particular circumstances of families
and individuals have been overlooked. Nevertheless, it is clear that
two sorts of social division are very important to any description of
schooling: social class and ethnicity.

Our best indication of the social-class positions of individuals is
occupation, as reported to the census and in other records. This tells
us the kind of work they did (baker, clerk, laborer, lawyer), whether
or not they were self-employed, and sometimes the sector of the
economy in which they worked (clerk in textile mill, clerk in bank).
Optimally, one would wish to supplement the occupational information with knowledge of the income available to families. Individuals
in a given occupation may, after all, vary considerably in income.
Although information on family income is not available, related information is: the assessed value of the property (real estate and some
other forms of property) of a family.

The definition of social class, the major classes of different social
orders, the relationships among classes and class consciousness and
class struggle, the connection between all these and the state – these
themes have been central to the modern study of society throughout
its history. However, in conceiving of ethnic patterns of school attainment, and even of ethnic patterns of job attainment, we need not
grapple extensively with most of these issues. What matters most is
knowing how the economic characteristics of families – levels of material well-being, as well as social characteristics that often accompany
economic positions – explain the ethnic differences in children's
schooling and in their later job patterns.[30] In any case, even if we did
choose to grapple at length with the larger conceptual issues just
mentioned, we would be thrown back, in a historical survey of citywide trends, on the criteria of occupation and property values, for
these constitute the available evidence.

The mass of information on the occupations and property holdings
of thousands of individuals must be organized to highlight the class
distinctions inherent within them. One useful way is to group the
fathers of sample members into vertically ordered strata on the basis
of their occupations and property value: high and low white-collar;
skilled, semiskilled, and unskilled blue-collar.[31] Roughly speaking,

the white-collar workers can be thought of as middle-class, and the blue-collar workers as working-class. For some purposes, such as assessment of class consciousness or class conflict, such gross distinctions might well be inadequate. But our purpose is to arrive at a meaningful and efficient way to distinguish levels of socioeconomic well-being, and a vertical ordering of occupations and property values into strata and classes does serve that purpose. Other ways of approaching the evidence will be useful later.[32] For the moment, however, we consider these five strata.

The consistency in the sizes of these strata over time is striking. Of course, the occupational structure changed somewhat during the period. By 1925, more people than in 1880 no doubt worked in large factories rather than in small workshops or as artisans. Similarly, the prominence of various occupations changed as industries and services developed or declined. Nevertheless, roughly a quarter of those in the work force were in white-collar jobs in each sample. However, only 6–10% were in high white-collar occupations, enjoying positions as major managers and proprietors, or as professionals. The rest were petty proprietors, salesmen, or clerks. Another quarter of the workers held skilled manual-labor jobs or worked as foremen. These jobs generally required several years of training, for example, as an apprentice. They included machinists, carpenters, plumbers, goldsmiths, and the like. Below these were the low manual workers – the semiskilled and the unskilled, whose jobs could be learned in a few weeks or a few hours. Most of the former were factory operatives; most of the latter were described as laborers.

A very useful criterion of extended schooling for the period before 1930 is high school enrollment. High school represented a distinct level of schooling – a different institution, not merely an additional grade. Barely more than half the population entered, even in 1925, so that entry did distinguish those with relatively extended schooling. High school entry was determined by length of school attendance, of course, as well as by progress through the grades; the looseness of the age–grade fit makes it important to recall both determinants, and social origins clearly influenced both. The sample data are not well suited for assessing the measure of grade attainment social scientists typically seek in contemporary surveys, namely, the highest grade of school completed – too many records from the lowest grades are missing, as are too many records of college enrollment. But the research strategy was designed to maximize the accuracy of information on high school entry; for the moment, we can limit our attention to that measure of extended schooling.[33]

Table 1.2 shows the social-class differences in high school enroll-

Table 1.2. *High school entry and social-class origins, 1880–1925*

Gender of child	Father's occupation	1880 Rate (%)	1880 N	1900 Rate (%)	1900 N	1915 Rate (%)	1915 N	1925 Rate (%)	1925 N
Male	High white collar	40.1	(68)	64.4	(51)	63.9	(67)	83.3	(96)
	Low white collar	17.9	(119)	27.9	(151)	48.5	(179)	63.9	(171)
	All white collar	26.0	(187)	37.2	(202)	52.7	(246)	70.9	(267)
	Skilled	6.2	(213)	13.4	(263)	34.8	(223)	53.2	(258)
	Semiskilled	5.5	(142)	11.8	(199)	28.9	(208)	51.5	(231)
	Unskilled	2.3	(177)	8.0	(169)	12.3	(169)	29.7	(177)
	All blue collar	4.7	(532)	11.5	(631)	26.4	(600)	46.4	(666)
	Unknown	6.2	(64)	6.7	(47)	25.5	(48)	21.3	(132)[a]
	Total	9.9	(783)	17.1	(880)	33.6	(894)	49.4	(1,065)
Female	High white collar	44.3	(77)			61.7	(67)		
	Low white collar	30.3	(129)			52.3	(173)		
	All white collar	35.5	(206)			54.9	(240)		
	Skilled	11.7	(241)			39.1	(213)		
	Semiskilled	6.3	(210)			29.8	(243)		
	Unskilled	2.4	(172)			14.7	(163)		
	All blue collar	7.3	(623)			29.0	(619)		
	Unknown	17.5	(35)			44.0	(23)		
	Total	14.5	(864)			36.5	(882)		

Note: Sample sizes presented in this table have been weighted to reflect the correct relative sizes of the occupational strata. Actual sample sizes were substantially greater for males in 1880 ($N = 1,175$) and in 1915 (N for boys = 1,462) because of inclusion of supplemental samples of selected ethnic groups and because of gender-specific sampling ratios in the citywide sample of 1880.

[a] The proportion unknown is higher than in preceding years because information on father's occupations was not provided by the 1925 Rhode Island state census, requiring a trace to the city directory for the information.

ment rates by father's occupation over the course of nearly half a century in Providence. Sharp increases over time are evident in all groups, but of particular interest here are the differences across strata. They are not equally large. The patterns for children of semiskilled and skilled workers seem very similar, perhaps reflecting no more than weaknesses in the classification scheme. On the other hand, the similarities in all blue-collar rates before 1915 (especially among boys), and the sharp differences between blue-collar and white-collar rates, emphasize how much more common secondary schooling was among the children of the middle class. Within the high schools there were still many working-class children; the working class was so much larger than the middle class that even much lower rates of enrollment produced substantial representation. Nevertheless, the class differences are striking: 26% of middle-class boys compared with 5% of working-class boys reached high school in 1880, and 71% compared with 46% in 1925.

Table 1.3 shows the rates of high school entry in the same years for each of the major ethnic groups of the city. Because the 1880 and 1915 samples include both boys and girls, rates for the sexes are combined (gender differences are discussed in detail in later chapters). By no means all groups exhibited unique patterns; entry rates were similar in many groups. Yet there are some clear ethnic differences, differences that divided the city's children as sharply in ethnic terms as in terms of social class. At one pole, the largest immigrant groups, first the Irish and later the Italians, were especially unlikely to reach high school; so, too, were blacks through most of the period. Indeed, children from most immigrant groups (excluding the British children in the later part of the era) were relatively unlikely to enroll; Yankees were relatively likely to do so. Still, there were clear differences among the white groups beyond those an immigrant–native dichotomy could explain. For example, the Italians were much less likely to reach high school than were members of other immigrant groups. Nor did Jews behave like the other immigrant groups; Jews were at least as likely to reach high school as were the Yankees.

To some extent, of course, these ethnic differences were simply due to the fact that the heads of immigrant and black families were heavily concentrated in low-skill, low-paying jobs. They could not support extended schooling for children as easily as could others, if they could do so at all. To some extent, then, the ethnic differences may not be more than a reflection of social-class differences. The connections between social-class and ethnic differences in schooling are therefore important topics, which we shall carefully probe in subsequent chapters.

Table 1.3. Ethnic and social-class differences in high school entry, 1880–1925

Group	1880 Rate (%)	1880 N	1900 Rate (%)	1900 N	1915 Rate (%)	1915 N	1925 Rate (%)	1925 N
Father's ethnic group								
Yankees (NWNP)[a]	28.2	(614)	36.2	(185)	52.5	(263)		
NWIRP[a]	7.4	(56)	10.6	(104)	47.8	(191)	61.5	(296)[b]
NWOTHP[a]	24.1	(57)	23.0	(61)	40.1	(114)		
Blacks[c]	3.7	(216)	12.3	(114)	22.4	(264)	42.1	(107)
Irish[c]	6.6[d]	(774)	18.1[d]	(168)	41.4	(587)	73.5	(68)
English, Scots, Welsh	6.1	(244)	8.1	(99)	27.2	(136)	57.5	(40)
Italians[c]	[e]		3.5	(57)	9.9	(839)	33.0	(72)
Russian Jews[c]	[e]		[e]		42.3	(666)	69.4	(261)
All other immigrants	4.4	(112)	13.2	(144)	32.0	(400)	53.4	(189)
Father's social class								
White-collar	31.0	(500)	37.2	(213)	53.8	(1,038)	70.9	(276)
Blue-collar	6.1	(1,574)	11.5	(720)	27.7	(2,422)	46.4	(757)
Total: all groups[f]	12.4	(2,074)	17.7	(933)	35.0	(3,460)	53.0	(1,033)

[a]NWNP, native whites, native parentage; NWIRP, native whites, Irish parentage; NWOTHP, native whites, other parentage.

[b]Children of all native white groups (see Table 1.1, note a).

[c]Numbers are based on supplemental samples of blacks collected in each period and of Irish, Italians, and Russian Jews in 1915. Therefore, the numbers do not reflect the relative sizes of groups in the city. The supplemental samples are also included in the last three rows of rates, but weighted to reflect the actual ethnic compositions of the cohorts.

[d]Includes estimates of entry to some Catholic schools whose records are unavailable. See Chapter 2 and the Appendix for a full discussion.

[e]Too few for separate classification (included in "All other immigrants" category).

[f]Tables 1.3 and 1.4 exclude sample members whose social-class origins are unknown. The ethnic origins of a small number of sample members were also unknown (nearly all of these individuals were in the high school entrant samples included in Table 1.4); these individuals are included only in the rows for White-collar, Blue-collar, and Total.

1.5. *Jobs: social-class destinations*

Our study of the later social positions of the sample members must be limited to men, and limited further to those men who remained in the Providence metropolitan area as young adults. The limitations are dictated by the nature of the sources. The best available indicator of the social position that a sample member attained as a young adult is his occupation at that time, as listed in the city directory.[34]

Even among the men, only about half could be found in the city directories: 48%, 46%, 47%, and 52% for the four successive samples. The directories missed some men, and others had left the area; still others had to be eliminated because our search procedures simply could not identify them positively in the directories (as explained in the Appendix). Those men who could not be found may, of course, have differed in occupation from those who were found. But there is little reason to think that the patterns of attainment that interest us (differences by ethnic group, and differences in the effects of family background or education on attainment, for example) would have been sufficiently different among those who stayed to invalidate our conclusions.[35]

Sample members were traced in the city directories published a decade after the year of the census from which they were selected. Thus, the boys of 1880 were traced to the directories of 1890, those of 1900 to the directories of 1910, and so forth. The sample members, adolescents in the year of the census, would have been twenty-two to twenty-six years old in the year to which they were traced. It may seem unwise to focus on occupational information from such an early point in their careers. The practical reason for studying jobs of men in their early twenties is that during the course of their twenties and thirties, many more young men left the city. The choice of a later age would have meant still higher levels of missing data. There is, in fact, little reason to think that the relative socioeconomic positions of the men in their twenties changed dramatically later – particularly not in ways systematically related to ethnic origins. This contention is supported by some exploratory analyses. As part of the data-collection effort, the sample members had been traced two decades across time (as well as one), into their early and middle thirties. Most of the occupational patterns discussed in this book could be readily observed even in that exploratory analysis of the smaller, less representative samples. Also, the jobs of the men in their thirties correlated highly with those they had held in their twenties, suggesting that the critical relationships between occupations and background characteristics were also much the same for both sets of jobs.[36]

In Table 1.4, the jobs of young men have been classified into one of

Table 1.4. *Ethnic and social-class differences in young men's jobs*

Father's ethnic group or social class	Proportion obtaining jobs in each stratum[a] (%)			Total number in all strata[b]	Mean occupational score[c]
	White-collar	Skilled manual	Low manual		
1880 sample					
Yankees (NWNP)[d]	56.4	29.1	14.6	(249)	40.8
NWIRP[d]	21.8	32.6	45.6	(16)	28.7
NWOTHP[d]	53.4	17.8	28.9	(21)	33.8
Blacks	16.9	7.1	76.1	(35)	16.1
Irish	16.5	43.5	40.0	(214)	26.2
English, Scots, Welsh	35.3	36.3	28.4	(68)	36.0
All other immigrants	45.1	33.8	21.1	(25)	33.8
White-collar	64.5	20.0	15.6	(218)	41.4
Blue-collar	23.2	41.9	35.0	(423)	29.5
Total: all groups	35.9	35.1	29.0	(641)	33.0
1900 sample					
Yankees	56.0	23.4	20.6	(163)	40.2
NWIRP	30.7	31.4	37.9	(78)	30.3
NWOTHP	37.3	38.4	24.3	(47)	42.1
Blacks	25.7	6.8	67.5	(46)	20.8
Irish	30.9	22.9	46.2	(112)	28.8
English, Scots, Welsh	27.8	41.6	30.7	(70)	33.7
Italians	30.9	21.8	47.3	(20)	30.4
All other immigrants	17.0	44.5	38.5	(78)	31.0
White-collar	51.5	22.9	25.7	(215)	38.8
Blue-collar	29.5	32.6	37.8	(444)	31.7
Total: all groups	34.6	30.4	35.0	(659)	33.3
1915 sample					
Yankees	45.7	16.5	37.9	(77)	35.0
NWIRP	55.9	16.7	27.5	(68)	36.6
NWOTHP	57.8	3.4	38.9	(41)	36.3
Blacks	15.3	13.0	71.8	(46)	16.5
Irish	41.2	20.3	39.2	(238)	32.9
English, Scots, Welsh	36.4	37.0	26.6	(50)	35.7
Italians	33.2	20.3	46.5	(248)	26.8
Russian Jew	77.2	12.7	10.2	(158)	44.8
All other immigrants	38.3	20.6	40.8	(106)	33.2
White-collar	59.9	16.6	23.5	(300)	39.2
Blue-collar	38.4	20.3	41.3	(748)	31.7
Total: all groups	44.6	19.2	36.2	(1,048)	33.7
1925 sample					
Native whites	49.3	13.3	37.3	(150)	34.8
Blacks	8.5	12.8	78.7	(47)	16.3

Table 1.4 *(Cont.)*

Father's ethnic group or social class	Proportion obtaining jobs in each stratum[a] (%)			Total number in all strata[b]	Mean occupational score[c]
	White-collar	Skilled manual	Low manual		
Irish	60.0	14.3	25.7	(35)	35.9
English, Scots, Welsh	44.0	20.0	36.0	(25)	31.8
Italians	23.7	25.9	50.4	(139)	26.1
Russian Jews	74.4	5.1	20.5	(39)	41.2
All other immigrants	37.1	21.6	42.1	(97)	31.7
White-collar	66.3	12.4	21.2	(134)	39.9
Blue-collar	32.8	20.7	46.5	(398)	29.0
Total: all groups	41.7	18.5	39.9	(532)	31.9

[a]Based on the jobs of sample members ten years after the census year.
[b]Numbers include supplemental samples of high school entrants and of selected ethnic groups. All rates and means are based on appropriate weighting of sample members. N's, however, are unweighted and do not reflect each group's relative size in the age cohort. See also note f, Table 1.3.
[c]Each occupation was assigned a score based on a 100-point scale (O.D. Duncan's socioeconomic index; see text and its notes for full description). The mean of scores found in each ethnic group is reported.
[d]NWNP, native whites, native parentage; NWIRP, native whites, Irish parentage; NWOTHP, native whites, other parentage.

three major strata: white-collar (including both high and low white-collar jobs), skilled, and low manual (including both semiskilled and unskilled jobs).[37] Young men fared better, on average, than their fathers: More of the sons entered white-collar work, and fewer took low manual jobs.[38] It may seem surprising that sons would have had such an advantage, particularly by their middle twenties, over their fathers. However, it should be recalled that large proportions of the sample members' fathers were immigrants, whereas the vast majority of their children were native-born, and even the rest had spent much of their youth in the United States. The American-born were generally much more successful in avoiding the most unattractive jobs, having had the training and the familiarity with the American scene to know how to do so.

Although many ethnic groups fared similarly, some ethnic differences in job patterns were as glaring as those in school patterns. In particular, occupational differences between Irish and Yankee in the first part of the era, between blacks and all others, between most immigrants and natives, and between Italians and other whites are clearly important. Again, the Jews were in a relatively favorable position compared with others, including natives. Many of these ethnic differences were as large as those across class lines. As in the case of ethnic differences in schooling, some of these ethnic differences in occupations simply reflect the fact that the class origins of young men in different ethnic groups varied widely. Moreover, another important part of the story of ethnic differences in job destinations may have been ethnic differences in educational attainments – whatever the sources of the educational differences.

In considering all these issues, it will be useful to think of occupations in a somewhat different way than we have thus far. Earlier, occupations were classified into a small number of strata (high and low white-collar; skilled, semiskilled, and unskilled blue-collar); usually it will be more useful to assign each occupation a score on a scale. The scale used here was developed by Otis D. Duncan from 1950 U.S. Census data and from survey data on the prestige of particular occupations; it has been used widely in social research for more than two decades. In essence, instead of assigning an occupation to one of five levels (strata), it is assigned a score on a scale of 0 to 96. Moreover, the social distance between any two adjacent scores is assumed to remain constant: 1 point on the scale. In its use of many levels equally separated, the occupational scale bears some analogy to measuring social position in terms of income levels of families. On the other hand, the differences between the occupational strata (e.g., low white-collar vs. skilled, compared with skilled vs. unskilled) are not defined precisely on any scale.

An initial obstacle to thinking about occupations in terms of scores, of course, is the abstract nature of occupational scores. For example, it seems more natural to think in terms of skilled and unskilled than in terms of occupations 20 points apart. It may be useful, for overcoming that obstacle, to consider Table 1.5, which indicates the scores assigned to selected occupations. It also may make the meaning of scores easier to grasp if we relate it to the more familiar blue-collar–white-collar distinction: The average score for all blue-collar occupations was about 28 points below the average score for all white-collar occupations.

Each method of classifying occupations – by strata or on an occupational scale – has advantages and limitations for the study of social behavior generally and for a historical study of ethnic-group experience in particular. However, for a great many purposes, the occupational scale has proved no less useful than the five strata, and for others far more useful. One key advantage is that it captures more of

Table 1.5. *Scores for selected occupations on the occupational scale*[a]

Occupation	Score
Physician	92
Banker	85
Manufacturer	61
Toolmaker	50
Merchant	49
Clerk	44
Foreman	44
Grocer	33
Machinist	33
Mason	27
Cabinetmaker	23
Carpenter	19
Barber	17
Longshoreman	11
Teamer/driver	8
Peddler	8
Laborer	6
Spinner	5
Woolsorter	2
Bobbin carrier	1

[a] O.D. Duncan's socioeconomic index; see text for full description.

the effect of the father's occupation, for example, on children's schooling, because it makes nearly 100 distinctions (rather than only 5) between kinds of occupations. This difference is especially important in comparing individuals alike in terms of father's occupation but differing in ethnicity or in length of schooling – in "controlling for father's occupation." The occupational scale is also useful in studying the occupations of the sons as young adults, because a mean occupational score can be easily calculated for individuals in each ethnic group, and differences in the mean occupational scores can be compared. Thus, a single number captures the situation of a group, rather than a set of three or five proportions (the proportion reaching each stratum). The mean also provides a more tractable measure for sophisticated analysis of relevant problems, for example, of the relative impact of family background and schooling on the sizes of ethnic differences in job outcomes.[39]

Obviously, there are comparisons in which the mean occupational score would be a poor substitute for occupational categories. For example, if our purpose were to describe a social structure, or to discuss social conflict that is related to social-class position, the five-category scheme might well be preferable. More generally, classifying occupations into categories is especially useful if the social behavior being explored can be explained by the factors that unite people into the particular categories used; the most important example concerns the Marxist categories of social class that are used to explain particular social behavior because that behavior is based on class interest and on class consciousness. However, discussions of the effects of social-class origins on schooling or on social mobility usually do not have that character; they do not explain outcomes as resulting from the particular nature of the unifying class character of an occupational category. Rather, the occupational categories are used primarily to convey a vertical scale, simply to assess the advantages of being more highly placed in social-class origin. For better or worse, the connection of those advantages to other aspects of social-class analysis usually is not an important part of the discussion. Given the use of social strata to convey a vertical scale, often the purpose is better met by the occupational scale.[40]

Another issue concerns the validity of using the particular occupational scale developed by Duncan for historical study. How accurate can a scale based on 1950 data be for the 1880s? In fact, the vertical positions of occupations in the scale and in the five strata correlate highly. Consequently, if the scale is unreliable, the strata can hardly be much better. Moreover, the available research uniformly suggests that changes in the vertical positions of occupations over time have been small, much smaller than many apparently have supposed. In the present study, a large part of the entire analysis was conducted using both methods: the occupational scale and the five strata. The conclusions simply were not affected. However, the analysis can be presented more concisely (and some details will stand out much more clearly) when the occupational scale is employed.[41]

The mean occupational scores for fathers' and sons' jobs demonstrate again the stability over time and the advantage of the sons over the fathers that the occupational categories revealed earlier: The means for fathers' occupations were 24.1, 24.1, 25.9, and 27.8 in successive years; for sons' occupations they were 33.0, 33.3, 33.7, and 31.9. The difference in occupational outcomes by ethnic or class background also shows up clearly using the occupational score instead of the occupational strata (Table 1.4).[42]

One other distinction should be borne in mind in thinking about the social positions of the young men. Their positions can be conceived in terms of occupational attainment or in terms of occupational mobility. The two ideas are similar, but not identical. Attainment indicates simply the position the sample member reached. Mobility indicates the difference between that position and his father's. Both perspectives can be useful, and both should reveal much the same patterns. In most of the work that follows, the focus is on attainment, because it is much simpler to assess and present findings in those terms. Issues of mobility are simply recast into an attainment framework by asking how important a factor the father's occupation was in determining the son's occupational attainment. By recasting the issue in this way, the father's occupation is treated as one of a number of relevant factors – along with ethnicity, schooling, number of siblings, and others.[43]

1.6. *Education and social destinations, 1880–1935*

Before turning to distinctive ethnic patterns of behavior, it is important to consider briefly the importance of education in determining job destination. The crucial role of education in helping people to get ahead is a staple of contemporary American ideology, and today's sociologists confirm that educational attainment is indeed at least as important as any other aspect of an individual's background in determining career.[44] However, their studies provide much less evidence about the importance of education in determining careers before World War II, and virtually none at all pertaining to the period before 1920. The Providence data provide a unique opportunity to examine the impact of education on later occupations. This examination, in turn, provides a context for understanding ethnic differences in schooling and social destinations.

Specifically, we can consider both the magnitude of the occupational advantage enjoyed by those who had enrolled in high school and the proportion who had enrolled. Both must be kept in mind in order to understand the role that education played in enhancing or inhibiting social equality. For example, the advantages of secondary schooling reached only a relative handful of working-class children in 1880 and even in 1900. The average social position of all working-class children could hardly have been much affected by any advantages enjoyed by that handful.

We can consider each issue in turn: first, the advantage of an extended education to those who received it, and second, its role in determining the patterns of inequality in the population as a whole. The analysis focuses on the impact of high school entry as a measure of extended schooling. Other measures of schooling would be possi-

Table 1.6. *Extended schooling and social destinations: men, 1890–1935*

Group	1890	1910	1925	1935
A. *Advantage (in mean occupational score) of men who had entered high school*				
All men	19.6	15.0	12.9	15.0
Sons of low manual, immigrant workers	22.6	11.5	11.4	11.6
All men, controlling for 5 family background characteristics[a]	11.4	11.6	9.3	10.4
B. *Advantage (in mean occupational score) of social class origins: difference between sons of white- and blue-collar origins*				
Advantage of white- collar origin	12.0	7.1	7.5	10.9
C. *High school entry and social-class mobility: proportion who had reached high school among all men of blue-collar family origin holding white-collar jobs (%)*				
Sons of:				
Natives	29.3	30.1	57.2	84.1
Immigrants	9.1	18.5	48.2	73.0
All	18.1	24.3	51.7	77.1

[a]Characteristics controlled include the father's occupation (occupational score), assessed value of the family's property, ethnicity, number of siblings, whether or not both parents were present in the census year.

ble and would add some subtleties, but for the purposes at hand, this measure is simple and sufficient.

The experience of the Providence sample members could hardly be clearer regarding the advantages associated with schooling: Those who entered high school were able to attain higher-status occupations. The occupational score for those who received some secondary schooling was nearly 20 points higher than that for others in the 1880 sample and some 13–15 points higher in each of the three later samples (Table 1.6, first row). How large is that difference? We can compare the magnitude of that difference to another: the difference between the occupations attained by middle-class and working-class boys. The advantage of having come from a middle-class home amounted to 7 to 12 points in each of the four samples (Table 1.6, part B). Thus, the difference associated with secondary school entry was notably larger in each sample.

The occupational advantages enjoyed by high school entrants were only partly due to that schooling itself. After all, most who received extended schooling had other social advantages; for example, they were more likely to be of middle-class origin. These other advantages, rather than their schooling, could have accounted for their later good fortune in the job market. So it is important to consider how much of their advantage remains when high school entrants are compared with nonentrants of comparable social origins.

Table 1.6 presents the evidence relevant to this question. First, by way of concrete illustration, it indicates (in the second row) the impact of high school entry among a particular group: the sons of immigrant blue-collar workers. Did it really make any difference to these boys whether or not they reached high school? Were they not trapped in difficult social conditions regardless of schooling? They were not. The suspicion that secondary schooling did not help working-class boys, or immigrant working-class boys, who received it cannot be sustained. Education did not merely reflect the advantages of birth. Immigrant working-class boys who reached high school entered much more attractive occupations than others of similar social backgrounds, occupations averaging about 11 points higher in the three later samples and higher still in the 1880 sample.

Table 1.6 also presents a more general measure (in the third row): the occupational advantage resulting from high school entry among individuals comparable in regard to many aspects of social background. The father's occupation (classified into the nearly 100 levels of the occupational scale described earlier), the value of the property held by the family of origin, the number of children in the family, and whether or not both mother and father were present are all taken into account. Finally, many categories of immigrants and their children, as well as blacks, are distinguished – seven to twelve ethnic categories, depending on the ethnic composition of the city in different years. The measure of the occupational advantage resulting from high school entry among individuals comparable in terms of all these background characteristics was obtained by multiple-regression analysis.* That occupational advantage was still between 9 and 12 points in each period.

Clearly, other, unseen differences could have mattered as well, but the differences controlled are immensely important, and their impact, though not negligible, is modest enough to suggest that others would not greatly affect the results. Indeed, most other important differ-

---

* Multiple regression, a statistical procedure used throughout the study, can be thought of as averaging differences in outcomes within categories of each of the family background factors taken into account; in this case, it averages the differences in occupational scores between entrants and nonentrants (the occupational advantage of high school entry).

ences in family origins were related to these, and much of their effect
has therefore already been taken into account.

In sum, with no controls, the advantages associated with high school
entry amounted to 20 points in 1880 and 13–15 points later; with controls, these advantages still amounted to 9–12 points in each period.
Even in 1880, half the advantage was independent of measurable family
origins, and in later periods at least seven-tenths. That independent
advantage may in turn be compared with the total advantage associated with being raised in a middle-class rather than a working-class
home (including those class advantages realized through schooling).
The independent advantages of high school entry (9–12 points) were
about as large as the total advantages associated with class origins in
1880 and 1925, and larger than these in 1900 and 1915 (A and B in
Table 1.6).

Thus, the answer to the first question posed earlier (How much of
an advantage did extended schooling give those who received it?) is
unambiguous: That advantage was very considerable. However, we
can now consider the second question: How many indeed received
that advantage, and, particularly, were they numerous enough to
matter to the outcomes generally – for example, to the fate typical of
all working-class boys?

The answer to this second question turns on the proportion of children who received secondary schooling, and particularly on the proportions who did so within different social classes and ethnic groups.
Until after the turn of the century, secondary schooling was rare, affecting but one boy in ten in 1880, and even in 1900 fewer than two
boys in ten. Its impact on inequality in the society as a whole was
bound to be restricted. True, it was comparatively common among
the children of middle-class native whites as early as 1880; very nearly
two-fifths of the boys from these origins enrolled. By 1900, secondary
schooling was not uncommon among the middle-class sons of other
ethnic origins as well (nearly three in ten reaching high school), but
it remained rare among working-class families in both periods. Indeed, among black and immigrant working-class families, only one
boy in fifty reached high school in 1880.

The large improvement in social position accruing to the individual
who reached high school must be seen in this context. Before 1915,
secondary schooling cannot be said to have had much impact on the
overall standing of young men from working-class origins, particularly among blacks or immigrants. In 1880, the impact of the 22.6-
point advantage accruing to the one working-class boy in fifty who

reached high school raised the average occupational score of the group by less than half a point ($22.6 \times 0.021 = 0.47$). In later years, especially in 1915 and after, the larger proportions enrolling, coupled with the large advantages to those who did, meant that the institution had much more of an impact.

The impact of high school entry should be distinguished from the impact of schooling generally. It is possible, although by no means certain, that other, less exclusive levels of educational attainment – completing grammar school, for example – also conferred large occupational advantages on those who attained them, compared with those who did not. If so, the role of schooling in helping people to get ahead in the nineteenth century may have been greater than is indicated by our analysis (limited to the effects of high school entry on occupations). We need not resolve this issue here. The critical points for our purposes – to provide background for the discussions of ethnic differences that follow – are two: Extended schooling, measured by secondary school enrollment, did have important advantages for individuals who received it throughout the period, but it had little effect on the fate of working-class boys as a whole, especially those of immigrant and black origins in the first half of the era.

An important corollary of the preceding discussion concerns the means by which working-class boys achieved upward mobility into the middle class. Our best measure of this mobility is the proportion of boys whose fathers held blue-collar jobs and who themselves obtained white-collar jobs. How many of those who made this transition had enrolled in high school? Table 1.6 (part C) indicates that among the children of natives, extended schooling was important for working-class mobility into middle-class jobs as early as 1880. Very nearly 30% of the upwardly mobile came from the ranks of those who had received secondary schooling. That the rate is so high is striking, because only one boy in eight from this stratum enrolled in high school. Upward mobility of this sort was comparatively rare among those who had not enrolled in high school (one in four accomplished it) and very common among those who had (four in five did so). As a result, a significant proportion of the upward mobility of boys from native, working-class homes was indeed accomplished with the aid of secondary schooling even in the years when 88% of such boys never reached high school.

Moreover, because the rate of entry in 1880 probably was not significantly different from what it was in 1850 or 1860, and because working-class mobility into white-collar jobs was not vastly more common in the early years either, it is probable that the same conclusion – the considerable connection between secondary schooling and upward mobility among boys from native, working-class homes – will hold for the entire second half of the nineteenth century, at least in the urban North.

Among the sons of immigrant workers, the proportion of high school entrants who obtained white-collar work was nearly four in five. However, only 2.1% of the sons of immigrant workers enrolled in high school. Consequently, they accounted for only a small fraction of the upward mobility by men of immigrant stock. Less than one in ten of the upwardly mobile accomplished that goal with the aid of secondary schooling. By 1900, the comparable fraction had doubled, to reach nearly a fifth; by 1915 it had shot up to nearly half, and by 1925 to nearly three-quarters. In twenty-five years, then, upward mobility among the sons of immigrant workers was transformed from something rarely accomplished with the aid of secondary schooling to something rarely accomplished without it.

We have dealt with two measures: the rates of high school entry and the magnitude of the occupational advantage conferred by entry. They help clarify a final point as well. We have seen that the magnitude of the occupational advantage enjoyed by high school entrants amounted to 9–12 points in each sample (Table 1.6), on average. Obviously, it varied from one individual to another, but did it also vary systematically across important social groups? For example, perhaps among the children of native-born workers, high school entrants enjoyed a 25-point advantage over nonentrants, whereas among the children of immigrant workers, high school entrants enjoyed only a 5-point advantage over nonentrants. The answer is that such variations in the magnitude of the advantage enjoyed by entrants did not exist. Nor, for example, was the occupational advantage that Russian Jewish high school entrants enjoyed over Russian Jewish nonentrants particularly different from the advantage that Italian entrants enjoyed over Italian nonentrants. Indeed, in general, this measure, the occupational advantage of extended schooling, did not vary systematically across ethnic groups, at least among whites.* Consequently, if ex-

---

* Or, more precisely, we cannot observe variations that did occur in this measure, and so we surmise that they must have been reasonably small. In part, the issue is methodological: It is difficult to determine the differences across groups in the occupational advantages of schooling – because results involving the interaction of three variables (occupation, schooling, and ethnicity) are less likely to reach levels of statistical significance than results involving the interaction of two variables. On the other hand, because each group is studied on the basis of samples from at least two different years, and because samples are large, the absence of large, consistent ethnic differences in the occupational advantages of extended schooling (even those that are not statistically significant) does suggest that whereas subtle differences of this sort may well have existed, we are not overlooking an essential part of the story by ignoring them.

tended schooling helped some ethnic groups to get ahead more than it helped others, the explanation lies in our other measure – that is, in the proportion who received extended schooling in each group. Of course, education is by no means the only explanation for ethnic differences in occupations. So we shall examine the proportion receiving an extended education in each ethnic group, as well as how fully these differing educational attainments account for the differing occupational outcomes for the groups.

2   The Irish

The famine migration, the massive Irish immigration of the mid-nineteenth century, was over well before 1880; however, the Irish continued to immigrate in great numbers for decades after the famine years. The number of later arrivals was never as great in any one decade as it had been in 1845–55, but impressive numbers arrived in every decade thereafter. By 1900, a majority of Irish immigrants living in the United States had arrived after the famine years. About 1.9 million had come between 1830 and 1860, and another 1.9 million arrived between 1860 and the turn of the century. Nearly three-quarters of a million more came between 1900 and the Great Depression. The American descendants of these immigrants probably number well over 15 million today. The coming of the Irish is a major theme in American history, a long, often painful process of accommodation by immigrants and their children and grandchildren – a theme not merely of one era but of successive eras.[1]

Many studies of Irish-American communities in the late nineteenth and early twentieth centuries have appeared recently. These have stressed, first, that the concentration on the northeastern states in earlier histories was misplaced; the Irish, particularly after the famine migration years, settled throughout the country. Moreover, those who settled outside the Northeast may have fared better economically than the rest. Finally, these recent studies have stressed that most earlier historical work concentrated on the famine migration and ignored the social accommodation of later generations. These criticisms, particularly the last, have some merit. On the other hand, throughout the nineteenth and early twentieth centuries, Irish immigrants were in fact concentrated in the Northeast. As late as 1900, 60% of them lived in six core northeastern states: New York, Pennsylvania, New Jersey, Massachusetts, Connecticut, and Rhode Island. Evidence about their success elsewhere is important, but what happened in the Northeast remains central.[2] Moreover, in the cities of New England they constituted an especially important presence, because until the 1880s their numbers were not matched by those of other immigrants. Elsewhere in the Northeast, a large mid-nineteenth-century influx of Germans accompanied the Irish immigration.

43

The importance of the Irish in the cities of New England is clear from the Providence sample of 1880, in which 41% of the children, the largest ethnic group, were the offspring of the Irish. Another 3% were the grandchildren of the earliest Irish arrivals. By contrast, the children of the Yankees accounted for 32% of this age group.

The children of the Irish in the 1900 and subsequent samples, of course, were the offspring of later waves of migration. By 1900, also, the grandchildren of the Irish immigrants, the third generation, composed a large group, and by 1915 they were nearly as numerous as the children of the immigrants.[3]

The Providence samples spanning 1880–1925 allow us to examine the Irish experience in a long, crucial period. Although the initial Irish adjustment to American life came earlier, much of it occurred during the years covered here. Indeed, change in the Irish educational and occupational patterns during the course of these years is one of the central themes of the following pages. The first section of this chapter concerns the amount of schooling Irish children received and the jobs the boys obtained when they reached their early twenties. The second and third sections cover patterns of Catholic school enrollment and some differences between public and Catholic schools.

2.1. Patterns of schooling and occupational attainment

Very few of the children of Irish immigrants had been born abroad: in 1880, about one in eight; by 1915, barely one in thirty.[4] The Irish children, then, generally did not personally suffer the consequences of transatlantic migration – such as arriving in the first grade at the age of nine. However, they certainly did suffer the disadvantage of immigrant working-class origins and often (especially in the early years) the disadvantage of severe poverty as well.

Throughout the period, the Irish-American households in Providence were overwhelmingly working-class (Table 2.1). Indeed, they were heavily concentrated in the lower levels of the working class, in the semiskilled and unskilled strata. In 1880, fully 60% of the household heads were employed in low manual labor, and that proportion did not change by more than five percentage points until 1925. Only tiny proportions reached the highest strata, and fewer than one in five households were headed by a white-collar worker of any kind before 1925.

Still, there was improvement over time. It can be seen most clearly in the mean occupational score for the group, which rose gradually between 1880 and 1915 and more sharply (by nearly 5 points) between 1915 and 1925. It can be seen, too, if less clearly, in the gradual

Table 2.1. *Occupations of Irish-American fathers*

Occupational stratum	Census year			
	1880 (%)	1900 (%)	1915 (%)	1925 (%)
Irish father				
High white-collar	2.4	2.2	2.1	2.7
Low white-collar	9.3	14.3	15.6	21.6
Skilled	21.0	19.8	23.0	18.9
Semiskilled	22.3	18.1	25.6	37.9
Unskilled	37.9	39.0	29.3	10.8
Unknown	7.0	6.6	4.4	8.1
Total (100%) N^a	837	182	646	74
Mean occupational score	15.9	18.6	21.4	26.3
Father native white, Irish parentage				
High white-collar	3.2	2.9	3.7	[b]
Low white-collar	9.5	16.2	23.6	
Skilled	47.6	27.6	24.6	
Semiskilled	11.1	39.0	32.5	
Unskilled	19.0	13.3	12.6	
Unknown	9.5	1.0	3.1	
Total (100%) N	63	105	191	
Mean occupational score	22.1	25.3	32.4	

[a]The numbers do not reflect the relative sizes of the groups. Different sampling ratios were used for each census. In 1915, the sampling ratio used for the Irish also differed from that used for the native whites of Irish parentage. [b]The 1925 Rhode Island State Census did not provide information on the sample members' grandparents.

increase in white-collar workers. By 1925, that proportion among Irish fathers had increased to a quarter of the household heads, which was about the norm in the city as a whole.

There was also improvement across generations. The households headed by a native of Irish parentage were better off than the Irish of the immigrant generation; in 1900, their mean occupational score was nearly 7 points higher, and in 1915, 11 points higher. Far fewer were in unskilled work, and by 1915 notably more were in white-collar work.[5]

The second-generation Irish reached the mean score for all fathers' occupations in the city by 1900 and passed it by 1915; the immigrant generation reached it in 1925. More and more immigrants came from southern and eastern Europe in the years after 1900, usually with few resources and few skills; the advantages of the Irish in job and language skills and in connections helped place them closer to the city-wide norm.

There was clearly improvement, then, both for later immigrants compared with earlier immigrants and for the second generation compared with the first. Nevertheless, the social position of the Irish was distinctly working-class, and the immigrant generation was heavily concentrated among the low manual workers.

It is critical to bear this perspective in mind in studying the schooling of the Providence Irish. The resources for extended schooling were surely lacking in many of these homes. Indeed, often child labor must have been necessary to make ends meet. Irish school attendance and child labor rates clearly reflect that reality. However, they reflect other influences as well.

We can measure the length of schooling in two ways. High school enrollment rates are available for 1880–1925. Unfortunately, the high school data for 1880 and 1900 are flawed because the records of the Catholic high school are incomplete for those years. For most purposes, the gap in the records is trivial. However, because the Irish were the clientele of the Catholic institutions, it is important here. The numbers of missing high school records were therefore estimated with great care, and the observed Irish enrollment rates adjusted accordingly. The results were encouraging: Several independent procedures yielded consistent outcomes (see Appendix, Section 4D). Nevertheless, given the problem of missing high school records, it is especially fortunate that the census records themselves provide some relevant supplemental information. School attendance rates are available for 1880 and 1900, and child labor rates for 1880, 1900, and 1915. We can most fruitfully consider school attendance and child labor among children thirteen to fifteen years old, the most critical ages for the transition from school to work and the ages included in all three samples, 1880–1915.

In 1880, differences in schooling and child labor between the children of the Irish immigrants and the children of the Yankees were huge (Tables 2.2–2.4). Among the Yankees, only a fifth of the boys and a tenth of the girls worked during their early teens; among the Irish, nearly two-thirds of the boys and half the girls did so. Patterns of school attendance tell the same story. The high school enrollment rates of the Irish, even when every allowance is made for the missing records at the Catholic high schools, also indicate how starkly the city was divided along ethnic lines. An impressive minority of the Yankees reached high school, but almost none of the Irish children.

The Irish, as we have seen, came from less well-to-do homes. Surely, within all groups, the poor left school first. Yet the social-class differ-

Table 2.2. *High school enrollment of Yankees and Irish-Americans,*
1880–1925

Year and group	Rate (%)	N	Odds ratio: each group compared with Yankees[a]	
			No controls	Social background factors controlled[b]
1880: sons of				
Yankees	23.7	(355)		
Irish immigrants: observed[c]	2.1	(440)	14.48	4.68 (3.82)[d]
1880: daughters of				
Yankees	32.4	(259)		
Irish immigrants: observed	3.9	(335)	11.81	6.03 (4.99)
1900: sons of				
Yankees	36.2	(185)		
NWIRP[e]: observed	10.6	(104)	4.79	2.45 (2.28)
Irish immigrants: observed	14.9	(168)	3.24	1.18 (0.49)
1915: sons of				
Yankees	49.6	(123)		
NWIRP	47.9	(94)	1.07	0.82 (0.67)
Irish immigrants	40.7	(405)	1.43	0.85 (0.71)
1915: daughters of				
Yankees	55.0	(140)		
NWIRP	46.4	(97)	1.41	0.95 (0.17)
Irish immigrants	41.8	(201)	1.70	1.05 (0.20)
1925: sons of				
Native whites[f]	61.5	(296)		
Irish immigrants	73.5	(68)	0.58	0.43 (2.63)
Corrected for missing data[c]				
1880 sons of Irish	2.9–6.8		4.1–10.0	1.3–3.3
1880 daughters of Irish	5.5–10.8		4.1–8.5	2.1–4.2
1900 sons of NWIRP	13.4–18.6		2.3–3.4	1.3–1.9
1900 sons of Irish	16.2–20.0		2.1–2.7	0.8–1.0

[a] The odds that the children of Yankees (native whites of native parentage) would enroll in high school compared with the odds that the children of Irish immigrants would do so. In the NWIRP rows, the children of Yankees are compared with the grandchildren of Irish immigrants.

[b] Father's occupational score, assessed value of the family's property (high, low, none, missing), number of siblings, both parents present (yes, no). The second column of odds ratios are exponentiated coefficients from logit regression analyses.

[c] Some records of the Catholic high schools for 1880 and 1900 are missing. The corrected figures are based on estimates of the number of entrants to those high schools who were incorrectly classified as not having entered high school (see Appendix for the estimating procedure).

[d] *t* values.

[e] Native whites of Irish parentage.

[f] The 1925 Rhode Island State Census did not provide information on sample members' grandparents' places of birth. In 1915, 45.0% of the children of all native whites enrolled in high school ($N = 298$).

Table 2.3. *School attendance and child labor among Yankees and Irish-Americans age 13–15, 1880–1915*

Year and group	Proportions of sample members (%)				
	At school	At work	Both	Neither	N (100%)
1880: sons of					
Yankees	77.7	14.1	5.9	2.4	(170)
NWIRP[a]	33.3	46.7	13.3	6.7	(15)
Irish immigrants	31.5	46.1	17.0	5.4	(241)
1880: daughters of					
Yankees	77.2	9.7	0	13.2	(114)
NWIRP	50.0	33.3	16.7	0	(12)
Irish immigrants	40.2	45.6	8.9	5.3	(169)
1900: sons of					
Yankees	72.5	21.4	2.3	3.8	(131)
NWIRP	53.3	33.8	10.4	2.6	(77)
Irish immigrants	54.4	35.1	8.8	1.8	(114)
1915: sons of					
Yankees	[b]	12.8			(94)
NWIRP		18.6			(70)
Irish immigrants		21.1			(308)
1915: daughters of					
Yankees		5.8			(104)
NWIRP		15.5			(71)
Irish immigrants		12.8			(148)

[a] Native whites of Irish parentage.
[b] The 1915 Rhode Island State Census did not gather information on school attendance.

ences explain only part of the huge Irish–Yankee difference in schooling. Consider, for example, the minority of Yankee children from homes headed by a low manual worker. Nearly 100 such children were found in the Providence samples, enough to permit us to generalize confidently from their experience. Some 17% of them reached high school. This rate may be compared with the rate among *all* Irish children – those from low-manual-worker homes as well as the considerable minority (one-third) from skilled-worker or white-collar homes. We may also take the upper limit of the range estimated for the rate of Irish high school enrollment in 1880. Even with the comparison constructed in this way, the Irish enrollment rate is barely half the Yankee rate (8.8%).[6]

Table 2.4. *School attendance among Yankees and Irish-Americans age 13–15: a multivariate analysis*

| | | | Odds ratio: each group compared with Yankees[a] | |
Year and group	Rate (%)	N	No controls	Social background factors controlled[b]
1880: sons of				
Yankees	83.6	(170)		
All Irish immigrants	48.5	(241)	5.41	3.97[c] (4.42)[d]
Literate Irish immigrants[e]	52.1	(167)	4.69	3.88 (4.20)
1800: daughters of				
Yankees	77.2	(114)		
All Irish immigrants	49.1	(169)	3.51	2.04 (2.03)
Literate Irish immigrants	51.9	(129)	3.14	1.91 (2.15)
1900: sons of				
Yankees	74.8	(131)		
NWIRP[f]	63.7	(77)	1.69	1.19 (0.46)
Irish immigrants	63.2	(114)	1.73	0.90 (0.31)

Note: The 1915 and 1925 Rhode Island State Censuses did not provide information on school attendance. Consequently, comparisons are restricted to the first two periods.
[a]The odds that the child of a Yankee (native white of native parentage) would attend school at age 13–15 compared with the odds that the child of an Irish immigrant would do so.
[b]See note *b* in Table 2.2.
[c]The 1880 male ratio is significantly different from the 1900 ratio ($t = 3.12$).
[d]*t* value.
[e]Based on the head of household: ability to read and write.
[f]Native whites of Irish parentage.

The same point may be made more systematically with the help of multiple regression. We can take into account several family background characteristics at the same time. In addition to the father's occupation, the assessed value of the family's property, whether or not both parents were present, and the number of children in the household were controlled. The first two are measures of social-class origin, as already explained. The larger the number of children, the fewer the resources (material and other) that parents could devote to each one. The absence of a parent, other things being equal, also made material and other forms of support scarcer. Consequently, children from larger families, or those with one parent, were less likely to participate in extended schooling. All of these family background characteristics were related to both schooling and ethnicity. How much of the Irish–Yankee difference in school behavior, then, resulted from Irish–Yankee differences in the prevalence of these characteristics?

The format of Tables 2.2 and 2.4 is used throughout this book. The first column of the table indicates high school entry rates, and the second column the number of sample members on which these rates are based. The third and fourth columns provide odds ratios. The odds ratio offers a particularly useful comparison of the behavior of groups, in this case of Irish and Yankees. For example, the first row of odds ratios in Table 2.2 compares the odds that Yankee children would enroll in high school and the odds that Irish children would do so. A ratio more than 1.00 indicates that the Yankees were more likely to enroll, a ratio less than 1.00 indicates that the Irish were more likely to enroll, and a ratio of 1.00 indicates that children in the two groups were equally likely to do so. The odds ratio in the third column is based simply on the proportions in the first column.* The odds ratio in the fourth column is based on a comparison in which the family background characteristics noted earlier have been taken into account. The t statistic, in the last column, is an indicator of the statistical significance of the ethnic difference that is unexplained by family background. A t statistic greater than 1.96 is regarded as statistically significant.†

Table 2.2 presents the results of the regression analyses for high school entry, and Table 2.4 presents those for school attendance rates. Whichever measure is used, the story is the same: In 1880, a large ethnic difference remains unexplained even when the family background characteristics discussed earlier have been taken into account. The difference is just as clear for both sexes.[7]

---

* The odds that a child of a particular group would enter high school is the proportion who entered divided by the proportion who did not. An odds ratio is the ratio of the odds for two groups. Thus, in the first line of Table 2.2, the proportions in the first column (23.7% and 2.1%) may be converted into the odds ratio in the third column: $[0.237/(1-0.237)]/[0.021/(1-0.021)] = 14.48$. Note that in some subsequent tables (e.g., those that deal with occupational attainment), means rather than rates (and differences between means rather than odds ratios) are presented.

† However, lower t values, particularly if comparisons with all other groups are in the same direction, should not necessarily lead one to ignore the results. On the other hand, t values below 1.00 suggest great caution in taking an individual result seriously. The t value indicates the probability that a particular difference between groups is merely an artifact of sampling (that in the population from which the sample was drawn, the relevant odds ratio is actually 1.00, or the relevant difference in means is actually 0). A t value of 1.96 indicates that a given observed difference between groups would be expected as an artifact of sampling in 5% of the relevant samples that could be drawn from the population; a t value of 1.65 indicates that the observed difference would be expected as an artifact of sampling in 10% of the samples; a t value of 1.00 indicates that the observed difference would be expected in about 30% of the samples.

Several historians have suggested that Irish parents' desire for the security of homeownership led them to send their children to work at early ages, sacrificing schooling in the process. Irish rates of home-ownership in working-class strata did exceed those for Yankees, and Irish children did leave school earlier. However, the prevalence of Irish homeownership is not evidence that the Irish sacrificed their children's schooling to attain that goal. On the contrary, the children from Irish homeowning families were more (not less) likely to have received extended schooling than were the children of Irish renters (even after controls for other family background characteristics have been imposed). Apparently these families had reached their goal of homeownership by following other strategies.[8]

Of course, various other factors may have helped create this ethnic difference in schooling, such as economic and demographic characteristics of families that we cannot measure, or imperfect measurement of those we can. Such concerns can be addressed more conveniently following our analysis of the Italians in Chapter 3 (Section 3.5). Here we note only that relevant omitted characteristics, such as family income, probably were highly correlated with those that were included in the regression analyses. Consequently, much of the connection between these additional factors and schooling has already been taken into account. Even if we could control them, they probably would not reduce the ethnic differences in school patterns to insubstantial levels.[9]

Thus, the regressions lead us to conclude that the glaring Irish–Yankee difference in schooling and child labor patterns in 1880 was partly due to differences in social class and family structure between the two groups – but also that it was partly independent of these background characteristics. Later we shall consider the sources of that large residual ethnic difference, the difference not due to family background characteristics. First, however, we should turn to the change in patterns of Irish schooling over time.

The sharp differences between Irish and Yankee schooling seen in 1880 had all but disappeared by 1900. True, Irish rates of school attendance, child labor, and high school enrollment still differed from those for Yankees. However, in 1900 and 1915, these ethnic differences were due largely to social class and the other family background factors that distinguished Irish from Yankee. When these factors are controlled, the residual ethnic difference is trivial in magnitude and in statistical significance. Indeed, by 1925, the figures suggest, the Irish had pulled ahead.[10]

Much of the change seems to have occurred since 1880, although there may have been a further spurt between 1915 and 1925. In any case, the consistency of the evidence for 1900–25 makes it clear that the shift after 1880 was not an artifact of some quirk in the 1900 sample. On the contrary, there are some peculiarities to the 1900 patterns, but in the context of the samples from other years, these suggest an interesting interpretation. The peculiar feature of the 1900 data is the decline in the rates of school attendance by adolescent Yankees between 1880 and 1900, when one might have expected a rise, as extended schooling became more common (Table 2.3). The decline is admittedly not great and could perhaps be due to sampling variability. But given the expectation of an increase, the drop is noteworthy. Indeed, none of the city's ethnic groups – except the Irish-Americans – registered more than a trivial increase in rate of school attendance during these years, and some showed a decline. The reason may have to do with the condition of the economy. Whereas 1900 was a good year in which to look for work, 1880 may still have shown some effect of the depression of the 1870s.[11] The change among the Irish, then, should be considered in that context: Despite the greater incentive to look for work in 1900, which acted to reduce rates of school attendance in general, the rate of Irish-Americans had risen.

How are we to understand both the sharp difference between Yankee and Irish school behavior in 1880 and its later disappearance? Because measurable family background factors only partly explain the phenomenon, and additional, unmeasured factors are unlikely to do so, we turn to other dimensions of the Irish-American experience. Two kinds of explanations are especially relevant. One concerns the cultural heritage that the immigrants brought from Ireland. The other concerns the nature of Irish–Yankee relations and of Irish accommodation to American urban life generally.

These explanations deal with influences on behavior that cannot be easily isolated and measured. Moreover, partly as a result of this difficulty, these explanations can be easily abused. It is, in particular, notoriously difficult to generalize convincingly about the values that distinguish one culture from another. Nevertheless, these explanations are worth our cautious consideration because they are based on the Irish historical experience and if formulated with care, they can help us comprehend the patterns of behavior we have observed.

We begin with the question of the world view that traditional Irish peasant culture, the culture of the immigrants, may have encouraged. Whatever the hazards of generalizations about cultures, social historians across an impressive range – from at least Oscar Handlin's earliest writings through Kerby Miller's 1985 synthesis of the Irish immigration – have argued for just such a generalization. In Miller's summary, traditional Irish peasant culture was more communal than individualistic, more dependent than independent, more fatalistic than optimistic, more prone to accept conditions passively than to take initiatives for change, and more sensitive to the weight of tradition than to innovative possibilities for the future. Indeed, their perspectives seemed so premodern that to bourgeois observers from business-minded cultures, the native Irish often appeared "feckless," "child-like" and "irresponsible": inclined to behave or justify behavior in ways which avoided personal initiative and individual responsibility, especially as to livelihood.[12]

Such a culture would not have encouraged schooling as a means toward economic advancement; indeed, it would not have encouraged any means toward such advancement. How much this cultural outlook was particularly Irish, and how much it shared with peasant cultures generally, we cannot resolve.

Whatever its origins, such a cultural heritage would help explain the specifics of Irish educational patterns, including their change over time. The recent descriptive literature suggests a transformation of Irish peasant attitudes during the nineteenth century and consequently the likelihood that the outlook of later migrants differed somewhat from that of the earlier migrants.[13]

The trends in rates of Irish literacy offer some support for these descriptions of a changing peasant outlook. Literacy rates in mid-nineteenth-century Ireland were still low, but rising rapidly. The figures for Ireland suggest that the parents in the 1880 sample were part of a cohort about half of whom were literate; the parents in the 1900 sample were part of a cohort three-quarters literate (Table 2.5).[14] The immigrant Irish parents in Providence were actually more literate as a group than the Irish cohorts they left behind. Nevertheless, the trend in literacy rates among these parents reflects the trend in Ireland. In 1880, 22% of the Irish immigrant fathers and 37% of the mothers were illiterate; by 1900, only 6% of the fathers and 14% of the mothers were.

Increasing levels of literacy may erode the attitudes characteristic of the older culture directly, by introducing new ideas. Literacy may be particularly relevant to attitudes of parents concerning their children's education. Alternatively, increased literacy may accompany the economic and social transformations that hasten such attitudinal changes. As such, even if not directly a source of change, it may still be an indicator of that change.[15]

Were the literate Irish really more supportive of their children's schooling than the illiterate Irish, as this line of reasoning implies they would be? The Providence data from 1880 can provide a direct

Table 2.5. *Literacy in Ireland, 1841–1901*

British Census year	Percentage of population who could read and write	
	Entire population	Children age 10–15 years
1841	28	
1851	33	
1861	41	48
1871	49	59
1881	59	73
1891	71	87
1901	79	94

Sources: Great Britain, Parliament, *Parliamentary Papers,* 1882 (Commons), vol. 76 ("Census of Ireland, 1881. Part II, General Report," London, 1882), and *Parliamentary Papers,* 1902 (Commons), vol. 129 ("Census of Ireland, 1901. Part II, General Report," London, 1902).

test: a comparison of the schooling of children from literate and illiterate Irish immigrant homes.

That test offers only a modest confirmation of the idea that literate parents supported schooling more than others (Table 2.4). The children of the literate were indeed more likely to attend school (even after other family background characteristics have been controlled), but only slightly so. The school attendance rates among the children of the literate and illiterate Irish were much more similar than the former were to Yankee rates.[16]

In sum, the one attempt we can make to confirm possible changes in attitudes brought from Ireland – using parental literacy as a proxy for such changes – provides only modest support for the hypothesis. We cannot rule out the possibility that such changes were important; literacy may simply be a poor proxy for them. Nevertheless, we do well to consider additional sources of difference between the earlier and later immigrants.

In nineteenth-century Providence, Irish–Yankee animosities, often stemming from religious issues, were bitter, just as they were elsewhere.[17] If a Protestant mob never destroyed a Catholic convent in Providence, as occurred in Boston in 1834, perhaps it was only because, on at least one occasion, the Providence Irish answered the call of their bishop and, armed to the teeth, stood guard over church property. Such open threats of violence receded in later years, but other forms of confrontation remained common throughout the century. Among the most important issues was the "school question." In 1874, in the *Providence Journal*, the bishop challenged the fairness of taxing Catholics for public schools. Two years later, the Rhode Island Commissioner of Education openly pronounced that the Protestant Bible was read in public schools. That same year (1876) the state legislature limited the tax-exempt status of religious institutions, with the result that Catholic schools were excluded from the exemption. Court challenges to this law in 1878 and 1883 failed, but they must have kept the issue in the public mind. The law was not repealed until 1894.[18] Perhaps its repeal indicates some accommodation between the Irish and Yankees, or at least the emergence of the Irish as a political force.

Whatever the degree of affection between groups in the city, the Irish could feel more at home by the turn of the century simply because they had gained a modicum of political control. Irish political power was more restricted in Providence than in many other cities, such as Boston, because of local political arrangements. Until 1888, the foreign-born could not vote in municipal or state elections unless they possessed real estate; until 1928, citizens without real estate could not vote for the city council. Although the Irish vote did become important in the elections for mayor after 1888, the power of that office was severely limited. Indeed, many issues affecting the city's affairs were settled in the state legislature. These arrangements, in turn, were preserved through the 1920s by a notoriously corrupt state legislature. As a result, Yankee control of city government lasted much longer than it did in Boston.

Nevertheless, the Irish presence in politics became increasingly important in the 1880s. Although the Irish could not seize control of the city council, they did conquer the Democratic Party. Between 1888 and 1900, Irish representation on the party ward committees increased from 35% to 73%, while Yankee representation fell from 61% to 23%. The Providence School Committee (like the mayor) was elected by the full electorate, and consequently Irish representation there was notable by 1900. In 1880, when the School Committee included sixty members, only one member (and perhaps a second) had a father born in Ireland. By 1900, the committee's size had been reduced to thirty. Of these, six had Irish-born fathers. No doubt, too, Democratic members of the School Committee who were not of Irish descent would still have been very sensitive to issues of Irish concern when three-quarters of the Democratic ward committeemen were Irish.

Changes were palpable at the level of the classroom. Less than 4% of the public school teachers in 1880 were children of Irish immigrants; by 1908, almost a quarter were, and many more must have been granddaughters of the immigrants by then. It is hard to judge whether so many teachers were of Irish background because the increasing political power of the Irish made their appointment possible or simply because, given the city's ethnic composition, Irish girls would in any case have constituted a large fraction of those entering teaching. But the combination of these factors seems to have worked as effectively in Providence as in Boston, whatever the differences in Irish political clout in the two cities may have been. In 1908, the Irish fraction of the teaching force was the same in both cities.[19]

In short, it is reasonable to suppose that by 1900, the Irish were keeping their children in school longer because by that time they felt more comfortable with the public schools. They felt more comfortable, in turn, because the bitter feelings between them and the Yankees had diminished, because they exerted more control over the schools than they had formerly, and because their own daughters were now heavily represented among the teachers.[20]

Support for the conclusion that by 1900 the Irish felt more at home in Providence generally, and in its public schools in particular, than they had earlier comes from a Catholic observer of the era. A historian of the diocese of Providence, writing in 1899, noted that the local parishes had only recently been able to afford the construction of decent schools. However, he added, "now the enthusiasm for these schools is far less than it would have been thirty years ago, when Catholics were smarting under the affronts and insults of 'Nativism' and 'Know-Nothing-ism'."[21] Although there is no way of determining precisely how much of the change in Irish behavior between 1880 and 1900 was due to such cultural and political accommodation, some of it probably was.

This explanation of Irish school patterns (that the Irish felt more comfortable in the Providence public schools) can be contrasted with the first explanation discussed (a shift in Irish peasant values and attitudes concerning schooling). This second explanation does not necessarily imply any shift in basic values among the Irish. It need involve no more than an increasing Irish Catholic confidence that the schools would treat their children decently and not malign their faith – quite possibly an accurate assessment of the changing reality. Both are arguments about cultural change, but quite different changes are involved. Indeed, a related argument concerns the sharp rise in the number of Irish teachers. These teachers must have made these institutions appear not merely less hostile to Irish parents, but also more salient – in discussions about relatives and friends, for example. These explanations are not, of course, mutually exclusive. However, it is worth stressing that having controlled for various economic and de-mographic characteristics of groups, we are still confronted with a range of plausible "cultural" explanations. Moreover, differences in the perceived value of schooling between groups need not always be the most important of these explanations.

An expansion of Irish job opportunities may also have influenced the group's school behavior. If the friends of the Irish were more often in positions to hire them by 1900, if fewer announcements proclaimed that no Irish need apply, preparation for more attractive employment may have seemed more valuable. Most new occupational opportuni-ties did not require the extensive schooling that teaching did, al-though some of the new clerical jobs opening up for women in these years may have had comparable educational requirements. In any case, for some, the preparation for jobs that did require schooling, and the increased awareness of opportunity, may have encouraged extended schooling. In part, this source of the change in Irish school behavior was simply a rational response to the changing availability of jobs requiring schooling. In part, it was based on a general diffusion of positive attitudes toward schooling that in turn stemmed from changes in the labor market. In any case, such transformations were not in the heritage brought from Ireland, but in the influences prevalent in the American city.

Finally, the presence of a large, settled, second-generation com-munity, natives of Irish parentage, must have eased the later Irish immigrants' accommodation to urban America. That community was growing rapidly. In 1880, only 7% of the Irish-American children were from homes in which the fathers had been born in the United States. By 1900, the comparable proportion was 37%. Even if the pre-migration culture had not changed at all between 1880 and 1900, the very presence of these more acclimated individuals would have helped make the adjustment of later Irish immigrants more rapid. We may seek evidence of this influence in a comparison of the school patterns for the third generation compared with those for the second. The be-havior patterns of the grandchildren might be expected to fall be-tween those of the children of the Irish immigrants and those of the Yankees. However, no such neat pattern appears. The behavior pat-terns for both generations of Irish-Americans are quite similar in 1900 and in 1915 (Tables 2.2–2.4). The immigrant households may have absorbed the outlook of the second-generation households, at least with regard to schooling. Or perhaps the balance of the other influ-ences we have considered – pre-migration culture and patterns of accommodation in Providence – operated to create similar school be-havior among both generations.

In any case, the finding that by 1900 the children of the Irish were receiving as much schooling as Yankees of similar socioeconomic status deserves to be stressed in the light of other interpretations of Irish patterns of behavior. These interpretations often fail to distinguish the Irish of the early twentieth century from those of the middle nineteenth century. A particularly glaring instance is found in the work of Thomas Sowell:

> The ancient Celtic culture was "hostile to literacy" and Ireland was the only major Western nation that did not build a single university during the middle ages. Even a sympathetic historian acknowledges that there has been "almost no intellectual tradition among them."
>
> Against this background it is perhaps not surprising that early twentieth century Irish youngsters in New York finished high school at a rate less than one hundredth of that of youngsters from a German or Jewish background. . . . The importance of education was simply seen very differently by [the Irish] and it had been for centuries.[22]

Both the theory of cultural heritage and the evidence on Irish-American schooling in Sowell's discussion should be scrutinized. His view of the Irish pre-migration heritage is based on a cultural force that retains its power not merely over decades but over centuries and even millennia, and apparently does so independent of the social structural contexts in which it exists. It would not be surprising, if this legacy were indeed operative, that the Irish migrants of the famine years and those who came in the twentieth century shared the same outlook. Such a cultural explanation may be contrasted with the more limited and tentative explanation offered earlier that rests on a "peasant outlook." But can the medieval history of the university seriously be proposed as evidence for the attitudes of late-nineteenth-century peasant migrants? Surely, at the very least, the two phenomena are results of some differing causes as well as some similar causes. And if such murky appeals to medieval intellectual life are in order, what of the Irish monks whose literacy and dedication preserved so many texts for Christendom?

Moreover, Sowell's evidence is inaccurate. It is simply untrue that the Irish graduated high school at less than one-hundredth the rate for Jews and Germans. Sowell relied on an erroneous report of a questionable study.[23] Much more straightforward evidence is available from the 1960 U.S. Census. It reported the years of schooling completed for groups in each region of the country by age. Those who were sixty-five to seventy-four years old in that year would have been fifteen years old in the years 1901–10. Among the children of Irish immigrants in that age group, 23.5% were listed as high school graduates, whereas 29.6% of the children of Russians (nearly all Jews) and 14.9% of the children of Germans had reached that level of schooling. Admittedly, graduation rates were higher among the Jews than among the Irish, but by no means to the extent Sowell suggested.[24] In any case, graduation rates were higher among the Irish than among the Germans. Finally, it seems worth recalling, in the light of Sowell's conclusion, that even in the period in which Irish schooling was greatly different from that of Yankees in Providence, it is difficult to sort out how much of the difference was due to attitudes concerning the value of education and how much was due to attitudes resulting from Protestant domination of schools, the labor market, and other important institutions.

Stephan Thernstrom's judicious and influential examination of ethnic groups also concluded that Irish educational attainment was low in the early twentieth century. He also cited aspects of the premigration culture as sources of the pattern. He noted the educational, occupational, and income status in 1950 among the sons of immigrants from several countries: Ireland, Italy, England, Sweden, Germany, and Russia. This evidence suggests that Jewish and Swedish attainments cannot be attributed merely to their family origins. Swedes, and especially the Jews, did outdistance the other three groups. However, Thernstrom seemed to believe that the Irish peasants were especially low achievers, not merely that the Swedes and Jews were especially high.[25] Yet whereas the Irish do indeed fall a few points behind the English and the Germans, their social origins were much less advantageous, so that the difference in attainment hardly seems remarkable.[26]

On the other hand, the detailed national evidence in the 1960 U.S. Census, referred to briefly earlier, supports the conclusion about twentieth-century Irish-American schooling suggested by the Providence samples. It provides unusually detailed tables on educational attainment among ethnic groups. The native-born children of Irish immigrants were among the highest of any group in median years of school completed (Table 2.6). They matched the children of other British immigrants, Germans, and native whites, for example.[27] True, the Swedes had slightly higher attainments, and the Russian Jews much higher attainments (at least by the 1920s), but these groups' attainments were the very highest reported. If Irish rates appear low by comparison, so must all others. The proportion of Irish entering college in the early cohorts was lower than for some of these other ethnic groups, but only slightly lower.

A great difference between Yankee and Irish patterns of schooling had existed in the nineteenth century, a difference that cannot be explained by family background characteristics. This is one major

Table 2.6. *Educational attainments of selected ethnic groups, 1960 U.S. Census data*

| Gender and age cohort: 15 years old in | Median years of school completed (U.S. and Northeast region[a]) for children of fathers born in selected countries | | | | | | | |
| | United States | | Northeast | | | | | |
	Natives	Ireland	Ireland	U.K.	Russia	Germany	Sweden	Italy
Males								
1941–50	12.3	12.6	12.6	12.6	14.1	12.5	12.6	12.1
1931–40	12.1	12.5	12.4	12.3	12.7	12.2	12.4	11.1
1921–30	10.4	11.7	11.3	11.4	12.5	10.2	11.7	8.9
1911–20	8.8	9.5	9.2	9.3	11.1	8.7	9.5	8.4
1901–10	8.4	8.7	8.7	8.7	9.0	8.4	8.7	8.0
1900 or before	8.2	8.5	8.5	8.5	8.5	8.3	8.6	7.8
Females								
1941–50	12.3	12.5	12.5	12.5	12.7	12.4	12.5	12.2
1931–40	12.2	12.4	12.4	12.4	12.5	12.2	12.4	11.0
1921–30	11.4	12.1	12.0	11.9	12.2	10.5	12.2	8.7
1911–20	9.4	10.4	10.0	9.9	10.7	8.7	10.5	8.3
1901–10	8.7	8.9	8.8	8.9	8.9	8.4	8.8	7.8
1900 or before	8.6	8.7	8.6	8.7	8.7	8.4	8.7	8.0
Males only, selected cohorts: proportion completing at least 1 year of college								
1921–30	17.6	21.9	18.4	20.9	38.3	16.2	21.6	9.4
1911–20	14.5	15.8	13.7	16.0	27.2	11.3	16.6	8.1

[a]Region of residence in 1960.
Source: U.S. Bureau of the Census, *Census of Population: 1960:* subject reports: "Educational Attainment" (Washington, 1963), Table 5, and "Nativity and Parentage" (Washington, 1965), Table 12.

finding of our study.[28] The pre-migration cultural heritage probably influenced these patterns, and the value placed on learning by the Irish peasantry may well be a particularly influential element in that heritage. The other major finding is that those earlier Irish patterns of schooling had changed by the twentieth century. There is good reason to think that transformations in pre-migration culture, as well as in the cultural and political context into which the Irish came, were sources of the change in school behavior.

The later careers of the young men in the samples provide a second perspective on the Irish experience in the United States. Male sample members, it will be recalled, were traced from the years of the census to later years, by means of city directories, which provided their occupations at the time they were twenty-three to twenty-six years old.[29] The results confirm the two striking patterns evident in school behavior. First, in 1880 the occupational positions of the Irish were considerably below those for the Yankees, even when family background is taken into account. Second, by the later years, 1915 to 1925, the situation had changed dramatically, so that the Irish were in a much more favorable position.

Even in 1880, the children of the Irish held more attractive jobs than their fathers had held. The mean score for the fathers' jobs had been 16; for the sons it was 26 (Table 2.7). However, the mean occupational score for Yankees' sons was 41! Much of this huge ethnic difference was due to differences in family background – particularly, of course, to the relatively comfortable economic situation of the Yankee families. Many more Yankee sons also enjoyed the benefit of an extended education. However, family origin, not education, appears to have been the more important factor in creating the ethnic difference in job outcomes (as comparing the magnitudes of the ethnic differences in the third through sixth columns of Table 2.7 suggests). Also, the ethnic difference that remains when both education and family background are controlled is large: 6 points in 1880, and 7 points in 1900, on an occupational scale with a standard deviation of some 18 points.

The Irish, of course, included a large number of illiterate fathers in 1880. Their sons suffered a handicap that does not fully disappear even when all the other background factors are taken into account. However, as in the case of the school patterns, most of the differences between Yankee and Irish were unrelated to this background characteristic: The sons of literate Irish differed from those of Yankees by 6 points.[30]

Despite the Irish disadvantage of the early years, by 1915 the average Irish young man had a slightly better occupation than the average

Table 2.7. *Ethnic differences in occupational attainment, males, 1890–1935*[a]

			Differences in means			
				Controlling for		
Year and group	Means	N	No controls	Family back-ground	Educa-tion	Both
1880 sample: sons of						
Yankees	40.8	(249)				
Irish immigrants[b]	26.2	(214)	−14.6	−6.8	−11.1	−6.4
1900 sample: sons of						
Yankees	40.2	(163)				
NWIRP[bc]	30.3	(78)	−9.9	−7.3	−6.9	−6.3
Irish immigrants[b]	28.8	(112)	−11.4	−7.3	−8.8	−7.2
Irish immigrants compared with all except Irish-Americans	35.3	(469)	−6.5	−4.0	−5.7	−4.4
1915 sample: sons of						
Yankees	35.0	(77)				
NWIRP	36.6	(68)	1.6	4.4	3.9	4.3
Irish immigrants	32.9	(238)	−2.1	3.2	0.1	2.9
Irish immigrants compared with all except Irish-Americans	33.4	(742)	−0.5	1.5	−0.8	0.5
1925 sample: sons of						
Native whites	34.8	(150)				
Irish	35.9	(35)	1.1	4.9	1.0	3.5
Irish immigrants compared with all others	31.7	(497)	4.2	5.2	2.5	3.6

Notes: (1) All differences shown for 1880 and 1900 are significant ($t > 1.96$); for the later periods, only the fourth and sixth columns for 1915 NWIRP are. (2) In 1880, the difference between the sons of literate Irish and the sons of Yankees, with both family background and schooling controlled, was −5.9.
[a]Male sample members' occupational attainment a decade after the census year (e.g., 1890 for 1880 sample members). Available only for those sample members found in the Providence area in the later year. Based on a numeric score for each occupational title (the Duncan score). The differences in means are coefficients on ethnic dummy variables in OLS regressions. Also, supplemental samples are included in the regressions, weighted to reflect their true relative magnitudes (samples of blacks in all periods, high school entrants in the first three periods, and Russian Jews, Irish, and Italians in 1915). Results without weights, and results omitting the high school entrant sample, were comparable to the above. The N's reported are for actual sample size.
[b]Compared with Yankees.
[c]NWIRP, native whites of Irish parentage.

Yankee, once family background is taken into account. Some of this change was due to a drop in the Yankees' position relative to the position of all others. However, there is no mistaking the Irish advance. It is apparent in both 1915 and 1925, whether the sons of the Irish (or the grandsons) are compared with the Yankees, with all native whites, or with all young men not of Irish descent.

Some of the sources of behavior surveyed earlier are specific to schooling; others may also have influenced Irish occupational attainment. If there was indeed a "fatalistic" streak in the pre-migration culture of the early Irish migrants, as some observers noted, that surely would have influenced jobs as well as schooling. In the United States, the conflict between Protestant Yankees and Catholic Irish no doubt resulted in job discrimination against the Irish, discrimination that was more virulent in the early years of their migration history. Later, the discrimination may have abated, not only because the Irish became more familiar by dint of long acquaintance but also because they seemed less alien than the later newcomers from southern and eastern Europe. For example, the Italians, like the Irish, were Catholics, but, in addition, they did not speak English, and they came from less developed regions than the Ireland of 1915.

Discrimination also would have abated because increasing Irish influence in city government meant some district control over job opportunities. It was not merely that the Irish could be hired as firemen or policemen; despite the common image of the Irish policeman, relatively few of the young men in the sample held such jobs. However, the city probably employed many young men in a variety of jobs. Given the nature of most job titles, we cannot, unfortunately, identify those who worked for the city. We cannot determine, for example, how many of the young Irish-American clerks were on the public payroll. In any case, many who would have profited from political influence probably were not public employees at all. Rather, they worked for Irish employers who did an important share of their business with the city, much more than Irish employers would have done in earlier years. Such transformations are simply too deeply buried in the texture of economic relations to be reflected clearly in the job descriptions of the census or city directory. These transformations, however, may well be reflected in the changing relative positions of the Irish sons.

Whereas the processes underlying the transformations in educational and occupational attainments were broadly the same, the timing of changes in these attainments may well have varied somewhat. Whatever the specifics of the timing, however, the evidence of transformations in Irish achievements, both in schooling and in jobs, is unambiguous.[31]

2.2.   Growth of the Catholic school system: Providence, Boston, and beyond

Everywhere they settled, the Irish have been among the most important clientele of the Catholic schools. Indeed, in Providence, the vast majority of the children in these institutions were Irish-Americans. The Catholic schools probably represent the largest project undertaken by voluntary associations in American history, with the exception of the churches themselves. In many places they enrolled substantial fractions of the entire school population, dwarfing, at least by the late nineteenth century, all other private initiatives in schooling. In Providence, throughout our period, one schoolchild in six attended a Catholic school. These schools faced many of the same issues as the public schools, but always in a somewhat different way – issues of bureaucracy, local control and community feeling, class and ethnic divisions, concerns about curriculum and self-image, and recruitment and supervision of teachers. The significance of these issues bears not only on religious and educational history but also on working-class history and ethnic history.

Only a tiny fraction of the social history of education produced during the past two decades has dealt with these schools.[32] Questions relating to the nature of the Catholic school clientele, especially, have received little attention. Almost none of the recent attention to attendance patterns in American educational history has concerned the Catholic school experience.[33] How many of the Catholic children did these schools reach? Which elements within the Catholic population were especially likely to enroll?

The remainder of this chapter deals with the social history of Catholic schooling, principally among the Irish. It explores ethnic differences in behavior, the central theme of this book, in noting the use that different Catholic ethnic groups made of the Catholic schools. However, it also deals with other themes, such as differences in the use of these schools among the Irish themselves. These sections are therefore somewhat more marginal to the exploration of ethnic differences than are other sections. Yet, in contributing to the social history of the Catholic schools, they illuminate crucial dimensions of Irish-American schooling.

Using the Providence data set, as well as published data, it is possible to study the prevalence of Catholic schooling in the city and to make comparisons with other places. We can also explore, to a limited extent, the social origins of Catholic school pupils among the Providence Irish.[34]

The most relevant studies of the prevalence of Catholic schools in different cities have been done by James Sanders.[35] Sanders found

Table 2.8. *Ethnic composition in Boston and Providence, 1880–1920*

Birthplace and parentage	Percentage of city population in each group					
	1880		1900		1920	
	Bost.	Prov.	Bost.	Prov.	Bost.	Prov.
U.S.	68.4	73.1	64.9	68.2		
U.S., U.S. parentage					26.7	29.3
Germany	2.0	1.1	1.9	1.3	0.9	0.6
U.S., German parentage					1.6	1.1
Ireland	17.9	16.2	12.5	10.6	8.2	5.5
U.S., Irish parentage					15.2	12.0
Great Britain	3.3	6.0	3.2	6.6	2.5	4.2
U.S., British parentage					2.4	5.4
Canada	6.4	2.4	9.0	4.4	5.1	4.6
U.S., Canadian parentage					5.9	2.4
Italy			2.4	3.6	5.1	8.2
U.S., Italian parentage					5.2	9.5
Russia			2.7	1.1	6.4	3.0
U.S., Russian parentage					5.1	2.7
Other	2.0	1.2	3.4	4.2	3.7	2.9
U.S., other parentage					6.0	8.6
Total population (thousand)	363	105	561	176	748	238

Source: U.S. Census Office, *Statistics of the Population of the United States at the Tenth Census* (Washington, 1883), Table 16, and *Twelfth Census,* "Population, Part I" (Washington, 1901), Table 35, and U.S. Census Bureau, *Fourteenth Census,* Vol. II, "Population" (Washington, 1922), Tables 9 and 11.

dramatic contrasts between the Catholic schools of Chicago and Boston. In 1880, 94% of all parishes in Chicago had schools; in Boston, a mere 37% did. Similarly, the proportion of the city's pupils enrolled in Catholic schools was much higher in Chicago, although Catholics there composed a smaller proportion of the population than in Boston. Chicago may have been an unusually well-developed diocese, but certainly Boston was unusually lax when it came to parochial schooling.

Here these comparisons are extended to Providence, providing a useful context in which to assess the prevalence of Catholic schools there, and shedding additional light on the contrast between Boston and Chicago. Providence and Boston were similar in several important ways that distinguished Boston from Chicago: The two New England cities are barely fifty miles apart, in 1880 they had existed for centuries, rather than decades, and (as Table 2.8 shows) their ethnic

Table 2.9. *Proportions of parishes with schools: comparison of Boston, Chicago, and Providence, 1865–1930*

Year	Chicago		Boston		Providence	
	%	N	%	N	%	N
1865[a]	82	(17)	42	(12)		
1870	71	(21)				
1880	94	(31)	37	(27)	63	(8)
1890	77	(81)	42	(33)		
1900	76	(114)	43	(44)	47	(17)
1907			45	(53)		
1910	72	(187)				
1915			49	(63)	54	(24)
1920	86	(227)				
1925			59	(64)	54	(28)
1930	93	(253)				

[a] Figures for Boston are from 1866.
Sources: Chicago figures from Sanders, *Education of an Urban Minority*, p. 4; Boston figures 1865–1907 from Sanders, "Boston Catholics and the School Question," p. 49; later figures for Boston and figures for Providence from *The Catholic Directory*.

compositions were similar throughout the period considered here. Consequently, the proportions of Catholics in the two cities surely were similar.

Throughout these years, the proportion of parishes with parochial schools was greater in Chicago than in either Boston or Providence (Table 2.9). The proportions of all pupils who attended Catholic schools were somewhat similar in Providence and Chicago in the early years (Table 2.10), but at least until 1900, Catholics composed a smaller fraction of the city's population in Chicago than in Providence – so these figures suggest a higher rate of Catholic enrollment in Catholic schools in the midwestern city.[36]

The comparisons between Boston and Providence are also revealing. At least until 1880, it appears that the two cities differed markedly. Three-eighths of the parishes in Boston had schools, and five-eighths of those in Providence did. Admittedly, the number of parishes in Providence was small, and so the comparison is not entirely satisfying. However, the enrollment trends unmistakably show the same point: The proportion of pupils in Providence who attended Catholic schools was twice as high as in Boston. By 1900, the two cities seemed more similar. In Boston, 43% of the parishes had schools,

Table 2.10. *Catholic school pupils as a proportion of all pupils in Boston, Chicago, and Providence, 1855–1930*

Year	Chicago (%)	Boston (%)	Providence (%)
1855			10
1859		4	
1865[a]	17	11	
1870	22		
1880	22	10	19
1890	19	13	18
1900	17	15	15
1907		16	17
1910	21		16
1915		16–19[b]	16
1920	25		16
1925		18–21	16
1930	28		

[a] Figures for Boston from 1866.
[b] Boston figures for 1915–25 are based on the daily average number reported in the Boston School Committee's *Report*. The first figure for these years is the proportion of Catholic school pupils among all Catholic and public school pupils. However, there were few Catholic high school pupils. Consequently, the second figure indicates the percentage of Catholic school pupils among all Catholic school pupils and all public school pupils below the high school level.
Sources: Chicago figures from Sanders, *Education of an Urban Minority*, p. 12; Boston figures for 1859–1907 from Sanders, "Boston Catholics and the School Question," p. 49. On later Boston figures, see note *b*. Providence figures based on the school census reports published annually in the Providence School Committee's *Report* after 1885 (figures from earlier years from the 1885 *Report*). See also the Appendix to this book.

and in Providence, 47%; in both cities, 15% of the school enrollment was in parochial schools.

Thus, comparison of the two New England cities suggests that in the late nineteenth century, the Catholic school situation in Boston was indeed distinctive, as Sanders argued. However, by 1900, the factors that earlier had distinguished the two cities had lost their power.

We cannot, with the data at hand, sort out just what factors distinguished the Providence pattern from the Boston pattern during the nineteenth century, but the fact that the patterns were different re-

veals the importance of local conditions in Catholic school arrangements. Moreover, this fact suggests that the particular local conditions involved were not merely due to the ethnic composition of the
Catholic population. It is important to stress this point, because ethnic compositions, coupled with the varying attitudes of different
Catholic ethnic groups toward the church institutions, clearly were
among the reasons the cities differed in the incidence of Catholic
schooling. This ethnic diversity among Catholics is easy to see in
Providence by comparing the two largest Catholic groups: the Irish
and the Italians.

The proportion of Irish Catholic pupils enrolled in parochial schools
can be estimated (see Appendix, Section 4D). Some 54% were enrolled in Catholic schools in 1880, 44% in 1900, 52% in 1915, and 50%
in 1925. Whatever may have created some decrease in enrollment in
1900, the Irish were sending half or nearly half their children to Catholic schools throughout the period.

Table 2.11 and Table A.2 in the Appendix allow us to observe the
contrast between the Irish and the Italians. By 1925, for example, the
children of Italians constituted 29% of the sample population, but enrollment in Italian-parish parochial schools accounted for less than
2% of the city's pupils. Indeed, the French Canadians, who probably
had less than one-fifth as many children in this age group as the Italians, enrolled more pupils in their parochial schools.[37]

Thus, the ethnic compositions of cities had an important impact on
the prevalence of Catholic schooling, but they cannot fully explain
that prevalence, as the Boston–Providence comparison in the nineteenth century suggests. Additional evidence demonstrates the same
point more forcefully for one moment in time. The Immigration Commission provided a breakdown of the proportion of children from
each immigrant group who attended parochial schools in several cities during 1908. The differences between the Irish and Italians were
everywhere great: The Irish were much more likely to be in the Catholic schools. Yet within each immigrant group, there were also striking differences from city to city.

James Sanders offered an explanation for the relative dearth of
Catholic schooling in Boston, particularly in the nineteenth century,
that is useful to consider for Providence as well, an explanation that
combines intriguing observations about ethnic differences with other
aspects of urban history. Part of his explanation concerns differences
between the Irish and the Germans, the other large group of immigrants to use Catholic schools in the second half of the nineteenth
century. In Boston and Providence, the Catholics were Irish; by contrast, Chicago received very large numbers of Germans as well as

Table 2.11. *Proportions of children enrolling in Catholic schools among the Irish and Italians*

A. Children of Irish-Americans,[a] Providence, 1880–1925

Year	Proportion of all pupils in Catholic schools[b] (%)	Males only: proportion of high school entrants in Catholic high schools[c] (%)
1880	54	28–65
1900	44	32–41
1915	52	33
1925	50	39

B. Children of Irish and Italian immigrants in 1908, selected cities[d]

	Proportion in Catholic schools			
	Irish		Italian	
City	%	N	%	N
Boston	26	(20,357)	11	(8,269)
Cleveland	71	(3,287)	3	(2,154)
Newark	76	(3,355)	13	(6,460)
New York	47	(54,795)	12	(67,946)
Philadelphia	69	(20,379)	36	(10,447)
Providence	38	(3,916)	1	(3,574)
San Francisco	32	(3,868)	3	(3,532)

[a] Children of native whites of Irish parentage and children of Irish immigrants.
[b] From Table A.2 in the Appendix.
[c] Based on sample data and on estimates for missing data in 1880 and 1900 (see Appendix). Limited to sons of Irish immigrants in 1925.
[d] Included are cities studied by the Immigration Commission that had 2,000 or more children of both Irish and Italian immigrants. Calculated from Howard Ralph Weisz, *Irish American and Italian American Educational Views and Activities, 1870–1900: A Comparison* (New York, 1976), 96, 401.

Irish. The Germans, Sanders argued, tended to construct parochial schools much sooner than the Irish. The difference is not simply a result of the more favorable economic situation of the Germans. Priorities were also involved. Boston's Irish Catholic parishes routinely erected expensive churches, but waited years and even decades before building schools. In other dioceses, especially among German Catholics, schools were built first; the school's main hall would be used for mass until funds for a church could be raised. That difference in construction priorities reflected different evaluations of the significance of Catholic schooling among Irish and Germans. One reason for the difference was that the Germans had a language to preserve and consequently had an added incentive to establish special schools. Moreover, Sanders argued, the Germans may have been more concerned about schooling generally than the Irish were, because primary schooling was more developed in Germany than in Ireland.[38]

Sanders also noted that the diocesan leadership in Boston did not act to counter the priorities of the Irish parishes; instead, the bishops tended to support education by promoting a small number of elite institutions of advanced learning, rather than primary schools.

Part of the explanation for parishes' and bishops' priorities also involved, according to Sanders, the interplay between Irish Catholics and Yankees. Boston, perhaps more than any other city, maintained a long tradition of public schooling. At least in principle, those schools reached out to all. The city's Yankee leaders were faced with the choice of compromising the Irish sensibilities or seeing common schooling disappear. For their part, the Irish Catholics of Boston were faced with an institution central to Yankee culture in the city in which that culture was preeminent. Each group was ambivalent about the other, but neither was willing to dismiss the other.

By the twentieth century, the school situation and the critical factors influencing it were changing. An energetic cardinal and changes in social conditions brought Boston into the American Catholic mainstream. The Irish were no longer the impoverished, defensive, resentful group looking in from the outside. Prominent in city politics, their own kind sat on the school board, in the superintendent's office (after 1918), and at the teacher's desk. In this context, however, Catholic parents faced an unclear choice. The Catholic schools differed from the public schools in less glaring ways than they had earlier – not only in personnel but also in the sort of curriculum these personnel would support. Moreover, given the nineteenth-century legacy, most leading Catholic leaders, as well as many priests, were products of the public schools. If they had escaped with little harm, why not the next generation? Finally, the ethnic composition of the city continued to affect enrollments: The most important of the later Catholic immigrants to Boston, as to Providence, were the Italians. By contrast, in Chicago, the largest new group were the Poles, who, like the Germans, had a language to preserve and, unlike the Italians, identified their national existence with the church. Enrollment figures for Chicago in 1908 suggest that the Poles were ten times as likely as the Italians to choose a Catholic school over a public school.[39]

Much of Sanders's discussion is relevant to Providence as well. His comparisons of Irish and German parish priorities are suggestive. In Providence, too, Irish construction priorities placed the church before the school building.[40] Moreover, the suggestion that Irish behavior before the last decades of the nineteenth century may have been prompted by less concern for schooling than other groups showed is consistent with the view of Irish educational behavior discussed in the preceding section.

These factors help explain why Providence, like Boston, differed from Chicago in the prevalence of Catholic schools. However, why Catholic schools were more prevalent in Providence than in Boston during the nineteenth century must be explained by factors other than the ethnic compositions of the two cities. The clash of Yankee and Irish cultures that occurred in Boston may not have occurred in just the same way in Providence. Differences in the attitudes of the mid-nineteenth-century Yankee elites toward the public schools in the two cities, although probably minor, may have had some impact. Similarly, Providence was not "the Athens of America," and whereas the images of the Yankee elite and their culture must have seemed reasonably similar to the Irish immigrants in the two cities, they may not have been identical. In particular, the unique cultural status of the Boston Yankee may have mattered at the level of church leadership. Bishops and priests in Boston may not have opposed the prestige of the public schools quite as strongly as such leaders did elsewhere. It is difficult to say more in the absence of a full-scale history of the Providence diocese.

In the early twentieth century, the Italian influx into both cities kept the proportion of Catholics who attended religious schools relatively low.[41] As in Boston, the change in Irish attitudes toward the public schools must have reduced the clarity of the choice between public and Catholic schools. Finally, in Providence, as in Boston, half the Irish population had attended public schools. Later generations of parents must have been influenced by the fact that their own schooling, like that of many Catholic leaders, had taken place in public institutions, reducing the sense that these schools necessarily were detrimental to one's faith.

These factors, then, help explain why Catholic schooling did not reach even more Catholics in Providence. Should we consider the numbers it did reach, between two-fifths and half of the Irish children, as high or low? If judged by the ideals of the church, formulated in Baltimore in 1883, the numbers were low: By no means was every child being educated in Catholic schools.[42] On the other hand, by comparison with contemporary America, the figures were respectable: In 1963, 44% of Catholic school-age children were enrolled in

Catholic schools, and in 1974, 29%.[43] By comparison with other cities during the period 1880–1925, the few figures available (Tables 2.9–2.11) suggest that the Providence experience was somewhere near the middle of the range for other cities, although perhaps in the lower half. However, the available data suggest above all a diversity in local behavior, so that it is not very meaningful to think in terms of a national norm. In the final analysis, that two to three children in five among Irish-Americans in Providence were enrolled in schools other than the public schools must be regarded as a major achievement of voluntarism in the sphere of education and as a central feature of the city's school arrangements.

2.3. Characteristics of Catholic high school students

Many Irish Catholics in Providence chose the Catholic schools; many others did not. What characteristics determined where an Irish Catholic child would enroll? The religiously committed families were surely predisposed to favor these institutions, but other subgroups among the Irish may have been especially likely to enroll as well.

The gender of the child was one social characteristic that may have predisposed families to choose one sort of school over the other. James Sanders and others have speculated that nineteenth-century parents considered the Catholic schools less relevant to worldly success than the public schools.[44] As a result, they may have enrolled boys more often than girls in the public schools. There the boys would learn to be breadwinners in America, whereas in the Catholic schools, girls might pick up values best suited for family life. The Providence school census, an annual enumeration by school authorities, offers some modest support for such a view. In the nineteenth century, 55% of parochial school pupils were girls, compared with less than 50% in public schools. After the turn of the century, the proportions of girls in the two types of schools converged (Table 2.12). Yet the same figures suggest that any preference for sending the children of one gender rather than the other to Catholic schools was quite weak. The fundamental point, surely, is that enrollments by gender were so similar. When one also considers that the Catholic school opportunities for older boys may have been limited by the availability of teaching brothers, the imbalance by gender, however intriguing, seems quite small.

What of the social-class origins of Catholic school pupils? Was the Catholic school the preserve of better-off Irish-Americans, who could afford a private school, or was it an institution for the working class? Unfortunately, the available records severely restrict our examination

Table 2.12. *Percentages of girls among Catholic and public school students, Providence, 1889–1925*

Year	Catholic schools	Public schools
1889	54.2	n.a.
1895	54.6	48.7
1900	54.6	49.2
1905	52.6	49.9
1910	51.3	49.4
1915	50.9	50.2
1921	50.5	50.2
1925	50.2	49.7

Source: Calculated from the school census reports published in the Providence School Committee *Report* for the years indicated from 1895; for 1889, see the *Report* for 1891/2, p. 33.

of primary and grammar schools, where most Catholic pupils were enrolled. Still, a few observations can be made.

The burden of financing these schools is relevant here. Generally, there were two major methods of supporting parochial schools, both of which placed the financial responsibility on the parish. One involved tuition payments from parents, the other direct support from general parish funds. Local arrangements often may have involved some mix of these methods. Schools that charged tuition may have had arrangements to waive the costs for poor families at the priest's discretion and to make up the costs from general parish funds. Many tuition-free schools apparently charged for books and supplies. Also, a parish with no tuition charges may have placed great pressure on parishioners to contribute to its support and may have singled out those with children in its school. The schools, in short, required money, and it had to come from parishioners one way or another. If the burden fell more heavily on parents than on others, its magnitude probably was not trivial. In a working-class family, in which the father might earn $400–600 annually at the turn of the century, a tuition of fifty cents to a dollar per month was appreciable, amounting (over a year) to 1–2% of the father's annual wage. Of course, in a large family, one with six children, for example, the expenditure would have been much larger.[45]

One way to respond to financial pressure was to get by with fewer teachers and tolerate larger classes. Horace Tarbell, the Superintendent of the Providence public schools, noted that the Providence parochial school student–teacher ratios in 1889 and 1893 were so great that public school teachers would have protested had they been faced with such work: fifty-eight students per teacher in 1889, and sixty-four in 1892. "It is a striking fact," he added, "that eight teachers in the school of the Immaculate Conception on West River Street teach more pupils than are taught in all the private schools of the city."[46] One advantage parents probably obtained for their children in the Catholic academies, which often taught grade school pupils (rather than secondary school pupils), in this era, and which charged higher tuition than the parochial schools, was a smaller class size. In the absence of more systematic work on Catholic school financing, these conjectures are the best we can do in describing how social class impinged on the use of the parochial school.

We are on firmer ground in studying the social-class origins of Catholic high school students, at least in the later years of our period, 1915 and 1925 (Table 2.13). The evidence is of considerable interest, because it was in that period that Catholic secondary schooling became salient for significant proportions of the Catholic population. Prior to that time, high school enrollment, public or Catholic, was rare for the children of Catholic immigrants.

The Catholic high schools of Providence were not outgrowths of the parish schools. They originated as academies that were meant to serve the entire diocese. In the nineteenth century, several academies had been established by various orders. Most were day schools, serving the diocese's students. Some (such as the Academy of the Sacred Heart) operated primarily as boarding schools, catering to an elite clientele from throughout New England. Several of these academies were small, weak institutions that closed after a time.[47]

In the early years, many of the academy students were actually enrolled in primary or grammar school grades. Eventually, however, the academies came to concentrate on more advanced instruction. Two of these academies were of preeminent importance: La Salle for boys and St. Xavier for girls enrolled the great majority of pupils in Catholic secondary schools. During 1915–25, these schools offered college preparatory programs ("classical" and "scientific" courses) and a terminal "commercial" course.

These secondary schools may be compared with the four public schools: Classical, English, Hope, and Technical. Classical High offered college preparatory programs, at first stressing languages and later rigorous training in a broader range of academic subjects. English High began by offering more "modern" academic subjects than

Table 2.13. *Social-class origins of entrants to Catholic high schools and public high schools with comparable programs: proportion of entrants who were children of white-collar workers, Providence, 1915–25*

Entrants	Male		Female	
	%	N[a]	%	N
1915				
All entrants				
Catholic high schools	35.9	(73)	44.4	(25)
Comparable public high schools	46.4	(549)	39.7	(734)
Children of Irish-Americans only[b]				
Catholic high schools	27.7	(65)	52.8	(18)
Comparable public high schools	17.4	(93)	29.4	(142)
1925				
All entrants				
Catholic high school	35.7	(56)		
Comparable public high schools	47.5	(201)		
Children of Irish immigrants only[b]				
Catholic high schools	47.4	(19)		
Comparable public high schools	20.0	(15)		

[a]Sample data are described in the text. The 1915 data are based on supplemental samples of the children of the Irish and of other ethnic groups, on supplemental samples of public high school entrants, and on the random samples. In calculating the proportions, the sample members were weighted down so that each group was represented in the same proportion as in the random sample. However, the N's shown are for the total number of cases. Consequently, the N's should not be regarded as an indication of the proportions entering each type of high school.
[b]Includes children and grandchildren of Irish immigrants in 1915, children only in 1925 (because the grandchildren of Irish immigrants in the 1925 sample cannot be distinguished from the children of natives). Generations were combined in 1915 because of small numbers.

did Classical High (at the expense of foreign languages), as well as commercial courses, and later came to focus increasingly on the commercial work. Hope High, situated across town from Classical and English, offered all the programs they did. Finally, Technical High School had begun as a manual-training institution; eventually it became simply a general-purpose high school, including many shop courses.[48] In the comparisons that follow, Technical High School is omitted. It offered programs that differed from those at the other schools, both Catholic and public. Consequently, La Salle and St. Xavier students are compared with those at Classical, Commercial, and Hope.

Had the Technical High School students been included, the differences between public and Catholic students discussed later generally would have been substantially greater.

Many of the students in the public high school were not Catholics and hence never seriously considered the Catholic high schools. Nor did the Italian Catholics do so; 212 of the Italian children in the 1915–25 samples were high school entrants, of whom 2 attended Catholic institutions. Therefore, the most interesting comparisons of students' social-class origins are limited to the Irish-Americans. Among them, middle-class children were more likely than others to enroll in Catholic secondary schools. That finding is not surprising: A private high school, one that probably charged considerably more than the parochial schools (given the likelihood of higher per-pupil costs), had a more advantaged Irish-American clientele than did the public high schools. Still, it is also important to notice that this statement is relative to other Irish-Americans. In all three samples, half the students in Catholic secondary schools came from blue-collar homes. If there was a sorting process on the basis of social class, it was a much more modest process than occurred at the socially exclusive private schools that were not Catholic.[49] It is possible, of course, that children of the Catholic upper crust attended other schools. The girls of such families might have attended the Academy of the Sacred Heart, for example. For boys, there was no Catholic alternative to La Salle Academy within the city. In any case, notwithstanding the possibility that a small elite group was sent elsewhere, the noteworthy fact is that the only Catholic institution available within the city, surely the one to enroll the vast majority of the Providence boys who received Catholic secondary schooling, was not particularly exclusive.

Some of the most striking characteristics of the Catholic high school students do not pertain to their social origins, but to their academic careers. Catholic high school students were more likely than those in the public institutions to enroll in college preparatory programs and more likely to graduate from high school.

Evidence about students' academic programs in the Catholic high schools is complete only for the 1925 sample,[50] but the pattern in that year is unmistakable (Table 2.14). Students at La Salle Academy were more likely to enroll in the college preparatory track than were students at the comparable public high schools; 48% of the public high schools' students enrolled in that track, compared with 75% of La Salle's. The pattern remains clear if we restrict our attention to the Irish, or even to particular social strata among them. Indeed, the great

Table 2.14. *Catholic and public high school entrants compared: rates of enrollment in college preparatory curricula, Providence, 1925*

Entrants	Catholic high schools	Comparable public high schools
All entrants	75.0% (56)	47.8% (201)
Irish only[a]	17/19	4/15
White-collar fathers	9/9	1/3
Blue-collar fathers	8/10	3/12

[a]Given the small number of sample members, results in this panel are presented as fractions rather than as percentages.

majority of the sons of the Irish immigrants who enrolled in college preparatory programs in 1925 did so at La Salle.[51]

The unique nature of the Catholic secondary school career is equally evident in the graduation rates, and here the data permit us to draw conclusions from 1915 as well as from 1925.

One of the most striking characteristics of American high schools during these years was the high rate at which students dropped out. That proportion was relatively stable in Providence between 1880 and 1915; it declined somewhat in 1925. In 1915, some 35% of the students who entered the comparable public high schools graduated; at the two Catholic high schools, 58% graduated (Table 2.15). By 1925, the graduation rate among entrants at the comparable public high schools had climbed sharply, whereas at La Salle it had not. Although the contrast between public and Catholic institutions was not as sharp in that year, there was a difference, with 57% of the entrants to the comparable public high schools graduating, and 66% of those entering the Catholic schools.[52] The differences in graduation rates may be most meaningfully seen when attention is restricted to the children of Irish-Americans. In 1915, three-fifths of those who enrolled in the Catholic high schools graduated, and one-fifth of those who chose the comparable public high schools. In 1925, the disparities were about as large.

The public and Catholic school pupils no doubt differed in many respects: Ethnicity, social class, and other family background factors may all have contributed to the difference in graduation rates. Also, graduation rates may simply have reflected the same academic commitments already encountered in connection with curriculum choice. Whatever made more Catholic pupils choose the college preparatory

Table 2.15. *Catholic and public high school entrants compared: Providence, 1915–25*

1. Graduation rates

Entrants	Catholic high schools		Comparable pub- lic high schools	
	%	N	%	N
1915[a]				
All entrants	58.2	(98)	34.8	(1,292)
Irish-Americans	59.5	(83)	21.0	(232)
1925				
All entrants	66.1	(62)	57.0	(214)
Sons of Irish immigrants	71.4	(21)	31.3	(16)

2. Odds ratios for graduation by school type

Factors controlled	Ratio[b]
1915	
No controls (calculated from the foregoing proportions, first row)	2.61
Five social background factors controlled[c]	4.08 ($t = 5.21$)
Curriculum choice also controlled[c]	2.65 ($t = 3.49$)
1925	
No controls (calculated from the foregoing proportions, third row)	1.47
Five social background factors controlled[c]	2.30 ($t = 2.10$)
Curriculum choice also controlled[c]	1.60 ($t = 1.13$)

[a]The 1915 data include males and females; the gender differences in rates were small. On the composition of the Irish-Americans and on cell sizes, see the footnotes to Table 2.13.
[b]The odds that a Catholic school entrant would graduate compared with the odds that a public school entrant would do so.
[c]The second and third odds ratios are exponentiated coefficients from logit regression analyses. The models included controls for father's occupation, assessed property value, ethnicity, number of siblings, and whether or not both parents were present. The regression model for the third odds ratio also included a control for whether or not the entrant had enrolled in a college preparatory curriculum. For details, see text note 53.

track also could have kept them in school longer. These issues can be addressed with the help of multiple regression (Table 2.15).

First, graduation rates were higher in Catholic high schools than in public schools, even when family background characteristics of students were taken into account. Second, the importance of controlling for curriculum choice was different in 1915 than in 1925. In the earlier year, the Catholic high school students were more likely to graduate, even after curriculum choice and family background were controlled.[53] In the 1925 sample, the findings are weaker, but in the same direction. Once again, a difference in favor of the Catholic schools remains even after all controls are imposed. However, in the 1925 sample, the difference in their favor is too weak to be statistically significant. Confronted with the 1925 data alone, we would be on risky ground in concluding that a difference between the two types of schools remained when both curriculum choice and social background had been controlled, but in the context of the 1915 data, it seems reasonable to conclude that although the pattern was probably weaker in the later year, it did exist.[54]

These differences in the academic behavior of students lead one to wonder about other possible differences in their later lives. In particular, did Catholic school students differ from others in regard to the jobs they eventually obtained? Apparently not, once family background characteristics have been controlled. The Providence data, in any event, reveal no consistent differences of this type. Perhaps the number of cases is simply too small to reveal a pattern. However, the distinctive characteristics of the Catholic high school entrants may have been exclusively academic in nature, lacking any consistent connection to the fate of an individual in the job market.

Whether or not they had a later influence in the job market, the distinctive academic characteristics of the Catholic high school students obviously were important in the academic realm. They are especially noteworthy in the light of contemporary discussions of American Catholic school achievement, stimulated by the research of James Coleman and his colleagues. That research argues that the academic achievements of Catholic school students are greater than those of public school students, even when social background characteristics have been controlled. The Providence findings raise the possibility that differences in student academic achievement between Catholic and public schools may have had a long history.[55]

Whether that difference resulted from the manner in which the schools are run or from unobserved differences between the families that selected Catholic schools over public schools has been a subject of debate.[56] We cannot identify with certainty the sources of the Catholic school advantages, which in any case may well have been reinforcing, but we can consider some plausible sources. They probably had something to do with unobserved differences between those who chose the public schools and those who chose the Catholic schools, and they may have had something to do with what may be called institutional cultures as well.

On average, the families who chose the Catholic secondary schools were no doubt more committed religiously than others, and committed in a way that expressed religiosity through an extended Catholic schooling. One group of pupils who would have chosen the schools on religious grounds in particular were those intent on becoming priests, nuns, or other brothers or sisters. The records of La Salle Academy include a list of graduates who joined the clergy. For the fifteen graduating classes beginning in 1917 (the years covering the 1915–25 samples), about one graduate in nine is identified in this way. That is surely a nontrivial proportion of the entire group. On the other hand, the great majority of the graduated did not join the clergy, which strongly suggests that the high graduation rate at La Salle Academy cannot be accounted for by the behavior of the future clergymen among them.[57]

The families who chose these schools should also be thought of as having chosen a private secondary school. It may be that the distinctive rates of enrollment in the classical programs and rates of graduation were not so much functions of Catholic private schools, but rather functions of private schools generally, that families choosing such schools showed greater initiative and commitment to their children's schooling, expressed, for example, through tuition payments, and that this commitment appears in the observed rates. The implications of tuition payments deserve particular consideration. Although there were social-class differences between the Irish choosing public and Catholic high schools, it is just as clear that social class by no means fully determined the choice. If tuition charges for Catholic secondary schools were relatively steep for a family of modest means, but not altogether prohibitive, those charges would have served to sift families. Those of modest means who had chosen the Catholic schools would have been especially committed to them.

Private schools, it should also be noted, were able to reject certain students, whereas schools in the public sector could not. In an era in which only a third to half of an age cohort ever entered high school – any high school – the luxury of rejecting an unwanted high school student may not have been as important as it is today, when enrollment is nearly universal. Nevertheless, it may have made some difference. Other constraints would have worked in a similar direction. In the years between 1910 and 1920, the demand for seats at La Salle appears to have been growing rapidly. Enrollment increased, and school authorities had to turn away applicants for lack of seats – fully 100 of them in 1919. Given the size of the school at the time (total enrollment 500), it is probable that a third of the applicants were turned away. In 1925, the Providence bishop concluded a successful fund drive for construction of Catholic high schools, and La Salle was given a new building. The restrictiveness of admissions must have quickly declined,[58] and the smaller public–Catholic difference in graduation rates observed in the 1925 sample may have reflected this difference in the restrictiveness of high school admissions. In any case, such restrictions probably were easier for private schools to impose.

Relevant differences in school culture could also have developed from the way the schools were run. Teachers may have conveyed a greater sense of mission and of expectations from students. In addition, Catholic schools may have had distinctive kinds of outside influences working on them – both more committed parents and different sorts of officials to whom the principal reported. In all this, the unique Catholic nature of the school may have been crucial, or its status as a private school may have mattered most.

School cultures could have differed at the level of student culture as well. If, on average, students with somewhat different sorts of commitments enrolled at the Catholic secondary schools, they may have reinforced these commitments in each other. In this way, an important peer influence would have operated: A student entering a Catholic high school with the same social background and commitments as one entering the public high school would have experienced stronger reinforcement for that academic commitment.

The social-class composition of a school may create peer influences as well, but they do not explain the Catholic school record.[59] In general, middle-class students probably were more likely to enroll in college preparatory curricula and to graduate. Pupils who were educated where the middle-class concentration was high would be influenced to do the same. However, middle-class students were as common at the public high schools (when all students, Irish and others, are considered; Table 2.13). So peer influences deriving from social-class composition would not have worked in favor of Catholic school achievement.

Finally, a theme running through the preceding paragraphs – that it may be useful to think of the Catholic schools in the same terms that one thinks of other private schools – suggests a broader point. One of the critical roles of Catholic schooling had to do with the new immigrant communities, among those who were poor, culturally distinct, and often contending with the older Protestant elites. However, in considering the Catholic high schools, we are closer to an institution that expresses the concerns of more well-established social groups, albeit in religious and ethnically distinct ways. The most impoverished, and hence also most of the less assimilated, were unlikely to reach any high school. That the Catholic secondary schools were diocesan and not parochial underscores the point: These were not schools of a small, tightly knit community. Small ethnic enclaves might have produced schools that were out of touch with American mainstream values of achievement. The Catholic high schools, however, did not emerge from such enclaves. Even in 1880, the diocese of Providence included forty-nine parishes and extended well beyond the city of Providence; by 1925, it included ninety-eight parishes.[60]

That the Catholic high schools and their pupils could nevertheless have been out of touch with mainstream American values regarding achievement seems unlikely. First, Irish-Americans were the principal clientele of these schools. The first section of this chapter makes it clear that by 1915, Irish-Americans as a group were not typified by academic or occupational achievements different from those of Yankees, and so there is no reason to assume that they differed in values regarding achievement. Second, it stands to reason that among all groups, those reaching high school were less likely than others to hold values that would have inhibited achievement. Finally, this section has shown that Irish-American high school students who chose the Catholic high schools over the public schools demonstrated higher attainments, at least in the academic (if not in the occupational) arena, as judged by the choice of a classical curriculum and by graduation rates.

3   *The Italians*

In the great immigrations of 1880–1920, the Italians composed the largest single group, with some 4 million of them reaching the United States. A great many, close to half, returned to Italy after a time. Despite the huge numbers who went back, however, the Italian immigration was so large that those who remained in the United States still outnumbered the arrivals in every other group.[1] In Providence, the Italian immigrant community was of negligible size in 1880; by 1900, however, its children constituted 7% of the sample, with 16% in 1915 and 29% in 1925. By 1915, Italian children were more numerous than those of any other immigrant group in the city; by 1925, they probably even outnumbered all those of Irish ancestry (both children and grandchildren of Irish immigrants).

Like the nineteenth-century Irish before them, the Italians were far less likely than others to receive an extended education. In 1915, for example, slightly less than one-tenth of the children of Italians, as compared with two-fifths of the rest of the city's children, enrolled in high school. The evidence also indicates that, on average, Italians received lower grades from their teachers than others did. Such patterns persisted throughout the years 1900–25. This chapter concerns the family background of the Italian children, their schooling, and their later jobs.

Many observers have suggested that the cultural heritage of the Italian immigrants predisposed them to underrate the importance of education. One of the earliest discussions of Italian schooling has remained especially influential. In 1944, Leonard Covello, an Italian-born educator who spent his career immersed in these issues, completed an exhaustive doctoral dissertation, *The Social Background of the Italo-American School Child*,[2] that sought to place school patterns in the context of the social structure and culture of southern Italy. Although not published until 1967, Covello's work was influential well before that.[3] He stressed the minimal school arrangements in rural southern Italy in the nineteenth and early twentieth centuries, the minimal relevance of the curriculum to the peasant, the imposed quality of the schools (coming as they did by edict from afar), the restriction of most schooling to a three-year course, and the great reluctance to provide formal schooling, especially extended schooling, for women (whose family roles did not require it, and might even be threatened by it). According to Covello,

> From the immigrant's point of view there was no obvious need for more than a trifling amount of formal education. All practical arts and skills should be acquired at an early age by working either in the parental household or through apprenticeship. Knowledge beyond the every-day requirements was a privilege and necessity for the "better" classes. His concept of wisdom had nothing in common with categories of knowledge and learning that are acquired in the school.[4]

Rather,

> To the *contadino* parent, education was the handing down of all the cultural, social, and moral value of his society through the medium of folklore, or the teaching, generation after generation, of the child by the parents. The peasant's desire for security in his way of living was directly opposed to education from outside the family circle. . . . This antagonism toward the school, which was definitely manifested in Italy and which constituted a part of the cultural tradition, was carried over to America and paved the way for the still current [1944] lack of rapprochement between the American school and the Italian parents.[5]

Resentment over compulsory schooling, which challenged the family's control of its children, also heightened tensions between the Italian immigrant household and the school. These tensions surely had an economic dimension, for the Italian immigrant families sought the contributions of child labor to the family economy. Covello was emphatic, however, that the sources of the conflict could not be reduced to economic necessity, but were to be found in cultural differences between the Italian outlook and the American norms. Finally,

> Since the Italian girl's sphere of activity was confined strictly to the home, adjustment was most difficult for her in the American milieu; her horizon was narrow and her scope of action very limited. In the struggle for a place in American life, she found herself unable to achieve anything like the status of Americans of other cultural groups whose female members were not so confined and restricted.[6]

Covello's influential formulations have been echoed by many others. For example, according to Alice Kessler-Harris and Virginia Yans-McLaughlin,

> Explanations for differences in educational attainment appear to lie directly in old country cultural values. The Italian peasant, suspicious of modern ideas and fearful of the extent to which American-

ization would disrupt the integrity of the family, withdrew his children from school as soon as possible. Economic needs [for child labor] conspired with culture in this respect.[7]

Nevertheless, other observers have strongly argued that economic factors (the class position of Italian families, their low starting place in the industrial economy) can fully or very nearly explain these patterns of schooling. Stephen Steinberg, for example, argues in *The Ethnic Myth* that "it is necessary to ask whether Italian attitudes toward education were simply a carryover from Europe, as is commonly assumed, or whether they were responses to conditions of Italian life in this country as well," and, indeed, he strongly emphasizes the primacy of their social-class position in the United States over such cultural attributes.[8] Similarly, John Briggs argues, against Covello and others, that the Italian heritage did include support for schooling and that Italian-American school achievement was not in fact much different from that of other working-class children.[9]

Moreover, even if the Italian-American school patterns cannot fully be explained by their social-class position, these patterns may have resulted from the propensity of Italians to return to Italy. As Michael Piore has stressed, immigrants set on returning to the old country faced many of their choices with a different attitude than other immigrants.[10] In particular, sending children to work in order to amass additional savings may have seemed a wiser investment than sending them to an American high school.

Solid evidence that will permit exploration of these issues and that is relevant to the early years of the century is available for the first time in the Providence data set. Information about social-class origins and family structure, of course, is particularly important. In addition, some evidence sheds light on the connection between return migration and schooling.

After assessing the nature of Italian schooling and the impacts of various social factors on it, this chapter turns to the later occupational attainments of the Italian sample members. Was their low level of school performance the result of factors that also produced low occupational attainments? Did that low school performance itself inhibit their socioeconomic attainments? Whereas the central concern in this section will be the relation between schooling and social mobility, we can also shed useful light on occupational advancement itself, quite apart from its relation to schooling. There have been numerous studies of the Italian absorption into American economic life, including some that have described the degree of economic advancement of the second generation. However, nearly all have compared the Italians to only one or two other immigrant groups in the city: to the Jews, or the Poles, or the Slovaks, for example. Here we have a chance to compare their performance with the norms for occupational advancement in the city as a whole. Second-generation Italians remained concentrated in somewhat less attractive jobs than was the norm. However, was their rate of advancement away from their origins relatively slow, or did they simply start at a lower point?[11]

Our best evidence pertains to those who were adolescents in 1915 or 1925. Supplementary samples of the children of Italian immigrants were drawn from the 1915 Rhode Island State Census. As a result, information is available on some 870 children of Italian origin who were then twelve to fifteen years of age. The 1925 sample was more restricted in scope; it was limited to boys, and no effort was made to supplement the numbers obtained by random sampling. Nevertheless, because the Italians constituted such a large proportion of the city's population, 289 of them were included in that sample.

3.1. Family background

In the early years of the Italian immigration, most adolescent children of the immigrants had been born in Italy themselves – 83% in the 1900 sample. Increasingly, however, the immigrant parents composed a group who had migrated when young and had established their families in the United States. By 1915, therefore, only 37% of the children were foreign-born, and by 1925 a mere 8%.[12] This sharp decline in the proportion foreign-born is easiest to understand in comparing the immigrant families of 1915 and 1925. During World War I (1914–18), the wave of immigration was cut to barely a trickle, and shortly thereafter Congress began to impose restrictions on immigration. Consequently, the decade between 1915 and 1925 brought relatively few new immigrants. More of the youngsters of 1925 were therefore from families who had lived in the United States for some time.

A less obvious process operated earlier, creating similar results even when immigration was at its peak. By 1915, the number of Italian immigrants who had arrived when young and were then raising families themselves was apparently growing much faster than the number of recent immigrants with children born in Italy. The sharply rising proportion of native-born children, of course, meant a comparable rise in the proportion of parents who had had years to establish themselves economically, as well as to learn American ways generally and the English language in particular.

In the early years, significant proportions of the Italian boys came to Providence with their fathers or brothers to work, rather than in

Table 3.1. *Occupations of Italian immigrant fathers*

Occupational stratum	Census year		
	1900 (%)	1915 (%)	1925 (%)
High white-collar	3.4	5.3	6.2
Low white-collar	15.3	13.4	12.5
Skilled	16.9	18.5	20.4
Semiskilled	15.3	23.2	20.8
Unskilled	45.8	36.9	30.8
Unknown	3.4	2.7	9.3
Total (100%) N^a	(59)	(863)	(289)
Mean occupational score	15.9	16.1	19.0

^{a} The numbers do not reflect the relative sizes of the groups. Different sampling ratios were used for each census.

complete families. Fully a third of the 1900 group seem to have been living in such arrangements, or else living in households with no identifiable relative present. However, by 1915, despite the tremendous preponderance of men among the Italian immigrants (75% in this era), very high proportions of the sample members were actually living in two-parent households – over 85%, and nearly all the rest with relatives. Few were in female-headed households. Whatever tensions migration and poverty imposed on these immigrants, it did not result in much family dissolution.[13] Most of the Italian families were large, including, on average, five children.

More than any other immigrant group, except perhaps the Irish in 1880, the Italian families were concentrated at the bottom of the economic order (Table 3.1). In 1900, fully 46% of the Italian fathers worked as unskilled laborers. Even among the Irish in the earlier year, the percentage had been somewhat lower. Only 17% of the Italians were in skilled work, and 19% in white-collar occupations. The Italian immigrant situation improved in subsequent years, but not markedly. By 1915, somewhat more worked in semiskilled occupations, somewhat fewer in unskilled labor; little else had changed. Because the occupations of over 800 Italian fathers in 1915 had been ascertained, we can closely examine the economic position of the group in that year.

Those who had lived in the United States for a relatively short time were, of course, most likely to be concentrated at the bottom. Although direct information on length of residence is unavailable, fathers of foreign-born adolescents can be assumed to have been more recent arrivals than fathers of native-born adolescents. Among more recent arrivals, some 4% were contractors, the most well-to-do group. A comparable proportion worked as carpenters. Both groups reflect the concentration of Italians in construction work. Peddlers and shoemakers were also comparably represented. Textile-mill operatives constituted another 7% of the workers. These were the largest concentrations – after laborers. Fully 35% of all the fathers were laborers, indicating the dearth of specific job skills and the poverty found among these immigrants.

Among the Italian fathers who had been resident longer, somewhat more had established themselves in small businesses, such as food stores. The proportion of laborers had also declined, but only to 24%. Generally, the changes between 1900 and 1915, and the changes resulting from extended residence, were relatively modest. The mean occupational score of the fathers in 1900 was 15.9. In 1915 it was 16.1 – 14.6 among recent arrivals, 16.9 among those resident longer.

In 1925, the proportion in skilled and white-collar work had increased very slightly, as the numbers of new immigrants dropped. Yet even in that year the mean occupational score had risen only to 19; more than half the fathers still held low manual jobs. By contrast, among the Irish, the mean occupational score was 26. Only the blacks were more concentrated at the bottom.

Although the Italian fathers were concentrated in low-skill and hence low-wage occupations, very few of the Italian mothers worked: 4% in 1915. Even in broken families, in which income from supplemental wage earners would be especially needed, a mere 9% of the mothers held jobs. The preferred way to increase household income was to send adolescent children, not mothers, into the labor force.

Our best evidence on child labor is once again from 1915. Among Providence boys fourteen to fifteen years of age, 30% were at work (Table 3.2). Among the Italian boys, the rate was higher: 37%. For the girls, the comparable figures were considerably more disparate: 26% and 47%. As these rates indicate, girls were generally less likely to work than boys at this age, but among the Italians the reverse was the case. The tendency to send girls to work sooner than boys may have been related to the structure of the job market for young workers, and especially for Italian workers. Many working boys in other groups obtained the juvenile jobs that did not involve actual machine work: especially as office, errand, messenger, and cash boys. A third of the city's working boys held these jobs, but only 10% of the working Italian boys did.

Table 3.2. *Jobs of children age 14–15 years, Providence, 1915*

Type of job	Boys		Girls	
	All sample members (%)	Sons of Italians only (%)	All sample members (%)	Daughters of Italians only (%)
White-collar workers[a]	6	4	17	10
Juvenile white-collar workers[b]	35	10	3	0
Skilled workers	8	14	4	5
Low manual:				
Textile workers	26	47	52	77
Service workers	4	3	6	2
All others	21	21	18	6
Total	100	100	100	100
Number working[c]	(132)	(99)	(117)	(61)
Percentage of age group at work	30	37	26	47

[a] Clerks and salesclerks.
[b] Messengers, delivery boys, errand boys, cash boys, office boys, and girls in comparable jobs.
[c] The first and third columns are based on samples of all children in the age range, the second and fourth columns on supplemental samples of Italians.

The working Italian youth were instead concentrated in manual labor, especially in the city's textile mills: 47% of Italian boys, compared with 26% of all boys; 77% of Italian girls, compared with 52% of all girls. Thus, more of the jobs available to girls generally were in mills, and more of the Italians of each sex obtained mill jobs than was typical for other groups.

The concentration of Italian children in the mills probably was the result of knowledge of employment opportunities and connections with employers through kin and friends working there. It may also have been due to employer discrimination elsewhere. However, other factors were also relevant. To many Italian parents, the work environment, including the presence of relatives and friends, may have seemed more appropriate for an adolescent girl than a high school. At any rate, the explanation based only on the employment opportunities in the Providence labor market must be supplemented by others, for Italian girls left school at younger ages than boys in a variety of cities, although the opportunities for child labor surely differed from city to city. The *Reports* of the Immigration Commission, based on a huge national survey of classrooms in 1908, provide the best evidence. In four major cities with large concentrations of Italians, fewer Italian girls remained in school to age fifteen than boys: 16% versus 24% in Boston, 9% versus 21% in Chicago, 11% versus 22% in New York, and 6% versus 14% in Philadelphia.[14]

3.2. Patterns of schooling

Our best evidence on Italian school patterns also derives from 1915 and 1925, because the samples are large and the school records are rich for those years. We shall concentrate on length of schooling and grades. These two aspects of schooling are, of course, related. Students who remained in school the longest, for example, typically received high grades. Nevertheless, the factors that influenced grades probably were somewhat different from the factors that influenced length of schooling.

One reason that Italian children received less schooling was that many of them had been born abroad. Of course, a child's chances of school success probably were not enhanced by having been born in the United States rather than brought here at age one or two. However, arrival in the United States at age six or seven meant learning English while starting school, which surely imposed academic hardships. Arrival at age eight or older would generally have meant sitting with much younger children – and quite possibly the humiliation of feeling that those children knew much more than did the new arrival.[15] In 1915, the proportion of children born abroad was nearly twice as great among Italians as among other immigrants: 37%, compared with 19%. As the preceding considerations would lead us to expect, these foreign-born Italian children were indeed far less likely to receive extended schooling than the native-born; among boys, for example, 5% of the former and 17% of the latter reached high school. We can therefore sharply reduce one source of difference between Italians and others in 1915 by focusing on native-born children of Italian immigrants. Because, by 1925, the children of Italian immigrants were nearly all native-born, we can ignore the issue of foreign birth in considering their experiences.

Nevertheless, even when attention is restricted to native-born children of Italian immigrants, their low school achievement relative to other groups is glaring. Two comparisons are especially useful. The first is to all other native-born children, those of both immigrants and natives. The second comparison is to the native-born children of some other immigrant groups, those not from the British Isles or Russia. These latter groups were excluded in order to maximize comparability. The Irish, English, Scots, and Welsh spoke English and had a longer history of settlement in the United States. The Russians were virtually all Russian Jews, who may have been especially committed to schooling. The remaining immigrants were an altogether heterogeneous group: roughly a third of them were Canadian, mostly of French Canadian background. Smaller proportions (about 10–15% each in 1915 and 1925) were Scandinavians, Germans or Austrians, and Poles. Finally, the Portuguese and Armenians each composed some 4–8% of this group. All others accounted for much smaller proportions.[16] Comparing this heterogeneous group of other immigrants with the Italians shows that Italian school patterns were not simply those common to all immigrants, nor to all but special groups like the English-speakers or the Jews.[17]

Consider first the high school entry rates for boys. Among native-born sons of Italians, 17% enrolled in high school; 40% of all other boys and 34% of the subgroup of other immigrants did so. In 1925, the comparable figures were 33%, 61%, and 53%. The Italians who did enter high school were as likely to graduate as other entrants, but because high school entrants were so much rarer among them, graduates also were rarer. Thus, in 1915, 6% of the Italians, 13% of all other natives, and 12% of the sons in the subgroup of other immigrants graduated. In 1925, the figures were comparable: 15%, 32%, and 28%. All these comparisons also reveal the similarity between the two groups with whom the Italians are compared, thus underscoring the striking distinctiveness of the Italian patterns.

One reason so few Italians reached high school is that poverty was more prevalent among them, even more than among other immigrants. For example, less than half as many families among the subgroup of other immigrants were headed by unskilled workers; almost twice as many were headed by skilled workers. Other economic and demographic characteristics of Italian families, such as family size, could also have operated to reduce Italian school achievement. Tables 3.3 to 3.5 are therefore arranged like the tables in the preceding chapter to compare the behaviors of groups while controlling for a variety of family background characteristics (for an explanation of the table arrangement, and of the odds ratio, see Section 2.1).

There is no doubt that the family background characteristics did matter, particularly poverty. When these characteristics are taken into account, the gap between the Italians and others is indeed reduced. For example, in 1915, the odds of high school entry were 3.17 times as great for other native-born boys as for Italians. With family background characteristics controlled, the odds ratio was reduced to 2.33. Nevertheless, as this example shows, these family background char-

Table 3.3. *Length of schooling by ethnicity, 1915 and 1925*

Group	Rate (%)	N^a	Odds ratio: each group compared with Italians[b]	
			No controls	Social background factors controlled
1915: high school entry rates, boys				
Native-born sons of				
Italians	17.2	(354)		
All others	39.6	(1,267)	3.17	2.33 (5.02)[c]
Some other immigrants[d]	34.4	(160)	2.52	2.15 (3.28)
Boys born in Italy[e]	4.8	(207)	0.24	0.29 (3.45)
1915: high school graduation rates, boys				
Native-born sons of				
Italians	5.9	(354)		
All others	13.3	(1,267)	2.45	1.43 (1.40)
Some other immigrants	11.9	(160)	2.15	1.55 (1.27)
1915: high school entry rates, girls				
Native-born daughters of				
Italians	8.7	(185)		
All others	44.1	(1,036)	8.28	6.24 (6.53)
Some other immigrants	34.1	(132)	5.43	5.12 (4.93)
Girls born in Italy[e]	4.3	(93)	0.47	0.53 (1.08)
1915: high school graduation rates, girls				
Native-born daughters of				
Italians	3.2	(185)		
All others	17.7	(1,036)	6.51	4.45 (3.42)
Some other immigrants	14.4	(132)	5.09	4.58 (3.06)
1925: high school entry rates, boys				
Sons of				
Italians	33.0	(261)		
All others	60.7	(678)	3.14	2.37 (4.98)
Some other immigrants[d]	53.4	(189)	2.33	2.18 (3.68)
1925: high school graduation rates, boys				
Sons of				
Italians	15.3	(261)		
All others	32.0	(678)	2.61	1.61 (2.23)
some other immigrants	28.0	(189)	2.15	1.78 (2.26)

[a] In Tables 3.3 and 3.4, supplemental samples of Russian Jews, Irish, Italians, and blacks in 1915 were included; supplemental samples of high school entrants were included in analyzing patterns of behavior within high schools. In computing the rates, means, and coefficients for "all others" in these tables, supplemental samples have been weighted to reflect the actual size of each group. The N's are unweighted sample sizes.

acteristics do not account for most of the difference between the Italians and others. With the controls imposed, the odds of high school entry for Italians rise, relative to the others, by a factor of 1.36 (3.17/ 2.33 = 1.36); however, for their odds of entry to have equaled those for others, a further rise by a factor of 2.33 would have been required.

By way of summarizing, consider two extreme but simple contrasts. First, in 1915, sons of white-collar Italians enrolled barely as often as sons of blue-collar immigrants in the comparison group: 24% versus 23%. In 1925, they actually enrolled less often: 46% versus 53%.[18] Similarly, the native-born sons of Italians were less likely to enroll in high school than were the foreign-born sons of the comparison group of immigrants: 17% versus 28%. Controls for family background, moreover, explain none of this difference.

However low the chances for extended schooling among the Italian boys, they were lower still among the girls (Table 3.3). In 1915, the year for which we have data on both, about half as many Italian girls as boys entered or graduated from high school. Among most other groups, by contrast, girls were somewhat more likely than boys to receive secondary schooling. Nor is the distinctive Italian pattern found among the children of most other immigrants in Providence. On the other hand, while in school, Italian girls did not perform notably different than Italian boys, and certainly they did not perform less well (Table 3.4). The evidence from grade-point averages (GPAs) for the sixth grade suggests that the girls received slightly higher grades, as was the case for girls in most groups. The reason the Italian girls left school sooner, then, was not that they were faring more poorly in their classroom work. Rather, the decision must have been based on other grounds.

These grammar school GPAs were available for substantial frac-

Table 3.3 (Cont.)

[b]Odds ratios without controls were computed from proportions at left; those with controls imposed are exponentiated coefficients on ethnic dummy variables in logit regressions. The variables controlled are father's occupation, family's assessed property value, number of siblings, whether or not both parents were present.
[c]t values.
[d]White immigrants from countries other than Italy, Russia, and the British Isles.
[e]In the last three columns of the table, these rates are compared with those for native-born children of Italian immigrants of the same sex. Comparisons involving high school graduation rates for the Italian-born, which were close to zero, are not shown.

Table 3.4. *Mean GPA by ethnicity, 1915 and 1925*[a]

Group	Mean GPA	N	GPA differences: each group compared with Italians	
			No controls	Social background factors controlled
1915: sixth-grade GPA, boys				
Native-born sons of				
Italians	2.02	(147)		
All others	2.39	(741)	0.37	0.27 (3.80)
Some other immigrants	2.42	(97)	0.40	0.35 (3.46)
1915: ninth-grade GPA, boys				
Native-born sons of				
Italians	2.10	(71)		
All others	1.97	(674)	−0.13	−0.25 (1.66)
Some other immigrants	1.95	(92)	−0.15	−0.26 (1.60)
1915: sixth-grade GPA, girls				
Native-born daughters of				
Italians	2.10	(91)		
All others	2.51	(640)	0.41	0.28 (3.17)
Some other immigrants	2.36	(73)	0.26	0.22 (1.83)
1915: ninth-grade GPA, girls				
Native-born daughters of				
Italians	2.13	(24)		
All others	2.25	(681)	0.12	0.10 (0.53)
Some other immigrants	2.31	(98)	0.18	0.38 (1.41)
1925: sixth-grade GPA, boys				
Sons of				
Italians	2.20	(198)		
All others	2.55	(538)	0.35	0.23 (3.42)
Some other immigrants	2.49	(135)	0.29	0.22 (2.65)
1925: ninth-grade GPA, boys				
Sons of				
Italians	1.85	(72)		
All others	2.06	(416)	0.21	0.13 (1.13)
Some other immigrants	2.15	(93)	0.30	0.25 (1.83)

[a]See notes to Table 3.3.

tions of the sample members (53% in 1915 and 70% in 1925). Some of the rest never reached grammar school; others had attended schools (mostly Catholic) from which these data were unavailable. Despite its limitations, the GPA evidence is of great value, and its limitations are reduced when controls for class and ethnicity are imposed.[19] These grammar school GPAs indicate a larger point: Italian children of both sexes received considerably lower grades than children in other groups. In 1915, for example, the mean Italian GPAs (on a scale of $4.00 = A$) were 2.02 (boys) and 2.10 (girls); the comparable GPAs for all others were 2.39 and 2.51. Because the standard deviation for these GPAs was about 0.8, these differences amount to fully half a standard deviation. Once again, some of this difference was due to family background characteristics. However, most of the difference in each of the three samples (boys and girls in 1915 and boys in 1925) was not due to the family characteristics we can observe.

High school grades are more difficult to interpret because of the large proportions of Italians who had already dropped out. Those who remained in school were likely to be especially high achievers academically. Nevertheless, in two of the three samples, the high school grades of Italian students were lower than those of other groups.[20] In sum, Italian children not only completed fewer grades of schooling than others did but also, in the judgment of their teachers, performed less well while there.

The GPA performance of the Italians in school sheds additional light on the group's low rate of high school entry. Reaching higher grades was, in part, simply a function of the length of time spent in school, but it was also a function of the rate of promotion through the grades. We can assume that that rate was, in turn, strongly related to schoolwork. There were many children whose grade levels were lower than their ages would suggest – in every ethnic group. However, the rate of this "grade retardation," as contemporaries called it (see Section 1.4), was higher for some groups than for others, and it was especially high among the Italians. The data of the Immigration Commission demonstrate these patterns clearly. Even when we consider a population much less likely than others to have been retarded in grade – native-born children who had started school by age six – we find many who were retarded in grade. Over a fifth of the children of native whites were retarded by two grades or more, and still higher proportions of immigrants' children were. Among the Italians, the rate reached 48%.[21] The retardation rate, then, as well as early school leaving, would have helped keep the Italian children from reaching high school. Whatever the exact mix of school processes that reduced participation in extended schooling – grade retardation and early school leaving being the two most important – they operated especially strongly on the Italians, even when social background factors are taken into account.[22]

3.3. *Patterns of occupational attainment*

The male sample members for 1915 and 1925 who remained in the Providence area have been traced in the city directories for 1925 and 1935, respectively, sources that indicate the occupations they held at ages twenty-two to twenty-five. These young men have been classified by family background characteristics and by levels of schooling completed: no high school, some high school, high school graduation, and college entry (1925 only).

The foreign-born sons of Italian immigrants, who were numerous in the 1915 sample, tended to work in much lower-level jobs than did native-born sons. Their mean occupational score was a full 9 points lower than that for the native-born (Table 3.5). Relatively little of the difference between them can be explained by social-class origin, family structure, or education; almost 7 points of the 9-point difference remained with these factors controlled. Clearly, the liabilities of foreign birth mattered to the Italians a good deal, for occupational success as well as for school success. The parents of the foreign-born probably had had less time to establish themselves economically and thus had had less success – in ways not captured by the economic variables controlled in the regressions. The foreign-born themselves no doubt had had less time to learn about American ways, and they also may have had fewer American contacts for jobs. It is also possible that some of them returned to Italy for various periods and that a less consistent residence in the United States reduced their opportunities for advancement, but the records are silent concerning this conjecture.[23]

For purposes of comparison with other groups, we can restrict our attention to the native-born boys in 1915. Italian young men in 1915–25 were working in somewhat lower-level jobs than were others (Table 3.5). In the earlier sample, the average native-born son of Italians held a job nearly 6 points lower on the occupational scale than did other natives. In the later sample, the difference between Italians and all others amounted to 8 points. Because the standard deviation for the occupational scores was 19 in the earlier year and 18 in the later year, these magnitudes are notable. Only the blacks, the Jews, and the Italians differed from the norm by such large amounts. Differences between the sons of Yankees and the sons of other immigrants, for example, were by no means as large.

Moreover, in one respect, the position of the Italians in the 1925 group was weaker than these figures suggest. In 1935, they obtained white-collar work much less often than did others, and also much less often than did the Italian sons of a decade earlier (Table 3.6). By 1935,

Table 3.5. *Ethnic differences in occupational attainment, males, 1925 and 1935*[a]

| | | | Differences in means: each group compared with Italians | | | |
| | | | No controls | Family back-ground | Educa-tion | Both |
Group	Means	N	No controls	Family back-ground	Educa-tion	Both
1915 sample						
Native-born sons of						
Italians	29.5	(175)				
All others	35.0	(685)	5.5*	2.4	2.4	1.2
Some other immigrants[b]	33.4	(89)	3.9**	0.9	1.4	0
Italian-born men (com-pared with native-born sons of Italians)	20.3	(73)	−9.2*	−8.1*	−7.4*	−6.9*
1925 sample						
Sons of						
Italians	26.1	(139)				
All others	34.2	(393)	8.1*	4.2*	4.0*	2.2
Some other immigrants	31.7	(97)	5.6*	3.8	2.9	2.1

Note: Statistical significance of differences from Italian means: *significant ($t > 1.96$); **$1.95 < t > 1.50$.

[a]Sample members' occupational attainment a decade after the census year (e.g., 1925 for 1915 sample members). Available only for those sample members found in the Providence area in the later years. Based on a numeric score for each occupational title (the Duncan score). The standard deviation of the occupational scores was 19.3 in the 1915 sample and 17.9 in the 1925 sample. The differences in means are coefficients on ethnic dummy variables in OLS regressions. Supplemental samples are included in the regressions, weighted to reflect their true relative magnitudes. See note *a* in Table 2.7.

[b]Immigrants from countries other than Italy, Russia, and the British Isles.

just about half of all other young men were entering such jobs, and 40% of the native-born sons of Italians had done so in 1925. But in 1935, the rate among Italians fell to 24%. The mean occupational score for the Italians reflects the same pattern, but much more weakly, dropping only from 29.5 to 26.1 over the decade. The mean, captur-ing not merely the proportion reaching a particular threshold, but rather the positions of all individuals, naturally conveys a somewhat

Table 3.6. *Occupational strata and mean occupational attainment, 1925 and 1935*

Group	Percentage entering			Mean occupational score
	White-collar	Skilled	Low manual	
1915 sample: native-born sons of				
Italians	39.5	19.1	41.4	29.5
All others	45.9	19.7	34.4	35.0
1925 sample: sons of				
Italians	23.7	25.9	50.4	26.1
All others	48.8	15.6	35.8	34.2

different picture than the white-collar entry rate. For example, among blue-collar workers, Italians were as likely as others to be skilled workers, rather than low manual workers. The sharp drop in white-collar employment, then, may not have been relevant to all Italian young men, but it did matter to many. The Great Depression, of course, probably had much to do with the difference between the jobs of 1915 and 1925 sample members, the latter seeking jobs during its worst years.

Whatever the temporal shifts, the occupational scores of the native-born sons of Italian immigrants were substantially lower than those for other native-born boys in both years. However, most of this ethnic gap in occupational attainment can be attributed to differences in family background or schooling.[24] These characteristics together account for all but 1.2 points of the 5.5-point difference in 1915 and all but 2.2 points of the 8.1-point difference in 1925. Perhaps these residual differences indicate that factors other than family background and schooling cannot be ruled out entirely – factors such as cultural attributes of Italians or discrimination against them. Nevertheless, the sizes of the residuals are not large enough to justify the argument that influences other than family background and schooling played critical roles in Italian occupation attainment.[25] The residual Italian differences in patterns of schooling and the residual differences in occupational attainment found among several other groups are much more impressive.[26]

Family background characteristics (our measures of class origin and family structure) accounted for roughly half the difference in occupational attainment between Italians and all others (compare the differences in occupational attainment presented in the third and fourth columns of Table 3.5). Clearly, some of the impact of family background factors was related to schooling: The children of better-off families were more likely to receive extended schooling, which in turn contributed to occupational attainment. At the same time, when only schooling is controlled, the difference between Italians and others also decreases by roughly half (compare the third and fifth columns). Some of this difference was also related to family background, for the reasons just noted.

Family background and schooling, then, operated partly independent of each other and partly jointly in creating the occupational-attainment difference between Italians and others. Especially interesting is the net effect of education on the ethnic difference in occupational attainment, the effect that was altogether unrelated to the measured family background characteristics. In order to measure the net effect, the family background characteristics are allowed to explain all they can, and then education is also taken into account (the difference between the fourth and sixth columns). This net effect amounts to a mere 1.2 points for 1915 and 2.0 points for 1925. It can be interpreted as a cost, in terms of getting ahead, that the Italians paid for their lower levels of schooling. In addition, some of the effects of schooling that operated jointly with the effects of family background can be considered part of that cost. That joint effect is the total impact of schooling less that part of its impact that is independent of family background (the difference between the third and fifth columns less the difference between the fourth and sixth columns). The joint effect is also fairly modest: 1.9 for 1915 and 2.1 for 1925.[27]

In sum, then, the cost the Italians paid for their lower levels of schooling, in occupational terms, amounted in 1915 to 1.2 points and to part of another 1.9 points; in 1925, it amounted to 2.0 points and to part of another 2.1 points. These are not negligible costs; yet, on a measure in which the mean was 32–34 and the standard deviation 18–19, they hardly amount to crippling handicaps.

However, for the individuals who did not enter high school, the costs take on a different significance. Such individuals constituted a higher percentage in the Italian group than in others: 22% higher in 1915, and 28% higher in 1925 (Table 3.3). Moreover, three-quarters of this 22–28% ethnic difference was not due to the constraints of family background characteristics. How much did these individuals who chose to forgo high school – roughly 20% of the native-born sons of Italian immigrants – lose in occupational success? The occupational advantage associated with high school entry (after controlling for all family background characteristics) was considerable: just over 10 points on the 100-point occupational scale. A substantial minority of the group, then, were absorbing a considerable loss by the choice to forgo high school.

Thus, the Italian patterns of schooling and occupational attainment may be interpreted in two ways. First, they may be considered from the point of view of those sons of Italians who did not attend high school while other boys in comparable social-class positions, and in comparably structured families, did. Second, they may be approached from the point of view of the entire Italian group. For those Italian boys who did not attend while comparably situated others did, ignoring secondary schooling meant a considerable eventual loss in occupational attainment. However, the experience of that subpopulation still had only a relatively small influence on the average occupational attainment of all Italian boys. Because roughly 20% of the boys lost 10 points on the occupational scale, the group as a whole lost 2 points.[28]

3.4.   Explaining the differences: other economic characteristics, remigration, and contextual effects

In sum, then, Italian school achievement differed from that for other groups in Providence, but their occupational attainments did not differ much (once schooling and family background factors are taken into account). The striking and distinctive feature in Italian behavior, then, is the pattern of schooling; explanatory efforts should focus on it. Clearly, patterns of Italian school behavior are in some measure due to family background factors – particularly the greater poverty among the Italians, deriving from their concentration in low-skill work. However, our concern now is with the sharp differences in schooling that remain when these family background factors have been controlled.

Other economic characteristics

There are, first of all, other ways in which the Italians' location in the social-class and economic structures of the city may have influenced their school behavior. Perhaps, for example, second-generation Italians could more easily obtain jobs in certain sectors, such as construction work, whereas others could more easily obtain jobs in business firms. As a result, upward mobility might have been as likely for Italians as for others, but not in the same fields of endeavor. The lower secondary school rates might be no more than a response to this reality. Young people prepared for the kind of work most readily available; in the case of the Italians, perhaps more of the jobs that promised economic advancement did not require extended schooling. Similarly, there might have been a paucity of jobs for Italian girls as clerical workers in the relevant sectors, which might explain the girls' distinctive school patterns.

Some reflection and evidence, however, suggest that little, if any, weight should be attached to this explanation. It is certainly true, of course, that Yankee boys had more access to white-collar opportunities, but was the same true for the sons of other immigrants, as compared with the Italians? They, too, were much more likely to enroll in secondary schools than were Italians. Moreover, at issue here is access to opportunity deriving from the group's concentration in certain sectors of the city's economy – as distinct from their concentration at relatively low levels of economic well-being. We have, after all, sought to control for the latter by taking note of the father's occupation and property value. The relevant argument, then, is that differences between Italians and other immigrants in industrial-sector locations mattered at comparable levels of the father's occupation and property holdings. One may well doubt that such differences were crucial, and the 1915 data allow us to investigate that hypothesis directly. They include the industrial sector as well as the occupation in which each father worked. Italians were indeed somewhat more concentrated in certain sectors than was typical for the city's work force as a whole (Table 3.7). For example, 13% were engaged in construction, as against 8% of the other workers; 13% worked in laundries, in shoe-repair shops, and in dressmaking, whereas 3% of the others did. Yet these were the most extreme contrasts. Thus, whereas 12% of the Italians worked in textile manufacturing, so did 9% of all others. Similarly, there is no reason to assume that work in laundries, shoe-repair shops, and dressmaking shops, no doubt often as petty proprietors, rather than ownership of other kinds of small shops, had a negative effect on schooling. In any case, the most critical evidence is a direct test: a regression analysis of the determinants of high school entry in which the economic sector was included as one of the independent variables. When fathers' positions in the industrial sectors of the economy (those indicated in Table 3.7) were controlled, in addition to the family background characteristics controlled earlier, the magnitudes of the ethnic differences in schooling left unexplained before (in Table 3.3) remain virtually unchanged.[29]

A further dimension of economic standing is employment status, that is, whether one is an employer or employee. Our occupational classification scheme routinely takes account of many employers.

Table 3.7. *Distribution of fathers by industrial sectors, 1915*

| Industrial sector | Italian fathers (%) | | All other fathers (%) |
	Of native-born	All	
Construction	11.6	13.1	7.6
Manufacturing			
Machinery	1.5	1.6	5.7
Textiles	10.6	11.6	9.1
Jewelry	2.1	2.3	6.3
Other	13.4	14.4	14.1
Transportation, communications, utilities	4.5	4.9	7.6
Wholesale trade	1.3	0.9	3.3
Retail trade			
Food (stores and restaurants)	13.0	10.4	6.8
Other	3.3	3.4	7.9
Finance and real estate	2.0	1.7	3.6
Laundering, shoe repair	15.4	13.1	3.1
Government	4.1	2.9	2.9
All other	17.5	19.6	22.0
Total (100%) N	(544)	(844)	(2,833)

However, some historians have argued that employment status remains a critical, overlooked dimension in studies of class standing in America.[30] Because the 1915 data provide explicit information as to whether each gainfully employed individual was an employer or an employee, we can fully control for that dimension. The added control adds nothing to the available explanatory power. What mattered most about the economic order, for rates of schooling, was vertical location in the class structure. Refining information about sector or employment status simply adds too little to the routine occupational and property information to deserve attention.

Remigration

The high Italian remigration rate may also be relevant to patterns of schooling. In the period between 1899 and 1925, 46 Italians departed the United States for every 100 who entered. The Italians were not the only immigrant group with a high rate of remigration. Nevertheless, among the ten largest immigrant groups (including three-quarters of all immigrants), only the Poles, with a rate of 33%, and the Slovaks, with a rate of 36%, had rates at all comparable. Indeed, for all immigrants other than Italians, the rate of remigration in those years amounted to 25%, barely half the Italian rate.[31]

A high rate of remigration could have had a number of effects that would have discouraged extended schooling among the second generation. If a family came to the United States with a clear intention of returning to Italy, its members may well have considered American schools irrelevant to their long-range goals. What mattered was to save as much money as possible in the United States for the eventual return, and sending a child to work at an early age would have made more sense, from that perspective, than extended schooling.[32]

The desire to return, of course, was itself a complex phenomenon; economic, political, and cultural factors all operated to make some immigrant groups more likely to return to Europe than others. Whatever its sources, the relevance of return migration to patterns of second-generation schooling requires closer scrutiny. In fact, most of the Italian families did not return to Italy, and many of these must have realized they would not do so. There are several sorts of evidence that point to this conclusion. First, it appears that relatively few whole families returned. The rate of remigration, the ratio of departures to arrivals, was radically different for men and women. True, even the rate for women, 21%, was higher than in most immigrant groups. However, among the Italian men, the rate of remigration was 55%. That so many more men were likely to leave is directly related to the fact that men constituted the great majority of all the Italian immigrants, 75% of them. A great many men were unattached, or had left their families in Italy while they came to work in America. It was primarily these men who went back. Our concern, on the other hand, is with those who established families in the United States. Among that group, the much lower women's rates of remigration is a better indicator of the tendency to return to Italy than the rate for both sexes.[33]

Even the rate of remigration among Italian women overstates the rate of return for the families of the second generation, for it appears that at least three-quarters of the Italian immigrants who later left the United States had spent less than five years in this country.[34] If recent arrivals were more likely to return, most of our sample members' families were not prime candidates. Over half the children of Italian immigrants had been born in the United States in the 1915 sample, and nine-tenths in the 1925 sample. The presence of a native-born child of age twelve to fifteen suggests that the family had been in the United States at least that long. Also, of course, several years may have passed between arrival and the birth of the child.[35]

Many of these families may have hoped to return to Italy despite long sojourns in the United States, despite the evidence that most did not do so in the end. How much such hopes may have influenced the school behavior of their children is difficult to gauge. On the one hand, several considerations suggest that plans to return would not have mattered much to the families of the adolescents we have observed. First, it seems unlikely that families in the United States for many years would have thought in terms of only a short additional stay. Moreover, the native-born children, who quite possibly had never seen Italy, and who were much more at home in America than the older generation, must have reinforced their parents' understanding that the family could not easily return.[36] Finally, the example of others in the immigrant community must have been a forceful reminder that few dwelling in the United States for very long periods ever returned. On the other hand, the desire to return may still have affected the plans of a few families, and it may have had a greater effect on plans in many households in earlier years, when the permanence of their stay was less certain – perhaps during the years when their children had been five to ten years old, for example. Decisions taken and attitudes held at that time may have had an impact on later schooling.

Of course, all these considerations about intentions and their effects amount to mere speculation. Empirical data that would bear directly on the commitment to return and on its effect simply do not exist. However, some indirect evidence is available in the Providence data, evidence that suggests some relationship between that commitment to return and school performance. The 1915 Rhode Island State Census ascertained the citizenship status of the foreign-born – whether they were citizens, had filed applications for citizenship, or were aliens. It stands to reason that those anticipating a return to the old country would have been more likely to remain aliens. Italians were indeed less likely than others to have applied for citizenship papers by 1915 (Table 3.8). Fully 41% remained aliens, even in families that had lived in this country for at least twelve to fifteen years (those with native-born children in the sample). By contrast, only 10% of the Russian Jews residing in the United States that long remained aliens, and only 12% of the Irish immigrants did so. However, the Irish and the Jews were especially unlikely to return. Those immigrants from countries other than Italy, Russia, and the British Isles – the immigrants to whom we have compared the Italians throughout – differed less markedly from the Italians in their patterns of citizenship: 29% of the long-time residents remained aliens.

These ethnic differences in rates of application for citizenship, of course, may reflect more than plans to return to Europe. For example, more Italians may have been illiterate (even in their native language), making it harder for them to learn about citizenship application pro-

Table 3.8. *Citizenship status of immigrant groups, Providence, 1915*

Group	Citizen (%)	Applied for papers (%)	Alien (%)	N^a
English, Scots, Welsh	62.8	11.6	25.6	(121)
Irish	85.4	3.0	11.6	(498)
Child U.S.-born				
Russian Jews	83.0	6.7	10.3	(341)
Italians	48.3	10.9	40.9	(514)
Some other immigrants[b]	64.9	6.2	29.0	(259)
Child foreign-born				
Russian Jews	35.2	24.7	40.1	(284)
Italians	15.2	15.2	69.7	(290)
Some other immigrants	20.2	21.3	58.5	(94)

[a] Numbers reflect different sampling ratios. Also, citizenship information was unavailable for some households selected from the census schedules (the households of 4–6% Italian and Russian Jewish Sample Members, and 11–15% of the sample members from the other immigrant groups). Those individuals for whom the information was unavailable have been omitted from this table and from the first panel of Table 3.9 (those individuals were, however, included in the regression analyses reported in Table 3.9).

[b] White immigrants from countries other than Italy, Russia, and the British Isles.

cedures and to learn the basics of American history and government that might arise in a citizenship hearing. Similarly, if fewer of them learned English (for example, because they lived in a large, relatively tight-knit immigrant community), they may have avoided the citizenship hearings, for these were conducted in English.[37] The very fact that so many in the Italian neighborhoods were short-term migrants probably also made information about citizenship application procedures less common than in other immigrant communities. Finally, if Italian immigrants were simply less familiar with institutions of the modern nation-state than were members of many other immigrant groups, the concern with citizenship also may have been less prevalent among them. An association between the parents' citizenship and children's schooling may have been due to some of these factors, rather than to the commitment to return.

Nevertheless, it is plausible that at least some of the connection between citizenship and children's schooling would be due to the commitment to return, particularly among the Italians, whose remi-

Table 3.9. *Household head's citizenship status and children's schooling*[a]

1. Children's high school entry rates

	Head citizen (%) N[b]	Head applied for papers (%) N	Head alien (%) N
Boys			
Italians	28.3 (166)	12.8 (39)	5.8 (139)
All other immigrants	42.0 (590)	38.1 (40)	16.7 (116)
Some other immigrants[c]	43.1 (102)	66.7 (6)	10.3 (39)
Girls			
Italians	13.4 (82)	0 (17)	2.8 (71)
All other immigrants	49.1 (359)	28.0 (32)	13.6 (85)
Some other immigrants	47.0 (66)	30.0 (10)	13.9 (36)

2. Odds ratios for high school entry by group[d]

	No controls	Controlling for		
		Family background[e]	Head's citizenship status	Both
Boys				
All others	3.17	2.33	2.20	1.76 (3.21)[f]
Other immigrants	2.52	2.15	2.18	1.87 (2.62)
Girls				
All others	8.28	6.24	5.67	4.89 (5.52)
Other immigrants	5.43	5.12	5.37	5.19 (4.88)

3. Sixth-grade GPAs[g]

	No controls	Controlling for		
		Family background[e]	Head's citizenship status	Both
Boys				
All others	0.37	0.27	0.33	0.25 (3.42)[f]
Other immigrants	0.40	0.35	0.36	0.32 (3.19)
Girls				
All others	0.41	0.28	0.31	0.24 (2.57)
Other immigrants	0.26	0.22	0.24	0.20 (1.66)

gration rate was so high. Because no study has assessed the impact of remigration on children's schooling directly, and because parents' citizenship status is our only measure relevant to the intention to remigrate, we should explore its connection to schooling – mindful that that connection may overstate the importance of the intention to remigrate.

Were patterns of parental citizenship and children's schooling generally related among immigrants? Table 3.9 reveals that they were. The children of citizens were more likely to enroll in high school than were the children of aliens (first panel of Table 3.9). Just how much of the distinctive pattern of Italian schooling, then, is related to the factors reflected in citizenship rates? The next two panels of the table provide an assessment. Panel 2 compares the odds of high school entry for various groups. It extends the information presented earlier in Table 3.3. There the odds ratios, with no controls imposed, were compared with those remaining when family background characteristics (economic standing and family structure) were controlled. Here the citizenship status of the household head is controlled as well. Similarly, the third panel presents ethnic differences in sixth-grade GPAs, extending the analysis in Table 3.4 to include control for household head's citizenship status.

The strongest case for the influence of citizenship status appears in connection with boys' high school entry rates. It clearly mattered for those rates, and in conjunction with family background characteristics, it accounted for a notable part of the difference between Italians and others. On the other hand, there still remained an important residual ethnic difference between the behavior of Italian boys and others. More specifically, with the household head's citizenship status controlled, the relevant odds ratio falls appreciably, indeed, by about as much as when social class and family structure are controlled. Thus, the odds that other boys would enroll in high school were 2.33 times

Table 3.9 (Cont.)
[a] U.S.-born sample members only.
[b] See note *a*, Table 3.8.
[c] White immigrants from countries other than Italy, Russia, and the British Isles.
[d] The odds of entering high school in each group compared with the odds the Italians would do so.
[e] See Table 3.3, footnote *b*.
[f] *t* values.
[g] Differences in mean GPAs: each group compared with the Italians.

as great as the odds the Italian boys would do so with these family background characteristics controlled, and 1.76 times as great with citizenship controlled as well. This ratio implies that whereas 40% of other native-born boys and 17% of Italian boys reached high school (Table 3.3), 27% of the Italian boys would have done so had family background characteristics and the household head's citizenship status been the same among the Italians as among all others.[38]

Among girls, high school entry rates were also related to the household head's citizenship status. However, Italian girls were so much less likely to enroll than other girls that even when the household head's citizenship status is controlled, a huge unexplained ethnic difference remains. The odds that other girls would enroll were 6.24 times as great as those that Italian girls would do so with family background characteristics controlled, and 4.89 times as great with citizenship controlled as well. Forty-four percent of other native-born girls and 9% of Italian girls reached high school (Table 3.3); the ratios suggest that only 14% of the Italian girls would have done so even if family background characteristics and the household head's citizenship status had been the same among the Italians as among all others. In sum, the much greater underrepresentation of Italian girls in the high schools had little to do with the issue of return. Finally, the household head's citizenship status affected GPAs less than it affected high school entry rates in the Providence samples.[39]

A reasonable interpretation of the evidence, then, is to assume that citizenship may well have reflected concern with remigration and that remigration did have some negative impact on patterns of Italian school attainment. However, the ethnic differences in patterns of male high school enrollment that remain, despite all the controls, clearly suggest that still other factors had important effects on Italian patterns of schooling. Such factors were stronger still in determining the length of schooling for Italian girls.

Contextual effects

The behavior of individuals was influenced not merely by the characteristics of their own families, but by the characteristics of their social context as well. And the characteristics of social context may have differed across ethnic lines, just as the characteristics of families did. Consider first the case of social class. Being a member of an ethnic group, such as the Italians, in which high proportions were unskilled laborers may well have influenced children's behavior even if their own fathers were not unskilled laborers.[40] The values of unskilled laborers, their more restricted access to information about opportunities for upward mobility, and especially their inability to provide jobs for youth of their own ethnic group would have made their predominance influential for all children of the group. The contextual effects of class composition, then, may have been partly economic and partly cultural in nature.

Second, consider again the issue of remigration. Even if many Italian children were raised in families that did not contemplate a return to Italy, they may have been influenced by growing up in a community in which there were unskilled, unattached young men working for relatively brief periods in the United States.[41] The presence of many such men in the community could, for example, have influenced attitudes toward school among the second generation. It could also have made information about opportunities for economic success relatively scarce among peers, because relatively few of the young, unattached male workers would have had that sort of information. If the children of the second generation really mixed socially with the younger among the unattached male laborers from Italy, these latter may have been the source of a peer context that discouraged schooling.

In evaluating the importance of these influences, we move from a consideration of family background factors (father's occupation, length of residence in the United States, number of siblings, whether or not both parents were present, and so forth) to a different kind of explanatory factor: the effect of being in a particular social context. Contextual effects are much less often assessed empirically than those related to family background.

Nevertheless, contextual effects are highly relevant to discussions of the relationship between class and ethnicity. Arguments about how the social-class compositions of ethnic groups influence their behavior may hinge on the contextual effects of class origin as well as on individual attributes. Indeed, contextual effects bear on any effort to understand how an ethnic group's location in the social structure mattered to the behavior of its members. Insofar as the structural location of the group is conceived to be important to each member of the group over and above the structural location of that member, contextual effects are in fact part of the argument.

How can these effects be assessed, and how strong were they? We must accept at the outset that they can be assessed only crudely. Moreover, that assessment does not suggest that contextual effects hold the key to understanding the ethnic differences in patterns of schooling left unexplained in the preceding analyses. Nevertheless, the assessment of contextual effects is worth considering further. At the very least, doing so should advance discussion; the concept of contextual effects helps to formulate explicitly and to explore, albeit tentatively, dynamics that often are either assumed or overlooked in thinking about the relationship between class and ethnicity.

Empirically, the relevance of these contextual effects arises, as it has in our discussion of the Italians, when measurable characteristics of individuals do not account for the entirety of the observed ethnic difference – characteristics that are related to structural location, such as the father's occupation and family property value. We may wonder whether these characteristics have been poorly measured with available data or whether other important aspects of social structural position have been omitted. However, it is also possible that contextual factors were influential in creating the ethnic patterns.

Contextual effects have been studied less often than individual-level variables because methods for assessing their importance empirically, particularly in studies of ethnicity, are not well developed, nor is it clear that such methods ever can be developed. Moreover, the study of contextual effects involves conceptual problems – for example, whether or not the contextual effects operate entirely through individual-level characteristics, whether a context is influential or, alternatively, individuals with certain characteristics choose certain kinds of contexts, and which of several possible contexts is most crucial for the determination of a particular behavior.

Even if we can bypass or ignore the conceptual problems raised by the study of contextual effects, some problems of measurement must be confronted. These and the quantitative analysis based on their resolution are left to the Appendix (Section 9).[42] In brief, differences between contexts are captured by using the group's mean (or rate) for a particular characteristic. For example, the mean for fathers' occupational scores in a boy's ethnic group is treated as a variable that characterizes each individual just as his own father's occupational score characterizes him. Similarly, the rate of return migration for a group is used to characterize each person. We can then explore how strongly these contextual variables were associated with measures of schooling, such as high school entry. However, these measures of contextual effects are not merely crude; they also carry a great potential for spurious positive findings. By definition, an individual's score for a particular contextual factor is perfectly correlated with the individual's ethnic identity, and therefore it has a good chance of being associated with whatever explains the ethnic differences. The results, then, are suspect precisely when the correlation is high.

Nevertheless, the effort to assess the effect of context (detailed in the Appendix) is of some use. It indicates that the contextual effects of social-class composition (measured in several ways) created virtually none of the differences in schooling between Italians and others. As we noted earlier, the odds that other boys would reach high school in 1915 were 3.17 times as great as the odds that Italians would, and with the family background characteristics and household head's citizenship status controlled, they were still 1.76 times as great. Controlling also the contextual effects related to the mean level of fathers' occupations only reduced the odds ratio only to 1.73. The impact of that factor on the odds that Italian girls would enroll in high school was still smaller. Apparently, then, most of the social-class effects were indeed those related to one's own family's position; the additional contextual effects related to being in an ethnic group whose social-class composition was distinctive were minimal.

The point is not that the social-class milieu in which a child was raised did not matter. The child of a laborer, for example, may have been influenced by a distinctive social context typical of laborers. However, that contextual influence would have been captured by controlling for his own father's occupation. The contextual factor at issue here, then, is solely the additional effect of membership in an ethnic group that included an especially high proportion of laborers. Apparently, this additional effect simply was not strong enough to be observed with the methods available.[43]

Assessing the contextual effects of a high remigration rate, on the other hand, offers an example of the dangers of spurious association. The remigration rate was indeed strongly associated with length of schooling, not merely in the Providence data, but in some useful national data as well. Nevertheless, further exploration revealed that the associations clearly were spurious.

The precise impact of the contextual effects of the remigration rate, then, cannot be determined, but the evidence suggesting a large impact is spurious. What we can say, by way of summary, is that class origins, family structure, and household head's citizenship status together reduced the odds ratio for boys' high school entry (the ratio of the odds that other would enter compared with the odds that Italians would do so) from 3.17 to 1.76. In stating the results this way, we ignore the ambiguities inherent in controlling for household head's citizenship status (which, as discussed earlier, may well control for more attributes than merely the intention to return to Italy). Yet these results still leave a considerable unexplained ethnic difference in patterns of schooling. In both cases, and especially among the girls, the remaining, unexplained odds ratio implies a substantial difference in enrollment rates. Finally, the contextual effects related to social class had virtually no effect on the ethnic patterns. The contextual effects of the remigration rate cannot be measured directly. However, the results of our other assessments – of economic and demographic background characteristics, parental citizenship status (itself related to remigration), and the contextual effects of class composition – suggest that it would be rash to assume that the contextual effects of Italian remigration can adequately explain the group's patterns of schooling.

3.5.   Explaining the differences: the European cultural heritage

What, then, does account for the distinctive Italian patterns of schooling – high school entry, GPA, and gender patterns not explained thus far? We are pressed back from a concern with the conditions of Italian immigrant life in the United States to the conditions of life in Italy. The magnitudes of the residual ethnic differences in schooling suggest that we should attribute considerable power to the heritage the Italians brought with them. Nor can the relevant dimension of this heritage be conceived exclusively in terms of occupational skills or other skills distinct from values, attitudes, and intellectual orientations. The influence of occupational and related skills surely affected the father's economic position, but that, in turn, was controlled in preceding analyses. Rather, what is at issue here are those values, attitudes, and orientations that, for the sake of brevity, we have termed pre-migration cultural attributes.

From regression analysis to pre-migration culture: on interpreting the residuals

This line of argument, admittedly, has an inherent weakness. The historical evidence available – with which we can study representative individuals and assess the impact of family background characteristics – does not permit us to measure the impact of cultural attributes directly. Moreover, our ability to assess the magnitude of social class, family structure, and other such influences is imperfect, as it is in every study. Some of the magnitude of the residuals may have resulted from imperfect measurement of the other characteristics controlled, as well as from other omitted variables, economic and demographic characteristics that we were not able to control.

These are serious considerations; others, however, tend to mitigate their force. First, the approach taken here is not novel. Rather, in most research contexts it is the best approach available for clarifying the sources of ethnic behavior; its limitations cannot be avoided. Second, the residuals comprise observed associations between ethnic origin and behavior (school performance or job attained). These residuals, then, should not be confused with the variance in behavior unrelated to anything measurable. We are assuming that the observed association reflects the influence of cultural attributes that are not directly observed – rather than only the influence of measurement error or other omitted variables, both of which are also unobserved.

That which we can observe suggests that measurement error and other omitted variables cannot completely explain the residuals. The occupational classification scale may seem particularly inexact as a measure of social-class standing. Nevertheless, an occupational classification scheme based on five strata left residuals at least as large. Various other modifications of the occupational control variable also proved inconsequential, including one that bypassed problems of classification entirely by controlling for each occupational title separately (treating each occupation as though it were an occupational stratum).[44] Therefore, mismeasurement in fathers' occupations – the most crucial and most complicated proxy for social-class origins – should not be regarded as a reason to dismiss the residuals.[45] Moreover, the ethnicity variable is also subject to various problems of classification, and our estimates of its strength are therefore also understated. For example, the place of birth of the sample member's father, the basis for determining ethnic identity, ignores whether a foreign-born father immigrated to the United States at age thirty-two or was brought by his own parents at age two. The criterion also ignores the place of birth of the sample member's mother.[46]

Our operational definition of social class, though resting heavily on occupation as a proxy, also includes the assessed value of the family's property and a control for family size (a measure of mouths to feed). Finally, adding controls for whether or not the father was an employer and for the industrial sector in which he worked did not appreciably reduce the residuals.

It is true that we have had no direct measure of family income. On the other hand, family income was surely highly correlated with the characteristics we have controlled. At issue is the influence of ethnic differences in income (within the same occupations, assessed-property category, family size, and so forth) on ethnic differences in schooling. The residuals that we think reflect the influence of cultural attributes generally account for half to three-quarters of the entire ethnic difference. In order to wipe out most of the residuals' magnitude, then, the net impact of family income (after the other, highly correlated characteristics have already been controlled) would need to be twice or three times the total impact of the characteristics already controlled. In the absence of any hint that the income variable would have such power, we should not assume that it would.

A control for parental literacy in the later samples (1915 and 1925) might also have been revealing. However, our analysis of Irish literacy patterns serves as a reminder that parental literacy may deserve most attention as a marker of pre-migration cultural attributes.[47]

Finally, the range of results encountered when imposing controls is important. In some instances – Irish schooling and occupational attainment in 1880, as well as Italian schooling – they have left large residuals. However, in other instances they have adequately explained the association between ethnic origin and behavior. These include Irish–Yankee differences in schooling and jobs in the later samples and Italian occupational attainment. Thus, the measured family background variables, the ones so central to any structural explanation of ethnic differences, seem adequate to some purposes. If they are not adequate for others, we should not rush to assume problems of method.[48]

Clearly, the competing explanations for the observed residuals (measurement error and the impact of omitted structural characteristics) would explain part of their strength; the part we assume they cannot explain poses the interpretive challenge. The presence of large ethnic differences unexplained by competing explanations cannot prove the influence of the pre-migration cultural attributes; still, the discovery of these large residuals makes the case for those attributes stronger than it would have been had the residuals been negligible. The appeal to cultural attributes, then, should be viewed as tentative, but reasonable, given the current state of the evidence and the methods available.

The cultural heritage: its character and historical origins reconsidered

The data on which we have relied cannot advance us very far in comprehending the nature of these cultural attributes; they do not, generally, allow us to sift among the elements in the cultural heritage that were most relevant. However, the differences between the patterns of schooling and occupational attainment can help narrow the search for explanations. The ethnic differences in school behavior that could not be accounted for by family background factors were large and consistent. The magnitude of the Italian lag in occupational attainment was much less striking – when compared with their educational behavior or with other ethnic differences in occupational attainment (for example, those between Irish and Yankee in 1880, and others we shall encounter in later chapters). Explanations specific to school behavior, then, should be of greater interest than those that would predict differences in job success. In particular, all explanations that suggest a distinct work ethic or a distinct attitude toward achievement should be treated with caution – explanations relying on the absence of the Protestant work ethic, preindustrial work habits generally, or a generalized suspicion of American values of success. Historians of immigration and sociologists of ethnicity have suggested all of these,[49] yet all would be expected to influence occupational attainment as strongly and consistently as school performance. Such factors, of course, may have had a small role in determining job or school patterns, but because they do not explain why school patterns would be especially affected, they are of marginal importance.

The cultural heritage of interest is one that made Italians less sensitive to the economic advantages of schooling, or less oriented to book learning generally, than other groups in Providence. Italian behavior was also, we noted, especially distinctive in connection with girls, suggesting either a belief that schooling in particular was less relevant to them or that for some other reason the school environment was less suited than others for girls (for example, because they could be more closely supervised in the teen years at home or even in some work contexts). Beyond this statement, the data do not allow us to probe; we must rely on the descriptions of Italian cultural attributes provided by others.[50] Leonard Covello's description was cited at the outset. In brief:

> The peasant's desire for security in his way of living was directly opposed to education from outside the family circle. . . . This antagonism toward the school, which was definitely manifested in Italy and which constituted a part of the cultural tradition, was carried over to America and paved the way for the still current [1944] lack of rapprochement between the American school and the Italian parents.[51]

However, Joseph Lopreato, in his study of Italian-Americans, cites Covello's summary with disapproval. Covello, Lopreato notes, was devoted to the notion of the "community school" concept

> which argues that in order to achieve its goal, the school must have a thorough understanding of the culture of the individuals and groups that it serves. Covello was thus naturally led to exaggerate the conflict between the American school and the southern Italian immigrants.[52]

Part of Italian parental behavior, Lopreato argues, was motivated by poverty. In any case, he argues, they may have been antagonistic to intellectuals, whom they had reason to distrust, and they were familiar with schooling only through the primary grades. However, they were not opposed to schooling or intellectual activity per se.

Yet Lopreato himself concludes that "this much can be said about the peasants of southern Italy prior to the great emigration. In general, they were so deprived and so far removed from what C. Wright Mills termed 'the educational elevator' that to entertain the thought of intellectual pursuits amounted, for most, to asking for a miracle." One would assume, as well, that they would have been less attuned to the relations between education and jobs generally than others were. Lopreato's criticism of Covello, followed by his own reformulation of a possible cultural legacy, suggests the futility of trying, on the basis of the Providence evidence, to state with precision the nature of the cultural legacy. Lopreato's differences from Covello are not trivial. However, even if one accepts Lopreato's descriptions completely, one can still conclude that Italian school performance differed from that of other groups for reasons derived from the Italian cultural past.[53]

The difference between the approaches of Lopreato and Covello also provides a useful way to understand the work of John Briggs, *An Italian Passage*. Briggs seems most intent to argue not that Italian school achievement was comparable to that for other ethnic groups, but that if it was not, the explanation is not intellectual inferiority or a lack of respect for intellectual activity.[54] Here we can certainly agree with him about the dangers of misstating the nature of the cultural legacy, but the issue for us is the operation of some sort of legacy and its power relative to other factors.[55] The Providence data strongly suggest that such factors were important, even if we cannot indicate their nature with precision.

Still less do the data permit us to describe the historical origins of these cultural attributes. Covello saw them developing out of the southern Italian peasant economy and the political realities that encouraged suspicion of governmental educational efforts. Such arguments are common in connection with Italians and other former peasant immigrants. Although we obviously cannot confirm them with the data at hand, we can offer some clarifications by surveying several related arguments.

These arguments are rarely clearly distinguished. One strand bears on the social structural position of the Italian immigrants, their origin in the lower strata of an agrarian social order. Still, more is surely involved. Farm laborers' children from rural New England or English Canada or Scandinavia did not follow the Italian pattern of school behavior. The particular nature of the rural social and economic structure from which the immigrants came, not merely their experience as agricultural laborers, was important. The Italian rural workers came from a society relatively unchanged by industrial development. There was less reason than in some other agricultural societies to take schooling seriously – less of a sense that schooling mattered for later work, or generally that the old order was passing and that old assumptions might no longer hold. In order to understand why some agricultural orders differed from others in producing a sensitivity to the value of schooling, perhaps it is necessary to go beyond changes due to industrialization to a vaguer conception of modernization generally, to the coming of newer attitudes that cannot be fully understood as responses to economic changes. Alternatively, perhaps economic changes were the central changes, but the transformations of agricultural capitalism, rather than those of industrialization, mattered most in increasing the sensitivity to the productive value of schooling. Perhaps, for example, managing one's own farm for sale of products in the marketplace was enough to stimulate such sensitivity.

All these strands of the argument assume that most Italian immigrants had been rural-dwellers, deriving their livelihood from the soil in a preindustrial, premodern, or precapitalist order: All assume that most of the immigrants had been peasants (or other agricultural workers) before the migration. However, some recent historical research has suggested that many of the European immigrants, including many from Italy, had not been peasants, but rather had come from many different social positions in their countries of origin.[56] Does this insight invalidate the line of explanation Covello and others have proposed? I think not. More work on these themes will be welcome. However, it is certainly plausible that many immigrants who were not former peasants had still lived within a social and cultural milieu dominated by the outlooks Covello described as characteristic of the peasantry; some other immigrants, although not peasants at the time of emigration, may have come from families that had lived as peasants a generation before. Moreover, even if many immigrants were not former peasants and did not hold the peasants' views, many others had been peasants. The presence of these peasants among the immigrants may have been sufficient to create the patterns we have observed. The low level of Italian school achievement, in other words, probably could have been created by the peasantry among the Italian immigrants even if that group comprised (for example) only two-thirds or one-half of all Italian immigrants.

In all these variants of the argument, the Italian immigrants' attitudes about schooling are thought to have had their source in the Italian social structure and economic order. Other sorts of explanations focus instead on the distinction between Catholic and Protestant societies. Some of these arguments stress the prevalence of a Protestant ethic that stimulated work, whether in school or in the marketplace. As already indicated, this explanation hardly seems central in the light of the small differences in occupational attainment between Italians and others; the issue is to account for the differences in schooling specifically. Other arguments about religious sources of behavior, however, concentrate on the tradition of literacy in Protestant societies, a tradition derived from the imperative to read and interpret the Bible directly, without the intervention of clerical authorities. This factor may have made immigrants from certain preindustrial agrarian economies (Scotland and Scandinavia, for example) more favorably disposed to schooling than others.

The extent to which European educational institutions had been available to the social strata from which the migrants came may well have been important in itself, familiarizing future migrants with school-going behavior and with its advantages. This factor, it will be recalled, may explain some of the changes among the Irish immigrants between 1880 and 1915. It also may have distinguished Italians from Irish in 1915. The availability of educational institutions, of course, is itself bound up with economic transformations, religious traditions, and political policies. But whatever its origin, that availability may have been a critical independent factor in determining the attitudes of immigrants.

All of the preceding explanations ultimately direct attention away from any characteristics of life unique to southern Italy and toward broader sorts of explanatory frameworks relevant to pre-migration life: social-class position, the economic order, religion, familiarity with schooling. At the same time, these and other factors – political arrangements, for example – may have come together in a unique way in southern Italian culture. That culture, then, may have had an independent force beyond its sources.

Italians, Slavs, and other immigrants

We cannot hope to disentangle these strands of argument completely. The Providence data are especially limited in this regard, for in Providence, as in New England generally, large communities of immigrant groups from other preindustrial, premodern environments were not to be found in the period after 1900. The Jews may seem to constitute an exception, but their patterns of schooling were in any case not typical of most new immigrant groups. The comparison with "other immigrants," as used repeatedly earlier, was useful because it ruled out the possibility that Italians were simply behaving like all immigrants, or at least like all except the English-speaking and Jewish immigrants. Still, in order to study whether the Italian experience was unique or was typical for immigrants from preindustrial peasant backgrounds, that comparison is imperfect. Ideally, the comparison should be with another such large immigrant community, not with a very heterogeneous group.

The principal immigrant groups from social positions most resembling those of the Italians were the Slavic groups, peasants from relatively less advanced economies and from societies not characterized by any special commitment to literacy. The Poles were the largest of these groups by far, but the other Slavic groups together provided nearly one immigrant in ten between 1899 and 1924. Indeed, taken together, the Italians, the Slavs, and the Jews (who are excluded from consideration here for reasons already given) constituted a large fraction of the immigrants, nearly 10 million among 17 million immigrants in all. Moreover, because those coming from the countries of western Europe and English Canada themselves numbered nearly 4 million, the Italians, Slavs, and Jews accounted for approximately three-fourths of all who did not come from western Europe or English Canada. In short, by considering the Slavs as the most significant groups to be compared with the Italians, we are indeed choosing not only groups relevant for theoretical reasons but also the great majority of such immigrants. Although we cannot compare Slavic and Italian schooling on the basis of the Providence data, we can exploit the 1960 U.S. Census figures on educational attainments of ethnic groups (described in the preceding chapter).

The median years of schooling completed by male members of the second generation are presented in Table 3.10. Virtually all of the Slavic groups' educational levels were similar to those for the Italians in the two oldest cohorts, those reaching age fifteen by 1905. In the later cohorts, all Slavs except the Poles pulled ahead of the Italians, narrowing the gap between themselves and the British and Irish, and then achieving roughly comparable educational levels as those groups. The Italians and Poles achieved levels comparable to those of the other groups only in the youngest cohort. The changing relative positions of groups may indicate changes in the nature of the immigrants' conditions in Europe, improving economic conditions in America for later arrivals in some groups, or the fact that later cohorts increasingly included families who had been dwelling in the United States for some time when their children reached adolescence. The critical point, however, is that if Italian school behavior was quite different from that for all other groups in Providence, it was not as different from that for all Slavs of the early twentieth century, and it was quite similar to Polish school behavior over a long period.

This conclusion is reinforced by considering gender differences in

Table 3.10. *Median years of schooling completed, selected ethnic groups (native-born males only)*[a]

Parents' country of origin[b]	Age in 1960					Group's rate of remigration[c]
	25–34	35–44	45–54	55–64	65–74	
"Old immigration"						
United Kingdom	12.7	12.5	12.0	9.8	8.7	20.2
Ireland	12.6	12.5	11.7	9.5	8.7	8.9
Norway and Sweden	12.6	12.4	11.1	8.9	8.5	15.4
Germany	12.5	12.1	9.9	8.6	8.3	13.7
Canada	12.3	12.2	11.1	9.2	8.7	14.8
"New immigration"						
Italy	12.2	11.4	9.0	8.4	8.0	45.6
Poland	12.4	11.5	9.2	8.3	7.6	33.0
Czechoslovakia	12.4	11.9	9.2	8.4	8.0	31.7
Hungary	12.5	12.0	10.1	8.9	8.7	46.5
Yugoslavia	12.4	12.0	9.5	8.4	7.7	47.6
Lithuania	12.8	12.3	10.9	8.9	8.7	20.3
Finland	12.5	12.2	9.5	8.5	7.6	22.0
USSR	13.6	12.7	12.3	10.4	8.7	12.3

[a]From 1960 U.S. Census Bureau, *Nativity and Parentage*, Table 12.
[b]Census data based on political boundaries of 1960; return rates on ethnic groups for 1899–1924. See Appendix, note 41, for details.
[c]Based on Archdeacon, *Becoming American*, 118–19.

schooling among different ethnic groups. Because gender differences were not large in most groups, the measure used earlier (median years of schooling completed) is too crude. We may focus, however, on the proportion who completed secondary school. In the American population as a whole before the 1950s, more girls than boys completed secondary school. Thus, among those age fifty-five to sixty-four in 1960 (the birth cohort most comparable to the 1915 sample), 31% of the women and 28% of the men living in urban places were graduates. Comparable differences were found in the younger and older cohorts and among the native-born children of the Irish (37% versus 31% in the cohort fifty-five to sixty-four years old), the English (40% versus 34%), the Swedish (39% versus 29%), and the Germans (38% versus 34%). Among the Italians, the rates showed the reverse pattern: 16% of the men and 12% of the women had graduated from high school. Was this a unique feature of the Italians? No. In every Slavic group, more men than women graduated: 18% versus 14% among the Poles, 31% versus 27% among the Lithuanians, 17% versus 15%

among the Yugoslavs. Among the Czechs, the figures were nearly equal for that cohort (15.4% versus 15.2%), but they were a bit higher for the preceding and subsequent cohorts.[57] The similarity of the Italian and Slavic patterns, in contrast to those for the other groups, also suggests a further reason for doubting the contextual effects of the high remigration rates noted in the preceding section. The gender patterns that characterized the Italians and Slavs seem explicable in terms of traditional peasant views of women, but not in terms of the contextual effects of high remigration rates.

These similarities between Italian and Slavic school behavior are consistent with the idea that pre-migration socioeconomic conditions shared by all these groups were important sources of their behavior. Whether or not local differences that distinguished the Italians from all others were also operating is difficult to say. That the Italians and Slavs were fundamentally similar in school behavior suggests that such differences probably were marginal. Still, if the Italians were not unique, they and the Poles apparently differed from the other Slavic groups to some extent. The difference may be related to specific cultural differences between these two groups and the others, but perhaps the difference also has to do with the difficulties faced by members of very large immigrant communities with few resources for economic advancement within the community itself.[58]

We need not resolve the issue; although structural or cultural factors specific to the Italians may have had some impact, there is surely good reason to stress the similar pre-migration socioeconomic positions of the Italians and Slavs. Those positions, in turn, appear central to an understanding of any cultural factors that influenced their children's school behavior in the United States. We assume, then, that the Italians differed from the "other immigrants" with whom we compared them in large measure because these others were not from rural backgrounds comparable to those of the Italians and the Slavs.[59] Thus, we may distinguish, first, the experience that Italians shared with all immigrants, second, the ways in which southern Italian culture may have been unique, and, third, pre-migration cultural attributes that Italians may have shared with Slavs or other peasant immigrants from preindustrial areas not characterized by any special commitment to literacy. This last is the most straightforward explanation for the differences between their school patterns and the patterns for others in Providence that remained unexplained by class and family structure.

The Russian Jews

The eastern European Jewish immigration was the critical event in American Jewish history. Like the Italians, the Jews from eastern Europe began arriving in the United States in large numbers just after 1880. The migration increased in magnitude with each succeeding decade, until American immigration restriction ended it in the early 1920s. Although Jews had come to the United States in earlier years, especially from central Europe, those earlier migrations were dwarfed by the numbers in the later migrations. By 1900, moreover, the Jews were the second largest immigrant group, after the Italians, to enter the United States each year. Many more Italians arrived between 1899 and 1924, the years for which the most reliable figures are available. However, a far higher proportion of the Italians also departed, so that there were nearly as many Jews among the immigrants who remained. In all, between 1880 and 1924, some 2.3 million eastern European Jews came to the United States.[1]

In the history of American immigration, the Jews hold a special place for reasons other than sheer numbers. Jewish immigrants and their offspring improved their economic standing more rapidly than other groups did. Moreover, the story of their rise is closely bound up with schooling. Finally, as we shall see, their schooling itself is a striking example of distinctive school behavior on the part of an ethnic group, quite apart from its relation to economic advancement.[2]

The evidence of the connection between Jewish schooling and economic advancement is plentiful for recent decades – for the period since 1930 and especially since 1945. During these recent decades, educational attainment has been likely to mean college attendance, and even enrollment in a professional school. A dominant pattern of upward mobility has involved entry into the professions by sons of reasonably well-established middle-class families. Consequently, in this later period, the role of education, though it does not explain all of the distinctiveness of eastern European Jewish patterns of mobility, naturally explains a good deal.

However, our understanding of schooling and economic advancement in the earlier stages of this group's adjustment to the United States is less clear. The evidence available on the eastern European

Jewish immigrants and their children indicates that economic advancement was unusually rapid for both; however, the connections between that economic advancement and schooling, especially in the second generation, are at issue. The children of the eastern European Jews were more likely to receive a relatively extended education than were those of other immigrant groups. Still, several important caveats must be noted.

First, the meaning of a "relatively extended education" should be clear. As Selma Berrol, Irving Howe, and others have observed, most children of the eastern European immigrants did not receive very extended educations.[3] More Jews than others may have graduated from college, but only a small fraction of any ethnic group reached college in the decades before 1920. More graduated from high school. Nevertheless, in 1908, well below 5% of the Russian Jewish children in New York City (where fully half of them lived) graduated.[4]

Second, the children or grandchildren of eastern European Jews have been especially well represented among American intellectuals and academics. However, the emergence of a sizable class of Jewish intellectuals may not tell us much about the role of education in the experience of the ethnic group as a whole. Their emergence may indeed have had something to do with the role of education in the ethnic group generally, but it also may have stemmed from other sources. Certainly, the emergence of such an elite is a poor basis for generalizing about the patterns of the whole group. Our concern here will be to understand the patterns of the ethnic group as a whole, rather than the creation of the intellectual elite. Those patterns provide the topic most directly connected with our larger theme (the school behavior of ethnic groups), and it is a topic for which we have useful information from Providence.[5]

Thus, the meaning of an extended education was not what it came to be later, and the experience of an elite is not to be confused with the experience of the majority. The statement that eastern European Jews received more extended education than others must be interpreted to mean that, at most, the eastern European Jews may have received a few more years of schooling than most others: a year or two of high school, for example, when most children left between the fifth and eighth grades.

Nevertheless, such ethnic differences could well have played a role in the economic advancement of the eastern European Jews, even though not making them professionals or intellectuals. As we have already observed in Chapter 1, differences of a few years in school mattered a good deal for economic attainment in the period 1880–1930, and they still do today. The initial advances of the Jews were, in any case, not into the professions but into business; there, such gradations may have been quite significant. Still, whether or not they fully explain the rapidity of the eastern European Jewish advance is another matter. Just how much of an educational advantage did the children of the eastern European Jews enjoy, and how much difference did it make to their economic advancement?

Finally, what accounts for the group's distinctive educational attainment, and for any distinctiveness in their economic advancement not due to their schooling? There is a clear division among the many writers who have addressed this issue, some stressing advantages the Jews enjoyed in American society at the turn of the century, mostly occupational advantages, and others stressing the pre-migration cultural heritage of eastern European Jewry. We turn first to those aspects of the social and cultural background of eastern European Jewry that have loomed large in these discussions, and then to a fuller description of the debate over its relative importance.

4.1. The eastern European Jewish background and the debate about its importance

It is useful to distinguish two sources of the eastern European Jewish heritage: the Jewish religion and the position of the Jews in eastern European social and political life.[6]

The religious influences, of course, were in some measure common to Jewish communities in other places and eras. However, the religion did not influence Jewish life in exactly the same manner in various times and places. The particular social position of the Jews helped determine the most dominant elements in the religious culture, as did internal intellectual developments in different Jewish communities. For our purposes, it is enough to note that the Jewish religion required the study and interpretation of God's law. That imperative for study and interpretation had important implications, not simply at the level of an elite, but for the mass of the population as well. The need was met by widespread schooling – though just how widespread is difficult to say. One useful source, the Russian census of 1897, showed that 55–70% of Jewish males in the older age cohorts (those over age thirty) were literate, compared with only 20–40% of other Russians. Moreover, it appears that many of these literate Jews (three-fifths of them in the oldest cohort) were literate only in a language other than Russian, offering some measure of the extent of the traditional schooling.[7] That schooling was meant to enable every man to read the prayers and to enable many (how many is again difficult to say) to follow, at least to some extent, the intricate discussions concerning religious law in the Talmud and its commentaries. A significant proportion of the male population was in fact able to devote considerable time to that study.

The role of the scholar, the individual who devoted himself to advanced study of the law and its interpretation, was an especially honored role, one to which it was natural for a boy to aspire. Honor also constituted a commodity one could join with wealth through marriage. The scholar was a desirable catch, and the wife of a scholar, other things being equal, came from a more well-to-do family than another man's wife. That system also increased the chances that the scholar would have the income for continued study. If he did not, his wife might herself operate a store or other business in order to provide it.

No doubt it was easier for the child of a well-to-do father to spend a lifetime in study, but wealth did not guarantee intelligence or desire for study. Also, examples of impoverished but brilliant students were legion, and these may not have been so rare, given the general levels of poverty and the number of scholars. Although we cannot be at all precise in describing the prevalence of scholarship in the population, we can assume that the heritage of several centuries must have made the ideal of male scholarship nearly universal by the middle of the nineteenth century. It was not the only ideal, of course. Wealth was surely another way one could achieve honor and power, and in terms of dealing with the secular world, it was a more secure path. Nevertheless, the important point for our purposes is the prevalence of respect for study, and the sense that learning was central to training the young.[8]

Or, rather, to training the young male. Women's functions were in the home, including, quite possibly, working in the family business. To be sure, good breeding in a woman might well include literacy, and it might include a basic education, but it did not include a life devoted to studying the law. That there may have been a handful of women in the millennia of Jewish history who became noted for attaining the ideal of scholarship hardly means we need modify the generalization: The sex difference was absolutely central.

Thus, the ideal of the scholar was limited to males and was realized by only a few of them. Nevertheless, the culture in which the majority of the eastern European Jews participated was a culture in which learning was central and familiar. First, unusually large proportions were literate before the coming of state-run schools; second, the activities of learning and study (over and above the acquisition of basic literacy) were visible to large numbers, and nontrivial numbers probably had some share, however modest, in these activities; finally, the accomplished scholar was highly visible and highly respected.[9]

The economic positions of the Jews in Europe had been strikingly different from the positions occupied by nearly all other immigrants, and these differences, too, could have produced distinct patterns of behavior. The Jews had not been engaged directly in farming; rather, they filled the peripheral economic roles found in an agricultural economy. They were artisans, tradesmen, storekeepers, innkeepers, and the like. They were generally poor, although they may well have fared better than the peasantry. Most Jews were involved in one way or another in commerce, at least in its broadest sense – in occupations in which one buys and sells with an eye to a profit, makes countless decisions and senses a connection between those decisions and exertions and the improvement of one's lot. This experience was generally different from that of the serf, that of the subsistence farmer, and even that of the wage worker.

We have concentrated on the role of learning in traditional eastern European Jewish culture and on the economic position of the Jews in eastern Europe. However, other aspects of their religious heritage and of their social circumstances also may have proved important to attitudes and behavior. For example, their strict adherence to literally hundreds of commandments concerning daily behavior distinguished the Jews from others. Moreover, the social and political standing of the Jews was distinct, and not merely because of their position in the economic structure. They lived as a threatened minority. Their lives and livelihoods might become endangered on short notice, and their day-to-day contact with non-Jews might well involve insult and even violence.

The preceding sketch is, of course, brief and schematic; it is also static. Economic, intellectual, and political transformations were occurring with great rapidity by the last half of the nineteenth century. The ideas that arose from the Enlightenment, socialism, and Zionism, as well as the social transformations created by industrialization and economic modernization generally, all became influential in a relatively short period. An extensive process of proletarianization was occurring in many eastern European Jewish communities, as a result of which Jewish shopkeepers and artisans could sustain themselves only by becoming factory operatives, producing textiles, garments, or other manufactured goods. Still, proletarianization was a matter of the last decades of the century, and surely most factory operatives could remember an earlier economic order.

If, then, the educational and economic advances of the eastern European Jews in the United States (and, indeed, in Europe) has been distinctive, was that because of the distinctiveness of their background, and, if so, how? In response to this question, a considerable literature has flourished around two opposing approaches. They are nicely captured by juxtaposing the formulations of Nathan Glazer and those of Calvin Goldscheider and Alan Zuckerman.

In the early 1950s, Glazer surveyed the socioeconomic advancement of American Jews in an influential article, "Social Characteristics of American Jews."[10] Near the end of his long survey, Glazer wrote:[11]

> We think that the explanation of the Jewish success in America is that the Jews, far more than any other immigrant group, were engaged for generations in the middle-class occupations, the professions and buying and selling. It has also been said that the urban experience helped them, but we think that is much less important. For in any case, very large proportions of Jews, German as well as East European, came from small towns and villages that were scarcely "urban." The special occupations of the middle-class – trade and professions – are associated with a whole complex of habits. Primarily, these are the habits of care and foresight. The middle-class person, we know, is trained to save his money, because he has been taught that the world is open to him, and with the proper intelligence and ability, and with resources well used, he may advance himself. He is also careful – in the sense of being conscious – about his personality, his time, his education, his way of life. The dominating characteristic of his life is that he is able to see that the present postponement of pleasure (saving money is one such form of postponement) will lead to an increase in satisfaction later.

In Glazer's view, these traits stem not only from the social position in which the Jews found themselves in Europe but also from prior sources in their religious world view itself and in their minority status. These were strengthened by the long commercial experience. Judaism

> emphasizes the traits that business men and intellectuals require, and has done so since at least 1500 years before Calvinism. . . . The strong emphasis on learning and study can be traced that far back, too. The Jewish habits of foresight, care, moderation probably arose early during the 2,000 years that Jews have lived as strangers among other peoples. . . . But certainly Jewish economic experience since the beginning of the Christian era can only have strengthened the bent given to them by religion and culture.

It is the cultural attributes derived from the long-term development of European Jewish history, according to Glazer, that are at issue, not so much the immediate occupational position of the Jews prior to migration. Thus, many had become workers in the years prior to migration,

> but they carried with them the values conducive to middle-class success, and they could, under the proper circumstances, easily return to the pursuit of trade and study, and thus to the ways of their fathers and forefathers. What is really exceptional, in terms of the large perspective of Jewish history, is . . . the degree to which in the Czarist empire and eastern Europe in general, they had been forced out of their age-old pursuits and proletarianized.

Perhaps because Glazer's concern in his article was primarily with socioeconomic advancement, rather than schooling, their "middle-class" outlook figures much more prominently in his formulations concerning the cultural heritage than does a commitment to learning, although the latter appears too. In any case, other formulations stress the relation between American Jewish patterns of schooling and the eastern European cultural heritage – both a middle-class outlook and a commitment to learning.[12]

Glazer's formulations will strike many as excessive, seeking to explain all, or nearly all, of the uniqueness of Jewish behavior by appealing to personality traits. They may appear far too confident, first, in asserting that ethnic differences in personality traits in fact existed, second, in describing the specific nature of those traits, and, third, in explaining their origins. His formulations seem heavily influenced by the early stages of the research on culture and personality popular in the 1950s and earlier.[13] However, what is most interesting for our purposes is the argument that some distinctive cultural characteristics (beliefs, attitudes, values, and personality traits) resulted from a distinctive pre-migration background and that these cultural characteristics help explain behavior. In essence, the argument is that (1) the tradition of learning may have influenced the orientation toward study and (2) the economic position of the Jews, their minority status, and even some aspects of their religious heritage may have influenced the orientation toward commercial occupations and toward economic advancement generally. They also may have influenced educational performance, because education was viewed as a means to these goals or as an arena of achievement in its own right.

The approach taken by Calvin Goldscheider and Alan Zuckerman is in glaring contrast to that of Glazer. Their work, *The Transformation of the Jews*, seeks to explain most social and cultural features of Jewish life without reference to differences in attitudes, values, or habits deriving from the past.[14] First, they are skeptical about reconstructions of the cultural background such as that of Glazer:

We know very little about the values held by contemporary Jews.
Few surveys exist to shed light on their beliefs and attitudes. Studies of the culture of those no longer alive are even more difficult to
carry out. Approaches that assume the existence of universal Jewish norms reduce an empirical problem to a theoretical assertion.

It is not merely the quality of the evidence that is at issue. Rather,
factors of a structural nature are simply much more important:

> What role did Jewish values play in the integration of American
> Jews? Did the poor, impoverished Jewish immigrants carry middle-
> class values? Did their religious traditions and culture result in their
> early successes in school and economic mobility? Those who have
> argued for the centrality of Jewish values as the explanation of rapid
> Jewish integration in America minimize the importance of social
> class and residential differences between Jewish and non-Jewish
> immigrants. . . . We emphasize the structural factors which distin-
> guish Jews from others.

Specifically,

> Working in more skilled occupations, Jews earned more money
> than did other immigrant groups. Their relative income and occu-
> pational security made it easier for Jews to invest in the schooling
> of their children. This combined with the permanency of their im-
> migration, urban residence, and the availability and access to pub-
> lic school education. Together, these structural features explain why
> . . . Jews accounted for relatively high percentages of those who
> attended schools and universities in the large cities of the North-
> east.

Goldscheider and Zuckerman argue that the structural features of
a particular time and place are the critical sources of behavior there.
These structural factors may in turn have been determined by earlier
ones. For example, American Jewish conditions were affected by the
occupational skills of Jews in Europe and by the self-selectivity of certain occupational groups among the Jewish migrants. However, in
contrast to Glazer's explanation, their view is that the attitudes, values, and habits that may have grown out of the structural situation in
Europe, or out of a particular religious world view, were, at best, of
marginal importance.[15]

In considering distinctive Jewish patterns in one city and in one
era, several of the structural factors raised by Goldscheider and Zuckerman can be ignored. Thus, differences that existed between places
of residence are avoided. Differences in the propensity to remain in
the United States are also less critical, since the eastern European Jews
can be compared with natives as well as with other immigrants. Besides, as noted in connection with the Italians, the immigrant parents

of native-born adolescents rarely left the United States. Consequently, the crucial factor these authors stress that is relevant to differences between Jewish immigrants and other individuals in a given American city is social class – the distinctive occupations that the Jewish immigrant fathers entered, particularly, they argue, occupations as skilled workers, especially in the garment industry.[16] Stephen Steinberg has developed much the same argument in *The Academic Melting Pot* and in *The Ethnic Myth*.[17]

However, such arguments have lacked the sort of data needed to establish the historical reality with any certainty – data on social origins, schooling, and occupational attainment in the period of settlement.[18] To borrow the words of Goldscheider and Zuckerman, the extent to which the structural factors they stress, or the cultural factors that Glazer stresses, determined American ethnic differences in the early years of the century is an "empirical problem"; it cannot be resolved by a "theoretical assertion," however plausible.

The Providence data provide an opportunity for empirical investigation. Our concern, as in the preceding chapters, is, first, with important characteristics of the eastern European Jewish immigrant families, particularly the social-class position of the group. We turn then to the patterns of schooling. To what extent, and in what specific ways, were the school patterns of the Russian Jewish children indeed distinctive? To what extent were distinctive patterns simply the result of social class and other family background characteristics that favored Russian Jewish attainment? We shall turn finally to the occupational patterns of the second generation. To what extent were they achieved through an edge in schooling, or because of the earlier success of the immigrant fathers? To what extent do they remain unexplained by either?

4.2. Family background

The eastern European Jews settled primarily in a few large cities: Half settled in New York City alone, and another one in five settled in Chicago, Philadelphia, Boston, and Baltimore, but the rest, three in every ten, settled in smaller communities like Providence. There, as elsewhere, they first constituted a noticeable presence during the 1880s; by 1920, the Russian-born numbered 6,269 in a city of some 237,000.[19] Their adolescent children were not to be found in the 1880 census, but they constituted nearly 3% of the 1900 sample, and about 7% in 1915 and 1925.

The U.S. Census, of course, did not ask respondents' religion. However, students of American immigration have long known that the overwhelming majority of the Russian-born immigrants in the United States were Jews (for example, by the high proportion listing Yiddish as their mother tongue). In Providence, even more direct evidence is available: The Rhode Island State Census of 1905 did ask respondents' religion. Some 95% of the Russian-born indicated they were Jews, and there is no reason to think that the proportion a few years earlier or later was any different.[20] Eastern European Jews migrated from countries other than the Russian Empire, of course, but by limiting our attention to the Russian-born immigrant community, we can be confident that we are studying a population almost exclusively Jewish. At the same time, we have no reason to think that the critical characteristics of the Russian-born differed from those of other eastern European Jewish immigrants.

Although the Jews composed a relatively small proportion of the Providence population, we can study their behavior intensively because supplemental data were collected from the 1915 Rhode Island State Census: Every twelve- to fifteen-year-old son, and three-quarters of the daughters, of Russian immigrants were included, 712 sample members in all. By concentrating on the patterns in 1915 and adding information from 1925 and occasionally from 1900, it is possible to probe deeply.

Fully 82% of all the Russian Jewish children in 1900 had been born abroad, but by 1915 that proportion had fallen to 40%, and by 1925 to only 11%. A similar drop in the proportion of foreign-born, it will be recalled, was found among the Italians. Increasingly, parents composed a group who had migrated when young and had therefore spent long periods in the United States by the time their children reached adolescence.

Also like the Italians of 1915–25, the great majority of the Russian Jewish children in all three samples, 88–96%, were raised in two-parent households. Similarly, too, migration to urban, industrial America did not rapidly influence the pattern of childbearing. The average number of children in Italian households was five; the Russian Jewish families average just below that in 1900 and 1915, and about four children in 1925. If there was some decline over time, it may have come not only as a result of an adjustment to American norms but also through the encounter of the Jews with more modern practices in Europe.[21]

Some information on the literacy levels of the Russian Jewish immigrants is also available. The immigration authorities, who kept records on the subject beginning in 1899, found that about one-fifth of males and two-fifths of female Russian Jewish immigrants were illiterate. The figures serve as an important reminder that the immigrants were by no means all well educated (in any kind of school). The gender difference probably reflects the lower regard for female learning in eastern European Jewish culture, as well as the advantage of literacy to the principal breadwinner.[22] Similarly, whereas the fathers in the Providence 1900 sample generally were listed as able to speak English, half the mothers could not, suggesting the extent to which their province was the home, while the fathers interacted with the larger world in the marketplace. Indeed, in the 1900 sample, none of the mothers worked, and less than one in twenty of those in the 1915 sample did so.[23]

The censuses provide extensive information about the social-class positions of the Russian Jewish families and about their changing levels of economic well-being. The 1900 sample shows a small group of families struggling to establish a foothold. Secure positions were few, and occupational levels relatively low. Nevertheless, the unique nature of the Russian Jewish position is unmistakable. The occupations for only eighteen fathers were available; yet their special nature emerges clearly. Seven of the eighteen worked in various manual occupations (dyer, a woolsorter, three instrument makers, a butcher, and a tailor), although none was a mere laborer. Two seem to have inched up to small proprietorships. Fully eight of the eighteen were peddlers. Thus, a majority were already in commerce, most of those having chosen work as peddlers over employment in the city's giant industries.

In the 1915 sample, these trends can be seen much more clearly.[24] That sample is large, and the Rhode Island State Census of 1915 is a splendid source because it includes three relevant questions on each individual's work, a format adopted by the U.S. Census only in 1930. It indicates the occupation (clerk, plumber, laborer, etc.), the industrial sector in which the individual worked (textile manufacturing, retail food sales, real estate, etc.), and the employment status of the individual (employer, employee, "own account").

Table 4.1 shows the proportion of the Russian Jewish immigrant fathers found in each major occupational stratum. The occupational position of the group was much improved over 1900. Nevertheless, more than one in every five of these family heads was still a peddler. These figures from one moment in time surely understate the proportion who worked as peddlers at some point in their lives.

Peddling suggests an entry into more solidly established commercial positions. Another one in five of the fathers was in fact a proprietor: a grocer, a merchant, a general storekeeper, a grain dealer, and so forth. Still another one in five was a self-employed worker in a manual occupation – primarily self-employed artisans, tailors, shoe-

Table 4.1. *Occupations of fathers in 1915*

Occupation	Russian Jews (%)	Other immigrants (%)	Natives (%)
A. Occupational stratum			
Professionals	3.2	1.7	4.7
Managers and officials	0.5	0.8	1.9
Proprietors	23.2	7.7	7.5
Self-employed manual workers	19.8	8.1	4.9
Clerical workers	0.7	1.7	7.3
Salesmen	7.1	3.3	10.2
Peddlers	22.3	2.9	0.2
Manual workers (employees)			
Skilled	10.5	24.6	26.9
Semiskilled	9.3	26.1	22.9
Unskilled	3.4	23.0	13.2
Total	100	100	100
B. Employment status			
Self-employed			
Employer	10.7	5.5	9.0
Other self-employed	59.5	13.8	7.1
Employee	29.8	80.7	83.8
Total	100	100	100
N^a	(561)	(761)	(532)
C. Industrial sector			
Construction	3.0	12.9	8.8
Manufacturing			
Apparel	2.1	0.7	0.2
Metal and machinery	2.7	12.5	11.0
Textiles	1.5	16.6	7.9
Jewelry	6.1	6.6	9.4
All others	6.4	12.8	11.0
Trade	54.9	18.5	19.3
Transportation	1.1	6.5	12.8
All others	22.2	13.5	19.6
Total	100	100	100
N^a	(528)	(682)	(491)

[a]Those who could not be classified by industrial sector (a total of 163) were more numerous than those who could not be classified by occupation (50). See also note 19 to text.

makers, and others. These men, too, may be thought of as operating their own businesses.

These three types of occupations (peddlers, proprietors, and self-employed artisans) together accounted for nearly two of every three Russian Jewish immigrant jobs (65%). A significant number of others described themselves as salesmen of various sorts (7%), and a few (although only a few) were clerks, accountants, bookkeepers, or managers and officials in some enterprise (together barely 1%). Finally, about 3% have been classified as professionals, but that small number hardly presaged the later concentration of Jews in occupations we think of today as "the professions." Far from being lawyers and doctors, nearly all were involved in traditional religious capacities: Of eighteen individuals whom the occupational classification system treats as "professionals," seven were rabbis, and eleven were "teachers" – and nine of those teachers were self-employed. Only two apothecaries, found among the proprietors, hint at the professional careers of a later generation.

All of the occupations described thus far usually would be classified as white-collar rather than blue-collar, and by a too-easy translation, they would be classified as well as middle-class rather than working-class. Clearly, the translation from white-collar to middle-class is inappropriate in this context. To understand that, we need only think of the peddlers. The average peddler was hardly to be envied, and to classify him with a shop owner seems a cruel distortion. Peddlers could more reasonably be likened to unskilled laborers in terms of the uncertainty of their income and the skill level of their work. On the other hand, there is an important grain of truth in thinking of these individuals as middle-class, or at least as related to that social class. A peddler with a pushcart was on a continuum of sorts with the owner of a small shop. The skills required, the buying and selling, were comparable. The peddler's capital accumulation was smaller, and his credit was not as good, but these are differences in degree. The similarities between a meat-and-poultry peddler and a butcher, or between a fruit-and-vegetable peddler and a grocer, a junk peddler and the owner of a junkyard, are important. In any case, none of the individuals classified as white-collar was a typical member of the working class as it is traditionally conceived in relation to this era – none was a wage worker engaged in manual labor. All these individuals, on the other hand, had links to the world of commerce that the more typical working-class members, at any level or skill, did not have.

The Jewish occupational pattern, of course, can hardly be attributed to the prevalence of peddlers, proprietors, and self-employed artisans in Providence economic life generally. There were virtually no native-born peddlers. Some immigrants other than Russian Jews did take up peddling, but the proportion of peddlers was seven times as great among the Russian Jews. Similarly, self-employed artisans were nearly twice as common among the other immigrants as they were among the natives, but they were twice as common again among the Russian Jews. Finally, the proportions of proprietors were about the same among natives and non-Jewish immigrants (about 8%); among the Russian Jews, the proportion was three times as great.

Another aspect of this social reality is captured by the employment status of the Jews: whether they worked for others, worked on their "own account," or employed others (Table 4.1, part B). In the city as a whole, eight of every ten fathers were employees, as compared with three of ten among the Russian Jews. Even excluding the peddlers, less than four of every ten of the remaining Russian Jewish fathers were employees. Nearly all of the self-employed, of course, were small operators who could not afford to employ others. Only 11% of the fathers were employers; yet even that figure is somewhat higher than the citywide norm (7%).

A final perspective on the occupations of the Russian Jewish immigrants is afforded by the information available on the types of businesses in which the Russian Jews were involved – the products they sold in business and the industries in which they worked (Table 4.1, part C). The garment industry, which was so closely linked with Jewish advancement in New York City, simply did not provide them many jobs in Providence – one in fifty. True, even this proportion was several times greater than the proportion among natives or immigrants. The occasional tailor in Providence was likely to be a Russian Jew, but he was likely to repair rather than produce garments.

Still, the Jewish concentration in industries was distinctive, even if it did not involve the garment industry. On the one hand, two industries that were of major importance in Providence hired few Russian Jews: Whereas 8% of the natives and fully 17% of the city's other immigrants were connected in some way with the city's textile industry, less than 2% of the Russian Jews were. They were also drastically underrepresented in the foundries and machine shops of Providence, which produced a wide range of metal products and machinery.[25]

On the other hand, the Russian Jews were somewhat more heavily concentrated than others in the costume-jewelry industry. The fact that Jewish employers had entered this industry, and the hope of progressing from a worker to an owner (the industry required only a small outlay in order to get started[26]), no doubt drew Jewish manual workers into it.

Occupational information alone leaves much ambiguity concerning the wealth of those engaged in commercial careers, particularly "proprietors." One may have been a corner grocer, barely better off than a fruit peddler; another may have owned a large store, a hotel, or even a mill. An additional perspective is provided by the assessed values of the property held by these men. Those whose real property was assessed to be worth at least $5,000, or whose personal property was at least $1,000, were considered major proprietors; the rest were petty proprietors. The criterion is admittedly crude, but it is simple and fairly exclusive. Only one-tenth of the sampled families in Providence had amassed property assessed at such a high value; indeed, six sampled families in ten had no taxable property whatever. As one would expect, among the Russian Jewish peddlers and self-employed artisans, very few had amassed enough property to be classified in the higher category (8% and 10%, respectively).

Of the 109 Russian Jewish proprietors for whom tax data could be obtained, 39 were major proprietors, the rest petty proprietors. The major proprietors, of course, remain a heterogeneous group; they might include the moderately successful grocer as well as the city's richest bankers and manufacturers. However, all these together constituted only a small upper crust of the city's population.

Thus, the economic classification based on the tax data indicates that the majority of the Russian Jews involved in commerce – and even the majority among those involved as proprietors – were not well-to-do. Nevertheless, a significant minority of the proprietors had already become well established by 1915.

Similarly, many more of the longer-term residents had become well established. During the years 1900–25, the positions of the fathers, who were increasingly likely to be long-term residents, improved considerably. Just as the proportion of Russian Jewish fathers who described themselves as peddlers had fallen from nearly half to a fifth between 1900 and 1915, it fell to only a twelfth by 1925. During the same years, the proportion of fathers in more attractive white-collar occupations rose. Especially striking is the proportion classified as high white-collar: zero in 1900, 13% in 1915, and 27% in 1925.[27] Even with the crude distinctions available here, it is clear that whereas most who entered commercial pursuits did so in a humble way, a substantial fraction of these individuals improved their economic conditions considerably during their own lifetimes.[28]

In Providence, then, the great majority of the Russian Jews in the immigrant generation were not members of the working class in any usual sense of that term. Rather, the Russian Jews' point of entry into American life was special. Many of them indeed were poor, but they confronted poverty in a different context than did other immigrant groups in the city.

The very existence of these occupational differences provides one of the most striking examples of ethnic distinctiveness. The explanation, surely, is bound up with the Jews' long familiarity with trade in Europe (whatever the experience in the decade or two before immigration). These occupations probably were chosen in Providence for a mixture of what might be called cultural as well as economically rational reasons. They seemed most highly desirable, most familiar, and they seemed the ones in which experience provided an edge.[29]

A competing explanation of the Jewish occupational pattern would be discrimination. No doubt anti-Semitism did close off certain jobs to Jewish immigrants. Perhaps Jews could not get jobs in the textile mills, for example. It has been argued that that was the case in steel mills in Pittsburgh – another case in which immigrant Jews avoided a dominant industry. Possibly, too, the fact that virtually no blacks were found in the Providence textile mills supports the argument for discrimination against Jews as well. Certainly, contemporary observers in Providence thought the Jews were subject to much antipathy. Yet discrimination cannot explain why so many Jews entered the commercial pursuits in particular. Discrimination in the case of the blacks led to enormous proportions of day laborers and menial-services workers among them (laundresses, janitors, and so forth). There were virtually no black peddlers. Moreover, it is unclear just how fully antipathy was translated into job discrimination in the mills. After all, the Italians were distrusted and disliked as well, but they filled the mills.

In any case, whatever the origins of the tremendous occupational differences between the Russian Jewish immigrants and others, such a difference can reasonably be expected to have influenced many other aspects of immigrant life. Upward mobility into the more solidly established reaches of the middle class may well have been one such implication. Hard work and diligence may have paid off more for the peddler than for the factory operative or day laborer. Even if most Jews began as impoverished as others, their occupational choices may have helped ensure a much more rapid escape from poverty.

Providence, of course, was not the typical place of settlement for most Russian Jewish immigrants. Whereas three in ten settled in similarly small cities, seven in ten were to be found in the five metropolises mentioned earlier, and half in New York City alone. Surveys of social structure and economic progress are not generally available for those communities in the degree of detail just reviewed for Providence. Nevertheless, Thomas Kessner's study of New York City in

1905 does provide a basis for comparison. It suggests that there were indeed clear differences in the occupational structures of the two communities. In New York, 54% of the Russian Jewish heads of households were manual workers; in Providence, a decade later, only 23% were.[30] That the Providence sample includes an older group, the fathers of adolescents, and that other differences between the data exist, surely does not account for the entire difference: The smaller city included fewer manual laborers among its Russian Jews.[31]

Why should many more have been engaged in commerce outside the large centers of Russian Jewish immigration? The explanation probably has much to do with the opportunities afforded by the garment industry. By 1900, the relation between that industry and the eastern European Jewish immigrants was well established. Both the industry and these immigrants were concentrated in the same few cities, and especially in New York. The garment industry was unique in providing so many opportunities in a labor market dominated by Jewish employers and employees.

These opportunities constituted an alternative to commerce, especially at lower levels of economic well-being: The immigrants could become skilled or semiskilled garment workers instead of peddlers. Faced with the choice, some would choose one, some the other. However, Jews living in the smaller communities were less likely to be deflected from a preference to enter trade.

Moreover, a city can support only so many small businesses. Everywhere, the Jewish immigrants probably were more likely than others to establish these businesses. Nevertheless, in cities in which the Jewish immigrants constituted a relatively high proportion of the total population, a kind of saturation point may have been reached; the ratio of small businesses to population may have been high, discouraging others who wished to establish businesses. Such an environment would discourage Jewish residents from entering trade or discourage those set on entering trade from remaining residents.[32]

Finally, the structure of trade in the metropolises may have been less conducive to the peddler, and even to the petty proprietor, than it was in smaller cities. Existing businesses may have been better established and larger, and relations between wholesale suppliers and retailers less conducive to interlopers.[33]

Beyond New York and the other metropolises, then, higher proportions of eastern European Jewish immigrants made their way into the American economy through small businesses, rather than as wage workers. This social-class difference between the metropolises and the smaller centers must have had repercussions in many domains of life. For example, Jewish political radicalism in such communities may have been less pronounced, because fewer Jews had had the experience of being wage workers. Possibly, too, and more relevant to our concerns here, Jewish youth sought education less avidly where the opportunities to enter trade directly were greater than elsewhere. To this issue we shall return later.

Nevertheless, the evidence from 1905 suggests that many Russian Jews, even in New York City, were engaged in commerce and rose to middle-class status in the course of one generation. After all, if just over half of New York's Russian Jewish household heads were to be found in manual occupations, just under half were not. The comparable proportion among the New York Italians, by way of contrast, was 20%. Still more striking is the evidence of upward mobility among New York's Russian Jewish immigrants. Among all gainfully employed (not merely household heads) who had arrived in New York City within the six years preceding the census, only 19% were in white-collar occupations; but of those who had arrived at least fifteen years before the census, 55% were. Thus, most Russian Jewish immigrants in New York apparently began their lives as manual workers, but even in New York, most did not remain workers.[34]

The preceding review indicates several critical features of the Russian Jewish immigration: the rapid economic advance of the first generation; the enormous importance of commercial pursuits for Jewish immigrants everywhere, especially those in Providence; the nature of the options the second generation would have perceived, options disproportionately concentrated in commerce. These features of the Jewish immigration clearly bear on the schooling and economic advancement of the second generation. Do they, however, fully explain Jewish distinctiveness in these domains?

4.3.   Patterns of schooling

In 1900, the schooling of Russian Jewish boys clearly reflected the recent arrival of their families. Most of the group left school, like other immigrant children, long before an extended education could have been completed. Eleven of thirteen boys age thirteen to fourteen had attended school in the previous year, but five of them were also listed as working. Several were, then, already in the process of leaving school. Among the ten boys age fifteen to sixteen, only two were at school, the rest at work. At the same time, two of these 1900 sample members remained in school long enough to complete high school, hinting at the possibility that Russian Jews were already graduating from high school at a notable rate.[35]

The crucial evidence is from 1915, because the supplemental sam-

Table 4.2. *Jobs of children age 14–15 years in 1915*

	Boys		Girls	
Type of job	All sample members (%)	Sons of Russian Jews only (%)	All sample members (%)	Daughters of Russian Jews only (%)
White-collar workers[a]	6	9	17	44
Juvenile white-collar workers[b]	35	56	3	11
Skilled workers	8	15	4	7
Low manual				
Textile workers	26	0	52	15
All others	25	21	24	23
Total	100	100	100	100
Number working[c]	(132)	(34)	(117)	(27)
Percentage of age group at work	30	19	26	17

[a]Clerks and salesclerks.
[b]Messengers, delivery boys, errand boys, cash boys, office boys, and girls in comparable jobs.
[c]The first and third columns are based on the samples of all children in the age range, the second and fourth columns on supplemental samples of Russian Jews.

ples selected for that year provide data on large numbers of children; the much smaller 1925 sample adds additional perspective. Before turning to the school patterns themselves, we can glance briefly at patterns of child labor (Table 4.2). The proportions working among the Russian Jewish youth (19% of the boys and 17% of the girls) were lower than the norm in 1915. More striking were the differences in the kinds of jobs obtained by those who were obligated to work. Among both boys and girls, the Russian Jews were much more likely than others to obtain some kind of white-collar work. True, the juvenile white-collar employment that so many of the boys obtained was hardly a clear stepping-stone to a career in the business world. Nevertheless, these jobs were taken instead of low-skill factory jobs or other forms of low manual work. Among those children employed as manual laborers, relatively fewer of the Russian Jews were in low-skill work, and strikingly fewer were in textile mills in particular, the largest employer of children. Whereas a quarter of all the city's working boys were in the mills, not a single Russian Jewish boy was, and whereas half the city's working girls were found there, only 15% of the Russian Jewish girls were.[36] Possibly discrimination at the factory helped to keep Jewish children away.

In any case, all these occupational choices suggest a more favorable economic position for the Russian Jewish children, as well as selection of the familiar – of the world of commerce, and to a lesser extent the light industries in which Jewish artisans worked. Even those who left school early, then, were in an ethnically distinctive position. What of the rest?

Three dimensions of schooling can profitably be considered: length, GPA (course grades), and curriculum choices (of children who reached high school). As noted in the preceding chapter, these dimensions of schooling are not unrelated; high achievement on one was associated with high achievement on the others. Yet each was influenced by somewhat different factors than the others, and so the associations among the three were by no means perfect, and a look at Russian Jewish behavior on each dimension is revealing.

Like the Italians, the Russian Jewish patterns of schooling differed by gender; we shall consider them separately for each sex. Also, our concern, as it was with the Italians, will be primarily with native-born children of Russian Jewish immigrants. By 1925, nearly all of these immigrants' children were native-born; in 1915, 40% were not (about the same percentages as found among the Italians). Because that proportion is much higher than for some other groups, and because the foreign-born were least likely in every group to receive extended schooling, it is easiest to observe whatever is special in the Russian Jewish behavior by focusing attention on the native-born in the 1915 sample.

The tables first present comparisons of Russian Jews with all others. Then comparisons with selected ethnic groups are presented: the children of Yankees, two groups of Irish-Americans, Italian immigrants, and other immigrants (excluding those from England, Scotland, and Wales; these were also used as a comparison group in the preceding chapter). The 1925 sources did not permit distinctions among the children of the native whites. Consequently, all native-born parents (including, among others, those from both Yankee and Irish immigrant homes) must be combined for that year.

Both sorts of comparisons (with all others and with particular other groups) have advantages and limitations. The first kind, of course, provides a summary statement. The second compares the Russian Jews and a range of historically important ethnic groups: the long-term residents, raised in the New England culture (Yankees); two generations of the massive Irish migration (children and grandchildren of immigrants); the Italians, the "new immigrant" group so often contrasted with the Russian Jews; and, finally, other immigrants in the city, non-English-speakers whose behavior did not contrast quite as starkly with that of the Jews as did the behavior of the Italians.[37]

The Russian Jewish boys progressed further in school than others (Table 4.3 and 4.4). Whereas 36% of the city's other native-born boys reached high school in 1915, and 12% graduated, 54% of the Russian Jews entered, and 22% graduated (see the first column of Table 4.3). The Russian Jewish rates exceed not only the city average but also the rates for every individual group in the city. Only the sons of some native white groups approached the Russian Jews in the length of their schooling. The comparison with the Italians provides striking evidence of just how different the experiences of these two groups really were. Whereas 54% of the native-born sons of Russian Jews entered high school, a mere 17% of the native-born sons of the Italians did so. The pattern in the 1925 sample may be somewhat weaker, but it is similar. Only the sons of the Irish immigrants reached high school more often than the sons of the Russian Jews, but that lead was very slight, and it was not maintained within high school, so that more Russian Jews graduated.

The consistency of the pattern, even after important family background characteristics are controlled, is also striking (on the arrangements of the tables and on the interpretation of the odds ratio, see Section 2.1). The characteristics that are controlled (father's occupation, family's property value, number of siblings, whether or not both parents were present) help account for the Russian Jewish distinctiveness, but they also leave much unexplained.

The contrast with the children of Yankees is actually stronger with these controls imposed, because their social-class position was higher than that of the Russian Jews, and they had fewer mouths to feed per family. However, for the most part, controlling these background characteristics does help to account for the Russian Jewish lead. Social-class position, in particular, favored the Russian Jews and contributed to their educational advantage, as Goldscheider and Zuckerman, Steinberg, and others have argued; yet it is just as striking that differences in family background characteristics do not erase the Russian Jewish advantage entirely.[38] Even after controls have been imposed, every one of the comparisons favors the Russian Jews in 1915, and only the Irish high school entry rate was greater in 1925. Indeed, often the magnitude of the ethnic difference changes surprisingly little when the controls are imposed. For example, the odds that others would enter high school were only about half as great as the odds that the Russian Jews would do so, with or without controls.

A great deal has been written about the contrast between Russian

Table 4.3. *Native-born boys' length of schooling by ethnicity, 1915*

Group	Rate (%)	N^a	Odds ratio: each group compared with Russian Jews[b] — No controls	Odds ratio: each group compared with Russian Jews[b] — Social background factors controlled
High school entry rates				
Sons of				
Russian Jews	54.3	(210)		
All others	36.1	(1,396)	0.48	0.54 (3.76)[c]
Yankees	49.6	(123)	0.83	0.75 (1.16)
Natives of Irish parentage	47.9	(94)	0.77	0.91 (0.35)
Irish immigrants	40.9	(391)	0.58	0.88 (0.68)
Italian immigrants	17.2	(354)	0.17	0.24 (6.77)
Other immigrants (non-Br.)[d]	34.4	(160)	0.44	0.52 (2.86)
High school graduation rates				
Sons of				
Russian Jews	21.9	(210)		
All others	12.0	(1,396)	0.49	0.51 (3.40)
Yankees	13.8	(123)	0.57	0.43 (2.49)
Natives of Irish parentage	19.2	(94)	0.85	0.91 (0.19)
Irish immigrants	13.8	(391)	0.57	0.89 (0.47)
Italian immigrants	5.9	(354)	0.22	0.36 (3.43)
Other immigrants (non-Br.)	11.9	(160)	0.48	0.56 (1.87)
Graduation rates of high school entrants[e]				
Sons of				
Russian Jews	39.8	(118)		
All others	30.5	(643)	0.66	0.62 (2.20)
Yankees	29.7	(107)	0.64	0.54 (2.07)
Natives of Irish parentage	34.6	(77)	0.80	0.78 (0.80)
Irish immigrants	32.2	(189)	0.73	0.80 (0.87)
Italian immigrants	35.2	(76)	0.82	0.89 (0.36)
Other immigrants (non-Br.)	28.6	(97)	0.61	0.55 (1.98)

[a] In Tables 4.3–4.9, the figures for 1915 pertaining to patterns within high schools include supplemental samples of entrants. Also, N's for Russian Jews, Irish, and Italians in 1915 include supplemental samples of these groups. In computing the rates, means, and coefficients for "all others" in these tables, and for trends within high schools in all groups, supplemental samples have been weighted to reflect the actual size of each group. The N's report unweighted sample sizes.

[b] Odds ratios without controls computed from proportions at left; those with controls imposed are exponentiated coefficients on ethnic dummy variables in logit regressions. The variables controlled are father's occupation, family's assessed property value, number of siblings, whether or not both parents present.

[c] t values.

[d] White immigrants from countries other than Russia, Italy, and the British Isles.

[e] The percentage of high school entrants who eventually graduated from high school. The percentage of all individuals from each group who graduated is shown in the preceding panel of the table.

Table 4.4. *Boys' length of schooling by ethnicity, 1925*[a]

| | | | Odds ratio: each group compared with Russian Jews | |
| | | | No | Social background |
Group	Rate (%)	N	controls	factors controlled
High school entry rates				
Sons of				
Russian Jews	69.4	(72)		
All others	51.7	(867)	0.47	0.56 (2.00)[b]
Native whites	61.5	(296)	0.70	0.64 (1.45)
Irish immigrants	73.5	(68)	1.22	1.49 (1.02)
Italian immigrants	33.0	(261)	0.22	0.32 (3.73)
Other immigrants (non-Br.)	53.4	(189)	0.51	0.69 (1.18)
High school graduation rates				
Sons of				
Russian Jews	45.8	(72)		
All others	25.8	(867)	0.41	0.53 (2.33)
Native whites	32.8	(296)	0.58	0.50 (2.36)
Irish immigrants	30.9	(68)	0.53	0.70 (0.94)
Italian immigrants	15.3	(261)	0.21	0.39 (2.91)
Other immigrants (non-Br.)	28.0	(189)	0.46	0.70 (1.14)
Graduation rates of high school entrants				
Sons of				
Russian Jews	66.0	(50)		
All others	50.0	(448)	0.52	0.61 (1.50)
Native whites	53.3	(182)	0.59	0.47 (2.08)
Irish immigrants	42.0	(50)	0.37	0.52 (1.49)
Italian immigrants	46.5	(86)	0.45	0.79 (0.62)
Other immigrants (non-Br.)	52.5	(101)	0.57	0.74 (0.77)

[a] See footnotes to Table 4.3.
[b] *t* values.

Jewish children and Italian children in particular.[39] Although both were the products of huge migrations, to many of the same cities, and in the same years, the contrast between the schooling patterns of the two groups could not be more stark. To what extent, however, can this be explained by social origins, particularly the Russian Jewish economic advantage reflected in fathers' occupations? In 1915, for example, the mean occupational score for Italian fathers was 16; it was 28 for Russian Jewish fathers.

   Without controls, the odds of high school entry for Italians were 0.17 as large as for Russian Jews in 1915; with controls, they were 0.24

as large. Family background, then, did account for some of the observed ethnic difference, raising the odds of Italian entry relative to those for the Russian Jews by a factor of 1.41 (0.24/0.17 = 1.41). Still, most of the large difference between the groups remains unexplained: The Italian odds of entry even after controls are imposed would have to have been 4.17 times as great as they were to equal those for the Russian Jews (1.00/0.24 = 4.17).

High school graduation rates were higher among the Jews not only because more of them reached high school in the first place but also because more who entered stayed on to graduate. One might well have expected a different outcome because of a pattern of self-selection. In ethnic groups with low rates of high school entry, those children who did reach high school probably were the ones most able and committed to schooling, other things being equal. For example, although the rate of high school entry among Italians was far below the citywide norm, the rate of high school graduation among Italian entrants equaled the norm. Because Russian Jews enrolled most frequently, these entrants were the least selected group. Nevertheless, this selectivity factor apparently was more than outweighed by factors that impelled the Russian Jews to remain in school, factors other than the family background characteristics already controlled.

At the same time, taking social background into account does change the relative standings of particular groups. The most notable shift concerns the Irish-Americans (the children and grandchildren of Irish immigrants). With controls, the odds that they would enter or graduate from high school were similar to those of the Russian Jews. The Russian Jewish lead in length of schooling, seen in the small sample differences, probably reflects the experience of the group accurately.[40] Still, the comparison with the Irish reminds us that there was a range of attainments among the ethnic groups of the city, and although the Jews were most likely to enter and graduate from high school, the behaviors of some other groups were not so different in this regard, at least when other family background differences have been considered. The relatively high Irish enrollments that came after 1880, and their sources, were discussed in Chapter 2. Some advantages that would have helped raise their enrollment relative to that of the Russian Jews include the fact that English was the language of the home, that the schools were staffed by many of their own kind, and that the school system generally, as a public agency, was sensitive to their political leaders.[41]

However, differences in attainment between Jews and others, including the Irish, increased at the collegiate level. During the 1920s, the Providence School Department began to keep track of the later schooling of the city's high school graduates.[42] Fifty-two percent of the male high school graduates were listed as having enrolled in some college; the rates were similar for most groups. Nevertheless, 67% of Russian Jewish boys who completed high school continued on to college. High continuation rates thus typified the Russian Jewish boys at all educational levels and resulted in one in four enrolling in college. Among others, the college enrollment rate was only half that.[43]

The conclusion from a review of the data on length of schooling among the sons of Russian Jewish immigrants, then, must surely be that their patterns of schooling were distinctive, even when the most relevant family background characteristics have been controlled.[44]

Russian Jewish boys were also much more likely than other high school entrants to enroll in a classical or other college preparatory program: 45% compared with 25% in 1915, for example (Table 4.5).[45] The Russian Jewish rate was the highest in the city and, at least in 1915, the highest even after controls have been imposed. Once the controls are imposed, however, it is clear that the Irish and the Italians were also likely to choose these curricula.[46]

The Irish-American patterns involved somewhat different kinds of curricular choices than those made by other groups. Among the Irish, as we have seen, college preparatory enrollment was concentrated in the Catholic La Salle Academy, rather than in the public programs, but the important point here is that it reached levels comparable to those for the Russian Jews. Two factors contributed to the Italian behavior. One was the self-selection noted earlier: Those who reached high school at all probably were especially committed to schooling, especially studious, and especially committed to advancement through learning. Also, the Italians were closest to the content of the classical curriculum. Much of it, after all, involved the history and language of Italy, a fact that must have been a source of pride in Italian homes. Moreover, the Latin language may well have been perceived as less of a hurdle to children from homes in which Italian was spoken.

In sum, then, the Russian Jewish boys' propensity to choose the classical and college preparatory tracks was not unique, but it was at the high end of the range of ethnic groups. Whatever may have driven up the rates for some of the other ethnic groups, Russian Jewish behavior is consistent with commitments to educational achievement: to long schooling and to study in the most academically prestigious programs.

What of the girls? Given the relative lack of concern in traditional eastern European Jewish culture for the schooling of girls, one might expect that gender differences in the schooling of the second generation would be large. However, Russian Jewish girls in Providence

Table 4.5. *Enrollment in college preparatory curricula, male high school entrants only, 1915 and 1925*[a]

Group	Rate (%)	N	Odds ratio: each group compared with Russian Jews	
			No controls	Social background factors controlled
1915: native-born boys only				
Sons of				
Russian Jews	44.6	(118)		
All others[b]	28.3	(643)	0.49	0.41
Yankees	25.0	(107)	0.41	0.27 (4.04)[c]
Natives of Irish parentage[b]	41.5	(77)	0.88	0.79
Irish immigrants[b]	34.5	(189)	0.65	0.75
Italian immigrants	26.2	(76)	0.44	0.48 (2.21)
Other immigrants (non-Br.)	23.1	(97)	0.37	0.30 (3.78)
1925: all boys				
Sons of				
Russian Jews	44.0	(50)		
All others	25.0	(448)	0.42	0.57 (1.65)
Native whites	27.5	(182)	0.48	0.40 (2.40)
Irish immigrants	36.0	(50)	0.72	1.42 (0.76)
Italian immigrants	29.1	(86)	0.52	1.05 (0.12)
Other immigrants (non-Br.)	17.8	(101)	0.27	0.37 (2.28)

[a]See footnotes to Table 4.3.
[b]The 1915 curriculum information in the La Salle Academy, the Catholic high school, was incomplete. The rates reported here are estimates based on the proportions entering La Salle in 1915 and on the proportion of the school's entrants who were in college preparatory programs in 1925. The ratios of these estimates to the uncorrected rates observed in the data were then assumed to be the same when social background factors were controlled, permitting calculation of the figures in the fourth column. The t ratios are omitted because the estimation affects them in ways that are difficult to estimate. However, the first one ("All others") is no doubt significant ($t > 1.96$), given the large size of the observed ratio and the small size of the correction. Because virtually all the students at La Salle were Irish-Americans, the corrections affect only the three rows indicated.
[c]t values.

received a considerable amount of schooling. Indeed, gender differences in length of schooling were insignificant, at least through high school (Table 4.6).[47] Still, in many ethnic groups, girls were somewhat more likely to enter and complete high school. Consequently, equivalent male and female rates among the Russian Jews implied some

Table 4.6. *Gender differences in length of schooling and in high school curriculum enrollment patterns, native-born children only, 1915*[a]

	High school entry rate (%)	High school graduation		High school entrants only			
		Rate (%)	N	Enrollment in a college preparatory curriculum (%)	Graduation		
Group					Rate (%)	N
Russian Jews						
Boys	54.3	21.9	(210)	44.6	39.8	(118)
Girls	47.5	21.3	(160)	6.7	44.2	(96)
All other native-born						
Boys	36.1	12.0	(1,396)	28.3	30.5	(643)
Girls	39.1	15.6	(999)	20.6	39.5	(658)

[a] See footnotes to Table 4.3.

favoring of the boys relative to the behavior of other groups. These gender patterns also meant that differences between Russian Jews and other groups were generally greater among the boys than among the girls – with the exception of the Italians, whose girls, as we have seen, were especially unlikely to receive extended schooling (Table 4.7).

Given the stark contrast between the schooling of boys and that of girls in traditional Jewish culture, their similarity in length of schooling (through high school) in Providence is striking. Moreover, because relatively few reached college, the similarity in the lower levels of schooling defined the experience of most Russian Jewish youth. The absence of a sharp gender difference in secondary schooling suggests a considerable transformation of the traditional heritage. For many families, that transformation began in eastern Europe, where the social order and values were undergoing dramatic changes. For others, it began in the United States. But the critical point is that by 1915, the secular schooling of girls was taken quite seriously. Perhaps this suggests some diffusion of the traditional esteem for learning once restricted to one sex. More likely, if there was any such diffusion, it occurred in the context of a second influence that must have been important in its own right: the rapid acclimatization of Jews to an American environment in which girls could find white-collar jobs – as teachers and as clerical workers.

Nevertheless, if Russian Jewish girls received considerable schooling by 1915, a sharp gender difference in college enrollment re-

Table 4.7. *Native-born girls' length of schooling by ethnicity, 1915*[a]

Group	Rate (%)	N	Odds ratio: each group compared with Russian Jews	
			No controls	Social background factors controlled
High school entry rates				
Daughters of				
Russian Jews	47.5	(160)		
All others	39.1	(999)	0.71	0.71 (1.85)[b]
Yankees	55.0	(140)	1.38	1.06 (0.23)
Natives of Irish parentage	46.4	(97)	0.97	1.12 (0.41)
Irish immigrants	41.8	(196)	0.79	1.02 (0.09)
Italian immigrants	8.7	(185)	0.11	0.14 (6.26)
Other immigrants (non-Br.)	34.1	(132)	0.59	0.71 (1.35)
High school graduation rates				
Daughters of				
Russian Jews	21.3	(160)		
All others	15.6	(999)	0.68	0.69 (1.60)
Yankees	23.6	(140)	1.14	0.74 (0.93)
Natives of Irish parentage	19.7	(97)	0.91	0.99 (0.04)
Irish immigrants	13.7	(196)	0.59	0.76 (0.88)
Italian immigrants	3.2	(185)	0.12	0.18 (3.63)
Other immigrants (non-Br.)	14.4	(132)	0.62	0.83 (0.57)
Graduation rates of high school entrants				
Daughters of				
Russian Jews	44.2	(96)		
All others	39.5	(658)	0.82	0.88 (0.54)
Yankees	44.2	(130)	1.00	0.85 (0.53)
Natives of Irish parentage	47.6	(77)	1.15	1.24 (0.66)
Irish immigrants	34.6	(133)	0.67	0.74 (1.06)
Italian immigrants	36.3	(28)	0.72	0.78 (0.54)
Other immigrants (non-Br.)	42.8	(97)	0.94	1.08 (0.24)

[a]See footnotes to Table 4.3.
[b]*t* values.

mained. The best evidence is from the 1960 U.S. Census.[48] In all groups, the college continuation rates were higher among men than among women. For example, among those most similar in age and region to the 1915 sample members, 53% of male and 40% of female high school graduates entered college. Among the children of immigrants, the comparable rates were similar: 55% and 37%. However, among the children of the Russian Jews, the gender gap was greater: 64% of male and 30% of female high school graduates continued on to college.[49]

In addition, Russian Jewish girls chose the classical and other college preparatory tracks in the Providence high schools far less often than boys (Table 4.6). Over 40% of the Russian Jewish boys, we noted earlier, chose those programs, nearly twice the city norm for boys. Among girls, the city norm was identical with what it was among boys: One-fifth chose those programs. Yet a mere 7% of Russian Jewish girls enrolled in those programs! Put another way, the odds that boys would choose them were about nine times as great as the odds that girls would do so among the Russian Jews. A clearer contrast could hardly be expected. It suggests deliberate, distinct uses of the schools for boys and girls, rather than simply passive acquiescence or a lightly weighed choice. A large minority of the boys obtained the most academically prestigious schooling, whether as an end in itself or in the hope that it might serve to prepare them for more prestigious collegiate education and possibly for a profession based on it; virtually none of the girls had this option. Perhaps, for some reason, the gender difference was unusually large in Providence. However, the predominance of Russian Jewish boys, compared with girls, in the academically elite programs probably was typical.[50]

The distinctive nature of the Russian Jewish enrollment patterns also appears among those who did not choose the classical and other college preparatory programs. For the city's boys, the most popular choice was the Technical High School.[51] Formerly the Manual Training High School, it offered extensive shop courses, as well as some advanced math and science that might help a minority of the boys prepare for careers as draftsmen or even engineers. Others chose either the classical programs or the English programs. The latter had come to include a great deal of commercial course work, and indeed by the 1920s the name of the program was changed from the English course to the commercial course. It prepared one, so the School Committee's announcements explained, for the world of business; Tech was a "general" high school, with an emphasis on shop courses.

In 1915, among the city's male public high school students, three-quarters of those who did not choose the classical and other college preparatory programs chose the Technical High School; only one-quarter chose English/commercial programs. But among the Russian Jewish boys, 45% chose the commercial programs. By 1925, Tech had lost some of its attraction for students who excelled academically because its advanced math and science courses were being offered at Classical High as well. The pattern was even clearer in that year: Two-thirds of the city's male clientele and only two-fifths of its Russian Jews chose Tech if they did not choose a classical or other college preparatory program. Among the girls, the same pattern obtained.

Although girls were much more likely to choose the commercial programs than the Technical High School, 30% nevertheless did choose Tech in 1915; among the Russian Jews, 18% did so. The Russian Jewish concentration in the commercial programs, rather than in the Technical High School, suggests their preference for commerce and their avoidance of programs that suggested a future in manual labor. Programs for the girls at Tech, for example, included cooking and sewing; in the commercial programs, secretarial and sales careers were stressed.[52]

The grades children received in courses deserve brief consideration. Generally, the patterns in the grade data were weaker. High school grades did not vary much across ethnic groups, as already noted in connection with the Italians, perhaps because of the degree of selectivity already occurring through the large dropout rates. The grammar school GPAs for 1925 also show no distinct Russian Jewish pattern, perhaps because of sample size. The 1915 grammar school grades indicate, however, that Russian Jewish boys received the highest grades in the city, although they differed from others by less than the Italians did (Table 4.8). The grades of Russian Jewish girls in grammar school courses also suggest school achievement near the upper end of the continuum for ethnic groups, but less exceptional than the achievement of the boys (Table 4.9), perhaps reflecting less emphasis on academic achievement for girls.[53]

Finally, do the Providence data indicate the prevalence of an intellectual elite among the Jewish students? Jews have been unusually well represented among intellectual elites in modern Europe and in the United States in this century. This "intellectual preeminence," as Veblen called it, can be observed among faculty and students at prestigious universities, among prominent intellectuals, among Nobel Prize winners, and even among the most influential figures in Western intellectual history (such as Marx, Freud, and Einstein).[54] Of course, the cultural and structural circumstances that encouraged this performance need not be the same as those operating on the mass of the Jewish population. At the same time, however, it is also possible that there are some continuities – if not between high school entry rates in Providence and the emergence of Marx, Freud, and Einstein, at least between those rates and some of the less rarefied indicators of an intellectual elite. Is there any hint in the Providence data that there were disproportionate numbers of Jews among those at the highest levels of intellectual attainment? There is not. We might, for example, consider the students who graduated from the classical programs of the high schools and inquire about the grades they received. Or we might ask about those with the highest GPAs in such programs. The

Table 4.8. *Boys' GPA by ethnicity, 1915 (native-born only) and 1925*[a]

Group	Mean GPA	N	GPA difference: each group compared with Russian Jews	
			No controls	Social background factors controlled
1915: sixth-grade GPA, native-born only				
Sons of				
Russian Jews	2.59	(165)		
All others	2.34	(775)	−0.25	−0.24 (3.46)[b]
Yankees	2.44	(74)	−0.15	−0.18 (1.68)
Natives of Irish parentage	2.46	(48)	−0.13	−0.14 (1.14)
Irish immigrants	2.38	(156)	−0.21	−0.13 (1.56)
Italian immigrants	2.02	(147)	−0.57	−0.50 (5.73)
Other immigrants (non-Br.)	2.42	(97)	−0.17	−0.15 (1.58)
1915: ninth-grade GPA, native born only				
Sons of				
Russian Jews	1.98	(111)		
All others	1.97	(594)	−0.01	−0.05 (0.38)
Yankees	1.99	(95)	0.01	−0.07 (0.53)
Natives of Irish parentage	1.77	(74)	−0.21	−0.25 (1.84)
Irish immigrants	1.95	(168)	−0.03	0.02 (0.12)
Italian immigrants	2.10	(71)	0.12	0.19 (1.06)
Other immigrants (non-Br.)	1.95	(92)	−0.03	−0.07 (0.55)
1925: sixth-grade GPA, all boys				
Sons of				
Russian Jews	2.54	(59)		
All others	2.43	(606)	−0.11	−0.04 (0.34)
Native whites	2.60	(197)	0.06	0.04 (0.34)
Irish immigrants	2.64	(33)	0.10	0.15 (0.95)
Italian immigrants	2.20	(198)	−0.34	−0.20 (1.85)
Other immigrants (non-Br.)	2.49	(135)	−0.05	0.02 (0.15)
1925: ninth-grade GPA, all boys				
Sons of				
Russian Jews	2.18	(46)		
All others	2.01	(406)	−0.17	−0.14 (1.04)
Native whites	2.05	(168)	−0.13	−0.15 (1.07)
Irish immigrants	1.86	(46)	−0.32	−0.25 (1.39)
Italian immigrants	1.85	(72)	−0.33	−0.23 (1.42)
Other immigrants (non-Br.)	2.15	(93)	−0.03	0.02 (0.12)

[a]See footnotes to Table 4.3.
[b]*t* values.

Table 4.9. *Native-born girls' GPA by ethnicity, 1915*[a]

Group	Mean GPA	N	GPA difference: each group compared with Russian Jews	
			No controls	Social background factors controlled
Sixth-grade GPA				
Daughters of				
Russian Jews	2.54	(141)		
All others	2.46	(590)	−0.08	−0.09 (1.25)[b]
Yankees	2.69	(100)	0.15	0.10 (0.96)
Natives of Irish parentage	2.46	(58)	−0.08	−0.08 (0.66)
Irish immigrants	2.45	(75)	−0.09	−0.08 (0.76)
Italian immigrants	2.10	(91)	−0.44	−0.37 (3.60)
Other immigrants (non-Br.)	2.36	(73)	−0.18	−0.15 (1.36)
Ninth-grade GPA				
Daughters of				
Russian Jews	2.23	(92)		
All others	2.26	(605)	0.03	0.06 (0.46)
Yankees	2.38	(114)	0.15	0.18 (0.46)
Natives of Irish parentage	2.18	(73)	−0.05	0.01 (1.26)
Irish immigrants	2.04	(122)	−0.19	−0.13 (0.95)
Italian immigrants	2.13	(24)	−0.10	−0.04 (0.19)
Other immigrants (non-Br.)	2.40	(91)	0.17	0.22 (1.57)

[a] See footnotes to Table 4.3.
[b] *t* values.

Russian Jewish boys were overrepresented in that population, and particularly within the public high schools' classical curricula, in which they accounted for approximately one-fifth of all graduates, whereas they numbered only 7% of the age cohort.[55] However, the GPAs of the Russian Jewish boys who graduated from these programs were not higher than those for other groups, nor was the GPA for the top one-fifth among them higher than that for the top one-fifth of other graduates.[56] There may have been no special academic elite among Jewish students in Providence; alternatively, the results may reflect just how small an intellectual elite tends to be, with evidence about their behavior being difficult to observe in a citywide sample.

In sum, then, the Russian Jewish boys received unusually long schooling, even when other factors are taken into account; they were more likely than most (although not all) other groups to enter a classical or other college preparatory curriculum, and their grades may also have been somewhat higher than those for other groups. Although evidence of extraordinary intellectual accomplishment is not to be found, a variety of data nevertheless reveal distinctive involvement with schooling. The data on the Russian Jewish girls suggest considerable accommodation to modern norms concerning the schooling of girls through high school. However, strong gender differences persisted in college enrollment rates, differences consistent with traditional norms.

4.4. *Patterns of occupational attainment*

The male sample members selected from the records of 1915 and 1925 have been traced in city directories of 1925 and 1935, respectively, sources that indicate the occupations of those found in the Providence area when they were twenty-two to twenty-five years old. The mean Russian Jewish occupational score was the highest in the city (Table 4.10). Some of the group's advantage is explained by the measurable family background characteristics we have routinely controlled: father's occupation, family's property value, and family size and structure. Nevertheless, when these family background characteristics are controlled, much of the Russian Jewish advantage remains unexplained. In the 1915 sample, for example, taking these family background factors into account reduced the differences between Russian Jews and all others only from 12.5 points on the Duncan scale to 11.1 points, and in the 1925 sample, from 10.1 to 7.6.

It is possible to enhance our information on the employment status of the fathers (employer, other self-employed, or employee) for the 1915 sample because employment is reported for every gainfully employed individual; yet adding this information explains little of the remaining ethnic difference. Also, controlling explicitly for whether or not a father was engaged in commerce (by exploiting the detailed 1915 information on the sector of the economy in which the father worked) adds very little explanatory power.[57]

The rapid rise of the second generation of Russian Jews has long been noted. Relatively little of their advancement seems to have been due to measured family background characteristics. The Providence data permit us to explore whether or not that occupational attainment was due to educational attainment. The sample members have been classified according to length of schooling: never reached high school, high school dropout, high school graduate, college entrant (1925 only).

A part of the Russian Jewish occupational advantage did result from their educational advantage: When the educational levels are con-

Table 4.10. *Ethnic differences in occupational attainment: males, 1925 and 1935*[a]

| | | | Difference in means: each group compared with Russian Jews | | | |
| | | | No controls | Controlling for | | |
Group	Means	N		Family background	Education	Both
1915 sample: native-born only						
Sons of:						
Russian Jews	45.5	(102)				
All others	33.0	(786)	−12.5	−11.1	−9.1	−8.7
Yankees	35.0	(77)	−10.5	−12.4	−9.2	−10.4
Natives of Irish parentage	36.6	(68)	−8.9	−8.1	−6.4	−6.1
Irish immigrants	33.4	(229)	−12.1	−9.0	−9.0	−7.3
Italian immigrants	29.5	(175)	−16.0	−12.0	−10.2	−8.6
Other immigrants (non-Br.)	33.4	(89)	−12.1	−11.1	−8.8	−8.6
1925 sample: all boys						
Sons of:						
Russian Jews	41.2	(39)				
All others	31.1	(493)	−10.1	−7.6	−5.4[#]	−5.4
Native whites	34.8	(150)	−6.4	−7.3	−3.7	−5.5
Irish immigrants	35.9	(35)	−5.3[#]	−2.4[&]	−2.7[&]	−2.0[&]
Italian immigrants	26.1	(139)	−15.1	−9.8	−8.1	−6.4
Other immigrants (non-Br.)	31.7	(97)	−9.5	−6.1	−5.3[@]	−4.3[@]

Note: All differences from Russian Jewish means are statistically significant ($t > 1.96$) unless otherwise indicated: @, $t > 1.50$; #, $1.30 < t < 1.49$; &, $t < 1.00$.

[a] Male sample members' occupational attainment a decade after the census year (e.g., 1925 for 1915 sample members). Based on a numeric score for each occupational title (the Duncan score). Available only for those sample members found in the Providence area in the later year. The standard deviation of the occupational scores was 19.3 in 1915 and 17.9 in 1925. The differences in means are coefficients on ethnic dummy variables in OLS regressions. Supplemental samples are included in the regressions, weighted to reflect their true relative magnitudes. See note *a* in Table 2.7.

trolled, the occupational advantage of the Russian Jew is seen to decline. It could hardly have been otherwise: The Russian Jews received more schooling, and schooling was related to occupational attainment. Of course, some of the explanatory power of schooling was in turn related to family background, because those from favored backgrounds were more likely to achieve extended schooling. However, when family background alone is controlled, it captures any occupational advantages associated with it, including those realized through schooling (the difference between the third and fourth columns of Table 4.10). On the other hand, the independent effects of education, the effects associated with education after family background has explained all it can, are generally also large (the difference between the fourth and sixth columns of the table). Thus, in the 1915 sample, the independent effects of education contributed more to the occupational advantage that the Russian Jews enjoyed over all others than did the total effects of the measured family background characteristics (including their effects realized through schooling: 2.4 versus 1.4 points). In the 1925 sample, although family background had the larger effect, the independent effects of education were not much smaller (2.2 versus 2.5 points).

In sum, education and family background should be considered to have operated jointly, as well as independently, to create the occupational advantages enjoyed by the Russian Jews. The independent effect of education is the occupational advantage that the Russian Jews enjoyed as a result of having obtained longer schooling than others, even when family background characteristics have been taken into account. The independent effect of education may not have been of great magnitude, but it was roughly as large as the effect that social-class origins, together with other aspects of family background, had in creating the occupational advantage of the Russian Jews (including any role of family background operating through schooling). Although the coefficients are small, they bear on a large theme. They do not support the hypothesis that Russian Jewish advancement in the early years was due to the class advantages of the Jewish immigrants rather than to schooling. Jews' use of a college education to enter the professions may indeed have been principally a third-generation phenomenon, occurring after families had solidly established themselves in the middle class. However, the second generation's occupational advancement seems to have had as much to do with schooling as with any social-class advantages.

As striking, surely, as any part of the explained occupational advantage is the large occupational advantage that remains unexplained even when family background and education are both taken into account (in the last column of Table 4.10).[58] In 1915, the year from which our best evidence comes, it amounted to no less than 8.7 points over all others, and in 1925 to 5.4 points. These are not merely large residuals, but also large fractions of the total observed ethnic differences (i.e., the differences observed without controls imposed): 12.5 in 1915, and 10.1 in 1925. An important part of the Russian Jewish advantage, then, is not explained by any of the factors we can take into account, including education.

Are these findings peculiar to Providence? We noted earlier the high concentration of Russian Jews in the largest American cities, and particularly in New York. Was their experience different there than in small cities like Providence? We cannot, of course, be sure. The unique nature of the Providence data makes precise comparisons impossible. However, one difference between the small and large cities noted earlier is important to recall here: The Jews were more concentrated in commercial occupations in Providence than in New York. That difference, in turn, could have made opportunities to enter business more plentiful and diminished the attraction of an extended education.[59] If so, the Russian Jewish patterns of schooling in New York may have been still more distinctive than they were in Providence. It is also possible that schooling may have accounted for more of the distinctive occupational attainment levels of the Russian Jews. There are, however, reasons for doubting that these intercity differences were great. The first concerns evidence on educational attainment by city. The Immigration Commission *Reports*, which were based on data from a score of cities in 1908, suggest that about 15% of Russian Jewish boys in New York entered high school and that only about 2% graduated. In Providence, seven years later, the rates were considerably higher (Table 4.3). The comparison is frustratingly imprecise, but it hardly suggests that the New Yorkers were notably more likely to obtain extended schooling.[60] Similarly, the Russian Jews of New York entered commerce at an impressive rate, as noted earlier, and a majority probably ended their work lives in business. In short, commerce may not have predominated quite so much in New York as in Providence, but it was crucial, and it would be rash to think that the difference produced a very different utility for schooling.[61] New York's Jews, it seems safer to conclude, probably were quite like those in Providence, both in their levels of educational attainment and in the distinctiveness of those levels. They probably were very similar, too, in enjoying a relatively large advantage in occupational attainment that was not due to longer schooling.

4.5. Explaining the differences

How are we to interpret the Russian Jewish advantages in educational and occupational attainment? Both are partly reducible to the family background characteristics of the group, and occupational attainment is partly reducible to educational attainment. But what of the residuals, the advantages unexplained when controls are imposed?

The sheer concentration of commercial occupations among the Russian Jews meant that even if a given family was not involved in commerce, a member of that family might nevertheless have obtained an advantage from being part of that ethnic group. These were the contextual effects of the ethnic concentration in commerce. Contextual effects are not captured by controlling for the occupation of each individual household head, and thus they are not taken into account in the regression results presented in the tables. Examples of contextual effects, and the methodological problems of studying those effects, were discussed in the preceding chapter.

At first sight, contextual effects seem to suggest a sufficient explanation for Russian Jewish patterns of schooling and occupational attainment. Quite apart from any contextual effects, a concentration in commercial occupations in Europe could have led to a similar concentration in the United States, because the Jews correctly perceived a competitive edge based on experience and felt most comfortable in familiar endeavors. A similar argument could be made about concentration in skilled trades, or at least in those skilled trades in which eventual self-employment was within the reach of many. Such concentrations would have led families engaged in commerce to rapid upward mobility, with important implications for the schooling and economic positions of their offspring. These outcomes are taken into account in the regressions. The possible contextual effects of concentration include information on available careers, contacts for jobs, and employer preferences for their own kind. All these would have shaped decisions about jobs and about preparation for jobs. Moreover, peer culture would have influenced the aspirations of young people: A child of a Russian Jewish laborer would have been familiar with many more examples of preparation for white-collar work than would the child of an Italian laborer. Thus, in rational calculations about opportunities, and in cultural manifestations such as aspirations, the Russian Jews may have reacted different than others as a result of the contextual effects of the initial concentration in commerce. As such, more of them may have prepared for college, and in turn entered classical or other college preparatory programs more often in high school. They also may have succeeded more often once in the job market, given the different structure of the opportunities available to them.

Still, the fact that contextual effects could have operated in all these ways hardly proves that they were the critical effects and that other plausible explanations should be ignored. Recall, for example, the rate at which Russian Jewish girls enrolled in high school classical programs in Providence. Their enrollment rate was lower than those common among the girls of other groups. Perhaps these enrollments can be said to reflect deliberate preparation for commercial jobs, compared with a less clear route to the world of work for girls in other groups. However, their enrollments in the classical curricula were also far lower than the enrollments of Russian Jewish boys, a pattern less easily explained by reference to the contextual effects of commercial concentration than by the pre-migration heritage of male study.

Also, a concentration in commerce may not have had the sorts of effects predicted earlier. For example, it is far from clear that such a concentration, particularly in small, family-owned businesses, would in fact have dictated longer-than-average schooling, including higher college continuation rates. Perhaps, one might argue, the concentration in commerce operated to raise expectations (for example, by encouraging the sense that the world was open to individual effort), and as a result it encouraged entry into the professions. However, there is no reason to assume that the European background in commerce did not also create such expectations long before migration. Perhaps, too, the American context operated in another way, making the Jews sensitive to the advantages of entering the independent professions, in which a member of a minority could be free from anti-Semitic employers. Yet, once again, it is hardly reasonable to assume that centuries of virulent European discrimination were inoperative and that only the sensitivity to the potential of discrimination in the United States operated. Indeed, if the latter alone operated, would it have been so much stronger against Jews than against Polish or Italian Catholics? Was discrimination really so much more virulent toward the former that it could produce such divergent responses?

The argument for the contextual effects, then, at first quite compelling, is far from self-evident. Moreover, the evidence that can be brought to bear does not encourage the belief that the contextual effects associated with the class position of the Russian Jews, or their concentration in commerce, can explain much of the distinctive quality of Russian Jewish behavior. Knowing the mean occupational score for Russian Jewish fathers helps only slightly to account for that behavior, as was also the case with the Italians. Similarly, because controlling for whether or not the father was engaged in commerce (or was an employer) adds practically nothing to the routine controls for the father's occupation and property value, it would certainly be rash to claim that the corresponding contextual effects would add a great deal. To argue that they would amounts to suggesting that member-

ship in an ethnic group concentrated in commerce (or a group including relatively more employers than others) was much more important
than having a father engaged in commerce (or one who was an employer).[62]

The magnitude of the unexplained ethnic differences we have encountered here leads us to return to the issue raised at the beginning
of this chapter: the ways in which the Jewish religion and the unique
socioeconomic and political situation of the Jews in Europe could have
encouraged attitudes, values, and habits conducive to economic advancement in a modern industrial society. We should consider not
only the explanations based on the social structural location of the
group but also those based in some way on its cultural heritage. There
is no question of excluding the former; it is a matter of taking the
latter seriously as well. This interpretation of the residual ethnic difference involves the weakness of placing great weight on an influence
we have not observed directly. The reasons for nonetheless accepting
this interpretation, given the data and methods available, were elab-
orated when large residuals were encountered in connection with Italian
schooling (Section 3.5).

The descriptions of particular beliefs, attitudes, and values such as
those of Glazer quoted at the outset may claim far too much certainty
about popular culture and its effects, as Goldscheider and Zuckerman
argued. In its barest essentials, the argument is that the particular
nature of the religion and the centuries of commercial involvement
and minority status may have encouraged a positive orientation to
schooling in its own right and characteristics useful for economic advancement (including an awareness of the utility of schooling). The
point here is not to argue that the nature of these characteristics can
be stated with confidence, but rather that the analysis of behavior
suggests that this category of explanations deserves attention.[63]

Nevertheless, it is worthwhile to consider, however cautiously, some
of the more obvious sorts of cultural characteristics that may have
been involved and some of the behaviors to which they seem relevant. The tradition of learning may have encouraged schooling and
indirectly contributed to occupational advantages insofar as these rested
on schooling. However, other cultural traits, quite apart from a tradition of learning, may have influenced school achievement, just as
they influenced occupational achievement. An achievement orientation may have operated on school behavior as much as on market
behavior. Moreover, the perception that school behavior might enhance market success, that schooling was useful for getting ahead,
would have stimulated academic achievement. We have, in sum, more

than one plausible relationship between the pre-migration background of the Jews and their distinctive educational attainment.

We should nevertheless recall here that the eastern European Jewish migration was hardly a migration of scholars; the level of learning typical in eastern Europe's Jewish communities would alone have guaranteed that. Also, it may well be that those Jews who chose to migrate from eastern Europe were especially unlikely to have had advanced Talmudic study and were less committed than others to the old religious life. The New World quickly took on a reputation for encouraging abandonment of the old ways.[64]

If the less learned and less religious predominated in the migration, how relevant could the tradition of learning have been to behavior in the United States? In fact, its relevance may actually have been enhanced as a result of these circumstances. The point is not so much the level of learning achieved, but rather the honorable place learning enjoyed in the traditional culture. An illiterate immigrant mother would have been as sensitive to that special role as would a scholar, although, of course, in somewhat different ways. That very difference may have spurred secular educational attainment. The traditional emphasis on learning was overwhelmingly concerned with religious learning. Those less religious and less well versed in traditional religious learning may have been best suited to blur the distinction between religious and secular schooling. Thus, insofar as the tradition of learning was salient, perhaps it is not the similarity of the subject matter that should be stressed, but rather the distance that existed between so many Jews and the substance of advanced Jewish learning – while they were nonetheless sensitive to the status of learning. From that perspective, for example, it is not the similarity between studying the Talmud and studying law that explains why Jews became eager law students. That similarity, in any case, hardly explains why Jews became eager medical students. Rather, it is the general status of learning and jobs based on it.[65]

It may also be helpful to summarize which particular strands of the eastern European Jewish heritage seem plausibly related to particular behavior patterns in the United States, even if we cannot explore their connections empirically. An orientation to achievement may have influenced many aspects of behavior. We can, however, be more specific about some other strands in the pre-migration background. Surely the orientation to commerce, as a cultural force and as a simple matter of differential experience, helps explain the fathers' concentration in particular occupations. Their concentration in those occupations, and the cultural preferences, in turn, help explain some of the patterns of child labor and some of the curriculum choices of Russian Jewish children. The tradition of learning may well have influenced the length of schooling and the enrollment of the boys in the classical and other college preparatory programs. The traditional difference between male and female education, though it had suffered considerable erosion, would explain the predominance of boys over girls in classical programs in high school and in college enrollments. Finally, the distinctive occupational attainments of the second generation may also have been related directly to some of the less obvious effects of the commercial past – to the preference for commerce.

Patterns of schooling and of economic advancement, then, were distinctive among the Russian Jews. A cultural heritage of considerable influence, together with important structural factors, must be considered to explain that distinctiveness. The advantage of schooling enjoyed by Russian Jews was itself a stimulus to occupational attainment. However, the occupational advantage that the Russian Jewish sons enjoyed was due to much else besides their schooling.

5   *The Blacks*

The great migrations of blacks from the South began during World War I, continued into the 1920s, slowed during the Depression years, and grew immensely during and after World War II. Prior to these migrations, black people were only a small proportion of the population in the northern cities. In some, such as New York and Chicago, they numbered in the tens of thousands; still, whites outnumbered them at least fiftyfold. The black community in Providence numbered some two to six thousand during the years 1880–1925; they were but a tiny fraction of the city's residents.[1]

Nevertheless, the Providence black community was large enough for intensive study. Data were collected on all blacks eligible for the random samples, 125–165 individuals in each of six supplemental samples (boys and girls in 1880 and 1915, boys in 1900 and 1925). Together they form the richest available evidence bearing on the early school patterns of blacks in the North and on the relationship between schooling and economic advancement. Because their school patterns were intimately bound up with poverty, discrimination, and family life, our study will bear on the often subtle connections among all these aspects of black social history.

The first section of this chapter describes some basic social characteristics of the black families from which the sampled children came – the prevalence of southern origin, parental illiteracy, family heads in low-skill, manual-labor occupations, broken families, and working mothers. The second section considers the strikingly low rate of child labor among blacks. The third and fourth sections describe patterns of black children's schooling, including (in addition to the aspects of schooling considered in earlier chapters) racial integration and segregation. These sections also stress the contrast between blacks' long attendance and low performance on some measures of school achievement. The discussion then turns to explanations of the school patterns. The fifth section explores the relative importance of low-social-class origins and a high incidence of broken families among blacks: Which mattered more for black children's schooling? The sixth section considers black culture and discrimination against blacks as the sources of the observed school patterns.[2]

163

Finally, the seventh section deals with the jobs that the male sample members obtained as young men. The differences between their jobs and those of whites were glaring. What accounts for that difference – class origins, family background, schooling, cultural differences between blacks and whites, or simply discrimination?

Throughout, when blacks are compared with whites, three groups of whites are distinguished: the children of Yankees (that is, children of natives of native parentage) and the grandchildren and children of immigrants. The information necessary to distinguish between the first two groups is unavailable for the 1925 sample; comparisons for that year must therefore be limited to the children of natives and the children of immigrants.

One might simply have compared blacks with all whites or, at the other extreme, with a much more differentiated list of immigrant groups. Considering whites as an undifferentiated whole is highly undesirable, because school attendance patterns differed in striking ways between some immigrant groups and the children of the Yankees. To distinguish several immigrant groups would complicate the discussion unduly. Blacks would then appear closer to some immigrant groups, and further from others. However, the basic thrust of the analysis would not change. Moreover, there is some advantage in asking how the experiences of blacks compared with those of immigrants generally. After all, the progress of blacks in the North, nearly all descended from southern migrants, often has been considered in comparison with the progress of migrants from abroad.[3]

5.1.   The social characteristics of black families

The black community in Providence traces its origins to early colonial times. Nevertheless, many of its residents in 1880 were recent migrants from the South (Table 5.1); about half of the sample members' parents had been born there. Migration continued during the last decades of the century, so that the proportion of parents in the 1900 sample who had been born in the South was about the same as in 1880. By 1925, it had declined slightly to about 40%. On the other hand, most of these migrants appear to have migrated as young people without children; less than a fifth of the sample members themselves had been born in the South. The point needs to be stressed: Given the availability of data indicating that as early as 1870, large proportions of the northern black population had been born in the South, it is easy to lose sight of the fact that most of the children of these migrants were born after their parents reached the North.[4] The northern-born children, of course, had not suffered the handicap of

Table 5.1. *Percentages of black sample members and their parents and grandparents born in the South*

Group	1880		1900		1925	
	%	N	%	N	%	N
Sample member	19.0	(232)	17.7	(119)	4.6	(153)
Father	58.3	(187)	52.6	(95)	42.1	(133)
Mother	45.9	(218)	53.6	(112)	37.9	(133)
Northern-born father: his own father[b]	10.3	(78)	31.1	(45)	n.a.[a]	
Northern-born mother: her own father[c]	8.5	(118)	25.0	(52)	n.a.	

[a] The 1925 Rhode Island State Census did not provide information on the birthplace of the sample members' grandparents.
[b] The sample member's paternal grandfather.
[c] The sample member's maternal grandfather.

southern black schooling. In Providence, this pattern had not changed even in 1925, after the unprecedented migration of blacks to the North during World War I.

Of those black parents who were native to the North in the earliest part of this period, most probably traced their northern roots far into the past. At any rate, only about one-tenth of the northern-born parents in the 1880 sample had a father who had himself been born in the South; however, by 1900 about three in ten did. The earlier migrants (the grandfathers of sample members) probably were free blacks, and a small number may have been runaway slaves.

One striking difference between those black parents who had been born in the North and those from the South concerns illiteracy (Table 5.2). The information on parental illiteracy in the North and South tells us a bit about the education of blacks in the period prior to 1900. Illiteracy among blacks in the North has been discussed to some extent, notably by Elizabeth Pleck, but it has received far less attention than other aspects of black social life in the nineteenth century, such as occupational and family structure.[5] It deserves closer scrutiny.

Illiteracy was not totally unknown among the northern-born blacks, even among those born in New England, where the common school system was most uniformly established, and where bars against blacks were no stronger than elsewhere in the North. Although the rates of illiteracy were quite low (in the range of 10%), it is important to realize that illiteracy among whites born in New England had been vir-

Table 5.2. *Illiteracy among parents of the black sample members and among blacks in the South, 1870–1900*

A. The Providence samples

Parents' birthplace	1880		1900	
	Fathers (%)	Mothers (%)	Fathers (%)	Mothers (%)
South	45.9	55.0	24.0	28.3
All other	12.8	18.6	11.1	17.3
New England only	6.8	12.8	10.3	9.4
All birthplaces	32.1	35.3	17.9	23.2

B. Estimates of illiteracy among blacks in the South, by age[a]

Age	1870 (males) (%)	1900	
		Males (%)	Females (%)
21 and over	88.2		
55–64 in 1900 (35–44 in 1880)		77.6	88.4
35–44 in 1900		47.9	66.6

[a]U.S. Census reports. See text and its notes for citations.

tually wiped out well before 1880.[6] The figures suggest that a fraction of the northern black community had not been reached by that school system.

However, if the very existence of illiteracy among northern-born black parents distinguishes them from northern-born whites, its relatively low incidence also distinguishes them from southern-born black parents. Among the latter group in the 1880 sample, about half were illiterate; in the 1900 sample, about a quarter were. Schooling for southern blacks in the late nineteenth century, however limited and discriminatory, was chipping away at the proportion who were growing up illiterate. The fact that half of the black migrant parents were illiterate in 1880 means that there were far more illiterates among them than among any group in Providence in that year. Even among the Irish immigrants, only a third were illiterate.

Nevertheless, literacy was far more prevalent among the black migrant parents than it was among the black population remaining in the South. The U.S. Census figures for the late nineteenth and early twentieth centuries provide sketchy information, but enough to make some comparisons, and thereby to learn something about the background of early migrants to the North.[7]

The 1870 U.S. Census indicates that in that immediate post-emancipation year, only 12% of adult southern black males could read and write. The figure is of some interest in itself as a benchmark for the evolution of black literacy rates. Some of these literate blacks had, of course, been free even in antebellum years. Nevertheless, census records suggest that about three-quarters of the literate black men in 1870 had been slaves.[8] Whether they learned to read and write clandestinely under slavery (when it was illegal throughout the South to teach a slave these skills) or whether they learned in the first years of freedom we cannot know. The later censuses provide other benchmarks of interest. In 1900, among black men fifty-five to sixty-four years old who were living in the South, only 78% were illiterate. That same age cohort had been thirty-five to forty-four years old in 1880 – as had many of the black fathers in the 1880 sample from Providence.[9] But among the southern-born black fathers in Providence, 46% were illiterate in 1880. More straightforward comparisons are possible for 1900. In that year 48% of the southern black men and 67% of the women thirty-five to forty-four years of age were illiterate. In Providence, 24% of the men and 28% of the women among the southern-born black parents were illiterate.

In short, the black migrants to Providence were far more literate than those in the age group they left behind. The same was true of the migrants to Philadelphia and to Boston.[10] Of course, some of them may have learned to read after they reached the North, as adults or as children. However, if most left the South knowing how to read and write, literate southern blacks must have been much more likely to migrate than others. Perhaps because getting work (or better work than that available in the South), and getting along in general, without literacy was especially difficult in the North, a far smaller fraction of the illiterate were willing to risk migration.[11] The literate, in all likelihood, were also in a much better position than others to learn about conditions in the North. Finally, they probably were more often city-dwellers, and their information may have come as a result of urban life as much as by virtue of literacy directly. As city-dwellers, they also may have felt more confident of their ability to make the adjustment than would others who had not lived in an urban setting. However, the possibility that literacy itself encouraged black migration is important. If it did, the low levels of southern black literacy and the slow development of adequate schooling for black children in the decades after the Civil War contributed to restricting black migration from the South before the second decade of this century. The flow and

Table 5.3. *Fathers' occupations in nativity and racial groupings*

Father's group	High white-collar (%)	Low white-collar (%)	Skilled manual (%)	Semi-skilled manual (%)	Unskilled manual (%)	Total (100%) N[a]
Native white of native parents						
1880	21.7	25.4	32.3	14.2	6.5	(614)
1900	16.8	30.8	29.2	16.8	6.5	(185)
1915	17.1	28.1	26.6	18.6	9.5	(263)
1925	—	—	—	—	—	—
Native white of foreign parents						
1880	9.7	17.7	38.9	14.2	19.5	(113)
1900	3.6	15.8	30.3	35.8	14.6	(165)
1915	5.1	21.6	27.7	34.8	10.8	(296)
1925[b]	13.5	19.3	32.1	25.0	10.1	(296)
Foreign-born white						
1880	2.9	11.5	27.4	27.0	31.2	(1,131)
1900	3.0	14.3	33.1	22.8	26.9	(469)
1915	6.8	18.6	25.2	26.7	22.7	(1,116)
1925	8.9	17.9	26.0	24.8	22.4	(630)
Black						
1880	2.8	5.1	10.2	25.0	56.9	(216)
1900	3.5	7.0	4.4	29.0	56.1	(114)
1915	1.1	8.7	6.1	20.8	63.3	(264)
1925	1.9	7.5	10.3	25.2	55.1	(107)

[a]Tables 5.3–5.7 are based on the samples of all children and on the supplemental samples of black children. N's for corresponding rows of these tables vary slightly because cases were omitted from a particular table if they were missing data relevant to it.
[b]Includes all native whites. See also note a, Table 5.1.

timing of that migration, in turn, shaped the contours of American history in countless ways.[12]

Once in the North, black parents were concentrated at the very bottom of the occupational structure to a much greater degree, and much more consistently over time, than any other group in the city. The mean occupational score for all household heads was 24–28 between 1880 and 1925; for blacks, the comparable mean was 14–15. In four census years, 80–85% of the black sample members came from families in which the head was a low manual worker (Table 5.3). Even among the Irish in 1880 or the Italians in 1900, that proportion did not exceed 65%. Moreover, by 1915, over a quarter of native-born family

Table 5.4. *Broken families by nativity and race*

Father's group[a]	1880		1900		1915		1925	
	%	N[b]	%	N	%	N	%	N
A. *Percentage of sample members living in households not headed by two parents*[c]								
NWNP	19.5	(650)	23.2	(194)	23.1	(277)		
NWFP	39.9	(133)	33.5	(173)	30.0	(317)	15.6	(327)
FBW	23.4	(1,215)	25.4	(501)	18.7	(1,157)	11.9	(666)
Black	44.8	(232)	39.5	(119)	39.1	(271)	39.2	(153)
B. *Percentage of sample members' families female-headed*[d]								
NWNP	7.7		8.8		10.1			
NWFP	23.3		15.6		15.8		2.8	
FBW	14.3		12.4		10.5		4.2	
Black	22.8		28.6		24.7		20.9	

[a] NWNP, native white of native parentage; NWFP, native white of foreign parentage (includes all native white in 1925); FBW, foreign-born white.
[b] See note *a*, Table 5.3.
[c] The households were headed by a single parent, or by someone other than a parent. In a negligible percentage of cases, both parents were present, but neither was the head of household. Sample members living with stepparents or with adopting parents (both present) were included in this category as well (8.7% of black sample members in 1880, 2.5% in 1900, 1.1% in 1915, 6.5% in 1925).
[d] A subset of the preceding group.

heads of Irish parentage were in white-collar occupations; among northern-born black family heads there was no such sign of the ethnic group's improvement in station since 1880.

A substantially higher fraction of black families than of white included only one parent. There is a voluminous literature on why this pattern existed; the prevalence of poverty, male underemployment, and early death among blacks are important factors. It is also worth noting in passing that there were white ethnic groups in Providence, particularly second-generation natives of immigrant stock, whose rates of parental absence were as great, or nearly as great, as those among the blacks, at least in some periods. Nor was the black–white difference overall as great as in our own time. Still, in 1880, an identifiable pattern already existed among black families in Providence (Table 5.4). That pattern usually is discussed in terms of the proportion of black families headed by females. Female-headed households were indeed more common among the blacks. However, it is also worth noting all forms of families not headed by two parents (families referred to here

Table 5.5. *Prevalence of working mothers by nativity and race*

Father's group	1880 %	N^a	1900 %	N	1915 %	N
A. *All strata*						
NWNP	3.6	(634)	7.6	(184)	9.8	(266)
NWFP	9.5	(127)	6.8	(163)	11.7	(309)
FBW	4.5	(1,146)	6.4	(466)	8.6	(1,112)
Black	27.5	(222)	38.1	(113)	46.2	(251)
B. *Low manual heads of household, both parents present*						
NWNP	2.0	(102)	6.3	(32)	8.7	(46)
NWFP	0	(24)	0	(54)	3.2	(95)
FBW	0.7	(539)	2.8	(177)	6.0	(453)
Black	12.6	(103)	25.9	(58)	39.1	(133)

^{a}See note *a*, Table 5.3.

as "broken" rather than "intact"). Two-fifths of the black sample members were living in such households.[13]

When fathers were absent, mothers were much more likely to work. In 1880, only about 4% of the mothers in Yankee or immigrant families worked for wages; among blacks, the proportion was 28% (Table 5.5). It was higher still in later samples, reaching 46% in 1915. Even among intact families, poverty spurred mothers to supplement the fathers' incomes. However, the race differences in the prevalence of working mothers were not due merely to family breakup or poverty. Even among intact families headed by low manual workers, black women were much more likely to work than white women. Among immigrants in such families, 1% of women worked in 1880, 3% in 1900, and 6% in 1915. Among blacks, the figures were 13%, 26%, and 39%. Even in these roughly comparable groups, the wages of household heads may have been lower among blacks than among whites.

Nevertheless, much of the difference probably was due to other factors. One element, Claudia Goldin has suggested, may have been the earlier experience of black women working as slaves, and consequently black families' greater familiarity with and willingness to resort to this option for supplementary income. Another may have been the greater need for supplemental income (because of the low and insecure wages of black men), which in turn made working wives more familiar and perhaps more acceptable than among whites.[14]

5.2. *Mother's work and child labor*

The most common way for immigrant families to supplement family income was child labor, particularly the employment of adolescents age thirteen and older. Black children were much less likely to be employed than were immigrant children (Table 5.6). Indeed, child labor in black families was no more common than in Yankee households. Whereas 39% of the eleven- to sixteen-year-old children of immigrant origin were at work in 1880, the figure was only 10% for the children of Yankees and blacks. Differences of comparable magnitude can be seen in the later years among both boys and girls. That black children were no more likely to work than the children of Yankees is striking because of the enormous differences in parental occupations between the two groups (Table 5.3) and because black families were much more likely to lack a male head. Both differences would have made income from child labor a much greater boon to black families.

One critical reason black children so rarely worked may have been that jobs were closed to them. The absence of child labor in Philadelphia, wrote W. E. B. DuBois, "is not voluntary on the part of the Negroes, but due to restricted opportunity; there is really very little that Negro children may do." We cannot, at this point in the discussion, distinguish the effects of discrimination from those of voluntary decisions by blacks to choose one form of activity over another. Still, evidence suggesting discrimination may be found not only in the opinion of astute contemporary observers but also in the complete absence of blacks from certain kinds of employment.

Consider the local textile mills, the largest industrial employer of children throughout the period under discussion. Not a single black child worked there. The published U.S. Census reports for 1890 and 1910, which cross-tabulated occupations by race, tell the same story for adults. In 1890, the 7,984 white mill workers constituted 13.5% of the white labor force. But among the blacks (and there were over 2,000 in the city's labor force), only twelve workers were employed in the mills – 0.6%. For 1910, the comparable figures are as follows: white, 8.8% of the labor force in the mills; blacks, 0.06%. Al Sisti, a mill worker from the age of thirteen, and a labor leader, recalling the period since World War I, remarked, "Hiring practices ran through the departments, and the bosses would generally hire their own kind. It wasn't frowned upon, and it wasn't exclusive. There wasn't the hue and cry and discrimination. But there wasn't a single black worker in the plant. I didn't think of it then, but I have since."[15]

Black children also may have worked so rarely because black moth-

Table 5.6. Children at work, at home, and at school by nativity and race[a]

Father's group	1880 School (%)	1880 Work (%)	1880 Home (%)	1880 N	1900 School (%)	1900 Work (%)	1900 Home (%)	1900 N	1915 Work (%)	1915 N
NWNP	83.4	10.2	6.5	(650)	65.0	30.9	4.1	(194)	7.2	(277)
NWFP	61.7	28.6	9.8	(133)	53.2	44.5	2.3	(173)	13.3	(317)
FBW	56.0	39.2	4.8	(1,217)	39.6	58.0	2.4	(502)	21.2	(1,158)
Blacks	76.7	10.3	12.9	(232)	63.9	30.3	5.9	(119)	8.1	(271)
Low manual heads of household										
NWNP	71.7	19.7	8.7	(127)	60.5	37.2	2.3	(43)	12.2	(74)
NWFP	51.3	38.5	10.3	(39)	44.6	51.8	3.6	(83)	14.8	(135)
FBW	50.7	43.9	5.4	(663)	35.0	61.1	3.0	(234)	26.3	(555)
Blacks	78.0	10.7	11.3	(177)	65.0	29.9	5.2	(97)	7.2	(222)

Child labor rates by sex (all strata)

Male

	1880 (%)	1900 (%)	1915 (%)
NWNP	12.0	30.9	9.8
NWFP	36.3	44.5	17.5
FBW	41.3	58.0	20.7
Blacks	14.0	30.3	9.7

Female

	1880 (%)	1900 (%)	1915 (%)
NWNP	7.6	n.a.	4.9
NWFP	17.0		8.9
FBW	36.4		21.8
Blacks	7.2		6.6

[a] Includes children 11–16 years of age. See note a, Table 5.3.

ers worked more than white mothers. Black mothers, in turn, may have worked for other reasons than to replace child labor. Certainly black female labor-force participation, including that of mothers, was high in many circumstances, North and South, rural and urban, in the context of good and poor educational opportunities for children (even after controlling for factors such as the presence and income of the spouse). In addition, as Claudia Goldin noted in work on Philadelphia's black families in 1880, black mothers may have worked in order to provide their children an education. Alternatively, black mothers may have worked because their children had more trouble finding adequate jobs (work at wages comparable to those for white children, steady work, or indeed any work). Discrimination, in other words, may have affected children's and mothers' job opportunities in different ways, and hence the choice of whom to send to work would be made differently among blacks and whites. Goldin found that in homes in which the mother worked, sons were less likely to do so. On the other hand, the negative relationship between child's work and mother's work did not hold for daughters (daughters were actually more likely to work when their mothers did, perhaps because the mothers helped their daughters find employment). Consequently, Goldin restricted her suggestion that mothers worked in order to permit the child's education, limiting it to sons.[16]

Nevertheless, the relationship between mother's work and child labor in black families does not appear to have been a simple trade-off, a strong negative relationship between the two (Table 5.7, part A). The evidence from Providence raises doubts about Goldin's second suggestion, in particular – that mothers worked in order to send their sons to schools. In only one of the five Providence samples of blacks, the boys in 1915, was the child less likely to work if the mother worked. With many family background characteristics controlled, the pattern remains the same (Table 5.7, part B).[17]

Families probably could choose among several economic strategies, of which child labor and mother's labor were only two; consequently they were not mutually exclusive. However, these families may also have faced a range of constraints not captured by the factors controlled in the regressions; if we could control these, perhaps we would observe a clearer trade-off between the two strategies. In any event, there were very few white families in which a fourteen- or fifteen-year-old child did not work and a mother did, even among the poor; yet over a fifth of the black children grew up in such circumstances. Whatever its sources, and whatever its precise connection to child labor, the prevalence of mother's work must have increased the flexibility available to black families in dealing with child labor issues,

Table 5.7. *Working children and working mothers: black families only,
1880–1915*[a]

A. Proportion of sample members at work

	1880		1900		1915	
	%	N	%	N	%	N
All black children						
Mother works	19.7	(61)	44.2	(70)	8.6	(117)
Mother does not	11.8	(161)	27.2	(43)	9.0	(146)
Boys only						
Mother works	26.9	(26)	44.2	(70)	5.9	(51)
Mother does not	15.8	(76)	27.2	(43)	14.7	(77)
Girls only						
Mother works	14.3	(35)	n.a.		10.6	(66)
Mother does not	8.2	(85)			2.9	(69)

B. Odds ratios for child's work by mother's work, controls imposed[b]

	1880	1900	1915
Boys	9.87 (2.12)[c]	2.29 (1.54)[c]	0.50 (0.97)[c]
Girls	3.46 (1.08)		1.34 (1.42)

[a] Includes children 11–16 years of age. See also note *a*, Table 5.3.
[b] The odds that a child would work if the mother did not compared with the
odds that the child would work if the mother worked. Family characteristics
controlled include father's occupation, assessed value of family's property,
whether or not only child, eldest, youngest, total number of siblings, whether
or not both parents present, age of family head, whether or not father un-
employed, any parental illiteracy, whether or not head born in South, whether
or not sample member; for 1915, information on last three unavailable.
[c] *t* values.

particularly in a context of labor-market discrimination against black
youth.[18]

5.3. *School attendance and grade attainment*

Most children who were not at work were attending school. Although there were somewhat more black children than others at home
(particularly in 1880), the strikingly lower child labor rates were clearly
reflected in higher rates of school attendance (Table 5.6). The ages in
which group differences in school attendance were largest were the

critical teen years, when more and more students in every group left school for work. During these years, the proportion of blacks who remained in school was almost as great as that among the children of Yankees, and greater than that among the grandchildren or the children of immigrants. These findings are particularly striking when we recall the differences in social-class composition between the blacks and the Yankees (Table 5.3). The social-class contrast, of course, is not as strong when we compare blacks with immigrants; yet that contrast, too, is sharp enough, as observed earlier. Social-class factors should have impelled blacks to leave the schools first; that they did not again underscores the point that other social forces were at work: discrimination in the job market, and perhaps others as well.

The point is especially vivid if we reduce the impact of the class differences among groups by focusing only on the bottom part of the occupational distribution, only on the children of low manual workers (Table 5.6). Such a comparison actually eliminates less than a fifth of blacks, but it compares them with a far more similar group of whites. In both 1880 and 1900, the school attendance rates for black children from low manual origins were the highest in the city. Similarly, in 1915 the rate of black child labor was the lowest in the city, suggesting that if the figures for school attendance had been available from that census, they would again have shown black rates of school attendance to be highest.[19]

Rates of child labor and school attendance rates are complementary measures of what might be described as a critical but external perspective on schooling. The perspective is external in the sense that we do not know what leaving school at a relatively advanced age meant in terms of academic characteristics – for example, in terms of GPA, high school entry, or curriculum choice. We would certainly expect that age of school leaving should be related to at least some of these other dimensions of schooling, but it is difficult to say more than that without examining behavior within schools. In this respect, the Providence data are unique. Looking only at the "external" measure – at the rates of school attendance – Timothy Smith found levels of school attendance among black youth to be surprisingly high. On that basis he inferred that blacks' school achievement generally was high in the early part of the century. Only later, he concluded, as more and more blacks realized that schooling would not provide them the access to good jobs that it provided whites, did their attitude toward schools change, and with it their achievement.[20] A closer look at the nature of black schooling inside the system calls into question the assumption that an advanced age of school leaving indicates high academic achievement generally.

Consider, first, the grade level that blacks attained. The highest grade reached in school, one might say, is the internal counterpart to the external measure of age at leaving school. Both capture aspects of length of schooling, and we might expect that the two measures would tell much the same story. However, age and grade were not always closely related in the nineteenth and early twentieth centuries, as we have already observed in general (Section 1.4) and in connection with the Italians in particular (Section 4.2). For blacks, the loose relationship between age and grade was especially important.

Our best indicator of grade attainment is whether or not blacks entered high school, because high school entry involved not merely attainment of an additional grade over the preceding year, but a recognized change in the nature of the institution attended. It marks, in other words, an especially important branch point. The figures are decisive (Table 5.8). If blacks were almost as likely as Yankees to remain in school into the later teen years, and more likely to do so than the other groups in the city, they were much less likely than Yankees to reach high school in each of the census years, and also less likely to do so than the grandchildren of immigrants. In 1915 and 1925, the years in which appreciable proportions of children, including children from lower economic strata, began to enroll in high school, the blacks also trailed somewhat behind the children of the immigrants. True, the differences in enrollment rates between blacks and immigrants were not particularly large even in 1915, and in the earlier years the rates were about equal. What is striking here, however, is the contrast with the rates for school attendance and child labor. The leading position of the blacks in the former is not reflected in the latter. Black school attendance rates were like those of Yankees, but black high school entry rates were like those of immigrants.

Thus, high levels of black school attendance in the teen years were not translated into comparably high levels of secondary schooling. Black teenagers attending school, the figures suggest, must have been in relatively low grades given their ages.

There is important supporting evidence for Providence, as well as for other cities, in the reports of the U.S. Immigration Commission that pertain to 1908. Although those reports do not permit the intensive individual-level analysis that the Providence data allow, they do confirm the particular patterns of age and grade fit described here.[21] The proportions of children fourteen and fifteen years of age who remained in school were calculated (by gender) for Boston, New York, Chicago, and Philadelphia, as well as for Providence. These other cities included the three with the largest numbers of urban blacks in the North and the large metropolis nearest Providence. Of twenty

Table 5.8. *School attendance and high school enrollment rates compared by nativity and race*

Father's group	School attendance[a] (%)	High school enrollment (%)
1880		
NWNP	83.4	27.4
NWFP	61.7	15.9
FBW	56.0	3.5
Black	76.7	3.7
1900		
NWNP	65.0	36.2
NWFP	53.2	15.2
FBW	39.6	11.5
Black	63.9	12.3
	Child labor[b] (%)	High school enrollment (%)
1915		
NWNP	7.2	52.5
NWFP	13.3	45.3
FBW	21.2	29.4
Black	8.1	22.4
1925		
NW	n.a.	57.8
FBW	n.a.	46.1
Black	n.a.	30.7

[a] Includes children 11–16 years of age.
[b] The 1915 and Rhode Island State Censuses did not provide information on school attendance. The 1925 census also did not provide information on child labor.

comparisons, nineteen show blacks remaining in school in larger proportions than the children of immigrants, as was the case in our sample data (Table 5.9, part A). By contrast, in each of the five cities, fewer sons of black families reached high school than did sons of immigrants. Among the girls, the pattern was less clear: Only in one city did immigrants reach high school much more often than the blacks; in three of the other cities the rates were only 1 percentage point apart, and in one city the rate was a few points higher for blacks (Table 5.9, part B). The critical point, however, is that the substantial

Table 5.9. *Supporting data from another source:*[a] *comparison of blacks and children of immigrants*

A. Estimated percentages attending school at ages 14 and 15[b]

| | Male | | | | Female | | | |
| | Blacks | | Children of immigrants | | Blacks | | Children of immigrants | |
City	14	15	14	15	14	15	14	15
Boston	84	53	68	40	75	53	70	45
Chicago	63	48	72	35	83	60	65	31
New York	88	45	66	30	74	45	63	29
Philadelphia	63	26	47	23	66	43	42	20
Providence	78	69	51	22	71	36	50	28

B. Estimated percentages enrolling in high school[c]

| | Male | | Female | |
City	Blacks	Children of immigrants	Blacks	Children of immigrants
Boston	24.2	40.7	25.3	46.8
Chicago	15.2	19.6	30.5	22.0
New York	10.7	14.7	14.6	15.5
Philadelphia	7.3	17.0	13.4	13.1
Providence	12.5	17.4	23.8	22.5

[a]U.S. Immigration Commission, *Reports* (1911). See text and its notes.
[b]Enrollment at each age/enrollment at age 12.
[c]Enrollment in ninth grade at any age/school attendance at age 12.

differences in school attendance in the teen years did not yield comparable differences in high school enrollment rates for either sex in any of the five cities.[22]

The Immigration Commission's tables also allow us to see directly the crux of the matter, which the commission referred to as grade retardation. At a given age, the average black had completed fewer grades of school than the average child of the immigrants. All twenty of the possible comparisons show this clearly: comparisons for age fourteen and for age fifteen, for boys and for girls, in each of the five cities (Table 5.10). A decade after the Immigration Commission reported its findings, the Chicago Commission on Race Relations noted that "negro parents are frequently more interested in keeping their

Table 5.10. *Supporting data from another source:*[a] *median grade attained, children age 14–15 years in school*

City	Male Blacks 14	15	Children of immigrants 14	15	Female Blacks 14	15	Children of immigrants 14	15
Boston	7.96	8.29	8.31	9.19	7.25	7.86	8.39	9.24
Chicago	6.48	7.08	7.56	8.37	6.90	7.67	7.88	8.76
New York	5.96	7.05	7.37	8.33	6.38	6.48	7.58	8.50
Philadelphia	5.33	5.86	6.84	8.66	5.89	6.26	7.38	8.62
Providence	6.10	7.60	7.92	8.73	7.31	7.83	8.04	9.28

[a] See Table 5.9, note *a*.

over-age children in school than white parents, especially foreign parents, whose anxiety to have their children leave school as soon as they are old enough to get work-permits is well known."[23]

The reason blacks had completed fewer grades by a given age was not simply because some were migrants who had begun their education in inferior southern schools (entering low grades on arrival in the North). Such a pattern did exist, but at issue is the magnitude of its impact; there are good reasons to think that it was insufficient to create the differences between blacks and immigrants. One reason is that a comparable factor would have affected the immigrants: Many of these children came from abroad, without knowledge of English and without schooling comparable to that of the American schools – indeed, perhaps without any schooling. In Providence, as already noted, less than a fifth of the black children in 1880 and 1900 were born in the South, and a mere 5% in 1925, and the proportions of immigrants' children born abroad were quite comparable. Moreover, regression analyses to assess the determinants of high school enrollment or of school attendance in the Providence data, which are discussed later, show that taking the place of birth into account does not much alter the relative standings of the groups on either dimension of schooling.

Finally, the Immigration Commission *Reports* contain some additional data from which one can conclude that if comparisons had in fact been limited to blacks born in the North and to native-born children of immigrants, the differences in grade retardation would have been even more unfavorable to blacks.[24] In the years after the Great

Migration, the picture may have changed, at least in the cities to which large numbers of black families came. More of the grade retardation of blacks in that later period may have been due to the influx of southern migrant children. However, it is important to realize that grade retardation was pronounced well before that time, a fact that suggests that in later years, too, it was not due solely to the presence of migrants.[25]

The social-class positions of the black groups worked against their school progress as well, because getting the most, academically, from a year at school was surely easier for children from economically better-off homes, but, once again, in Providence it was possible to control for this and for many other background factors. With these controls imposed, the relative positions of blacks and other groups in regard to rates of school attendance remained starkly different from their relative positions in rates of high school entry.

Thus, in this broader context, the finding of Timothy Smith, that black levels of school attendance in the early years of the century were strikingly high, must be interpreted in a new light. Taken alone, this finding seems to indicate that black school achievement generally was high in those years, and certainly that grade attainment also was high. Juxtaposing school attendance and grade attainment reveals the grim reality that the length of stay was not translated into grade attainment as fully as for other groups.

A few of the immigrant groups (according to the Immigration Commission data, the Italians and the Poles, for example) also had very high levels of grade retardation, comparable to those of blacks. Still, even among these groups, the native-born probably fared a bit better than the blacks.[26] In any case, the school situation of these groups was not really comparable to that of blacks, for the children of Italians and Poles also tended to leave school earlier than did children in other ethnic groups. The black situation was unique: Their attendance rates were as high as those of the Yankees, but their grade retardation was comparable to that of groups whose educational patterns contemporaries considered to be an acute social problem.

These findings also bear on the evidence of educational attainments that Stanley Lieberson presented. Using the retrospective data in the 1960 U.S. Census, he found that among the cohorts in school during the early years of the century, the median grade attainment of northern-born blacks was as high as, or even slightly higher than, that of the native-born children of some immigrant groups from southern and eastern Europe (most notably the Italians and the Poles). That finding is roughly consistent with the present analysis,[27] but the medians do not capture the uniqueness of the black educational patterns. Indeed,

Table 5.11. *Students' grades: differences between white groups and blacks, low-manual strata only*

Group	1915		1925	
	No controls	Controlling social background[a]	No controls	Controlling social background[a]
GPA, sixth grade				
NWNP	0.41 (3.07)[b]	0.36 (2.64)[b]		
NWFP[c]	0.40 (3.66)	0.32 (2.88)	0.43 (3.71)[b]	0.26 (1.93)[b]
FBW	0.33 (3.79)	0.28 (3.00)	0.19 (1.98)	0.17 (1.66)
Effort grade, ninth grade				
NWNP	0.45 (2.53)	0.48 (2.63)		
NWFP	0.67 (4.63)	0.65 (4.37)	0.33 (2.09)	0.29 (1.60)
FBW	0.45 (4.01)	0.44 (3.54)	0.18 (1.33)	0.20 (1.38)
GPA, ninth grade				
NWNP	0.25 (1.27)	0.23 (1.10)		
NWFP	0.18 (0.99)	0.15 (0.83)	0.10 (0.54)	−0.03 (0.15)
FBW	0.32 (1.89)	0.33 (1.92)	0.28 (1.71)	0.21 (1.19)

[a] Gender (1915), birthplace, father's occupation, assessed value of family's property, whether or not broken family, number of siblings. See also note 29 to text.
[b] *t* values.
[c] Includes all children of native white fathers in 1925.

in all likelihood, among the cohorts Lieberson was analyzing, the rate of black school attendance probably was substantially higher in the early teenage years than was the rate among the second generation of immigrants. Consequently, the gap in median grade attainments probably would have been even larger than observed had not black grade retardation also been greater than grade retardation among those white ethnic groups.[28] The next section will confirm that despite low rates of child labor and high school attendance, the black experience within the schools certainly had not escaped the harsh social realities in which it was enmeshed.

5.4. GPA, integration, and tracking

The grammar school GPAs of blacks were considerably lower than those of each group of white students in the 1915 sample (Table 5.11). The comparisons presented here are restricted to the children of low manual workers and also include other controls for differences in family background that might be thought to help account for the race difference in GPAs. Despite these controls, the difference remains strong (on the order of one-half to one-third of a standard deviation of grades). In 1925, the differences were not quite as great, but clear nonetheless. In both years, an effort grade was also given, and race differences on this measure were similar to those on the GPA measure. The pattern of low black GPAs is visible in most comparisons of high school grades, too.[29]

The Providence schools in which these patterns of academic advancement and GPA were found contrasted starkly, of course, with southern schools of the period, which were organized on a racial basis by law. Nevertheless, until the Civil War era, Providence maintained separate "colored schools." Although these were abolished in the late 1860s, following black protests, residential concentration as well as districting decisions ensured that two schools remained largely segregated for some time thereafter. Just how many of the black pupils in the late nineteenth century enrolled in these two institutions, and how many were in predominantly white schools, is unclear. In any case, one of the two predominantly black schools closed in 1887, and the other apparently included a dwindling proportion of all black students by 1900.[30]

During the early decades of the twentieth century, the school system was more fully integrated, indeed, more fully than is typical in many cities of our own time, because blacks attended schools that enrolled a majority of white students – at least in the higher elementary grades and in the high schools. That this was so in the high schools, and always had been, is obvious after a moment's reflection. Blacks composed 2% of the school population; whatever the racial feelings may have been, a secondary school devoted exclusively to them was never a possibility. Although, as we shall see, during the later years they were heavily concentrated at one high school, they still composed but a small proportion of the student body there. Blacks were also spread reasonably widely across the grammar schools, at least in 1915–25, the years for which good data are available. True, nearly a quarter of the blacks in the 1915 sample were enrolled in one school, and a fifth in another, but even in these schools, barely one student in twenty was black. It is possible that greater racial segregation existed at the primary school level, because there were far more primary schools than grammar schools, and maintaining a predominantly black school would have been possible. We have no information either way on this point. Nevertheless, the available data make it clear that the last academic experience for most black children was in an integrated, predominantly white school.[31]

The numbers of black high school entrants were large enough in the 1915 and 1925 samples to permit some observations about the curricula in which they enrolled. In order to grasp the patterns of racial tracking, it is important to appreciate the history of the Technical High School. Technical High had begun as Manual Training High School. However, by 1915, it had, for a dozen years, featured extensive offerings in math and science (more extensive than those available at Classical High). It served both those bound for manual industrial work and those interested in engineering or other technical jobs in industry. During the late 1910s and the early 1920s, Tech lost any special academic monopoly (because Classical High then offered the science courses as well) and became simply a general-purpose high school, which offered many shop courses. The shift in academic programs that occurred during 1915–25 was accompanied by a shift in the social-class composition of the high schools, with greater tracking by social class in 1925. By then, Technical High School was more clearly identifiable as an institution for working-class children.[32]

This evolution is relevant to race differences in enrollment patterns. Because curriculum patterns differed sharply by gender, race differences must be examined by gender too. In 1915, the black male enrollment in the Technical High School seems to have been just what it was for the city's male entrants generally (Table 5.12). But by 1925, black male entrants were much more highly concentrated at Tech. A regression analysis shows that this concentration was largely unrelated to social background factors other than race. Moreover, although there may have been a tendency to send children with lower grammar school grades to Tech, and although blacks had lower grades, low grades were not the principal reason they ended up there. Controlling for academic performance does not explain much of the black concentration at Tech. In short, by 1925, when the Tech program had become clearly identified as the less academically elite and less socially elite program, and the one more likely to prepare students for manual work, black males were concentrated there.

Black girls were overwhelmingly concentrated at Tech by 1915, rather than in the commercial programs, as other girls were (Table 5.12). With clearly defined training programs for white-collar female work in place, black female entrants were concentrated instead in the Technical High School, studying cooking and sewing rather than typing and stenography.

There was no absolute exclusion of blacks from any program, no rule, spoken or unspoken, that worked with the effect of a legal barrier. However, the pattern of enrollment strongly suggests that race, not merely class, was essential in determining curricular enrollments.

Table 5.12. *Enrollment in high school tracks by nativity and race, 1915–25*

A.   Percentage of high school entrants enrolling at Technical High School

	1915		1925
	Male	Female	Male
Black	49.9	70.3	78.7
NWNP[a]	62.6	31.7	
NWFP[a]	46.1	18.2	41.8
FBW	46.1	19.1	42.3

B.   Odds ratios for enrollment at Technical H.S. by group[b]

	Social background controlled[c]	Sixth-grade GPA also controlled
1915: Girls		
NWNP	0.06 (2.25)[d]	0.05 (2.38)[d]
NWFP	0.11 (2.87)	0.10 (2.97)
FBW	0.11 (2.99)	0.09 (3.07)
1925: Boys		
NW	0.23 (2.49)	0.23 (2.45)
FBW	0.19 (3.45)	0.19 (3.39)

[a] See note *a* in Table 5.4.
[b] The odds of enrolling at Technical High School for each group compared with the odds for blacks (low-manual-worker strata only).
[c] Gender (1915), birthplace, father's occupation, assessed value of family's property, whether or not broken family, number of siblings.
[d] t values.

5.5.   *Explanations of race differences in schooling: class and family structure*

Any effort to interpret race differences in schooling must consider how they were rooted in family background. Family characteristics generally had important influences on patterns of schooling, and black and white families differed considerably in social class and family structure. Indeed, much of the preceding analysis acknowledged the importance of these influences by controlling such characteristics. Although family background characteristics certainly do not explain all of the race differences, they are important. But what aspects of family background were most influential in determining patterns of schooling – social class or family structure?

In addressing this question, we can focus on one aspect of schooling: high school entry. Whatever the mix of factors that produced black grade attainment (long attendance, lower GPA, and grade retardation), grade attainment itself remains an important school outcome, perhaps the single most important factor for such later experiences as getting a job. High school entry, as already noted, is our best measure of grade attainment; it is also the measure of schooling for which data are available for all four of the years sampled in the period 1880–1925. To what extent, then, did blacks' rates of high school entry differ from those of whites as a result of poverty? To what extent because many blacks came from single-parent families?

Black high school entry rates were as low as those of immigrants in 1880 and in 1900 and the lowest in the city in 1915 and in 1925. But if our attention is limited to the children of the low manual workers in all groups, black rates of secondary schooling were much more similar to those of other groups (Table 5.13). They exceeded or nearly equaled the rates of the children of immigrants in every period and the rates of the grandchildren of the immigrants in two of the three periods for which comparisons are possible. All in all, when attention is restricted to those near the bottom, black rates of high school entry were generally within the white range.

It might be objected that the children of the poor – white or black – rarely enrolled in high school, and it is for this reason that race differences among them were not larger. The objection has considerable force for 1880, when only one child in about twenty-five from such a background reached high school; it has less force in 1900, and still less in the later years. By 1915, more than one-fifth, and by 1925, more than two-fifths, of children from families headed by low manual workers reached high school. In sum, substantial proportions of children from such backgrounds did make it to high school by the later half of our period, and therefore black rates could have been well below those of white children in the lower strata. They were not.[33]

White low manual workers may well have been more prosperous than their black counterparts. Consequently, limiting attention to low manual workers is not an adequate control for poverty. We can control, in addition, for the household head's specific occupation within the low manual strata, as well as for the assessed value of the family's property (another measure of economic well-being). Doing so reduces still further the black–white gap in high school entry (Table

Table 5.13. *High school enrollment rates by race and nativity*

Father's group[a]	Proportion enrolling in high school		Odds ratios: white odds of enrolling compared with black			
				Only low manual		
	All strata (%)	Only low manual (%)	All strata[b]	No controls[b]	Controlling for economic standing[c]	All strata (controlling for family structure)[d]
1880						
Blacks	3.7	4.0				
NWNP	27.4	17.3	9.82	5.02	3.13 (2.25)[e]	9.26
NWFP	15.9	2.6	4.92	0.64	0.57 (1.10)	4.91
FBW	3.5	1.7	0.94	0.42	0.39 (0.51)	0.89
1900						
Blacks	12.3	11.3				
NWNP	36.2	20.9	4.05	2.07	0.90 (0.18)	3.49
NWFP	15.2	7.2	1.28	0.61	0.36 (1.78)	1.14
FBW	11.5	9.0	0.93	0.78	0.90 (0.24)	0.79
1915						
Blacks	22.4	22.1				
NWNP	52.5	32.4	3.83	1.69	1.28 (0.80)	2.95
NWFP	45.3	35.6	2.87	1.95	1.43 (1.42)	2.31
FBW	29.4	18.9	1.44	0.82	0.84 (0.89)	1.07
1925						
Blacks	30.7	31.1				
NW	57.8	40.0	3.09	1.48	1.33 (1.02)	2.56
FBW	46.1	35.9	1.93	1.24	1.12 (0.51)	1.59

[a]NWNP, native white of native parentage; NWFP, native white of foreign parentage; FBW, foreign-born white; NW, native white.
[b]The first two columns of odds ratios are based on the proportions in the two columns that precede them.
[c]Father's occupational score and assessed value of family's property controlled (as well as gender and birthplace). See also note 29 to text.
[d]Whether or not both parents present, and whether or not mother worked (as well as gender), controlled.
[e]t values.

5.13, fifth column).[34] After 1880, with these controls imposed, the odds that blacks would reach high school did not differ much from the odds that whites would do so. Moreover, in 1880, when the Yankee rate was much greater than that of the blacks, it was greater still, with these economic factors controlled, than the rate for the other white groups (the children and grandchildren of immigrants).

Thus, the black children were entering high school at a rate well within the white range of entry rates, when we take into account their poverty. The balance of longer attendance, on the one hand, and grade retardation, on the other, was a situation in which blacks, overall, did reach high school at a lower rate than whites, but not at a lower rate than whites in comparable economic circumstances.[35]

How much of the race difference in high school entry rates can be attributed to family structure? Perhaps, indeed, much of the impact attributed to black poverty is in fact a manifestation more directly of black family structure. Broken families were generally more prevalent among the poor, and female-headed households, in particular, were more likely than others to be poor, lacking income from a male head. Another aspect of family structure noted earlier, whether or not mothers worked, also deserves consideration in this context. The frequency with which black mothers were employed could lie behind the black–white gap in levels of secondary schooling. Whether that factor would correlate positively or negatively with high school enrollment is not clear. Stanley Lieberson, for example, suggests, from contemporary data, that working mothers have less time to concern themselves with their children's schooling than do mothers who are at home, thus reducing the parental support for school success. That argument was also voiced in the early years of this century. But a competing argument is common among historians who concentrate on issues of family economic strategies: A working mother freed the child from the need to work. This second argument has already been considered in detail (Section 5.2).[36] However, only the first hypothesis is directly relevant in the present context: Our concern is to identify factors that may have had a negative impact on enrollments. If mother's work, instead, had a positive effect, as the second hypothesis predicts, it is not one of the factors we seek. In fact, mother's work has little explanatory power once the number of parents present has been taken into account. Nevertheless, because its effect on secondary school enrollment was negative, it was included in the regressions.

Those regressions reveal, with striking consistency, that family structure does not explain why blacks reached high school in fewer numbers than whites. Controlling for family structure does reduce the size of the black–white gap, but not by much (Table 5.13, last column). Restricting the comparison to those whose fathers were low manual workers has a considerably greater impact (Table 5.13, fourth column). The dynamics that explain this result are straightforward: Membership in the low-manual strata had a greater influence on whether or not any child (black or white) would reach high school than did family structure, and the difference in the proportions of black and white children growing up in families in the low occupational strata was greater than the difference in the proportions growing up in broken homes.[37]

5.6. Explanations of race differences in schooling: discrimination and culture

Clearly, the patterns of schooling of black children were unique. Blacks stayed in school, and out of the job market, as long as the children of Yankees. When we take into account their poverty, they remained in school longer than any group in the city. When other dimensions of schooling are studied, the educational situation for blacks appears far less favorable. Levels of grade retardation among blacks were very high; black GPAs were low; patterns of tracking by race were strong, at least once the social meaning of the curriculum was established and blacks began to enter high school in substantial numbers. Levels of grade attainment among blacks reflected the advantage of longer schooling and the disadvantage of high rates of grade retardation, as well as disadvantages due to background characteristics. The balance of these factors was such that with family background taken into account, the black handicap in grade attainment largely disappeared. The most critical of these aspects of family background was social class: Blacks were overwhelmingly concentrated among the poor. Family structure exerted a much weaker influence on schooling.

With the exception of grade attainment, then, the educational patterns of blacks cannot be fully understood as the result of differences between black and white family backgrounds. Moreover, even grade attainment is more clearly understood in the context of rates of school attendance and grade retardation that cannot be fully explained by differences in family backgrounds.[38] Other sorts of explanations, then, must also be examined. The most obvious of these is discrimination against blacks, in several forms. The literature about blacks also includes discussions of cultural differences between them and others that might account for some differences in schooling. Because no one doubts that discrimination operated in a multitude of contexts, the issue is how much, if any, of an observed race difference should be attributed to cultural factors.[39]

Any pattern that seems to typify blacks more than whites can be related ultimately to the treatment of blacks by whites, to the history of racism, South and North. If, for example, blacks attended high school less than whites in the northern cities, it may have been because black families were generally poorer than whites. But that so many more of them were poorer, of course, may in turn be explained by referring to their history of slavery, migration, and discrimination. Nevertheless, it is valuable to consider the issue of discrimination and black education in a narrower way. Discrimination may not have been equally virulent in all domains of life. Northern public schools, though surely exhibiting discriminatory practices,[40] constituted a particular domain – one run for children, by the state, and conditioned by principles in special ways. In that sphere, discrimination may have operated less virulently than in such other domains as the job market or the housing market.[41] In what ways and to what extent do patterns of schooling suggest that race differences were operating directly on children's schooling?[42] That proportionately more blacks than whites lived in poverty, to return to the preceding example, can indeed be related to the history of slavery and discrimination in America. But were black patterns in schooling simply like those of other poor residents of the same city? Or, even acknowledging the impact that poverty had on blacks, were there ways in which black patterns of schooling were special? To the extent that such patterns were not special, the pattern of black schooling itself does not require attention to the dynamics of discrimination (or of cultural diversity) in order to explain it.

To the extent that distinctive black patterns of schooling cannot be understood by reference to social characteristics of blacks, such as poverty, racial discrimination in the schools no doubt played a role in determining them; but other factors may have been influential too. When the different behavior patterns of two white ethnic groups are compared, differences in their cultural norms often are invoked as part of the explanation. In the case of blacks, it is certainly reasonable to assume that discrimination played a far larger role than among whites, but it need not necessarily have been the only influence.

However, recourse to cultural explanations for black–white differences is problematic for several reasons. One strand of discussion concerns the black commitment to schooling. The freedmen's hunger for education after emancipation is often cited. Blacks flocked to the schools in order to learn to read, in part because that right had been denied them, and the learning confirmed their freedom, in part because they wanted to be able to read the Bible. Hunger for education for their children has also been seen as a prime motive behind the northward migration of blacks.[43] Reading of these aspirations and struggles, whether in primary sources or in the descriptions of historians, we cannot fail to be moved. But these texts also leave us wondering about the prevalence of the phenomenon: Just how many flocked to the schools, and how many stayed how long? Such questions are by no means unique to the case of the blacks; they are exactly the sort that should be troubling when we read descriptions of alleged cultural norms among white ethnic groups. However, the black case is special in other ways. In discussions about most other groups, there may be disagreement concerning the importance of cultural norms in influencing behavior, but the direction in which those norms operated, if they did have much impact, usually is clear. No one argues that southern Italian culture drove children disproportionately into the high schools, nor that Russian Jewish culture led children to leave school early for the mills. In the case of the blacks, there is much less agreement about cultural norms. Despite the claims about unusually strong black commitments to schooling cited in the preceding paragraph, arguments that black cultural norms worked to depress school attainment have often been advanced too. One such argument is the same as that noted for many immigrant groups: Black migrants to the northern cities came from rural areas, where schooling was less extensive and less important in preparing for the future than in the city, and where there was no special concern with book learning in general. Another variant stresses factors unique to the black experience: Slavery, and indeed a particularly repressive form of it, did not prepare blacks for self-advancement or for self-assertiveness and competition with whites. Finally, a third argument rests on the nature of conditions since emancipation: Blacks came to perceive that racial discrimination was too pervasive and too strong, even in the North, for educational credentials to matter much, and therefore came to value them less. In short, cultural explanations have been invoked to explain both higher and lower educational attainments of blacks compared with those of whites.[44]

Another difficulty arises in assessing the extent to which explanations based on cultural norms are relevant to black patterns of behavior. The usual strategy of analysis in the case of other groups (used and evaluated in earlier chapters) is to isolate a residual ethnic difference that other social background factors cannot explain. If that residual is large, cultural norms could be an important part of the explanation for the ethnic differences in behavior. The strategy is far from perfect, because the power of the norms is not measured directly. In the case of blacks, however, there is an additional problem: The residual ethnic factor usually can be attributed either to cultural norms or to discrimination, whereas differential discrimination is rarely likely to be the crucial factor operating in the case of two white ethnic groups. It is difficult to believe that Italian children dropped out of school before Russian Jewish children because American teachers were so much more prejudiced against them.[45]

The effects of discrimination were, of course, also complex. Discrimination in the schools could have discouraged black achievement and attendance. However, labor-market discrimination could have had various countervailing effects. Discrimination in the labor market for young people, for example, could have encouraged black school attendance.

Finally, it is, important to recall the prevalence of black working mothers (discussed in Section 5.2) in this context. If discrimination operated to discourage black children more than mothers from seeking work, or if black families had a special commitment to education, they may have accepted working mothers instead of child labor. Finally, even in the absence of these two conditions, a greater acceptance of employment for mothers among blacks than among others could have depressed black child labor rates and encouraged school attendance.

Clearly, then, the race differences in patterns of schooling could be understood to result from numerous possible combinations of factors: (1) labor-market discrimination, (2) discrimination in the schools, (3) black cultural supports for schooling, (4) black cultural impediments to schooling, and (5) the prevalence of working mothers.[46] There is no need to belabor the point; the problem is that firm evidence to help rule out some of the plausible hypotheses and confirm others is, alas, extraordinarily difficult to find.

Perhaps the simplest interpretation is that discrimination in the youth labor market drove rates of child labor down and school attendance up. The child labor and school attendance patterns could also have been encouraged by a greater acceptance of working mothers in black families. Another factor, a special commitment to schooling on the part of blacks, could have encouraged these patterns as well. At a minimum, it would not be surprising, in the light of the preceding analyses, if their commitment to schooling was greater than that of various immigrant groups, for example, the Italians. However, in the context of other influences on behavior, particularly discrimination in the youth labor market, that probably operated to create the same outcomes as did a special commitment to schooling, the Providence data cannot provide any firm demonstration of such a commitment. One kind of relevant evidence could be the high proportion of black working mothers – if the reason so many of them worked was to extend their children's education. However, the evidence that so many of them did indeed work for this reason was found to be very weak (Section 5.2).[47] Also, the formulation of the argument for a special commitment to schooling among blacks would have to explain their high rates of grade retardation and low GPAs (found even when family background characteristics were controlled), for example, by reference to discrimination within the schools. Finally, the opposing hypothesis, that black cultural patterns operated in some way to reduce school achievement, cannot be ruled out conclusively. However, some relevant evidence fails to support it. That evidence can be explored most effectively in the next section, by treating school and work outcomes together.

If discrimination in the youth labor market (and the prevalence of black working mothers) did drive up school attendance, it may have had other, less obvious but related influences on black grade retardation and GPAs. Other things being equal, academically unsuccessful students dropped out sooner. Yet if discrimination in the youth labor market (and black working mothers) operated as an impetus to keep children in school, then at each age and level of economic well-being, relatively fewer of the academically unsuccessful and less interested students among the blacks should have dropped out than among the whites. Thus, more of the black students remaining in school at each age would have been academically marginal students: students more likely to have had low GPAs and low effort grades and to have been grade-retarded.[48]

Labor-market discrimination, rather than discrimination within the schools, could also have been the source of racial tracking by curriculum in the high school. True, teachers (and later, also guidance counselors) with little respect for black abilities may have guided them to these programs as the "natural" place for the race. Nevertheless, these curriculum assignments may have resulted from the expectations of sympathetic school authorities, or of the black students themselves, concerning the job-market prospects. If offices would not hire a black secretary, preparing for secretarial work was pointless.[49]

Of course, the fact that responses to job discrimination could have contributed to all these results does not mean that it actually contributed much to any of them. Discrimination in the schools and perhaps cultural differences could have been far more important.[50] It is striking, however, just how many features of black schooling could have been touched by youth labor-market discrimination.

We may conclude by considering how rarely contemporaries themselves must have tried to identify and weigh the sources of race differences in schooling. The various subtle explanations for those race differences – family background, various forms of discrimination, or cultural patterns – were surely less glaring than the simple fact that white and black school achievements differed, with the latter in many respects lower. To the extent that the complex social dynamics led to that simple reality in schools, beliefs about inherently low intellectual ability among blacks must have seemed confirmed.[51] Indeed, if the responses to job discrimination did operate in the subtle ways just suggested, that confirmation of racist beliefs was one of the most damaging consequences.

5.7. Black occupational attainment

Race differences in the jobs held by the young men in Providence were large, and devastatingly consistent, over the course of half a century. Somewhat smaller proportions of blacks than whites were to be found in the city directories, the sources indicating their occupations when they were twenty-two to twenty-six years of age. Perhaps more blacks had left town; perhaps the directory covered blacks less well than others. Whereas 46–52% of all male sample members in each of the four periods were found, only 35–40% of the blacks were. Moreover, the numbers of black sample members were not high to begin with; those for whom job information is available compose an especially small group (see Appendix Section 5). Nevertheless, the race differences are glaring.

As Table 5.14 shows, in each of the four samples the mean level of black occupations was at least 10 points below the lowest mean for white groups. In 1880, 76% of young black men worked in low manual occupations, in 1900, 68%, in 1915, 72%, and in 1925, 79%. Correspondingly small proportions managed to obtain white-collar work. Indeed, even those who had enrolled in high school were unlikely to receive such jobs. The experience of men from the two later samples is especially clear in this regard, for notable proportions of those black men had obtained some secondary schooling. Among those who had, 18% reached white-collar work in 1915, and 11% in 1925. The comparable proportions for high school entrants citywide were 68% and 60%.

Controlling for the family background of individuals naturally reduces the race differences in jobs somewhat (Table 5.14). Blacks, after all, were raised in some of the city's poorest families. Nevertheless, the size of the residual difference is enormous. Moreover, when educational attainment is controlled as well, the differences generally are not reduced at all, because, as we have seen, blacks were as likely as whites of comparable family backgrounds to attend high school.

Table 5.14. *Race differences in occupational attainment, males, 1890–1935*[a]

			Differences in means: each group compared with blacks				
				Controlling for[b] family background			
					And length of schooling		
Father's group	Means	N	No controls	Only	All strata	Low manual	And GPA (all strata)
1880 sample							
Blacks	16.1	(35)					
NWNP	40.8	(249)	24.7	17.5	17.6	14.3	c
NWFP	31.2	(37)	15.1	11.3	11.2	14.6	
FBW	28.7	(307)	12.6	13.0	13.8	13.9	
1900 sample							
Blacks	20.8	(46)					
NWNP	40.2	(163)	19.4	14.4	15.1	14.6	c
NWFP	34.0	(125)	13.2	10.5	11.9	12.8	
FBW	31.5	(280)	10.7	9.7	10.7	7.4[&]	
1915 sample							
Blacks	16.5	(46)					
NWNP	35.0	(77)	18.5	11.3	10.4	9.4	10.2
NWFP	36.5	(109)	20.0	15.1	14.4	15.8	14.2
FBW	33.6	(797)	17.1	14.5	14.1	15.4[&]	13.8
1925 sample							
Blacks	17.8	(60)					
NW	34.7	(158)	16.9	8.4	9.3	5.6[#]	9.4
FBW	30.7	(342)	12.9	8.7	10.1	8.3	10.3

Note: All race differences are statistically significant ($t > 1.96$) unless otherwise indicated: #, $1.50 < t < 1.96$; &, $1.10 < t < 1.49$.

[a]Male sample members' occupational attainment a decade after the census year. Based on a numeric score for each occupational title (the Duncan score). Available only for those sample members who remained in the Providence area ten years after the year of the census from which they were selected (e.g., until 1890 for 1880 sample members). The standard deviation of the occupational scores was 17.9–19.3 in each of the four periods. The differences in means are coefficients on ethnic dummy variables in OLS regressions. Supplemental samples of ethnic groups and of high school entrants are included in the regressions. In the regression analyses for 1880–1915, these samples were weighted to reflect their true relative magnitudes. The effect of including the supplemental sample of blacks from 1925, the only supplemental sample from that year, was controlled by the ethnic variables in the regres-

It also appears that blacks derived less advantage than whites if they did enroll in high school (as the rates of white-collar employment for high school entrants, mentioned earlier, suggest). In 1915 and 1925, the jobs of white high school entrants averaged roughly 10 points above those of white non-entrants. Although the sample sizes were too small to draw conclusions with much confidence, the advantages of high school entrants over nonentrants were uniformly smaller among blacks than among whites, and possibly negligible. The handful of black college entrants seem to have fared better than other blacks. They offer the only hint that at the very highest levels, the advantages of education may have been considerable for blacks as well as whites.[52]

Whatever the subtleties of the race differences, the most basic point emerges clearly: The great race difference in occupational advancement cannot be attributed to blacks' low social-class origins, nor to the proportion of broken homes among them, nor, finally, to their educational attainment. By far the largest part of the race difference in every one of the eleven comparisons in Table 5.14 remains unexplained by all these factors taken together.

Some of the race difference in occupational advancement could still have been related to educational patterns, but related in a way that eludes the controls for length of schooling. In particular, perhaps the quality of their schooling was poorer, independent of the length of time they remained in school. A number of scholars, particularly economists, have explored this issue in another context.[53] They have sought to understand how much of the race difference in American incomes is related to schooling, and how significantly changes in schooling have actually affected the income differential. They have wondered not only about the importance of the length of schooling but also about the quality of schooling. Blacks, nationally, have gained on whites in length of schooling throughout most or all of the period since emancipation. They may have gained in the quality of their schooling as well. In particular, the black schools in the southern segregated systems operated with smaller budgets, and as a conse-

Table 5.14 (Cont.)
sion model. The N's reported are for actual sample size. N's for the column "Low manual" are lower. See also note 29 to the text.
[b]Family background controls include birthplace, father's occupation, family property value, number of siblings, whether or not both parents present. Length of schooling is coded no high school, some, graduation, or (1925 only) college entry. GPA refers to sixth-grade academic grades in courses.
[c]Available for 1915 and 1925 only.

quence, they operated for less time each year and with less well-trained teachers, more pupils per teacher, and so forth. If the quality of education obtained in such schools was lower than that in the schools that whites attended, blacks who completed as many years of schooling as whites still suffered an educational handicap. Measures of length of schooling would not adequately capture differences in human capital gained by the races through education. Consequently, the changing returns to black schooling over time may reflect gradual improvements in the quality of black schooling, not merely the decline in employer discrimination. Direct measures of school quality are generally unavailable, and indeed most of the research has not tried to estimate its effect on labor-market outcomes directly. Rather, scholars have concentrated on the evidence that black schools were of lower quality and on the long-run changes in black–white income differences that school quality might explain.

The specific results of such studies are not directly relevant to our purposes here, for several reasons. Such work has had a national focus, and so the trends for our period have been overwhelmingly determined by the fate of blacks living in the South. Moreover, the separate and unequal school systems of the South were the chief focus of the argument for differences in school quality. In any case, most of the gain in black income, relative to white, that those studies sought to explain came after our period (the black–white income ratio was 0.44 in 1890 and 0.49 in 1930).[54] Nevertheless, the fundamental issue raised by those studies is of great interest here: Were employers simply choosing better-educated individuals, rather than discriminating against blacks? The Providence schools of 1880–1925 present a picture very different from that of the southern schools, organized on a racial basis by law. Blacks in Providence attended racially integrated schools, at least at the grammar school and high school levels (Section 5.4), and hence schools of the same quality as those whites attended.

On the other hand, the preceding analysis has shown that blacks, on average, achieved lower GPAs than did whites (Section 5.4). Consequently, this race difference in academic performance may indicate that blacks obtained less sturdy skills from schooling than did whites, even when they had completed the same number of grades in the same schools. Was this the reason employers favored whites?

The Providence data allow us to test this hypothesis directly. If employers selected by school skills, those who had received relatively poorer grades should have received poorer jobs. That blacks and whites attended the same grammar schools makes it all the more meaningful to consider the sixth-grade GPAs. The same teachers were judging the work of both.

It may seem strange to argue that such an early indicator as sixth-grade GPA, our best measure of grades, would be related to "human capital" as judged by employers. However, it should be recalled that most children, particularly those of low social-class origins, would have been at work by age sixteen or seventeen. These grades, then, provide a relatively current measure of the school-related skills of these young men. We know, too, that GPA did indeed measure something related to academic outcomes quite well, because it was a powerful predictor of high school enrollment.[55]

The association between boys' course grades and their later jobs offers no support to the idea that employers were discriminating on the basis of educational quality. Specifically, controlling for the sixth-grade GPA (or for children's effort grades) had no effect on the sizes of the race differences in occupations (Table 5.14, last column). True, the average child's academic performance had some relation to his later occupation, because it helped determine how long he would stay in school, and length of schooling, in turn, was strongly related to later jobs. But once the length of schooling has been taken into account, the association between grades and jobs is reduced to trivial levels.[56]

Because the net association between GPA and jobs was trivial, even blacks who received higher grades than whites could expect no diminution of the race handicap in jobs. A majority of blacks had sixth-grade GPAs over 1.83 (a C− average); roughly a quarter of all whites had GPAs that were lower than that. How did these blacks and whites – all of the former having higher grades than any of the latter – fare in the job market? The occupational differences between them in both 1915 and 1925 were as great as those separating all blacks from all whites (Table 5.15, part A).[57]

Thus, black grades were lower than white grades, and blacks received lower-level jobs than whites, but there was very little in the way of a causal relationship between the two social patterns. Consequently, in the Providence data, we can find no support for the idea that the quality of black schooling, over and above length of schooling, can account for any part of the race difference in occupational advancement.

Thus far, the differences in black family background and schooling have been considered as possible sources of the race difference in occupational attainment. Blacks may also have been handicapped by the contextual effects of living in a very poor ethnic community. Contacts for jobs, information of every type, and peer culture may all have worked to reduce black occupational attainment, even when an individual's family background and school attainment favored ad-

Table 5.15. *Race differences in occupational attainment, selected subgroups, 1925–1935*

A. Men classified by GPA

| | | Blacks with higher GPAs (>1.83) compared with whites with lower GPAs (≤1.83) | | | |
| | | | | Differences in means: each group compared with blacks | |
Father's group	All[a] (means)	Means	N	No controls	With controls[b]
1915 sample					
Blacks	15.5	15.9	(16)		
NWNP	38.8	33.6	(14)	17.7	12.4 (1.34)[c]
NWFP	38.5	38.5	(9)	22.6	18.2 (1.93)
FBW	35.3	32.7	(115)	16.8	16.5 (1.89)
1925 sample					
Blacks	17.5	15.0	(37)		
NW	35.4	30.7	(19)	15.8	15.1 (3.02)
FBW	31.1	28.1	(57)	13.1	18.2 (4.59)

B. Whites compared with blacks from families long resident in the North

| Father's group | Differences in means: each group compared with blacks (with controls[b]) | | | |
	1880 sample	1900 sample	1925 sample	All 3 samples[d]
NWNP	19.4 (2.81)[c]	9.9 (1.55)[c]		
NWFP	13.0 (1.78)	6.4 (0.98)	8.8 (2.52)[c]	12.4 (3.26)[c]
FBW	15.5 (2.26)	4.8 (0.75)	9.7 (2.90)	10.8 (2.83)

[a]These means differ from those in the first column of Table 5.14 because they exclude those for whom no GPA information was available and can thus be compared to figures in the second column. With controls, the differences from black means, which can be compared to figures in the fifth column, were NWNP 15.6, NWFP 17.2, FBW 15.5 in 1915 and NW 10.4, FBW 11.3 in 1925.

[b]Controls for family background and length of schooling. See Table 5.14, notes a and b.

[c]t values.

[d]Controlling for sample year. When all blacks (not merely those long resident in the North) are compared with whites in this way, the resulting differences are NW 13.0 (4.55) and FBW 11.3 (4.02).

vancement. Once again, the question is how large such contextual effects may have been. An effort to measure such effects was described in detail in the chapter on the Italians. Such an effort involves measuring that impact by assessing the relation between the mean occupational score of fathers (or other household head) in each ethnic group and the occupational scores of their sons, with other family background variables controlled. The dangers of spurious correlation make the procedure risky, but at least it offers some hints, and it is helpful in ruling out factors that are not strongly correlated. In thinking about the contextual effects of class origin on blacks, it is especially revealing to compare them with the children of the immigrants, for the differences in class origin, though still striking, were less than they were between blacks and other whites. The procedure for measuring contextual effects just described does indeed suggest that there was some relationship between context and jobs for blacks, but that association can account for no more than 1–2 points of the differences between blacks and the children of immigrants – differences that amounted to more than 10 points in every period.[58] The vast majority of that difference, then, remains unaccounted for by the contextual effects of class, as well as by the other characteristics we have considered.

Finally, then, we are left with a huge race difference in occupational attainments that cannot be explained by any of the factors we have considered: class origins, education, and contextual effects. In the case of white ethnic groups, the discovery of a substantial residual has led us to consider seriously various cultural attributes that could explain the group's distinctive school or work behavior. In the case of the blacks, racial discrimination commands our attention first. As to just how discrimination operated, we cannot determine much from the Providence data. Only on one point do these data offer any hints. Historians have noted that quite apart from employer behavior, blacks may have encountered great difficulty in entering skilled work as a result of labor's behavior in controlling the apprenticeships required for that work. Perhaps so; however, such training programs would have been much less relevant to white-collar work. Yet, as noted earlier, black high school entrants were drastically less likely to obtain white-collar jobs than were white high school entrants (18% versus 68% in 1915, 11% versus 60% in 1925), suggesting the importance of employer behavior rather than discriminatory unions in this instance. We cannot probe the actual concerns, goals, and behaviors of employers – such as simple dislike, thought processes that entailed generalizing from blacks with certain characteristics (such as poor jobrelated skills) to all blacks, and concerns about the attitudes of customers and white employees toward blacks.[59]

Was an important part of the unexplained race difference in occupations due to cultural attributes as well? There has been a great deal of heated debate on this issue. The arguments stressing dysfunctional cultural attributes were mentioned in the preceding section: rural origins (similar to those of European peasants), slavery's legacy, and responses to discriminatory behavior ("feedback" mechanisms). It is only fair to say at once that the Providence data cannot provide conclusive evidence to show either that cultural patterns were insignificant or that they played an important role in creating black occupational patterns. Nevertheless, several considerations suggest treating arguments that stress cultural attributes with much skepticism, particularly if those arguments minimize or dismiss the importance of discrimination.

One piece of evidence might, at first sight, seem to confirm the hypothesis that cultural attributes, and particularly a work ethic, were operating. The grades of blacks were lower than those of whites, and black occupational attainment was lower. The work ethic could be relevant to both. However, quite apart from the fact that discrimination alone could also have caused both, it should be recalled that in fact there was little connection between grades and later outcomes and that, indeed, whites with low GPAs differed occupationally from blacks with higher GPAs by as much as all blacks and whites (Table 5.15, part A). If a work ethic played a large role in determining both grades and job outcomes, the magnitude of the black handicap should have been substantially lower in this instance.

We can also attempt to test the version of the cultural hypothesis that stresses the pre-migration cultural heritage, particularly the legacy of slavery.[60] Consider the attainments of blacks whose families had lived in the North for a long time. If southern rural life, and slavery in particular, left an important negative cultural heritage that in turn affected attainments, children of more recent migrants should have suffered greater losses than children of families long resident in the North, who would have been influenced by other cultural constellations.

The Providence data provide relevant information in the 1880, 1900, and 1925 samples. In the first two, we can isolate those resident in the North for at least three generations (the sample members' grandfathers were northern-born). In all likelihood, then, the relevant black families had lived in the North for at least sixty years: since 1820 for the first sample, since 1840 for the second.[61] For the 1925 sample, we can at least isolate those families resident in the North for two generations (the sample members' fathers or, if fathers were absent, their mothers were northern-born). Did such individuals enjoy a more favorable record of attainment, compared with whites? They did not (Table 5.15, part B). The samples are very small (fifteen to twenty-five cases in each period), and numbers can be expected to fluctuate considerably. The race handicap in attainments does appear substantially lower for one of the three years (1900), but such a result is not unexpected when the samples are so small. For two of the three years, the remaining race differences are huge. Moreover, results from the three years can be combined (while controlling for sample years), thus conserving sample size. When that procedure is followed, the results indicate clearly that the family's length of residence in the North was irrelevant to occupational advancement for young black men. Once again, a pattern that probably would have existed if differences in cultural attributes had been influential is not found. Similarly, the Providence data indicate that among northern-born blacks, those whose parents had been born in the South did not obtain less schooling than those whose parents had been born in the North.[62]

We might also consider how large a difference in outcomes can conceivably be attributed to such cultural attributes. The other major example of an ethnic occupational disadvantage that we encountered involved the Irish in 1880 and 1900. Even after family background and schooling were controlled, Irish occupations averaged 6.4 points less than those of Yankees in 1880, and 7.2 points less in 1900. Those differences, in part, may have been related to cultural differences – the "fatalism" of the Irish, which many historians have stressed. But whereas Irish occupations averaged 6–7 points less than those of Yankees, black occupations averaged a staggering 11.4 points less than those of the Irish in 1880, and 8.4 points less in 1900. Just how great a cultural legacy could slavery have been? The Irish themselves are often thought to have suffered under a disadvantageous cultural legacy whose origins (in the political oppression and grinding poverty of Ireland) and character ("fatalism") were somewhat similar in nature to the putative cultural legacy of black slavery. Perhaps one would argue that the cultural legacy of slavery was more crippling. But how much more?[63]

Another version of the cultural hypothesis, already mentioned in connection with school patterns, stresses experiences in the North rather than the effects of slavery. According to this theory, discriminatory conditions produced attitudes and behaviors among blacks that were rooted in a hopelessness of producing any improvement in their lives. These attitudes and behaviors, in turn, were themselves sources of low achievement. Feedback theories usually are conceived in terms of the contemporary ghettos, or of the Depression years and after. However, in order to explain the huge race differences in attainment, such feedback would have had to operate as strongly in the northern black communities of 1880, for the race differences were as large in the 1880 sample as in the 1925 sample. Indeed, the job profile of the black parents in that year suggests that what needs to be explained was already in place much earlier still.[64]

As Robert Higgs has observed, the issue is the magnitude of feedback influences. This form of the cultural hypothesis lends itself still less than the pre-migration heritage hypothesis to investigation with the sort of data at hand. Nevertheless, the finding that the low black GPAs coupled with low occupational attainments do not demonstrate the influence of cultural attributes is, of course, relevant also to this variant of the cultural hypothesis. Moreover, we should recall that the very reason for a feedback loop is that it involves feedback from discrimination. Just how weak could the force of discrimination have been if the feedback was so strong?[65]

The black handicap was uniquely large throughout the half century covered by the Providence data. We have sought evidence that might test the theory that black cultural attributes played an important role in creating this handicap – evidence indicating the influence of such attributes that would not as easily be explained by discrimination. To repeat, no such evidence has been found. However, even if some part of that race handicap was nevertheless due to cultural attributes, it would still strain credibility not to conclude that racial discrimination in the job market was extraordinarily powerful and destructive.

Conclusion

We can now return to the interpretive challenge posed in the Introduction – understanding the sources of ethnic differences – by considering at once the school and work experiences of the four ethnic groups we have studied in detail. Many early efforts to grapple with the sources of ethnic differences appealed to biological explanations. Later efforts stressed how different cultures encouraged different beliefs, attitudes, and values. Much recent work has concentrated on "structural" or "compositional" explanations – on the extent to which a group's location in the American social structure explains its differences from others. These structural explanations focus on a group's social-class composition and may also include typical family size and structure, educational attainments, geographic concentration, and the like.[1]

An emphasis on structural location need not, of course, preclude attention to other factors, such as pre-migration cultural attributes or discrimination against a group. These sources of behavior may all interact, of course (as sociologist Stephen Steinberg and social historian John Bodnar have stressed). Nevertheless, current discussions that stress structural location typically minimize the independent roles played by other sources of ethnic behavior (except racial discrimination against blacks). One reason they do so is no doubt the intellectual context of their work – the need to counteract both the earlier emphasis on cultural attributes and the persistent strength of ethnic stereotypes in popular thinking.[2] There results a natural, and often healthy, tendency to wonder if ethnic differences in behavior deserve attention at all, or if they merely reflect other major social divisions, particularly social-class divisions (for example, to speculate that Italian children's distinctive patterns of schooling simply reflected the social-class composition of the Italian immigrants).

Our findings about the school and job experiences of the second generation in Providence bear on these interpretations. The social positions of their parents – immigrants and black migrants in the cities of the northern United States – surely owed much to the conditions of migration and to pre-migration characteristics, such as job skills.[3] However, once the migrants' structural locations had been deter-

203

mined, did a group's advancement in American society largely derive from that location? In particular, can the experiences of the second generation be adequately explained by reference to their social-class origins and to other structural characteristics of their families?

In virtually every comparison across groups, social-class origins and family structure played an important role in creating ethnic differences in schooling and work, and similarly, length of schooling was itself an important determinant of jobs.* In some important cases, these background characteristics (social-class origins, family structure, and in connection with jobs, length of schooling) fully explained why ethnic groups differed in the observed outcomes. However, in some other important cases, these explanatory factors left large unexplained ethnic differences in school or work outcomes. Pre-migration cultural attributes of a group, or discrimination against it, can help account for those ethnic differences.

The ethnic differences remaining after other factors had been taken into account bear on a very large theme, the relationship between class and ethnicity in American history – for they bear on the nature of ethnic distinctiveness: distinctiveness in schooling and job attainments, behaviors central to social and economic life. They suggest that whereas some patterns of apparent ethnic distinctiveness merely reflect the social-class composition of the ethnic group, or other structural characteristics, an impressive number of ethnic patterns cannot be explained adequately in these terms. Insofar as they cannot, ethnicity is not a redundant category of explanation. Rather, to that extent, the distinctive ethnic patterns operating within and on the class structure were not merely derivative of it, and their distinctiveness was not barely noticeable, but of considerable importance.[5] That the distinctive ethnic elements interacted with and were reinforced by class divisions made them still more salient to contemporaries and to the student of American history. The following pages ground these observations in our findings concerning the Irish, Italians, Russian Jews, and blacks of Providence.

Family background characteristics and schooling.   Tables C.1 and C.2 provide a synthesis of relevant data drawn from the preceding chapters. Table C.1 concerns ethnic differences in high school entry rates, before and after controls for family background characteristics have been imposed. Other dimensions of schooling were also studied

---

* We did not usually evaluate the individual contribution of social class and family structure, but when we did (particularly in the case of the blacks), social-class influences were clearly the more important ones.[4]

in the preceding chapters, of course, but including them here would add little. Table C.2 concerns ethnic differences in job attainment, before and after controls for both family background characteristics and length of schooling have been imposed. These tables are arranged differently from the tables presented in the preceding chapters: Tables C.1 and C.2 do not include all of the groups we have studied in each period, but only the groups whose patterns of schooling or occupational attainment were clearly distinctive even after controls were imposed.

The family background characteristics we regularly took into account included the father's occupation, the assessed value of the family's property, whether or not both parents were present, and the number of siblings. On occasion, we supplemented these with other economic and demographic indicators of family origins (for example, whether or not the father was an employer or parents were literate). These family background characteristics accounted for all, or nearly all, of the differences in high school entry rates between Irish and Yankees after 1880 and between blacks and whites in all periods.*

At the same time, each of the four groups also exhibited patterns of schooling that could not be explained by family background characteristics (see Table C.1). High school entry rates were lower among the Irish of 1880, lower among the Italians and higher among the Russian Jews than among other relevant groups. Black high school entry rates, admittedly, differed little from those for whites once family background characteristics were controlled, but the social dynamics creating these rates were complex and actually involved more than family background characteristics. In any case, race differences in two other measures of schooling could not be wiped out by controlling family background characteristics – those in GPAs and in high school curriculum choice.

Family background characteristics, schooling, and job attainments. Family background characteristics also had a substantial part in creating ethnic differences in job attainments. Patterns of schooling contributed to these differences as well. We found, first, that extended schooling provided individuals with a strong advantage in job attainments as early as 1880 (Section 1.5). Consequently, the ethnic differences in length of schooling enhanced the advantage of the Yankees

---

* As we saw in the preceding chapter, many factors may have affected the black high school entry pattern. However, the relevant point here is that a substantial black–white gap was observed before family background characteristics were controlled, and it was wiped out by the controls.

Table C.1. *Selected ethnic and social-class differences in high school entry rates, 1880–1925*

Gender	Father's group	1880 Rate (%)	1880 Odds ratio[b] No controls	1880 Controls	1915[a] Rate (%)	1915 Odds ratio No controls	1915 Controls	1925 Rate (%)	1925 Odds ratio No controls	1925 Controls
Male	Yankee[c]	23.0								
	Irish[d]	4.9	5.8	1.8						
Female	Yankee	33.2								
	Irish[d]	8.3	5.5	2.8						
Male	Italian				17.2			33.0		
	All other				39.6	3.17	1.76[e]	60.7	3.14	2.37
Female	Italian				8.7					
	All other				44.1	8.28	4.89[e]			
Male	Russian Jew				54.3			69.4		
	All other				36.1	2.08	1.85	51.7	2.13	1.79
Female	Russian Jew				47.5					
	All other				39.1	1.41	1.41			
Both	White-collar	31.0			53.8			70.9		
	Blue-collar	6.1	6.92		27.7	3.04		46.4	2.81	
	Occupational scale: 1 SD difference[f]		2.56			1.85			1.76	

[a]Limited to native-born children in 1915.

[b]The ratio of the odds of high school entry in the two groups (ratio of higher to lower odds in each case). Controls: odds ratio controlling father's occupational score, family property value, number of siblings, and whether or not both parents present.

[c]Yankees are defined as native whites of native parentage.

[d]Because of missing Catholic high school records in 1880, these rates and ratios are estimated (see Chapter 2 and the Appendix for details; midpoint of range used as estimate here). School attendance rates of 13–16-year-old children (no estimation required) were as follows:

Male:	Yankee	79.1%		
	Irish	42.1	5.20	3.52
Female:	Yankee	73.9		
	Irish	41.4	4.01	2.54
Both:	White-collar	76.5		
	Blue-collar	45.6	3.88	
On occupational scale: 1 SD difference			2.26	

[e]Head's citizenship status also controlled. With only the other controls imposed, the ratio for boys was 2.33, and for girls, 6.24.

[f]The increase in the odds of high school enrollment associated with an increase of one standard deviation in father's occupational score.

as a group over the Irish in 1880 and the advantage of the Russian Jews over all others; they also created disadvantages for the Italians, compared with all others. The magnitude of the occupational advantages or disadvantages created for ethnic groups by their school patterns may seem relatively small. For example, we noted that high school entry created an advantage of roughly 10 points on the occupational scale for the average individual, and roughly 20% fewer Italians than others received such an education (after family background characteristics were controlled) (Section 3.3). The distinctive educational pattern, then, reduced the group's mean occupational score by only 2 points ($0.2 \times 10 = 2$). Nevertheless, a substantial minority of the group (20%) lost a substantial amount (a 10-point advantage).

The implications of extended schooling for jobs were different for blacks. Their occupational disadvantage was not due to any lack of extended schooling among them, for blacks were as likely as whites to obtain that schooling (once family background characteristics were controlled). The data also suggest that although the occupational advantage an individual obtained from extended schooling did not vary much among white groups, it was lower for blacks (Section 5.7).

The dynamics of family background characteristics, length of schooling, and ethnicity in influencing job attainments were presented in preceding chapters. By contrast, Table C.2 is restricted to a presentation of ethnic differences in jobs when both family background characteristics and length of schooling are controlled. With the controls imposed, some ethnic differences in job attainments disappear entirely (and are therefore excluded from the table) – those involving the Irish in the later years and the Italians. However, the Irish in the early years and the blacks in every period suffered substantial occupational disadvantages that these controls do not explain; the Russian Jews enjoyed a substantial advantage.

The magnitude of the residual ethnic differences.   The portion of the entire ethnic difference in schooling (Table C.1) or in occupational attainment (Table C.2) that remained unexplained even after the controls were imposed we have called the residual. As just discussed, some of the residuals were of trivial magnitude, but the residual ethnic differences presented in Tables C.1 and C.2 were generally at least as large as, and often much larger than, the portions of the ethnic differences that could be accounted for by the controls.

Just how large were these residual ethnic differences in schooling and jobs? The question immediately suggests comparisons: How large were other differences in schooling and jobs among social groups? Tables C.1 and C.2 address this issue by comparing the magnitudes of ethnic and social-class differences in schooling and jobs. As al-

Table C.2. *Selected ethnic and social-class differences in mean occupational scores, men, 1890–1935*

Father's group	1880 sample			1900 sample			1915 sample			1925 sample		
		Difference			Difference			Difference			Difference	
	Mean	No controls	Controls[a]	Mean	No controls	Controls	Mean	No controls	Controls	Mean	No controls	Controls
Yankee[b]	40.8			40.2								
Irish	26.2	14.6	6.4	28.8	11.4	7.2						
FBW	28.7			31.5			33.6			30.7		
Blacks	16.1	12.6	13.8	20.8	10.7	10.7	16.5	17.1	14.1	17.8	12.9	10.1
Russian Jew[c]							45.5			41.2		
All other							33.0	12.5	8.7	31.1	10.1	5.4
White-collar	41.4			38.8			39.2			39.9		
Blue-collar	29.4	12.0		31.7	7.1		31.7	7.5		29.0	10.9	
Occupational scale: 1 SD difference[d]		7.4			5.0			5.4			6.6	

[a]Controls include family background characteristics (father's occupational score, family's property value, number of siblings, and whether or not both parents present in census year) and length of schooling (no high school, some, graduate; in 1925, college entrants distinguished from other graduates). Comparisons between blacks and the children of the foreign-born were also controlled for place of birth of the son (northern or southern, native or foreign, respectively).
[b]Yankees are defined as native whites of native parentage; FBW, foreign-born whites.
[c]1915 comparisons limited to native-born sons.
[d]Mean increase in son's occupational score associated with an increase of one standard deviation in father's occupational score.

ways, our best indicator of social-class origin is the father's occupation. Two measures are offered. The first compares the children of white- and blue-collar fathers. These differences in behavior we have loosely translated into differences between middle-class and working-class children. Second, the tables compare children whose fathers' occupations differed by a standard deviation on the occupational scale (the scale described in Chapter 1). The standard deviation measures the dispersion of occupational scores around their mean.

Consider first the occupational attainments of blacks. In the job market, race mattered even more than social-class origin. In three of the four samples (and very nearly so in the fourth), the *residual* occupational disadvantage of blacks – the disadvantage unaccounted for by family background characteristics and schooling – was greater than the *entire* disadvantage that working-class boys suffered in comparison with middle-class boys (including disadvantages operating through schooling, or, for example, because fewer working-class boys were of native stock).

On the other hand, differences in schooling and jobs among the white ethnic groups were often smaller than the social-class differences, even when no controls were imposed. The residual ethnic differences were smaller still, of course. Nevertheless, these residual differences were impressive; nearly all were at least half as large as the social-class differences in schooling and jobs. Several were considerably larger than that, and a few actually exceeded the social-class differences.

The advantages associated with an increase of a standard deviation in the father's occupational score were not as great as those associated with middle-class compared with working-class origin. The standard deviation amounted to some 18–20 points on the occupational scale, whereas the difference between middle-class and working-class occupations was roughly 28 points. Still, a difference of a standard deviation is considerable – separating a clergyman from a boilermaker, or a glazier from a bootblack, for example. In many populations (those that statisticians call normally distributed), two-thirds of the individuals are found within one standard deviation of the mean.[6]

Nearly every ethnic difference presented in Tables C.1 and C.2 – including the residual ethnic differences – was as large as the difference associated with a standard deviation in the father's occupation. Many were larger. Individuals from these different ethnic groups, then, typically differed in schooling and jobs – even after background characteristics had been taken into account – by as much as or more than the child of a clergyman and the child of a boilermaker, or the child of a glazier and the child of a porter. The residual ethnic differences among white groups, in short, were large judged in comparison with social divisions that we readily acknowledge to be crucial – albeit generally smaller than those between middle-class and working-class families.[7]

The ethnic behaviors presented in these two tables, of course, do not pertain to all ethnic groups in the city. Tables presented in Chapter 1 showed patterns of schooling and occupational attainment among all groups. They revealed that many groups did not differ sharply from each other.[8] Our focus has been on the most salient ethnic differences; yet these differences pertain to groups that were large and important, both in Providence and elsewhere.

Contextual effects.   We explored several ways in which the social positions prevalent in the group may have affected the individual, even if the individual's own family did not occupy those positions. Social contacts limited to the poor, for example, reduced the supply of information about jobs and the chances for being hired, even if one's own family was not poor. Perhaps such contacts also stimulated distinct attitudes and values. Conversely, contacts with many people engaged in commerce could have been an asset even if one's own father did not work in commerce. Living among many people who planned to remigrate may have had distinct effects as well.

Assessing the importance of these contextual effects, it must be admitted, is frustrating and inconclusive. No method captures such effects as clearly as standard statistical techniques capture the effects of family origins. The available method – based on ranking the ethnic groups in terms of the context of interest, for example, the mean occupational score for fathers in the ethnic group – suggested that contextual effects were weak (see Section 3.4 and Appendix, Section 9).

Further work on the role of contextual effects in ethnic differences would be welcomed – work on conceptualization and on measurement. Considering these effects should at least stimulate explicit discussion of ways in which the structural location of a group mattered to an individual – beyond the individual's own structural location. That issue is important to any adequate statement of the relationship between class and ethnicity in American history, and it has received too little attention. But pending further work, the assessments noted earlier must stand: There is no evidence that the contextual effects of an ethnic group's structural location were particularly important, once family background characteristics were controlled.[9]

Ethnicity and social structure.   We are therefore confronted with large ethnic differences unexplained by other social characteristics that we can measure. We turn later to interpretations of these differences. First, however, it is worth noting that these results bear on another study of social divisions in the American city during the same period, that of Olivier Zunz. From a study of Detroit, Zunz concluded that nineteenth-century ethnic divisions constituted crucial social fault lines, but by 1920, class lines were at least equally important. This change in the nature of major social divisions occurred as a result of economic transformations: In the earlier period, entire economic structures could exist within an immigrant community. By the twentieth century, major industries dominated, and the compositions of groups, as well as their places of employment, were determined by that reality. Zunz's stimulating suggestion has been questioned on the grounds that the contrast between nineteenth- and twentieth-century social divisions has been overdrawn and that conditions in Detroit may well have been special (given the nature of the giant automotive industry).[10]

Zunz's criteria for judging the salience of ethnic and class divisions were residential patterns and, to a lesser extent, a few other indicators of social behavior (fertility, homeownership, family structure, and the like). The present study offers two other indicators of social behavior as criteria for the extent to which ethnicity and social class were important fault lines: patterns of schooling and occupational attainment. These behaviors, after all, are no less salient to social history than those Zunz studied. Yet in terms of these behaviors, Providence appears to have been noticeably divided along both class and ethnic lines, rather than primarily on ethnic lines, even in 1880. Moreover, the city remained divided along both dimensions throughout the period 1880–1935. Admittedly, Tables C.1 and C.2 do not provide any single, neat measure of the changing degrees to which class and ethnicity determined outcomes, but they surely show the continuing salience of both forms of social division. Italian schooling differed from that of other groups (especially natives and Jews, but even other immigrants), much as Irish schooling had differed earlier from that of Yankees. Jewish rates of occupational attainment also suggested the continuation of sharp ethnic differences in important behaviors. The presence of such differences, of course, depends on the ethnic composition of a given city. In Providence, in any event, the magnitudes of differences do not seem to have changed in the time period Zunz suggests, notwithstanding changes in the scale of urban industry. The ethnic divisions may well have become less crucial in later decades, but, if so, the cessation of large-scale European immigration and the shift from ethnic to racial differences (following massive migrations of blacks from the South) – not the transformation of industry in the early twentieth century – would seem to provide the reasons for the change.

Pre-migration cultural attributes and discrimination. The discovery of the large residual ethnic differences in schooling and jobs led us to consider seriously other sorts of explanations for these differences, namely, differences in pre-migration cultural attributes of groups and discrimination against some groups. There is a weakness inherent in this line of argument. The historical evidence available (with which we can study representative individuals and assess the impact of family background characteristics) does not permit us to measure the impact of cultural attributes directly. Moreover, our ability to assess the magnitude of the effects of social class, family structure, and other such influences is imperfect, as it is in every study. Some of the magnitude of the residuals might result from mismeasurement of the other characteristics controlled, as well as from other economic and demographic characteristics that we were not able to control. We considered these issues fully in connection with the Italians (Section 3.5). Several considerations lead us not to dismiss the residuals by appealing to such possibilities. We have exploited several indicators of social-class origins in order to improve our estimates of its impact, and in any case measurement error probably also weakened our estimates of ethnic influences on schooling and jobs. Moreover, the residuals refer to measured associations between ethnic origin and schooling or job attainment (not to unexplained variance in the dependent variable). Finally, in some instances, the background variables controlled did account for all, or nearly all, of the observed ethnic differences. Black–white and, later, Irish–Yankee differences in high school entry rates involve little or no unexplained residual, nor do Italian differences from others in occupational attainment. The variables we have controlled, then, seem adequate to some purposes. If they were not adequate for others, we should not rush to assume that problems of measurement can explain away the results.[11]

Invoking cultural attributes and discrimination as explanations does not mean that the entire strength of the residuals is derived from these sources. Clearly, the other explanations just reviewed (measurement error and the impact of omitted structural characteristics) would explain part of their strength. The rest poses an interpretive challenge. The presence of large ethnic differences unexplained by various competing explanations cannot prove the influence of cultural attributes or discrimination, but the discovery of these large residuals makes the case for cultural attributes and discrimination much stronger than it would have been had the residuals been negligible. The appeal to cultural attributes and discrimination should be viewed as tentative, but reasonable, given the current state of the evidence and the methods available.

Discrimination against the Irish and especially against the blacks will command our attention later. Discrimination against Italians and Russian Jews no doubt existed as well. However, though evidence is scant, it seems unlikely that the discrimination leveled against them was much greater than that leveled against others with whom they have been compared. In any case, the relevant ethnic differences do not readily suggest discrimination: low school (but not job) attainments by Italians, and high job and school attainments by Russian Jews. Consequently, in considering Italians and Russian Jews, we concentrated on possible cultural attributes – particularly differences in orientations to school or work derived from the pre-migration heritages. We were able to say relatively little about the particular cultural attributes that may have created these ethnic differences, and instead had to rely on the descriptions of others. These descriptions stressed attitudes of estrangement from schooling among southern Italians (and related attitudes favoring child labor contributions to the family economy), especially positive attitudes toward learning and toward socioeconomic advancement generally among Russian Jews, and finally lower valuations of schooling for girls than for boys. Although the Providence data set shed little light on the specific content of these descriptions, it did reveal the importance of the gender differences, and it did permit us to eliminate other explanations for Italian behavior, namely, those based on a distinctive work ethic (because their job attainments were not distinctive).

We could, of course, have dwelt on the pre-migration cultures at much greater length, drawing on countless available descriptions of their supposed influence on the migrants,[12] but doing so would have added nothing new. The problem has not been to find such descriptions, but rather to find evidence of the existence of such influences and their impact on behavior. We have found evidence consistent with the impact of cultural attributes, however poorly defined they may be.

Some might argue that describing the nature of these cultural attributes should, in fact, be the principal aim of a historical study of ethnic groups. That view, however, implies a peculiar value judgment about historical topics. Describing beliefs, attitudes, and values prevalent in communities of the past is surely of interest, but there is no reason that that goal should be of greater interest than describing the

impact of these beliefs, attitudes, and values on important social behaviors.

Nevertheless, further work on the nature of pre-migration cultural
attributes themselves would certainly be welcomed. For much of that
work, historians' traditional methods, supplemented by anthropologists' approaches, would be preferable to the quantitative techniques
used here. Such qualitative work could produce better descriptions of
cultural attributes than we now have – more precise, more rooted in
the insights of recent social history than in the psychology and an-
thropology of the 1940s and 1950s. If could also produce hypotheses
about the ethnic differences in social behavior that such cultural attributes generated. However, techniques of the type used in this study
still will be required to support descriptions of cultural attributes drawn
from necessarily restricted, unrepresentative historical evidence, as
well as to test the influences of these attributes on behavior.[13]

We can also pause here to consider several connections between
social structure and cultural attributes. First, the origins of pre-migration
cultural attributes usually can be found in the economic and social
history of the country of origin, particularly in the future migrants'
social-class positions there. For example, many migrants' peasant
origins in regions relatively unaffected by industrial capitalism help
explain their pre-migration cultural attributes.[14] To ignore this pre-
migration class analysis, as Stephen Steinberg has urged, is to mis-
represent the central mechanisms of migration and cultural change
and to make a mystique of ethnic cultural differences. Moreover, following migration, specific cultural attributes will be more advantageous for success in some societies than in others; in this sense, as
well, the social advantage of particular cultural attributes depends on
the social structure itself.[15]

These observations are useful to recall. Nevertheless, they do not
bear on the most important intellectual challenge posed by the notion
of pre-migration cultural attributes. Indeed, many writers who have
stressed the influence of cultural attributes assume the truth of these
observations. For example, Nathan Glazer and Thomas Sowell, like
Steinberg, typically explain the origins of immigrant cultural heritages in terms of pre-migration social structure,[16] and informed discussion of these cultural heritages certainly need not include any implication that the same cultural attributes will be advantageous in every
society. Rather, the intellectually significant debate has been about
whether the behavior of an ethnic group within American cities in the
late nineteenth and early twentieth centuries can be understood exclusively, or at least largely, as the outcome of the group's location in

the social structure of these cities or, alternatively, whether pre-migration cultural attributes seriously influenced that behavior as well. The broad generalization that cultural attributes generally derive from and are shaped by social structures will not resolve that issue for us; what matters here are the nature, strength, and persistence of particular attributes in a given social context over several decades. What, then, is the empirical record? The Providence data cannot directly prove the point, but they strongly suggest that in the cases of the Italians and the Russian Jews (critical, given the importance of these groups in American history and their roles in the debate), pre-migration cultural attributes cannot be dismissed or even treated as afterthoughts, but rather constitute an important part of the explanation for group differences in behavior.[17]

Of course, immigrant culture interacted with the American social context; outlooks and behaviors did not exist in a vacuum. Thus, the school behavior of the Italians changed, approaching the American norms in later generations. Nevertheless, it matters how quickly these transformations occurred; they did not require centuries, but in some cases they apparently required decades.[18]

Similarly, the salience of particular cultural attributes may depend on the social-class position of the immigrants within the American social structure. Any Russian Jewish predisposition for schooling and mobility may have received greater encouragement in the middle-class (or upper working-class) context in which many of the second generation grew up; the Italian conception that child labor should contribute to the family economy may have been encouraged by the working-class context in which most of these children grew up.[19] Nevertheless, simply noting the interaction between class and culture does not permit us to slight the cultural element involved in it. Moreover, and most important, the process of interaction envisioned does not necessarily explain most, or even much, of what requires explanation. Italian children from middle-class homes left school earlier than Russian Jewish children from working-class homes and earlier than other children from working-class homes as well.

As this example shows, the interaction of pre-migration cultural attributes and social-class position in America is a concept that is partly subject to empirical research. In particular, we can explore whether or not ethnic differences themselves differed across social classes. For example, did Italians and Russian Jews from middle-class origins differ more than those from working-class homes? The results of such exploration suggest caution in attributing too much importance to such interactions. Any interactions in the Providence data between ethnicity and class origins were less important to the schooling and jobs of individuals than was the ethnic identity shared by individuals from a particular ethnic group, regardless of their class origins.[20]

Of course, cultural and structural factors did operate together. Perhaps an adequate conceptualization can be advanced by focusing on the family economy, especially for issues involving children. Families had to make choices about resources and needs; these were determined partly by shared material constraints, and partly by other factors. The result was a range of ethnic behaviors – a range of family strategies that varied across ethnic lines. Mothers' work, children's job prospects, and views on the value of schooling, the proper role for an adolescent, and whether or not children should contribute to the family economy – these issues blended objective constraint and cultural differences. Although this study has not been built explicitly around the concept of the family economy, it can be thought of as an effort to assess the extent to which strategies related to schooling differed across groups and to assess the factors determining them.

Finally, the experience of the Italians offers at least a hint about distinctive behavior patterns of Slavs and of other groups composed largely of peasants from preindustrial environments. We have not studied the distinctive patterns of the Providence ethnic groups in such detail only now to generalize crudely about others. Nevertheless, the Italian patterns suggest that some apparently distinctive behavior patterns of these groups probably can be fully explained by structural characteristics, that some other patterns cannot be, and that pre-migration cultural attributes are plausible explanations for these latter. The school patterns of these groups may well be important examples of the latter type, as was the case for the Italians.[21]

Our interpretation of distinctive Italian and Russian Jewish patterns of behavior (reflected in the residuals) has directed attention to pre-migration cultural attributes; our interpretation of distinctive Irish behavior directs attention to several different influences. Although family background factors accounted for all the important Yankee–Irish differences in the later years, they left large residuals in 1880. One source of the ethnic difference in 1880 may have been pre-migration cultural attributes. The regularity of historians' appeals to a cultural legacy involving a fatalistic attitude, as well as the restricted familiarity with schooling (reflected in nineteenth-century Irish illiteracy), support this hypothesis. Changes in pre-migration culture may have occurred in the later years, resulting, in turn, from changes in Irish economic, social, and political life. However, a second source of the Irish pattern may have been alienation of the Irish Catholics from a hostile school system, as well as discriminatory hiring in the job market, and these, too, probably declined in later years. It seems worth considering alienation and discrimination in the case of the Irish more seriously than in the case of the Russian Jews and Italians. First, the Irish were compared principally with the Yankees, rather than with other immigrants; Yankees, surely, suffered less discrimination than others. Second, the virulent Protestant–Catholic hatred that reinforced ethnic divisions in the nineteenth century became more muted later. Finally, the position of the Irish, first as a numerous and threatening group to the established order, and then as a rising political power (amidst the new immigration of southern and eastern Europeans), suggests fundamental changes in the social status and power of the Irish that could explain their changing behavior.

Like the mix of factors operating to explain Irish behavior, those affecting black schooling could not be fully disentangled. We did, nevertheless, observe the important impact of social class, especially compared with the impact of family structure, and the presence of some mix of other factors – perhaps cultural characteristics of various sorts, the prevalence of working mothers, and discrimination within schools and in the youth labor market. By contrast, the pattern of black occupational attainment indicated uniquely virulent discrimination. An important competing explanation was rejected: Schooling – including quality as well as length of schooling – cannot explain much, if any, of the very large residual race differential in occupational attainment. Like other analyses, ours, admittedly, cannot distinguish the role of black cultural attributes – if indeed they played any role at all – from the role of job discrimination in a fully satisfactory way. Nevertheless, our analysis strengthened arguments that stress racial discrimination over cultural attributes of blacks for several reasons. First, no evidence was found that could not be explained as easily by discrimination as by cultural attributes. Second, one kind of evidence that might seem to indicate the influence of a poor work ethic among blacks can be rejected (namely, the lower GPAs of blacks, for whites with low GPAs differed occupationally from blacks with higher GPAs by about as much as all blacks and whites). Third, nineteenth-century blacks whose families had lived in the North for generations generally differed from whites by about the same margin as did all blacks, calling into question the impact of slavery's cultural legacy. Fourth, the magnitude of the occupational disadvantage the blacks suffered far exceeded the occupational disadvantage of the late-nineteenth-century Irish, the other group for whom a disadvantageous cultural legacy of somewhat similar character has often been argued. Finally, the argument that dysfunctional cultural attributes developed among northern blacks of this period as a response to racial discrimination itself implies the importance of that discrimination.

One generalization will not serve to describe or explain the ethnic differences found in American social history. Many groups behaved in similar ways; others differed for a range of special reasons. Neither culture nor discrimination nor class origins in the American city can alone provide a credible summary. Rather, ethnic groups are products of distinct histories. We need not seek the single, consistently primary factor creating ethnic distinctiveness, nor even a single generalization that will cover the relationships among several factors; far better, with a comparative perspective and an eye on theory, to explore the individual ethnic histories.

Appendix: The Research Design, the Data Collection, and the Use of Regression Analyses

The purpose of this Appendix is to provide enough information to enable the reader to understand how the samples were gathered, coded, and processed and how regression analyses were used to construct the tables in the text. I have discussed all these issues, particularly the research design and data collection, in several other contexts. Consequently, the discussion here is not meant to be exhaustive.[1]

This Appendix is divided into nine sections:
1. An overview of the research design
2. Selecting the samples
3. Obtaining additional information on family background
4. Obtaining information on schooling
5. Obtaining information on the male sample member's career
6. The coding and classification of occupations
7. The organization of the data collection and processing
8. The use of regression analysis
9. Assessing contextual effects: the case of the Italians

1. An overview of the research design

In its essentials, the research design is simple. Manuscript schedules were available from censuses taken by the federal government in 1880 and 1900 and by the state of Rhode Island in 1915 and 1925. Male sample members were drawn from these manuscripts and then traced in their school records. Samples of girls were gathered in the same way from the sources for 1880 and 1915. Finally, all male sample members were traced one decade forward in time in city directories, which indicated their occupations. They were traced in the directories for Providence as well as those for nearby towns.[2]

Other data gathering involved variations on this basic design: an age cohort selected from census records, traced through school records, and its males traced forward in time in city directories and tax books. One variation was to trace all sample members' guardians in the city directories and tax books for the census year. This procedure provided information about their property holdings and added information (beyond that available in the census) about their occupations and the spelling of their names (critical for tracing across time). The second, and more extensive, variation involved collecting samples to investigate special populations more closely. There were two types of such samples:

Supplemental ethnic samples. In order to study immigrant groups in detail, I selected large supplemental samples of blacks in every period and of Irish, Italian, and Russian Jewish children in 1915. These samples were collected from the census manuscripts and traced in other sources in exactly the same way as were the random samples.

Samples of high school entrants. Most adolescents did not attend high school at all during most of the period under consideration. In order to investigate the high school population in detail, a separate sample of high school entrants in the census years was selected from high school records. It was traced back in the census records and then in other sources in the same way as the census sample. Table A.1 provides a summary of these samples and the number of individuals in each.

2.   *Selecting the samples*

A.   *The census samples*

In order to obtain a representative sample of adolescents, individuals were drawn from the entire city rather than from only selected neighborhoods. The age range for the sample members was chosen in order to maximize the probability of successfully tracing them in records of grammar school graduation or high school entrance. The age range included the three most common ages of grammar school graduation, as well as the ages one year younger than these (in order to increase the size of the group sampled). In the 1880 and 1900 periods, these ages were thirteen to sixteen, and in the 1915 and 1925 periods, twelve to fifteen. The change is due to the fact that the grammar school course was shortened by one year in 1904. In addition, for the 1880 period, the age range was extended to include individuals eleven to sixteen years old.[3]

Only about 2% of the population fell into the four-year age ranges in which I was interested. Therefore, a pure random sample – for example, one based on combinations of randomly chosen census enumeration districts, page numbers, and lines – would have involved rejecting some 98% of the lines selected, an unnecessarily inefficient

Table A.1. *The size of each sample*

Period	Sample	Number in sample of boys	Number in sample of girls
Selected from the census			
1880	11–16-year-olds in Providence	1,223	898
	11–16-year-old blacks	125[a]	142[a]
1900	13–16-year-olds in Providence	914	
	13–16-year-old blacks		
1915	12–15-year-olds in Providence	915	903
	12–15-year-old blacks	155[a]	158[a]
	12–15-year-olds whose fathers were born in Russia	388[a]	324
	12–15-year-olds whose fathers were born in Italy	581	291
	12–15-year-olds whose fathers were born in Ireland	446	215
1925	12–15-year-olds in Providence	1,090	
	12–15-year-old blacks	165[a]	
Selected from public high school records			
	Individuals entering high school in		
	The 1880 period	216[b]	112[b]
	The 1900 period	581[b]	367[b]
	The 1915 period	349[b]	416[b]

[a] Includes entire population in age range – not a sample.
[b] Includes entire classes in selected years – not a sample.

procedure. A common alternative to a pure random sample is a systematic sample, in which every nth individual is chosen, but for my purposes, such a procedure would have exactly the same drawback as a true random sample. I chose instead to sample every nth page of the census and to include every individual in the age range on sampled pages. Because there were fifty individuals listed on each page, there tended to be few sample members chosen from any given page. Indeed, on average, one was chosen from each page. Strictly speaking, the samples probably should be defined as cluster samples (each page constituting a cluster chosen by systematic sampling), but with the number of clusters so high and the number of sample members selected from each cluster so low, they approach systematic samples.[4] When two (or more) siblings in a family fell into the appropriate age range, both were included in the sample.

The supplemental ethnic samples.   These included (1) all black boys in the age range in all four periods and all black girls in the age range in 1880 and 1915 (the years for which random samples of girls were collected)[5] and (2) samples of Irish, Italian, and Russian Jewish boys and girls in 1915. Supplemental samples of those groups in other periods were not drawn because the critical comparisons could be made among individuals selected from one point in time, and because large numbers of the Irish were found in the 1880 random sample and large numbers of the Italians in the 1925 sample.

The criterion for inclusion in the black supplemental samples depended, of course, on the race of the individual (the few listed as "mulatto" were also included). For the other supplemental samples of ethnic groups, the criterion was the father's place of birth. In Providence (as in the United States generally), the vast majority of immigrants from Russia were Jews. The 1905 Rhode Island State Census, which ascertained respondents' religion, showed that fully 95% of those Providence residents who had been born in Russia were Jews.[6] Although no figures are available for 1915, there is no reason to assume that the proportions had changed in the intervening decade.

One use of the supplemental samples was to make all results less subject to sampling error. The sample members in the random sample who came from ethnic groups for which supplemental samples had also been selected were replaced by the supplemental sample members from the appropriate ethnic group. The latter, however, were weighted down to equal the number replaced. The same procedure was used in the analysis of occupational attainment. In these, the supplementary samples of high school entrants were also included, and weighted down to equal the number of high school entrants in the random samples.[7]

Sample representativeness.   The most straightforward way to assess whether or not the samples adequately reflected the populations from which they were drawn would be to compare the distribution of specific characteristics (such as age or ethnicity) in sample and population. That procedure, however, proved difficult to follow because the sample members are adolescents. There were few tables in the published census data that reported figures on adolescents or, of course, on their parents. However, a few comparisons with published data were possible, and many comparisons between the independently collected samples of boys and girls could be made. The results of these, reported elsewhere, raised no problems of representativeness due to the research design.[8] Although we are, of course, ultimately dependent on the adequacy of the census enumerations, we may be confident that the process of sample selection did not create important biases.

B.   The sample of public high school entrants

In the 1880 period, there was a single public high school in the city – the Providence High School. It included the Classical, English and Science, and Girls' Departments. By the 1900 period, this institution had been replaced by Classical, English, Hope, and Manual Training (later Technical) High Schools. These same institutions provided the city's public secondary schooling until the Great Depression.

The samples from the public high schools included all boys and girls entering the ninth grade in the year of the corresponding census sample. Thus, all those entering high school in 1880, 1900, and 1915 were included. Because the numbers of boys who entered in 1880 and 1900 were too small for an adequate sample, those entering in the years before and after were included as well.[9]

No sample of high school entrants was selected from the 1925 period because the boys in the census sample enrolled in sufficient numbers to make supplemental data unnecessary. Also, no special sample was selected from the Manual Training (Technical) High School. Its records had been interfiled alphabetically in an enormous file of other records; tracing a person in that file was easy, but selecting a sample of one school's students from it would have been difficult. The information on entrants to this school is based on the census sample members who enrolled there. Because the school admitted large numbers of boys (and, by 1915, of girls as well), the absence of a supplemental sample did not prove to be a serious limitation. Finally, no supplemental samples of private school students were selected. Full student academic records (as opposed to lists of entrants) were unavailable for some private schools; in the case of others, the special data-collection effort was deemed unnecessary.

3.   Obtaining additional information on family background

A.   Tracing sample members' guardians in the city directory and tax book

The city directory lists individuals in alphabetical order, providing address, occupation, and often business address. The guardians of sample members were traced in the directory of the census year in order to supplement the information on their occupations and to provide additional information on the spelling and commonness of names (useful in tracing to still other sources).

For each period except 1880, a biennially published house directory was also available. It ordered entries by street address rather than alphabetically by name. The house directory appears to have been far less inclusive than the city directory, perhaps limiting listings to heads of households. Nevertheless, it was of considerable use in locating those individuals whose names had been hopelessly misspelled in the census manuscripts. All guardians not successfully matched to a listing in the city directory were traced in the house directory.

The city directory also listed tradesmen by occupation in a "business directory" – a separate list of names printed in the same volume as the list of residents. Finding an individual in the business directory would have indicated that he was self-employed. However, it also would have required an additional trace and therefore was not undertaken. Fortunately, in Providence, the city directory itself often indicated the name of a proprietor's enterprise (in parentheses following his name). Consequently, it was possible to identify many owners merely by using the list of residents. Whether or not this procedure revealed all the self-employed individuals who could have been identified by using the business directory is uncertain, but probably the more important proprietors were indeed noted. In any case, a critical additional perspective on self-employment, no doubt more complete than the business directory, was available for one sample: The 1915 Rhode Island State Census provides information on the self-employment status of all gainfully employed (indicating whether employee, employer, or other self-employed).

The *Providence Tax Book* has been published annually since the early nineteenth century. It includes the name of each individual owning taxed property, the assessed worth of that property, and the amount of the tax. The property is divided into two categories: real property and personal property. The latter includes all property other than real estate. After 1912, it was subdivided into tangible personal property (such as machinery or furniture) and intangible personal property (such as bonds or savings accounts). The actual assessment for any individual was only a very rough estimate of his financial status. Salaries were excluded, savings accounts may have been routinely ignored, and other property escaped assessment through loopholes in the laws. Moreover, different assessors evaluated property differently, and all assessed at only a fraction of true value. Finally, of those fathers who could be traced unambiguously in the tax book, most owned no assessed property (67–70% in different samples). Nevertheless, the tax records supplemented the use of occupation as a measure of class origin. As a rough approximating of the relative wealth of families, and especially in marking those who possessed something more than the average, the assessed value of property was useful.

The tax book rarely listed the address of a property owner. Consequently, only those with uncommon names could be traced in the tax book, roughly between half and two-thirds of the guardians in each period.

B. Tracing the high school entrant sample to the census manuscripts

The census manuscript schedules are not arranged alphabetically. An index exists for the heads of households in the 1900 U.S. Census. All the guardians of sample members selected from the high school records were traced in it. However, only a partial index exists for the 1880 U.S. Census, and none at all for the 1915 Rhode Island State Census. Therefore, the 1880 sample members not found in the index, and the entire 1915 sample, required a special strategy.[10]

Every street address fell between two cross streets. These cross streets were found with the help of a special street directory (published in the city directory). Then the census enumeration district that included the address could be determined (descriptions of district boundaries were obtained from the National Archives). Knowing the relevant enumeration district made it fairly simple to find the address by skimming the street names on each page of the census manuscript schedules for that district. If an individual was not found by this method, directories were consulted to determine any recent change of residence, and the alternative addresses were then checked in the census.

4. Obtaining information on schooling

Information on education in this study pertains especially to secondary schooling: entry or nonentry, curriculum, GPA, and graduation. The other major type of information drawn from school records is sixth-grade GPA. Far less central evidence of college entry patterns in 1925 was briefly discussed in Chapter 4 and used throughout the study as a control in analysis of occupational attainment. Finally, the U.S. Censuses of 1880 and 1900 had ascertained whether or not children had attended school during the preceding year; this evidence was particularly useful in the case of the Irish in 1880 (when it supplemented incomplete evidence on high school entry) and in illuminating the contrast between teenage school attendance and high school entry among blacks.

We have focused heavily, then, on one dimension of school behavior: extended schooling (reflected in high school entry and other measures of grade attainment). For the study of educational differences in whole populations (rather than elites, for example), the importance of this dimension can hardly be overemphasized, as the uniform concern with it among social scientists and social historians studying school patterns suggests.[11]

Throughout, the available measures of grade attainment, high school entry, for example, have been preferred to those bearing purely on length of school attendance, notably responses to the census-takers' question about school attendance in the preceding year. One simple reason is that every choice of a measure involves some limitations, and whereas the data on high school enrollment are available for all four years sampled, school attendance was not a question in the 1915 and 1925 Rhode Island State Census. But there are more important reasons for the choice.

High school entry (and grade attainment generally) was determined by progress through the grades as well as by length of school attendance; the looseness of the age–grade fit makes it important to recall both determinants, and both were affected by social origins. Consequently, the relations of social origins and schooling typically are clearer when a measure of grade attainment, such as high school entry, is studied than when length of school attendance is the measure. Moreover, when it comes to assessing the influence of schooling on later social destinations, grade attainment has still other advantages as a criterion; for employment opportunities, the child who completed two years of high school surely had an edge over the one who left in the eighth grade, even if they had both spent ten years in school. Finally, the information bearing on length of school attendance in historical studies derives from the census-taker's question whether or not the child had attended school in the past year. The answer does not in fact provide us with the length of the child's school attendance – first, because children entered school at a range of ages and, second, because the answer tells us only the child's attendance status that year, not the age at which he left school.[12]

Of course, both measures, high school entry and school attendance in the preceding year, could have been studied in depth, but the relative positions of ethnic groups on these two measures were not so different that the discussion should be complicated by adding more details about the less revealing of the two. Exceptions were noted in the case of the Italians (Section 3.2) and especially the blacks (Section 5.3).

The school records, and the collection of data from them, are described next.

A. Descriptions of the high school and grammar school records

1. The high school records

Public high school records. These were kept in register books until about 1900, and then on record cards. The information given was quite consistent over the entire period of the study: name, guardian's name, address, age, previous school, date entered, date left, whether or not graduated (and sometimes the curriculum followed), attendance data, and grade in each course each quarter, semester, or year.[13] Grading systems (5-point scale, 10-point scale, A–F, and others) varied over time, but often were stated explicitly on the card and in any case were easy enough to determine.[14]

Catholic high school records. The register book for the boys' Catholic high school, La Salle Academy, had been discarded. By the 1915 and 1925 periods, however, record cards were in use, and these remained intact. Luckily, a list of all graduates of the school since its establishment had been prepared from the missing register. Also, some teacher registers were available from the 1900 period. The records of the Catholic girls high school, St. Xavier's Academy, were preserved in a similar form. For the 1915 period, sheets indicating the name and grade of each student (arranged by class) were used, as well as a list of graduates. For the 1880 period, only a list of graduates was available. On the estimation of missing Catholic high school records, see Section D1.

Other private high school records. The more elite private schools of the city published annual catalogs. These often listed the names of the students, sometimes with their addresses, and often by grade level. Lists of past graduates were often included as well. Thus, information was available on length of schooling, but not academic achievement. The clientele of these schools came disproportionately from among the wealthy and included no more than 1–2% of the age cohort. For some purposes, this elite would be an important subject of study; in considering ethnic differences, they were not. Other children, still fewer in number, attended out-of-town boarding schools. Given these circumstances, complete coverage of private high schools was impractical. However, available information covered the most important of the select schools in Providence and therefore most entrants to elite private schools.

2.   The grammar school records

Prior to about 1905, the public grammar school records seem to have consisted of register books, which have been lost. The public grammar schools' student academic records are available for the 1915 and 1925 periods on record cards. During the Depression, WPA workers created a single alphabetical file of old public elementary school records. Intensive checks indicated that records of five grammar schools in the 1915 period (of some fifteen) were incomplete. Moreover, because parochial (and other private) grammar school student records also were incomplete, and because those preserved were not interfiled, no effort was made to exploit them. Consequently, grammar school GPA data are available only for 53% of the sample members in 1915 and 70% in 1925. Not every unavailable grammar school record reflects missing or untapped sources; some children left school before reaching grammar school, probably some 11–20% of the population. Thus, the grammar school GPA data would reflect the population's academic performance with some bias even if they were complete (this problem is considerably more severe, as noted in preceding chapters, in connection with high school GPA data, because only a minority of sample members entered high school).

Despite these limitations, the GPA data remain useful. The most important biases due to loss of a particular public school's records probably would be related to social class and ethnicity (because of residence patterns and attendance at neighborhood schools). Controls for social class and ethnicity surely reduce such biases. The largest single omission, the Catholic records, is less serious to the preceding analyses because grammar school GPAs were not included in the study of the Irish, by far the most frequent users of these schools in Providence. Finally, the selectivity bias probably would tend to mute rather than create the ethnic differences observed, because, other things being equal, those with the lowest GPAs were most likely to drop out, and more of them were found among groups characterized by low school performance.[15]

B. *Descriptions of other records pertaining to schooling*

1. Post-secondary schooling

The inclusion of information on post-secondary schooling involves many of the same difficulties as the inclusion of information on private school students: There were innumerable institutions that sample members may have attended. However, the overwhelming majority of sample members could not possibly have reached college, because they dropped out at lower grade levels. By 1925, somewhat more were reaching college than before, but by then, other school sources provide information on post-secondary education of high school graduates (the school census card and high school graduate follow-up card, described later).[16]

2. Other records kept by the Providence School Committee

The sources described earlier included all the student records used in this study. Other information on schooling was available from lists of graduates of grammar schools and other institutions published in newspapers (and occasionally in reunion books) and from additional documents kept by the Providence School Committee other than student academic records. These latter included working papers, school census cards, and high school graduate follow-up cards. Working papers were required by the laws regulating compulsory education and child labor. They certified that a youth was legally entitled to work by virtue of his age and, in some cases, length of schooling. The school census, also an outgrowth of compulsory-education legislation, was an attempt to keep track of all youths in the city. It ascertained whether or not they were enrolled in school and, if so, in which school and in what grade. It was introduced in the late 1870s as an annual enumeration. In 1927, an ongoing census was begun in which records of individuals were periodically updated. It included all in the age range from five to twenty. The records of the effort begun in 1927 have been preserved.[17] Both the census cards and the working papers have the advantage of indicating private as well as public schooling. Finally, a follow-up card on each public high school graduate of the 1925 period is also available. In addition to listing the student's entire academic record, it listed the father's occupation, birthplace, religious background, occupational aspirations, further schooling, and/or early employment.

3. Marginal institutions

Other private institutions offering instruction in various skills abounded
– schools of music, dance, or art, for example. No effort was made to
include information on attendance at these. One kind of institution
does deserve special attention, however: the business or commercial
school. Throughout the years 1880–1925, a number of such schools
thrived in Providence. Most have disappeared completely (Schol-
field's Commercial College, Max Magnus's School for Shorthand,
Spencerian Business College, and others); the rest have evolved into
other kinds of schools (one as the Katharine Gibbs School, another as
Bryant College). Most of their student records were no doubt destroyed. Extant catalogs, which are very few, generally do not list
enrolled students.

Such institutions offered a very different range of training than the
public school "commercial programs" (which were begun partly in
response to the success of these business colleges). Some offered
courses in traditional disciplines that were useful for business careers
– especially grammar, writing, and arithmetic. Principally, however,
they offered a wide range of courses and work programs to provide
business skills. These included courses of a year or more, but also
many others that lasted two to three months. The Providence data set
does not identify sample members who completed such courses. Such
information also may well have been missed when the federal census-
takers inquired about respondents' "years of schooling" (beginning
in 1940). How, for example, did respondents report a three-month
bookkeeping or shorthand course taken after leaving grammar school?
Yet such schools may have been important for individuals entering
the business world. Information about the clientele of these schools
(class and ethnic origins, and even gender) is at a minimum. Our
inability to probe this question is unfortunate, particularly given our
concern with the mechanisms of social mobility for those starting near
the bottom.[18]

C. *Linking sample members to school records*

Tracing sample members in files of student record cards was tedious
but straightforward (the largest file even included soundex information on alternative spellings of names). Tracing them in high school
register books was more complicated. The names of students found
in these sources were copied, along with any information that would
identify them (address, guardian's name, year of entry or gradua-

tion). Every student who by virtue of age might have fallen into the census samples was included. The resultant list of student names was then alphabetized, and all sample members could be traced to it. Determining whether or not a sample member and a student listed in the high school records with the same name were indeed the same individual was generally simple because the registers included the age, address, and guardian of the student.[19] Linking sample members to lists of students that did not provide that information required more careful attention to the probability of erroneous matches, but the use of such records in this analysis was limited to a few private school records and therefore was altogether minimal.

How complete are the data based on the school records? The grammar school data, as already indicated (Section 4B2), covered only part of the sample; however, controls for indicators of social class and ethnicity mitigate the effects of biases due to missing data. The high school records, our basis for measuring length of schooling, were nearly complete. The exceptions include the Catholic high school records of 1880 and 1900 and the elite private school records. With regard to the rest, there is no reason to suspect incomplete records. Abundant published information made clear the schools existing in each period, their courses, and approximate size. Extensive exploration in the manuscript records confirmed their completeness.[20] Errors due to difficulties in tracing from source to source were likely minimal as well, because, as already explained, a good deal of information on a student's identity was available. The actual tracing work of research assistants was also carefully checked (see Section 8). Difficult names were treated with special care; for example, a second-generation Italian individual reviewed the linkages involving Italian names.[21]

D.   Estimating Catholic school enrollments

This subsection provides details relevant to two estimates of Catholic schooling discussed in Chapter 2. Catholic school enrollments have not received much attention from social historians. Consequently, these details are also provided to stimulate consideration of sources and methods. Nevertheless, because they bear on a narrower topic than the rest, many readers may wish to skip them and turn to Section 5.

Estimating the proportions of Irish-American sample members who entered the Catholic high schools in 1880 and 1900. The Catholic high schools' student academic records for 1880 were lost; those for 1900 are incomplete. For both periods, lists of graduates remain at the schools. Consequently, the sample members who had entered these schools, but had not graduated, were not identified. In the 1880 sample, all of these students were erroneously classified as not having reached high school; in the 1900 sample, some were so classified. In order to estimate their number, it was first necessary to estimate the total number of entrants and then subtract the number of known graduates.

A variety of independent sources provided figures that could be used in estimation. The Providence School Committee's annual reports gave public school enrollment figures by level (primary, grammar, high school). The school census report (published with the School Committee's report) presented the number of children five to fifteen years old who were attending public, Catholic, and other schools. Beginning in 1891, the reports of the Rhode Island Commissioner of Public Schools, published annually, included the numbers enrolling in and graduating from each Catholic school. The *Catholic Directory*, published annually, included the number of pupils enrolled (or the number of seats) in each Catholic school. Newspapers listed graduates of many public grammar schools beginning in 1881 and for Catholic schools beginning in the 1890s.

The number of Catholic high school entrants was estimated in three ways, based on (1) the rate at which the public system produced high school students and the ratio of the number of pupils in the public and Catholic systems, (2) the rate at which the public system produced grammar school graduates 1881–1900, the rate at which the Catholic system did after 1892, and continuation rates in the public schools between grammar school and high school (published for a few years in the School Committee reports), and (3) the number of Catholic high school graduates at La Salle Academy and St. Xavier's Academy in the 1880s (available from their lists of graduates), the number of pupils in other academies, estimated rates of attrition in these schools, and estimated proportions of Providence residents among the pupils. This third method was also used to estimate the number of entrants at La Salle Academy in 1900.

The first and second methods also required estimates of sex ratios in the high school classes. Similarly, the estimates assume, conservatively, that all Catholic pupils in 1880 were the children of Irish immigrants; in 1900, the proportion they constituted among all pupils was estimated. Gaps in series of enrollment figures required further estimates.

Despite the many estimates, however, the methods are largely independent, and yet the results accord reasonably well. For example, the three estimates for the number of Catholic high school entrants in the 1880 sample of boys were six to twenty, fifteen to twenty-five, and twenty-one to twenty-eight. The figures, and the extent of consistency, were similar for the girls. In a sample of 488 Irish boys, the entire range of six to twenty-eight covers but a small fraction of the whole and is adequate to the purposes at hand.

On the basis of the estimates, the odds ratios comparing Yankee and Irish enrollments could be corrected for the missing data among the Irish (Table 2.2, last section). The odds ratios with no controls imposed were calculated directly from the corrected proportions of high school entrants. The odds ratios with controls imposed (obtained from logit regression analysis) were adjusted by the same factor as those without controls.*

Estimating the proportion of Irish Catholic pupils in Catholic schools. In order to determine the proportion of Irish Catholic pupils in Catholic schools directly, one would need complete primary and grammar school records. Because these were not available, the proportion was estimated for each census year, as shown in Table A.2. The estimates were surely rough. On the other hand, two partly different methods of estimation produced very similar results – one is shown in line 9; the other is calculated as (line 1)/(lines 1 + 6).

There were two published sources for the number of pupils in Catholic schools: The *Catholic Directory* and the school census. The first probably provided an administrator's estimate either of the number of seats or of the average number of children registered. The numbers of students listed for a parish were therefore certainly rough; for example, they often were round numbers that remained unchanged for several years. The *Catholic Directory* also distinguished the national parish schools from the rest, allowing us to exclude high school students. These were found in academies, not parish schools. However, because in the early years many of the students in these academies were in fact grade school pupils, their numbers had to be estimated and included in the figures in line 1.

The second source, the school census, ascertained for all children ages five to fifteen which schools they attended, if any. At best, it, too, surely provided only a rough count.[22] The census was also published annually, and it provided figures for public, Catholic, and other

---

* $D = (B/A) \times C$, where A is the observed odds ratio, no controls, B is the corrected odds ratio, no controls, C is the observed odds ratio with controls imposed, and D is the corrected odds ratio with controls imposed. This adjustment assumes that if the sample members who attended the Catholic high school could have been identified correctly, the sum of the logit coefficients for the family background characteristics controlled in the regression analysis would remain the same; the coefficient for the Irish dummy variable would change.

Table A.2. *Proportions of Irish Catholics enrolled in Catholic schools, estimates for Providence, 1880–1925*

Components of the estimate	1880	1900	1915	1925
A. Enrollment in Catholic and public grade schools[a]				
1. Total Catholic grade school enrollment	3,571	4,070	5,873	7,872
2. Less French national parish school enrollment		300	628	845
3. Less Italian national parish school enrollment			231	655
4. Subtotal: territorial parish school enrollment	3,571	3,770	5,014	6,372
5. Territorial proportion of all Catholic enrollment	1.00	0.926	0.854	0.809
6. Public grade school enrollment	11,759	21,863	33,260	41,020
B. School census enrollment figures[b]				
7. Catholic school enrollment	2,759	4,256	5,997	7,523
8. Public and non-Catholic private school enrollment	12,408	24,130	32,910	39,861
9. Proportion Catholic	0.182	0.150	0.154	0.159
10. Estimated proportion territorial Catholic (line 9 × line 5)	0.182	0.139	0.132	0.129
C. Proportion of school-age population in major Catholic ethnic groups (from sample data)[c]				
11. Children of Irish	0.411	0.202	0.131	0.073
12. Children of U.S.-born, Irish parentage	0.031	0.117	0.108	0.150
13. Children of French Canadians	0.001	0.049	0.045	0.036
14. Children of Italians	0.003	0.065	0.158	0.286
D. Adjustment for ethnic differences in school enrollment[d]				
15. Irish enrollment rate compared with city average rate, 5–15-year-olds only	0.767	1.00	1.07	1.16
E. Estimated proportion of Irish Catholic schoolchildren enrolled in Catholic schools: [(line 10)/(line 15)]/(line 11 + line 12)	0.537	0.436	0.516	0.499

[a]Lines 1–5 are based on the *Catholic Directory* (see text); line 6 is based on the Providence School Committee's annual reports. All pupils in Catholic grade schools other than those in national parish schools (i.e., the schools of French Canadian and Italian parishes) were assumed to be Irish Catholic.
[b]Figures are based on the school census and on line 5.
[c]The ethnic composition of the school-age population (part C) is based on the sample data (the composition of the sampled age range representing that of the entire "school-age" population). Lines 12 and 13 for 1925 had to be estimated from earlier years (and from line 11).
[d]The 1880 adjustment was estimated from school attendance data on sample members 11–15 years of age and from a hand count of attendance rates for ages 5–10

private schools. It is reasonable to assume that it offers the advantage of comparing enrollments from different kinds of schools using the same definitions of school populations (presumably enrollment of a certain age range on a certain day).

James Sanders, who made similar computations for Chicago and Boston (see Chapter 2), calculated the following: (line 1)/(lines 1 + 6). Although that method ignores enrollments in the non-Catholic private schools, they were small and their exclusion affects the estimates only slightly. Nevertheless, a different strategy was adopted here. Wherever possible, the school census was used (rather than the *Directory* and the public school enrollment reports). However, the data from the *Directory* still were needed in order to estimate the proportion of Catholic school pupils enrolled in territorial parish schools (line 10). The calculation in part E does not require lines 6, 13, and 14 of the table; they are included to provide a fuller context.

5. Obtaining information on the male sample member's career

Tracing sample members across time in the city directory involved correctly matching them with names listed there.[23] Name changes posed one problem. One frequent kind of change was the Anglicizing of non-English first names (e.g., Luigi to Louis) by the individual himself or by others – a census-taker or a schoolteacher, for example. Another involved small changes in spelling that did not substantially affect the sound of a name, for example, Di Meo to De Meo, Brown to Browne. Both sorts of changes were routinely considered. Other changes usually were not. The dropping of a suffix or prefix from a name, and similar changes, would have made the pool of similar-sounding names too large, thus probably increasing rather than decreasing error, and it would have made the rules for tracing too unsystematic and too time-consuming.

Table A.2 (Cont.)

(not broken down by ethnicity). Because 1900 Irish-American attendance rates at ages 13–16 were about the same as the city average, no adjustment was made. Attendance data were not available in the Rhode Island State Census schedules for 1915–25; attendance rates at ages 5–12 in 1915 and 5–13 in 1925 were assumed to be about the same among the Irish as in the city as a whole (compulsory school laws having some effect). Attendance rates at 13–15 in 1915 and 14–15 in 1925 were estimated from high school entry rates in the sample data (i.e., rates of entry among second- and third-generation Irish-Americans in the 1915 sample, and among the second generation in the 1925 sample, were compared with the rate for all children).

Table A.3. *Male sample members traced across time: results of the tracing effort*

Father's ethnic group, by period (selected groups)	Unsuccessful traces[a] (%)	Successful traces: residential information		
		Not available (%)	Available	
			Not needed (%)	Needed for trace (%)	Total (100%) N^b

Father's ethnic group, by period (selected groups)	Unsuccessful traces[a] (%)	Not available (%)	Not needed (%)	Needed for trace (%)	Total (100%) N^b
1880					
Yankee (NWNP)[c]	46.9	23.1	24.3	5.7	(449)
Irish	53.0	20.1	13.9	13.0	(452)
Black	64.6	20.4	12.1	2.9	(101)
All	51.6	20.9	18.7	8.9	(1,307)
1900					
Yankee	53.3	18.0	24.4	4.3	(339)
Irish	52.9	16.1	18.3	12.7	(219)
NWIRP[c]	48.7	19.1	21.3	10.9	(149)
Black	59.8	18.3	21.0	0.9	(115)
All	54.3	18.2	19.7	7.7	(1,379)
1915					
Yankee	52.9	16.5	24.8	5.8	(162)
Irish	45.3	15.0	24.7	14.9	(427)
NWIRP	40.4	14.8	34.9	9.9	(109)
Black	64.5	15.3	19.5	0.8	(130)
Russian Jew[d]	52.5	11.7	28.8	7.0	(214)
Italian[d]	52.4	12.1	27.8	7.8	(368)
Other immigrants[d,e]	56.7	16.3	24.5	2.4	(202)
All	52.8	16.6	24.5	6.2	(2,248)
1925					
Native white	49.3	13.2	30.7	6.8	(296)
Irish	48.5	11.8	26.5	13.2	(68)
Black	60.8	15.0	22.2	2.0	(153)
Russian Jew	45.8	11.1	40.3	2.8	(72)
Italian	46.7	10.0	34.5	8.8	(261)
Other immigrants[e]	48.7	12.2	31.8	7.4	(189)
All	47.7	11.8	32.9	7.6	(1,086)

[a] Includes those individuals not found in the directory and those found for whom no occupation was listed.
[b] Included are the random sample members as well as members of the supplemental samples of ethnic groups (both drawn from the census manuscripts) and samples of high school entrants (drawn from the school records). The N's reflect the numbers of observations. For the proportions, cases were weighted (as in all text tables dealing with occupational attainment) by sample of origin.

Individuals with common names presented a greater problem. Because the directory did not provide information on identifying characteristics such as age, place of birth, and race, it was difficult to match a sample member with a directory listing if several individuals with that same name were listed. When the research strategy was designed, it seemed wise to avoid limiting the sample to individuals with uncommon names, because no information was available on how such a limitation would bias the results.[24] Preliminary work with the samples indicated that those with common names were concentrated by ethnicity, most notably among the Irish in Providence. Within an ethnic group, no consistent differences emerged between those with common and uncommon names. However, the effects of including sample members with common names had been to reduce the number who could be found as adults in the directories. Middle initials could be used to differentiate some individuals from others, but often no initial was available, or, if it was, the directory listed more than one individual with the same name and initial.

The directory included some additional information that could help identify individuals, namely, address. Sometimes an individual with the same common name as a sample member lived at the same address that the sample member had lived at ten years earlier; in other cases, such an individual lived at a different address, but another individual was listed at that address too, and that second individual had the same name as the sample member's father (or mother, or sibling). In such cases, the probability of a correct match between sample member and directory listing was, of course, sharply increased. The trouble with exploiting this information was that it biased the sample in the direction of those who still lived with their families.

Table A.3 shows the results of the tracing efforts. No occupational data could be obtained from the directory for one large group of sample members. The names of many of these individuals did not appear in the directory, either because they no longer resided in the city or because the directory compilers had missed them. Many others in this group could not be matched because their names appeared more than once, and no residential information revealed the correct match. Still others were matched with a name in the directory, but no occu-

Table A.3 (Cont.)
[c]NWNP, father is native white of native parentage; NWIRP, father is native white of Irish parentage.
[d]Native-born sample members only in 1915.
[e]Immigrant fathers from countries other than the British Isles, Russia, and Italy.

Table A.4. *Comparison of multiple-regression results for occupational attainment: samples weighted by residence status and not weighted*

Selected coefficients	Not weighted by residence status		Weighted by residence status	
	Coefficient[a]	SE[b]	Coefficient	SE
A. Ethnicity: all groups compared with Yankees for 1880–1915, and with all native whites for 1925				
1880 sample				
Irish	6.4	(1.8)	6.2	(1.9)
Black	−17.8	(5.0)	−17.7	(4.7)
1900 sample				
NWIRP[c]	−6.3	(2.3)	−6.9	(2.4)
Irish	7.2	(2.3)	8.2	(2.3)
Black	−15.7	(4.9)	−15.3	(4.7)
1915 sample				
NWIRP	4.3	(2.1)	4.7	(2.2)
Irish	2.9	(2.1)	2.9	(2.2)
Black	−11.0	(4.8)	−11.2	(4.7)
Russian Jew[c]	10.4	(3.4)	10.2	(3.5)
Italian[c]	1.8	(2.4)	1.6	(2.4)
Other immigrants[c]	1.8	(2.1)	1.6	(2.0)
1925 sample				
Irish	3.5	(2.8)	3.9	(2.9)
Black	−11.4	(6.2)	−11.0	(6.1)
Russian Jew	5.4	(2.7)	5.4	(2.6)
Italian	−0.9	(2.0)	0.9	(2.0)
Other immigrants	1.2	(2.0)	1.4	(2.0)
B. High school: occupational advantages associated with high school entry[d]				
1880	11.4	(2.3)	11.5	(2.3)
1900	11.6	(2.0)	11.6	(2.1)
1915	9.3	(1.3)	9.1	(1.3)
1925	10.4	(1.5)	10.2	(1.5)
C. Residence status as predictor of sample member's occupational score[e]				
1880	−2.4	(1.3)		
1900	−2.6	(1.4)		
1915	−0.5	(1.2)		
1925	−0.7	(1.6)		

[a] Occupational score regressed on background factors; coefficients on dummy-variable terms for selected ethnic groups are shown. Also controlled; father's occupational score, property value, number of siblings, whether or not both parents present, educational attainment.
[b] Standard error.
[c] See notes for these groups in Table A.3.
[d] The coefficients on high school dummy variable (treated here as dichoto-

pation was listed with that name. If we were interested in levels of persistence and turnover in the community, it would be important to assess the proportion of individuals classified here for each reason. For our purposes, the reasons matter much less; the critical point is that we lack the information on their occupations. The other three groups of individuals include those who could be matched to an occupation in the directory. Those in the second and third groups had uncommon names; in the case of the third, residential information confirming the match was also available (although it was not used to make the match). The fourth group includes those with common names who were matched with a directory listing – but only because confirming residential information was found. Thus, individuals found on the basis of name only are those in the second and third categories. The possibility of bias due to residential status is introduced when the individuals in the fourth category are also included in the analyses.[25] These individuals, it can be seen, are not a large proportion of all sample members; however, it should be recalled that they compose about twice as large a proportion among those found.

My original plan had been to exploit information on the fourth category and to correct for biases by weighting down members of the third and fourth categories to the number in the third category alone, with separate weights for each ethnic group. However, that procedure was not followed. Rather, the cases were included without being reweighted. After perusing preliminary results, I began by tentatively ignoring the weighting issue (subject to later reweighting) because of complications with some of the codes that indicated how individuals had been traced. By the time the coding issues were resolved, much of the analysis had been completed, and so, for consistency, all results pertaining to occupational attainment that are reported in the text are based on samples in which the individuals found with the aid of residential information are included. Had the regressions included weighting for residential status, the results would have changed by utterly trivial magnitudes. This conclusion can be confirmed by studying Table A.4.

In Table A.4, occupational attainment was regressed on the same variables used throughout the preceding chapters. The results for critical

Table A.4 (Cont.)
mous: compared with no high school). Except for education, the other terms in the regression equation are those specified in footnote *a*.
[e]Occupational attainment regressed on variables indicated in footnote *a*; in addition, a dummy variable for residential status (living with family of origin, or not, at time of ten-year trace) is included; the coefficient on that variable is indicated here.

coefficients, particularly the relevant ethnic terms, are presented. For convenience, all groups in these tables were compared with Yankees in the first three periods and with native whites in the fourth. The regressions were run twice, first with no weights for residential status, then with weights for residential status (assigned separately for each ethnic group). The comparison shows that the impact of the reweighting was negligible – for the coefficients on high school entry (studied in Chapter 1) as well as for the ethnic terms.

Another set of regressions (not shown) were run without reweighting the residential variable, but including it as a control. This procedure, too, demonstrated that the weighting variable had no impact on the results of interest. It also produced estimates for the connection between residency status and occupational attainment; these are presented in the table. In the first two periods, young men living with their families of origin seem to have averaged slightly lower occupational scores than others. In the later periods, even this difference nearly disappeared.

In sum, any residential bias involved in the tracing procedure has not determined the conclusions of this study. That finding is not really surprising. The proportion of individuals found by virtue of the residential information was not large, and there is no evidence that ethnicity or schooling influenced occupational attainment in a distinctive way among them.

Another issue arising in any directory trace concerns the similarity between the individuals found and the entire group. Table A.5 shows comparisons between the entire sample and the successfully traced subsample for each period (the attributes of those in all four categories of the preceding table compared with those in the last three categories). There are biases inherent in such tracing – by ethnicity, by class, and also by education. However, they are actually quite modest, suggesting that those for whom we could find information in Providence and nearby towns were, at least on these criteria, quite representative of all.

In order to increase the number and representativeness of those successfully traced across time, sample members not found in the Providence directory were also traced to the city directories of some surrounding towns. They were sought in all the towns contiguous to Providence (Central Falls, Pawtucket, East Providence, Johnston, North Providence, and Cranston in 1910 and after), as well as in Warwick in the period in which it was important as a suburb of Providence (in 1920 and after). These towns were chosen partly for practical reasons: available sources, time and effort. However, the choice was also guided by Sidney Goldstein's study of suburbanization in Rhode Island history. He defines a first ring of suburbs for the period 1900–30 and a

Table A.5. *Comparisons of all male sample members and those found ten years later*

Sample members' characteristics	Proportions of sample members		Sample members' characteristics	Proportions of sample members	
	All (%)	Found (%)		All (%)	Found (%)
A. Ethnic composition: selected groups			C. Fathers' occupational strata		
1880			1880		
Yankee (NWNP)	32.1	35.2	High white-collar	9.7	12.4
Irish	40.8	39.5	Low white-collar	16.6	18.4
Black	2.4	1.8	Skilled	29.5	30.7
1900			Semiskilled	19.4	17.6
Yankee	20.7	21.2	Unskilled	24.9	21.0
Irish	19.6	20.2	1900		
NWIRP[a]	12.7	14.3	High white-collar	6.4	7.5
Black	2.4	2.1	Low white-collar	17.8	15.5
1915			Skilled	31.4	33.4
Yankee	13.8	13.7	Semiskilled	23.7	22.7
Irish	12.1	14.0	Unskilled	20.7	20.9
NWIRP	10.1	12.7	1915		
Black	2.0	1.5	High white-collar	8.0	8.4
Russian Jew[a]	3.2	3.2	Low white-collar	19.8	20.2
Italian[a]	10.7	10.8	Skilled	27.2	28.5
Other immigrants[a]	17.4	15.9	Semiskilled	24.7	24.1
1925			Unskilled	20.2	18.8
Native white	31.5	30.6	1925		
Irish	7.2	7.1	High white-collar	10.2	9.8
Black	1.4	1.2	Low white-collar	18.2	16.6
Russian Jew	7.7	7.9	Skilled	27.7	30.8
Italian	27.8	28.3	Semiskilled	24.8	25.8
Other immigrants	20.1	19.8	Unskilled	19.0	17.0
B. Proportion entering high school			D. Mean occupational scores for fathers		
1880	10.1	12.7	1880	25.1	27.3
1900	16.8	19.6	1900	25.0	25.7
1915	33.6	41.0	1915	26.1	26.4
1925	53.0	55.9	1925	27.8	27.3

Note: Proportions and means in this table may differ slightly from those in preceding chapters, because the weighting used for the group traced across time (which includes the high school supplemental sample) differed from that used for the entire age cohort selected from the census and used to study patterns of schooling. In this table, to maximize comparability across columns, the high school samples are included in the "all" group (as well as in the "found" group), and both are weighted like the group traced across time. In addition, many text tables pertain to both males and females, whereas this table pertains to males only.
[a]See notes for these groups in Table A.3.

second ring for the period after 1930. With the exception of two small towns (Barrington and Smithfield), all of his first ring was covered in the tracing.[26]

6. The coding and classification of occupations

Chapter 1 surveyed the issues that arise in using occupations to capture the important social distinctions among individuals. This section covers the specifics of occupational classification.

Total flexibility of coding was preserved in order to experiment with various classification schemes, in particular those of Stephan Thernstrom and Otis Dudley Duncan. Their work, in turn, rests on earlier efforts by Alba Edwards at the U.S. Census Bureau and on modifications in his classifications undertaken by the bureau.[27]

It is worth distinguishing three levels of generality in occupational classification. The most detailed level comprised (a) the descriptions respondents gave the census-takers – tens of thousands in every federal census; these were collapsed to (b) several hundred categories of occupations used for detailed tabular presentation. Census Bureau coders converted (a) into (b) by means of an alphabetical index of occupations that the bureau has published in conjunction with each census since 1910. A similar broad categorization was used to classify industries. Finally, the detailed categories were collapsed into (c) a few broad categories.

In the 1920s and 1930s, Alba Edwards created a version of the broad categories (c) that he believed were vertically ordered social strata, categories that would be useful descriptions of socioeconomic position (professionals, clerical workers, semiskilled workers, and so forth). He simultaneously overhauled the detailed list of occupational categories (b) and assigned each new detailed category to one of the broad strata he had proposed. He made the crucial judgments about vertical order on the basis of his knowledge of occupations derived from several decades of Census Bureau work. He did not systematically apply criteria such as average income, education, or surveys of occupational prestige, but Edwards made it clear that he was thinking of each of these, and more particularly of the skills required for the work.

The Census Bureau modified his scheme, most notably by diluting its purely vertical character. Specifically, it added broad categories of service workers to Edwards's list of strata. These service categories included a wide vertical range. Also, the bureau modified Edwards's detailed categories. He had included an enormous number of jobs in residual categories, particularly "operative, not elsewhere classified" and "laborer, not elsewhere classified." The bureau subdivided these larger categories by industrial sector. Finally, it reassigned categories on Edwards's detailed list to different strata. Many, for example, were shifted from the unskilled to the semiskilled stratum. This Census Bureau scheme was used in the 1940 U.S. Census and in each census thereafter, with some modifications introduced each time.

Thernstrom relied on the Census Bureau scheme, but modified it. First, he reassigned the occupations that the Census Bureau had placed in the anomalous service groupings back into the appropriate vertical category. Second, he subdivided the white-collar workers into high and low. The clerical and sales workers were clearly low, and professionals clearly high. Remaining were "managers, officials and proprietors." Those individuals who were unambiguously relatively wealthy ("banker, manufacturer") were classified as high white-collar. The rest were classified low white-collar, subject to revision later if they possessed a certain amount of assessed property (and if tax data were available).

Duncan's classification scheme, widely used by sociologists, assigned to each of the detailed occupational categories in the 1950 census a two-digit numeric score. The score was based on the educational attainment and income level typical of individuals in that category. These criteria were used because they had been found to predict the prestige value of occupations exceedingly well in survey data.

I assigned distinct codes to each occupational description – each combination of occupational title and industrial sector. These occupational descriptions, along with my code for each, were made machine-readable, alphabetized, and printed out as an occupational codebook. Research assistants who coded occupations with the help of the printout were therefore not required to make decisions about occupational classifications, but only to look up occupations in the codebook, much as Census Bureau coders use the alphabetical index mentioned earlier.

I also determined the Census Bureau code for each occupational description listed in my codebook (from the 1950 version of the bureau's alphabetical index).[28] Once each individual's occupation had been assigned the appropriate code from my codebook and made machine-readable, a program also assigned it the corresponding Census Bureau code. Finally, on the basis of these census codes, each occupation was assigned its score on Duncan's scale, the "occupational score" referred to throughout this study.

My own occupational code had been constructed in a way that also made it easy to classify individuals into Thernstrom's major occupational strata, high and low white-collar, skilled, semi-skilled, and unskilled blue-collar. Some tables in the text exploit Thernstrom's classification. In all of the regression work, the father's occupation is controlled using Duncan's occupational score. Assessed property value is controlled as a separate variable. Virtually all analysis of occupational attainment as a dependent variable is based on Duncan's scale.[29]

7. *The organization of the data collection and processing*

I studied the various sources, determined the research design, drew up directions for use of the sources, designed forms on which to record the information collected, pilot-tested them, and supervised all stages of the data collection. The data were actually collected by student research assistants, several score having been hired at one time or another. They spent, in all, many thousands of hours on the project. I trained each one, and frequently checked samples of their work.[30]

Large samples often are easier to collect from historical records than in contemporary surveys, because interviews and mailings are not involved. In the present case, however, the sample size (some 12,000 cases) does not convey the true scope of the effort, because each sample member had to be traced by hand in six to eight other sources. Each of those traces, on average, required nearly as long as the original process of selecting a sample member from the census. One may liken the effort, then, to the collection of a census sample of some 85,000 – except that the start-up effort of mastering new sources and working with new directions was much greater. These start-up costs may be understood by considering the directions required to collect the data (e.g., directions for the use of out-of-town directories or Catholic high school records). In all, I produced 125 single-spaced typewritten pages of directions for the project. The directions for the use of each source (city directory, census schedule, etc.), on the other hand, were generally three to six pages, and thus proved manageable.

Once the data were keypunched and verified, a considerable effort was made to check carefully for errors in keypunching or coding. Programs were written to check for incorrect values in every variable and to check for combinations of values on several variables that were logically inconsistent or improbable. The keypunching of all such cases was all rechecked by hand, and often the coding was rechecked by consulting the primary sources.

A professional programmer worked with the project through the data-collection and processing periods on a consulting basis, and several students contributed considerable amounts of programming time as well. However, I worked very closely with each of these programmers. I undertook nearly all the programming for the data analysis, principally in the SAS package.

8. *The use of regression analysis*

In studying rates – of high school entry or graduation, curriculum choice, or white-color employment – logit regression analysis was used. In studying means – GPAs and occupational scores – ordinary least-squares (OLS) regression was used.[31]

School variables typically were regressed on (1) the father's occupational score (using Duncan's scale of occupational scores), (2) the assessed value of the family's property (four categories: high, low, none, or unknown because of common-name problems),[32] (3) the number of children in the household, (4) whether or not both parents were present (yes, no), and (5) ethnicity. Ethnic groups were classified differently for each sampled year. These classifications follow; each category of ethnic origin among whites refers to the sample member's father. Regressions using 1880 data included dummy variables for the following: Yankees (native whites of native parentage); native whites of Irish parentage; native whites of other parentage; blacks; English, Scottish, and Welsh; Irish; and all others. For 1900, a dummy variable for Italians was added, and for 1915, another for Russian Jews. In addition, in 1915 (and only in that year) both native-born and foreign-born sample members were numerous among the children of Italians, Russian Jews, and the miscellaneous group of "all others." Accordingly, two separate dummy variables were included for each of these three groups. For 1925, the three categories of native whites had to be collapsed into one because the Rhode Island State Census of that year did not provide information on the sample member's grandfather's place of birth.

In many of the tables, a particular group (e.g., the Russian Jews) is compared with specific groups as well as with "all others." For the comparison with specific groups, regressions included the ethnic terms just indicated. For comparison with "all others," the regressions were rerun with all groups except the one of interest (e.g., the Russian Jews) placed in one category. Finally, when blacks were compared with three groups of whites (children of Yankees, of other native whites, and of immigrants), dummy variables for these four groups were created.

Regression for occupational attainment also explored the role of education. Three categories were distinguished: those who had not enrolled in high school, high school entrants, and high school graduates. For the 1925 data, a fourth category, those high school graduates for whom evidence of college entry was available, was added.

The figures reported from OLS regressions are the coefficients, typically the coefficients on ethnic dummy variables. These indicate the

difference in the means on the dependent variable between two ethnic groups, with other variables controlled – for example, the difference in mean occupational score between Russian Jews and Yankees,
or Russian Jews and all others. The t statistics for the coefficients are
included as well.

The figures reported from logit regressions are also the coefficients
and t statistics, but the coefficients have been exponentiated. In exponentiated form, a logit coefficient can be interpreted as an odds
ratio – the ratio of the odds that members of one group would behave
in a certain way compared with the odds that members of the other
group would do so (would enter high school, for example). Thus, in
comparing all others with the Italian boys for 1915, the logit coefficient was 0.8459; exponentiated, it was 2.33. That figure indicated
that the odds that all others would enter high school were 2.33 times
as great as the odds that Italians would do so.[33]

Sample members usually were weighted by sample of origin. The
exception occurred when two conditions were met: (1) only the ethnic
samples, not the sample of high school entrants, were included, and
(2) ethnicity was controlled. Unless otherwise indicated, regression
analyses excluded the tiny fraction of sample members who were living with no relative and the small fraction of others whose father's
occupation (or other guardian's occupation) was unavailable. The
numbers of cases indicated in each table always refer to the numbers
included in the particular analysis presented in that table.[34]

Regressions for each census year (1880, 1900, 1915, and 1925) and
those for boys and girls were nearly always run separately (exceptions are noted in context).

Typically, the first column of a table presents rates (or means), and
the second shows the odds ratios (or differences in means) based on
the first column (i.e., with no controls imposed). Then a column reports results from regression models in which controls were imposed
(or several columns show the effects of imposing various combinations of controls in different regression models). For a fuller description of the table arrangement, see Section 2.1.

9.   *Assessing contextual effects: the case of the Italians*

This section supplements the discussion of contextual effects in Section 3.4. It provides more detail on the methods employed and on
their limitations. It also calls attention to some national data relevant
to the relationship between return migration rates and length of children's schooling.

How, in the first place, is a contextual factor to be measured? Social scientists have relied on group rates (or means) for measures of contextual factors.[35] For example, remigration rates for immigrant groups would serve to order the groups according to how prevalent remigration was in each and thus how great its effect on each would be expected to be. The contextual effects of the class composition of the group can similarly be crudely gauged by arranging groups according to the mean of the fathers' occupational scores in each. In fact, a number of measures for the contextual effects of class composition were examined; the mean fathers' occupational score will serve as well as any of them.[36]

Each ethnic group in the city was assigned a score on each of these two measures. One was based on the rate of remigration for the group in the United States as a whole; the other was the mean score for fathers' occupations in the Providence sample.[37] We can now proceed to consider how strongly these factors are associated with measures of school behavior. For exploratory purposes, we can consider the rates of high school entry in 1915. How strongly, then, are rates of remigration for ethnic groups, and their mean occupational scores, correlated with high school enrollment rates?

Stated in this way, the second measurement problem is immediately clear: If there is in fact a strong association, is it due to these contextual factors, or is it simply spurious, due to some other factors associated with both (for example, with both the remigration rate and high school entry)? We can reduce the chances of spurious correlation to some extent because the Providence data make it possible to control for some of the obvious differences between groups, namely, the family background characteristics we have routinely controlled throughout. Thus, we can consider the contextual factors in a regression analysis that considers high school entry to be a function of several family background factors (father's occupation, value of the family's assessed property, number of siblings, whether or not both parents present) and of the rate of remigration for the group in which the individual is a member (or the mean occupational score of that group). In effect, the contextual factor replaces the ethnic categories in our analysis, and the question becomes to what extent the net ethnic differences in high school enrollment observed earlier (the ethnic differences that were not due to family background) can be explained by the rate of remigration (or mean occupational score). How much remains unexplained even after the rate of remigration (or mean occupational score) has explained all it can?[38]

Still, the problem of spurious association remains critical. Spuriousness is always a possibility, but in the present case (the study of contextual effects of ethnic-group membership) it assumes vastly greater importance. It does so because there are only a few ethnic categories, and individuals are classified on contextual variables on the basis of their ethnic identity alone. Consequently, the effective sample size for the purposes of sorting among competing explanations is less than a dozen. If, for example, the rate of remigration is found to be strongly associated with schooling, we cannot explore whether other features of these groups are more critical or whether the rate of remigration remains strongly associated with schooling even when controlling for these other features.

Checking for contextual effects, then, may be more useful in eliminating factors that are not strongly associated with school patterns than in confirming the operations of those contextual factors that are strongly associated with schooling.[39] Indeed, in the light of these difficulties, the preferable course usually is to study the effects of a relevant factor at the individual level – for example, class origins – and if those individual-level effects explain most of the ethnic difference, we may assume that the contextual effects associated with it explain the rest. If, on the other hand, they leave much of the ethnic differences unexplained, it would be rash to assume that the corresponding contextual effects can account for the rest of that difference. However, because of the explanatory importance of social class and remigration, an attempt to assess their contextual effects directly was made.

In fact, the contextual effects of social class apparently created virtually none of the differences in schooling between Italians and others. The association between the mean occupational score of the group and high school entry (with family background factors, including the occupation of each particular family head, controlled) was negligible, and, as indicated in the text, the relevant odds ratios dropped by negligible amounts.[40]

The association between rates of remigration and the schooling of second-generation children provides an example of the dangers of misinterpreting a strong correlation between a contextual effect and the behavior of interest referred to earlier, for that association was very strong, and statistically significant. Indeed, the association between remigration and schooling can explain *all* of the difference between Italian rates of high school entry and those of others that had not been explained by family background characteristics. The odds ratio measuring the ethnic difference in male high school entry rates will drop from 1.76 with family background characteristics (including household head's citizenship status) controlled to 0.60 (indicating Italian rates of entry substantially *higher* than those of others) when the remigration rates of groups are also controlled! The results for female high school entry rates are similar.

Table A.6. *Correlations between remigration rate and median years of schooling*

	Age cohort (in 1960)	
Group	45–54	55–64
All groups included	−0.70[a]	−0.58[a]
"Old immigration" only	0.21	0.25
"New immigration" only		
All groups	−0.67	−0.61
USSR excluded	−0.38	−0.17

Note: The remigration rates and medians for schooling are presented in Table 3.10.
[a]Statistically significant ($t > 1.96$).

The strong relationship between the rate of remigration and school achievement is visible also in national data that include over a dozen ethnic groups (Table 3.10). The 1960 census data on median years of schooling completed by age cohort permit us to examine two especially relevant cohorts: those who would have reached age fifteen in 1910–20 and 1920–30 (i.e., those age forty-five to fifty-four and fifty-five to sixty-four in 1960). The remigration rates for the European groups are strongly negatively correlated with median years of schooling completed: −0.58 and −0.70, respectively (Table A.6).[41] Of course, this correlation does not control for other family background factors, as the associations discussed in connection with the Providence data do, but it is surely suggestive.

What, then, is the explanation for the strong association between remigration rate and school achievement? Is it indeed due to the contextual effects of the former, or is it a spurious association, an association due to some other aspect of the ethnic differences?

Most of the association is almost certainly spurious. In the first place, it is striking that in the national data, those classified as part of the "old immigration," the British, Germans, Irish, and Scandinavians, were characterized by lower return rates. The "new immigrant" groups (those predominating after 1880) generally had higher rates (the Jews are the notable exception), although there was a considerable range among them. Within the old immigrant group, the association between schooling and return rates is trivial, and within the new immigrant groups, it is trivial once the Jews are excluded from the calculation. If the return rates were influential, why should they appear so much less so when the groups are classified in this way?

A second argument concerns the Providence data. We have solid estimates of the impact of family background characteristics (social class and family structure) on ethnic differences in schooling. We are faced with the suggestion that the contextual effects of the remigration rates were much more important in distinguishing the school patterns of the Italians from those of others than were class, family structure, and household head's citizenship status together.[42] Common sense argues against such a strong effect. Also, controlling the household head's citizenship status should capture some contextual effects of remigration – much as controlling the father's occupation appears to capture most contextual effects of the mean occupational score. It stands to reason, after all, that the children of aliens probably were closer to the contextual effects of remigration than were the children of citizens (even if most return migrants were not parents). Only those contextual effects of remigration not captured by the individual-level variable (household head's citizenship status) would therefore be left to be captured by the contextual variable (the remigration rate) – reducing still further the possibility that those effects could be as great as the regressions suggest.

A third consideration involves the relationship between the school and occupational outcomes. The supposed contextual effects of remigration noted earlier (restriction of information, restriction of opportunities for employment by members of one's own group, and establishment of a peer culture less oriented toward American patterns of mobility) could be expected to have influenced occupational attainment as well as schooling. Yet, in fact, only the school patterns of the Italians require explanation; occupational attainment differs hardly at all once family background characteristics and schooling have been controlled.

That is the best we can do in considering the impact of the contextual effects in creating the ethnic difference in schooling. The contextual effects of the remigration rate cannot be measured with precision. However, as the concluding paragraph of the text in Section 3.4 indicates, in the context of other findings, it would be rash to assume that it could adequately account for the residual difference between the schooling of Italians and that of others.

Notes

Introduction

1 Fox Butterfield, "Why Asians Are Going to the Head of the Class," *New York Times, Educational Supplement,* August 3, 1986, 18.

2 See Charles E. Silberman, *A Certain People: American Jews and Their Lives Today* (New York, 1985), chap. 4 and references cited there, as well as those cited in Chapter 4 of this book.

3 United States Bureau of the Census, "Population Profile of the United States: 1982" (*Current Population Reports,* Special Studies Series P-23, no. 130; Washington, D.C., December 1983), 20; *Nativity and Parentage* [Final Report PC(2)-1A, 1960 Census of Population, Washington, D.C., 1965], Table 12; also see Chapter 3 of this book.

4 On contemporary ethnic differences in economic attainment, see, for example, David L. Featherman and Robert M. Hauser, *Opportunity and Change* (New York, 1978), 452–61; Thomas Sowell, *Ethnic America: A History* (New York, 1981), passim.

5 Philip Gleason, "American Identity and Americanization"; Michael Olneck and Marvin Lazerson, "Education," in Stephan Thernstrom, ed., *Harvard Encyclopedia of American Ethnic Groups* (Cambridge, Mass., 1980).

6 A similar survey of explanations of ethnic differences, particularly those in the sociological literature, may be found in Roger D. Waldinger, *Through the Eye of the Needle: Immigrants and Enterprise in New York's Garment Trades* (New York, 1986), particularly chap. 1–2.

7 The distinction between these two sorts of pre-migration heritage is far from perfect. A strong work ethic, for example, could well be called an occupational skill. Nevertheless, a working distinction is possible by considering as beliefs, attitudes, habits, and values those features that are not restricted to one sort of occupational task (if any). Thus, a work ethic would qualify as a cultural attribute.

8 Stephen Steinberg, *The Ethnic Myth: Race, Ethnicity, and Class in America* (Boston, 1981), x, passim.

9 Sowell, *Ethnic America;* Steinberg, *The Ethnic Myth.* Neither Sowell nor Steinberg was concerned only with explanations for ethnic differences, although both treated the subject very extensively. Steinberg did not deny the importance of cultural factors in determining group behavior, but rather argued that culture has been overrated as a determinant. An adequate theory, he claimed, is one that sees culture operating to distinguish groups in the context of the constraints of class, which is primary (ix–x,

102–3, 137–8, passim). As stressed later in the text, the extent to which groups could have differed as a result of cultural attributes cannot in fact be deduced from the general formulation that class and culture interact. However, the thrust of his work is in fact to suggest a rather minimal role for cultural attributes. In part, this thrust may be the result of his concern to show that cultural attributes have been overrated.

10 In some historical studies, such as studies on social mobility, the theme appears in much the same terms as among social scientists. See Stephan Thernstrom, *The Other Bostonians: Poverty and Progress in the American Metropolis, 1880–1970* (Cambridge, Mass., 1973), 160–75, 203–19.

11 John Higham, "Current Trends in the Study of Ethnicity in the United States," *Journal of American Ethnic History*, vol. 2 (Fall 1982), 9. See also Olivier Zunz, "The Synthesis of Social Change: Reflections on American Social History," in O. Zunz, ed., *Reliving the Past: The Worlds of Social History* (Chapel Hill, 1985), 53–114, especially 86–92.

12 Herbert Gutman, "Work, Culture and Society in Industrializing America, 1815–1919," *American Historical Review*, vol. 78 (1973), 531–88.

13 Daniel T. Rodgers, "Tradition, Modernity and the American Industrial Worker: Reflections and Critique," *Journal of Interdisciplinary History*, vol. 7 (Spring 1977), 655–81; David Montgomery, "Gutman's Nineteenth-Century America," *Labor History*, vol. 19 (Summer 1978), 416–29, especially 421, 425, 428; Lawrence T. McDonnell, " 'You Are Too Sentimental': Problems and Suggestions for a New Labor History," *Journal of Social History*, vol. 17 (Summer 1984), 629–54, especially 636.

An interesting point about the intellectual history of the 1970s is that Gutman's enormous influence did not manifest itself more strongly in the use of his essay by those, like Sowell, who stressed the role of premigration cultural attributes to explain group differences and to urge nonintervention by government. It should be recalled that Gutman particularly emphasized work-ethic differences between industrialized and preindustrial workers, a subject with great potential for exploitation in this context. That he would have found such a use of his views revolting is not a complete explanation; the views of Oscar Lewis apparently were appropriated for purposes different than those he had intended in the discussion of the culture of poverty several years earlier (see Steinberg, *The Ethnic Myth*, chap. 4). More important, I suspect, were, first, Gutman's emphasis on characteristics common to many preindustrial cultures (which in turn results from his contrast of "preindustrial" and "industrial," a contrast for which the authors cited earlier all criticized him, but which made it less obvious how to use his work to explain differences between, say, Italians and Jews) and, second, the fact of his location well within the historical profession, rather than in the social sciences, where those concerned with policy questions would have been more likely to encounter his work. Third, and probably most important, his concern was with how working-class immigrants managed to resist the destructive pressures of migration into industrial capitalist society and succeeded in forging family and worker solidarity. His essay appeared in the intellectual context of the early seventies, when the culture-of-poverty concepts were being criticized and attention to class issues was great. Gutman's formulations became part of the effort to understand the strengths of working-class communities, rather than part of the explanations for the slower economic progress made in some ethnic groups than in others.

14   The population explosion in Europe, though partly due to factors only distantly related to these developments, was also directly stimulated by them. Similarly, persecution of European minorities surely contributed to the flow of migration, but the particular circumstances in which the minorities chose to migrate can hardly be separated from the wider expansion of capitalism. On the wider context of capitalism, see, for example, John E. Bodnar, *The Transplanted: A History of Immigrants in Urban America* (Bloomington, Ind., 1985), especially chap. 1.

15   Steinberg, *The Ethnic Myth*, 80, 87, 103, passim; Bodnar, *The Transplanted*, xvi–xxii, 210, passim.

16   That the class position of blacks at a given historical moment was the result of earlier discrimination is an important, but separate, issue. Note, too, that in the case of blacks, the distinction between culture and discrimination as sources of behavior is also relevant.

17   David B. Tyack, *The One Best System: A History of American Urban Education* (Cambridge, Mass., 1974); Olneck and Lazerson, "Education"; Stephan Thernstrom, *The Other Bostonians;* Thomas Kessner, *The Golden Door: Italian and Jewish Immigrant Mobility in New York City 1880–1915* (New York, 1977); Christopher Jencks et al., *Inequality: A Reassessment of the Effect of Family and Schooling in America* (New York, 1972). For an example of work by educational historians using published aggregate records to study school achievement, see Michael Olneck and Marvin Lazerson, "The School Achievement of Immigrant Children: 1900–1930," *History of Education Quarterly,* vol. 14 (Winter 1974), 453–82. Recently, social historians have used data from the manuscript schedules of the census to study social origins and attendance patterns. See, for example, Carl F. Kaestle and Maris A. Vinovskis, *Education and Social Change in Nineteenth-Century Massachusetts* (New York, 1980). For a comparison of attendance and school-record data, see the introduction to Section 4 in the Appendix of this book. Although the wealth of detail drawn from the Providence school records remains unique, as do the scope and size of the samples, others have also begun to exploit data from school records, in at least one case to study social mobility. See Reed Ueda, *Avenues to Adulthood: The Origins of the High School and Social Mobility in an American Suburb* (New York, 1987), chap. 7.

Chapter 1

1   Useful material on the history of Providence may be found in William G. McLoughlin, *Rhode Island, A Bicentennial History* (New York, 1978); Peter J. Coleman, *The Transformation of Rhode Island, 1790–1861* (Providence,

1963); Charles C. Carroll, *Rhode Island, Three Centuries of Democracy* (4 vols.) (New York, 1932). As the titles suggest, most relevant histories treat the state, rather than focusing directly on the city. As a result, there are yawning gaps in the historical writing about the city itself. There is, for example, no modern political history of Providence. Patrick T. Conley and Paul Campbell, *Providence: A Pictorial History* (Norfolk, Va., 1982), focuses on the city and is helpful.

2 Carroll, *Rhode Island*, vol. 2, chap. 29, deals with Rhode Island manufacturing establishments after 1860.

3 Providence city registrar, *86th Annual Report Upon Births, Marriages and Deaths in the City of Providence for 1940* (Providence, 1941), 126–8, presents the figures for successive state and federal censuses. A useful discussion of the timing of the economic decline of Providence is found in John P. Colangelo, "Italians in Providence: 1900–1930" (unpublished undergraduate thesis, Brown University, 1974), chap. 2.

4 U.S. Bureau of the Census, *Fourteenth Census of the United States Taken in the Year 1920*, vol. 1 (Washington, D.C., 1921), 81.

5 John H. Cady, *Civic and Architectural Development of Providence 1636–1950* (Providence, 1957); William Kirk, ed., *A Modern City: Providence, R.I. and Its Activities* (Chicago, 1909), provide some information on neighborhoods and buildings.

6 U.S. Department of the Interior, Census Office. *Statistics of the Population of the United States at the Tenth Census* (June 1, 1880) (Washington, D.C., 1883), vol. 1, 536–41; U.S. Bureau of the Census, *Thirteenth Census of the United States Taken in the Year 1910*, vol. 3 (Washington, D.C., 1913), 624; *Fourteenth Census*, vol. 3 (Washington, D.C., 1922), 920.

7 On the early history of Providence schooling, see Charles Carroll, *Public Education in Rhode Island* (Providence, 1918); Providence School Committee, *Report* (title varies; Providence, published annually; henceforth abbreviated *PSCR*) for 1899–1900 (which includes "Centennial Celebration of the Establishment of the Public Schools: Historical Addresses and Reports"); Thomas B. Stockwell, *History of Public Education in Rhode Island 1636–1876* (Providence, 1876); Emit Duncan Grizzell, *Origin and Development of the High School in New England before 1865* (New York, 1923); Providence School Committee, *A Brief Sketch of the Establishment of the High School, Providence, together with the Dedicatory Exercises of the New Building* (Providence, 1878).

The reformers of the 1830s and 40s were well aware that the high school was highly controversial, because it was a large public expenditure for relatively few students. They nevertheless convinced a considerable majority of the voters to support a referendum calling for creation of the institution as the logical pinnacle of free public instruction. The vote to support the high school took place a few years before a vote in Beverly, Massachusetts, to abolish a high school. Referenda on the creation of these new and expensive institutions also took place in other towns and cities in the first half of the nineteenth century. See, for example, S. Willis Rudy, *The College of the City of New York: A History 1847–1947* (New

York, 1949), chap. 2. These referenda are interesting because they reveal something about how individuals from different social backgrounds perceived extended schooling. On the intriguing Beverly case, compare Michael B. Katz, *The Irony of Early School Reform: Educational Innovation in Mid-Nineteenth Century Massachusetts* (Cambridge, Mass., 1968); Maris A. Vinovskis, *The Origins of Public High Schools: A Reexamination of the Beverly High School Controversy* (Madison, 1985). See also my own essay review of the latter (*Journal of Interdisciplinary History*, 1988, in press).

8 *PSCR* for 1884, 64. The two most important changes of the intervening years occurred in the 1850s: First the high school was reorganized so that it offered a classical program and an English program, leading to diplomas (which had not been awarded in earlier years). Second, following various short-lived arrangements, the School Committee came to be elected on a ward basis directly by the voters. *PSCR* for 1899–1900, 157, 268; Carroll, *Public Education in Rhode Island*, 391.

9 The proportion for ten-year-old children is based on a hand count of children of that age selected from the manuscript schedules of the census. The proportion for fifteen-year-old children is based on the 1880 sample described in the next section.

10 *PSCR* for 1902–3, 87; Carroll, *Public Education in Rhode Island*; Barbara Tucker Cervone, "Rounding Up the Children: Compulsory Education Enforcement in Providence, R.I., 1883–1935" (doctoral thesis, Harvard Graduate School of Education, 1983).

11 *PSCR* for 1899–1900, 157–9; Joel Perlmann, "Curriculum and Tracking in the Transformation of the American High School: Providence, R.I., 1880–1930," *Journal of Social History*, vol. 19 (Fall 1985), 29–55.

12 *PSCR* for 1899–1900, passim; *PSCR* for 1900–1, 92.

13 Carroll, *Public Education in Rhode Island*, 239–42; Carroll, *Rhode Island, Three Centuries*, 956; *PSCR* for 1923–4, 37. The laws also required that older children attend school if they were not at work. This provision applied to children one to two years older than the legal employment age (the requirement was altered from time to time, and in some years those who had completed a certain amount of schooling were exempted from this requirement).

14 *PSCR* for 1902–3, 69; *PSCR* for 1886, 55; *PSCR* for 1890, 31–55; *PSCR* for 1895, 31–48. Age–grade tables appeared annually in the reports for a decade after 1917.

15 *PSCR* for 1902–3, 78 (on evening schools); *PSCR* for 1911–12, 41–50 (on industrial education); *PSCR* for 1915–16, 31 (on prevocational schools); *PSCR* for 1917–18, 35–43 (on the trade school).

16 *PSCR* for 1899–1900, 136–7; *PSCR* for 1911–12, 19–33; *PSCR* for 1916–17, 10–11 (on special schools); *PSCR* for 1917–18, 49–70; *PSCR* for 1921–2, 31–5; *PSCR* for 1922–3, 23 (on IQ tests); *PSCR* for 1917–18, 43–9; *PSCR* for 1919–20, 30–7 (on guidance); *PSCR* for 1919–20, 26–8 (on Americanization).

17 *PSCR* for 1922–3, 31–2; *PSCR* for 1924–5, 15–17 (on the Gary Plan).

18 *PSCR* for 1921–2, 28–31; *PSCR* for 1931–2, 5–14 (on junior high schools);

PSCR for 1925–6, 5–9 (on the size of the School Committee); Division of Field Studies, Institute of Educational Research, Teacher's College, Columbia University, *Report of the Survey of Certain Aspects of the Public School System of Providence Rhode Island, School Year 1923–1924* (New York, 1925).

19 *PSCR* for 1935–6, 12–14, 36.

20 On the Catholic schools, see especially Americo D. Lapati, "A History of Catholic Education in Rhode Island" (unpublished doctoral dissertation, Boston College, 1958); Carroll, *Rhode Island, Three Centuries*, chap. 34, deals with Catholic and other private schools.

21 See, for example, David B. Tyack, *The One Best System: A History of American Urban Education* (Cambridge, Mass., 1974); Michael B. Katz, *Class, Bureaucracy and Schools: The Illusion of Educational Reform in America* (expanded edition, New York, 1975); Edward A. Krug, *The Shaping of the American High School 1880–1920* (Madison, 1964); Marvin Lazerson, *Origins of the Urban School: Public Education in Massachusetts 1870–1915* (Cambridge, Mass., 1971); Selwyn K. Troen, *The Public and the Schools: Shaping the St. Louis System, 1938–1920* (Columbia, Mo., 1975); Raymond E. Callahan, *Education and the Cult of Efficiency: A Study of the Social Forces That Have Shaped the Administration of the Public Schools* (Chicago, 1962).

22 State-of-birth information was available only in the 1880 and 1900 censuses. The generalizations in the text therefore are based only on data from the first part of the period under consideration.

23 There is no consistent difference between the occupations of Yankee fathers who were migrants and those who had been born in Rhode Island. Similarly, the children of Yankee migrants enrolled in high school about as often as the children of Yankee nonmigrants. For a fuller discussion, See Ari Joel Perlmann, "Education and the Social Structure of an American City: Social Origins and Educational Attainments in Providence, R.I., 1880–1925" (doctoral dissertation, Harvard University, 1980), 164–73.

24 Figures in the text are based on mothers, fathers, and grandfathers of sample members. Had information been collected on grandmothers as well, it could only have reinforced the conclusion that very few families were unfamiliar with recent migration.

25 Ninety-one percent of the eleven-year-old children had attended school during the year preceding the census. All school attendance rates discussed in this section are based on the census question concerning children's school attendance during the year preceding enumeration – not, strictly speaking, attendance at the time of the census. On the history of school attendance earlier in the century, see Carl F. Kaestle and Maris A. Vinovskis, *Education and Social Change in Nineteenth-Century Massachusetts* (New York, 1980), especially chap. 3 and 4; Lee Soltow and Edward Stevens, "Economic Aspects of School Participation in Mid-Nineteenth-Century United States," *Journal of Interdisciplinary History*, vol. 8 (Autumn 1977), 221–43.

26 Figures on age at school entry by ethnicity and class are not available in the Providence data set because it covers children ages eleven to sixteen. Nevertheless, a hand count of children five to twenty years old in the

1880 census manuscripts showed roughly equal attendance rates at each age from seven to eleven. This suggests that the pattern among children of age eleven in the Providence data set – nearly universal attendance in all social groups – also existed in the rest of the seven-to-eleven age range. See also Kaestle and Vinovskis, *Education and Social Change*, 98, and Tables A4.4–A4.9, which also suggest nearly universal schooling in this age range well before 1880.

27   Joel Perlmann, "After Leaving School: The Jobs of Young People in Providence, R.I., 1880–1915," in Ronald K. Goodenow and Diane Ravitch, eds., *Schools in Cities: Consensus and Conflict in American Educational History* (New York, 1983), 3–43.

28   The median was estimated to be 8.8 years. Beverly Duncan, *Family Factors and School Dropout: 1920–1960* (Ann Arbor, 1965), 148–50, indicates a method for calculating average length of schooling from the proportions enrolled at each age. It assumes "that a child enters school only once and entry occurs before the age of peak attendance, that a child leaves school only once and leaving occurs after the age of peak attendance; and age of entry is independent of age of school leaving."

29   One reason for this pattern is simply that the primary and grammar school program in Providence, as in many other places in New England, included nine grades, not the eight with which we are familiar today. In addition, however, many did not progress at the rate of a grade per year; there was a considerable tendency to hold students back to repeat grades. As a consequence, the age–grade fit was loose indeed. On the age–grade fit in the early nineteenth century, see Joseph F. Kett, *Rites of Passage: Adolescence in America 1790 to the Present* (New York, 1977), 14–21.

30   In particular, given the questions of interest here, there will be virtually no attention to definitions of social class that stress the importance of the changing class consciousness of historical actors, forged in interaction with other classes; E. P. Thompson, *The Making of the English Working Class* (New York, 1963), 9–10; for a recent discussion, see, for example, Olivier Zunz, "The Synthesis of Social Change: Reflections on American Social History," in O. Zunz, ed., *Reliving the Past: The Worlds of Social History* (Chapel Hill, 1985), especially 86–92. Or, rather, insofar as changes in class consciousness affected the behaviors of interest here, those effects should be reflected in the behavior of children of different social backgrounds defined in terms of the characteristics we do study – the father's occupation and wealth, insofar as we can measure it. Otherwise, the states of consciousness affected groups defined on some other basis.

31   Or, more precisely, the heads of households are grouped into the five strata; a mother or other relative was taken as the head when the father was not present. The occupational classification scheme described in these paragraphs follows Stephan Thernstrom, *The Other Bostonians: Poverty and Progress in the American Metropolis, 1880–1970* (Cambridge, Mass., 1973); see especially his Appendix B and the section on occupational classification in the Appendix to this book.

32   Another vertical ordering of occupations is presented later in this chap-

ter. Other aspects of economic position – notably, comparisons of employees versus employers and of individuals in different economic sectors – will be considered, especially in connection with the Italians and Russian Jews. Information on self-employment is available from the city directories; in one period, 1915, it is also possible to distinguish employers from others.

33   Because social origins clearly influenced both length of school attendance and progress through the grades, the relations between social origins and schooling typically are clearer when a measure of grade attainment, such as high school entry, is studied than when merely length of school attendance is considered. For a fuller discussion of the two measures, see the introduction to Section 4 of the Appendix.

In later chapters, information on high school graduation is exploited, as well as information on college entry in 1925 (the one period for which it is available); here it would add little.

34   Directories excluded most women even if they were gainfully employed. The limitation of the study to male patterns of mobility is one shared by nearly all studies of social mobility, and especially historical studies, because data on men's jobs are much more readily available. The 1915 Providence data include women's occupations (drawn from marriage records). However, the issues arising in the study of women's attainments in the context of overwhelming gender segregation in the labor market led me to defer that study for a separate treatment. The complexities of using two quite different kinds of occupational data (one from a given age, the other from age of marriage) suggested the same strategy.

35   The restriction of the study to those who remained in the city is common to virtually all historical studies of social mobility, because all rely on tracing individuals from one source to another of a later year. Also, the percentages mentioned in the text refer to individuals who were successfully located in the directory and whose occupation was given there. See Appendix, Section 5, for details.

36   An increase of a standard deviation in sample members' mid-twenties occupational scores was associated with an increase of 0.44–0.72 of a standard deviation in their mid-thirties scores. Also, in most of the samples, the earlier score explained more of the variance in the later score than did measurable family background characteristics and education together.

37   A three-strata classification of occupations is used here instead of the five-strata classification used earlier in order to conserve cell sizes. The initial sample has been reduced in size by the omissions discussed earlier; figures are presented for many ethnic groups, and very few of the young men had reached the high white-collar stratum.

38   Except in the 1925 cohort, who spent their twenties in the Great Depression.

39   The 100-point scale does not combine occupational information with evidence on the assessed value of the family's property, as the occupational strata can be constructed to do (see text). In controlling family back-

ground, the father's occupational score and the assessed value of the family's property were treated in regression models as two separate variables influencing the schooling and occupational attainment of the sample members. Tax data were not used in evaluating the social positions of the male sample members as young adults. For further details, see the Appendix, Sections 6 and 8.

Another dimension of social position, employment status, is often taken into account in the use of the 100-point scale, because the coding scheme for the scale calls for assigning a different score to the self-employed in many occupations. The evidence of self-employment was derived from the 1915 Rhode Island census schedules and the city directories.

40   The use of the scale instead of the strata might be less attractive (because interpretations of results might be less easily presented) if interactions between class background and ethnic background were critical in determining schooling, or if those between class background and educational experience were critical in determining occupational attainment, but they were not.

41   Otis Dudley Duncan, "A Socioeconomic Index for All Occupations," in Albert J. Reiss, Jr., et al. *Occupations and Social Status* (New York, 1961), 109–38; Robert W. Hodge, Paul M. Siegel, and Peter H. Rossi, "Occupational Prestige in the United States, 1925–63," *American Journal of Sociology*, vol. 70 (November 1964), 286–302; Christopher Jencks et al., *Inequality: A Reassessment of the Effect of Family and Schooling in America* (New York, 1972), 176–9; Donald J. Treiman, "A Standard Occupational Prestige Scale for Use with Historical Data," *Journal of Interdisciplinary History*, vol. 7 (Autumn 1976), 283–304; Robert M. Hauser, "Occupational Status in the Nineteenth and Twentieth Centuries," *Historical Methods*, vol. 15 (Summer 1982); Joel Perlmann, "Who Stayed in School? Social Structure and Academic Achievement in the Determination of Enrollment Patterns, Providence, Rhode Island, 1880–1925," *Journal of American History*, vol. 72 (December 1985), 598.

42   It is possible that the slight rise for fathers' occupations in the last year was due to the fact that occupations had to be determined only from city directories for that year's sample; the Rhode Island Census of 1925 did not include a question on the respondent's occupation.

If the last cohort of sons is ignored, their jobs having been obtained in the depths of the Great Depression, the mean occupational score of the sons varied by less than a point across three samples over thirty-five years. Somewhat greater numbers appear to have received white-collar jobs in the two later cohorts. Because the mean occupational score did not change, these probably were clerical and sales positions, whose relative standing was not much different from that of the skilled jobs that suffered a comparable decline.

The standard deviation for fathers' occupations was equally consistent over time: 19.1, 18.1, 19.2, and 19.8. Standard deviations for the sons' jobs showed a similar stability over time: 18.4, 18.4, 19.3, and 17.9.

The occupational scores of the fathers of those male sample members found in the later city directories differed hardly at all from the scores of the fathers of all male sample members: by two points in 1880, and by less than a point in each of the other periods. See Table A.5 in the Appendix.

43 Conclusions about attainment (or about mobility), of course, can be put in terms of occupational strata or in terms of the occupational scale. The choice will make virtually no substantive difference for the purposes of this book.

44 See, for example, Christopher Jencks et al., *Who Gets Ahead?: The Determinants of Economic Success in America* (New York, 1979), 316–27, which summarizes the correlations among background characteristics, occupational attainment, and income in eleven major contemporary data sets.

Chapter 2

1 Patrick J. Blessing, "Irish," In Stephan Thernstrom, ed., *Harvard Encyclopedia of American Ethnic Groups* (Cambridge, Mass., 1980), 528, 540.

2 See Blessing, "Irish"; David Noel Doyle, *Irish Americans: Native Rights and National Empires: The Structure, Divisions and Attitudes of the Catholic Minority in the Decade of Expansion, 1890–1901* (New York, 1976), 38–90; Kerby A. Miller, *Emigrants and Exiles: Ireland and the Irish Exodus to North America* (New York, 1985), 492–506. Miller (in note 186 to chap. 8) provides an extensive list of the recent work on Irish-American social structure.

3 In 1880, the third generation constituted 7% of the Irish-American children, in 1900, 37%, and in 1915, 45% (from Table 1.1). The 1925 Rhode Island State Census unfortunately did not ask for parents' places of birth. Consequently, whereas we can identify the places of birth of the 1925 sample members' own parents (by examining what the parents said about their own places of birth), we cannot distinguish the third-generation Irish-Americans from other children of natives.

4 See Table 1.1.

5 The small number of native whites of Irish parentage in the 1880 sample were also better off than the immigrant heads of that year.

6 The average of the upper estimates for high school entry rates of Irish boys and girls is 8.8% (from Table 2.2).

7 Child labor rates exhibited the same trend as schooling: With controls imposed, a large difference between Yankees and Irish remained in 1880, but only trivial differences were found in 1900 and 1915.

The tables present comparisons to the most relevant group, the children of Yankees (native whites of native parentage). Comparisons to all others (which are routinely made in later chapters) were omitted as misleading or redundant. In 1880, nearly all others were in fact Yankees. In later years, their composition changed considerably, making the comparison to 1880 less clear. Table 2.7 compares occupational attainments of Irish-Americans with those of Yankees, as well as with those of all others, because the relative position of the Yankees with respect to occupational attainment changed over time. The behavior of the children of the native whites of Irish parentage is not reported for 1880 because the number of cases is too small for meaningful multivariate analysis.

8　For a full discussion, see Joel Perlmann, "Working Class Homeownership and Children's Schooling in Providence, R.I., 1880–1925," *History of Education Quarterly,* vol. 23 (Summer 1983), 175–93, and the references cited there. For a different view, see David John Hogan, *Class and Reform: School and Society in Chicago, 1880–1930* (Philadelphia, 1985), 114–25, 287–8.

9　Some support for this argument is available if we look more closely at the factors we can control. In 1880, when no controls for social background are imposed, the odds that the sons of Irish immigrants, 11–16 years of age, would work were 9.45 times as great as those that the sons of the Yankees would do so. With all controls except father's occupation imposed, the ratio was 7.69; with father's occupation also controlled it was 4.99 (t = 5.69). Father's occupation is the most important measure of economic class in the data (property value being negligible for so many). Had family income data been available, it, too, would surely have had some independent effect, notwithstanding its correlation with father's occupation. But even if this second measure of economic class had as large an impact as the first, it would reduce the odds ratio from 4.69 to a ratio 0.65 as great (4.99/7.69 = 0.65) – to 3.24. That ratio would still constitute strong evidence that family background factors cannot adequately explain the ethnic differences in child labor patterns. Another category of influences on behavior, known as contextual effects, is discussed in the following chapter (Section 3.4). Concerning their relevance to Irish–Yankee differences, see Appendix, note 40.

10　For 1925, the Irish advantage in high school enrollment rates over native whites (to whom they are best compared in the absence of data on Yankees) is statistically significant. However, the high school graduation rate of the sons of Irish immigrants in 1925 was similar to that of the sons of natives, suggesting that the significantly higher Irish rate of high school entry observed was not sustained into the later teen years.

Other measures of school performance, including high school graduation rates and grades in courses in grammar school and high school (available only for 1915 and 1925), show no pattern that would lead one to doubt the conclusions drawn in the text from measures of school attendance, child labor, and high school entry.

When corrections for missing data have been taken into account in the table, the estimated range for the residual ethnic difference in male high school entry rates is frustratingly large, including a low minimum (an odds ratio of 1.3; see last rows of Table 2.2). If only this series had been available, it would, of course, be risky to conclude that a change had occurred. Fortunately, much less ambiguous evidence is available: the girls' high school enrollment rates, and especially the evidence from school attendance and child labor (which involves no estimation).

11　See Providence School Committee, *Report* for 1881, 20, and for 1899–1900, 90, which remark on the return of prosperity after the depressions of 1873 and 1893, respectively. Each indicates that economic improvement had reduced enrollments during that year to an unusual degree.

12 Miller, *Emigrants and Exiles*, 107. See also Oscar Handlin, *Boston's Immigrants: A Study in Acculturation* (Cambridge, Mass., 1941), chap. 5; Stephan Thernstrom, *The Other Bostonians: Poverty and Progress in the American Metropolis, 1880–1970* (Cambridge, Mass., 1973), 168–9, note 30.

13 See Miller, *Emigrants and Exiles*, 472–6, 508–9.

14 On the history of schooling in nineteenth-century Ireland, see Donald H. Akenson, *The Irish Education Experiment: The National System of Education in the Nineteenth Century* (London, 1970).

15 The arguments here could be rephrased in terms of theories of "modernization," but it is not necessary to complicate the discussion with an evaluation of such theories. For a recent discussion, see Walter Nugent, *Structures of American Social History* (Bloomington, Ind., 1981), 5–12.

16 Sample members were classified in terms of the literacy status of the head of the household, usually the father. Earlier work indicated that classifying them according to the mother's literacy status would not have altered the conclusions presented in the text. Ari Joel Perlmann, "Education and the Social Structure of an American City: Social Origins and Educational Attainments in Providence, R. I., 1880–1925" (unpublished Ph.D. dissertation, Harvard University, 1980), 341, 403.

17 See, for example, Handlin, *Boston's Immigrants;* Diane Ravitch, *The Great School Wars: New York City, 1805–1973* (New York, 1974), 3–76; James W. Sanders, *The Education of an Urban Minority: Catholics in Chicago, 1833–1965* (New York, 1977); James W. Sanders, "Boston Catholics and the School Question, 1825–1907," in James W. Fraser, Henry L. Allen, and Sam Barnes, eds., *From Common School to Magnet School: Selected Essays in the History of Boston's Schools* (Boston, 1979), 43–75; James W. Sanders, "Catholics and the School Question in Boston: The Cardinal O'Connell Years," in Robert E. Sullivan and James M. O'Toole, eds., *Catholic Boston: Studies in Religion and Community, 1870–1970* (Boston, 1985), 121–69; Michael R. Olneck and Marvin Lazerson, "Education," in Thernstrom, ed., *Harvard Encyclopedia of American Ethnic Groups;* William G. McLoughlin, *Rhode Island: A History* (New York, 1978).

18 Robert W. Hayman, "Catholicism in Rhode Island" (doctoral dissertation, Providence College, 1977), 491–6; Americo D. Lapati, "A History of Catholic Education in Rhode Island" (doctoral dissertation, Boston College, 1958), 130–5.

19 On the Providence Democratic Party, see Elmer E. Cornwall, Jr., "Party Absorption of Ethnic Groups: The Case of Providence, Rhode Island," *Social Forces,* vol. 38 (March 1960), 207. On the Rhode Island political background generally, see McLoughlin, *Rhode Island;* John D. Buenker, *Urban Liberalism and Progressive Reform* (New York, 1973), and, on Boston, Sanders, "Boston Catholics and the School Question" and "Catholics and the School Question in Boston." Figures on the School Committee come from hand counts traced to the census schedules; figures on the proportion of Irish teachers in 1880 come from a seminar paper by Vic-

toria MacDonald Huntzinger, Harvard Graduate School of Education, 1984; figures for 1908 come from U.S. Immigration Commission, *The Children of the Immigrants in School* (Washington, D.C., 1911), vol. 2, 265–7, vol. 5, 194–5.

20 The Irish increase in schooling did not come as a result of a great growth in Catholic educational institutions. The Catholic school system was indeed expanding, but in order for it to have been the source of the overall rise in levels of schooling among the Irish-Americans, that system would have had to sharply increase its share of their enrollment. That had not occurred. The Catholic share of all Irish secondary school enrollment did not sharply increase either (Table 2.11).

21 Austin Dowling, "Diocese of Providence," in William Byrne et al., eds., *History of the Catholic Church in the New England States* (Boston, 1899), 383.

22 Thomas Sowell, *Ethnic America: A History* (New York, 1981), 37–8. Sowell's references to sources in the quoted passages have been omitted.

23 Sowell cited Diane Ravitch, *The Great School Wars*, 178. In that context, she indeed mentioned the finding Sowell mentions, but also cited another, less dramatic, contrast among the groups found in another study from those years. She cited Leonard P. Ayres, *Laggards in Our Schools: A Study of Retardation and Elimination in City School Systems* (New York, 1912), and David K. Cohen, "Immigrants and the Schools," *Review of Educational Research*, vol. 40 (February 1970), 13–27. Ayres presented evidence (e.g., p. 107) that suggests that such extreme differences between the Irish and the Jews and Germans did not exist, and several of Cohen's tables suggest the same point (e.g., Table 2, which shows that, in a survey of several cities, among those born in the city surveyed, 27.6% of the children of the Irish were "retarded in grade," whereas 31.3% of the children of the Germans and 29.6% of the children of the Russian Jews were). However, Cohen, who surveyed many studies, also cited Joseph King Van Denburg, *Causes of Elimination of Students in Public Secondary Schools of New York City* (New York, 1911), 96; cf. Cohen, "Immigrants," 17. Van Denburg had reported that after eight semesters, only 1 Irish high school entrant of 73 in his sample had graduated, and 6 others were still enrolled ("retarded in grade"): a 1.4% graduation rate; Cohen's paper apparently mistakenly printed the 1% figure as 0.1%. In sum, Van Denburg found that 1% of the Irish graduated on schedule (and another 8% had persisted through eight semesters); this result, an atypically low summary statement for Irish school achievement, was lowered still further through an error, and then cited in Ravitch's and Sowell's widely read studies.

24 Calculated from U.S. Bureau of the Census, *U.S. Census of Population: 1960*, Final Report PC(2)-1A ("Nativity and Parentage: Social and Economic Characteristics of the Foreign Stock by Country of Origin") (Washington, D.C., 1965), 52, 55, 63 (Table 12). The figures used are for the northeast region.

Any use of retrospective data involves biases due to differential mortality; in this case, the poorly educated were more likely to die young.

Consequently, ethnic differences in the proportion poorly educated would appear less extreme among those sixty-five to seventy-four years of age in 1960 than among the same cohort in 1910, for example (when they had been fifteen to twenty-five years old). However, in order to explain how the Irish (who by 1960 appeared so similar to others) could have begun so much less well educated in 1910, one must assume unrealistically high educational differentials in mortality. Also, the comparisons with the Germans and with some others in Table 2.5 show the Irish rates to be higher. Assumptions of very high ethnic differentials in mortality within categories of educational attainment would be required to square this 1960 pattern with a 1910 pattern in which Germans had the higher rates. For evidence on educational differentials in mortality, see Evelyn M. Kitagawa and Philip M. Hauser, *Differential Mortality in the United States: A Study in Socioeconomic Epidemiology* (Cambridge, Mass., 1973), 17.

25   According to Thernstrom, "immigrants from Sweden closely resemble those from Ireland both in their low educational level and in their overwhelming concentration in blue collar jobs, and yet the second-generation Swedes outperformed the Irish by all three measures of achievement . . . differences in group culture played a significant role. Whether these cultures are best described with religious labels [or national labels] cannot be determined. . . . But . . . immigrants from . . . Catholic peasant societies . . . brought with them distinctive habits. . . ." *The Other Bostonians*, 174–5.

26   Eighteen percent of Irish, 40% of German, and 52% of English fathers held white-collar jobs. The median level of education among Irish fathers was two years below that of the English and German fathers. The importance of the Protestant–Catholic distinction (see preceding note) is not supported by this evidence. The Swedish experience was far more successful than those of the other two Protestant groups, and the Irish Catholic experience seems to have been about what one would expect when compared with the other two Protestant groups (after social origins are taken into account). If the Irish of the twentieth century can be thought of as peasants (and the Germans and English as something else), this evidence also does not support the idea that origin in a peasant society is of critical explanatory importance.

All this is not to discredit the largest of Thernstrom's points: Old World cultural values may well have mattered, as the success of the Swedes and the Jews (compared with all the others) suggests.

27   The U.S. Census provides figures on the children of native whites only for the United States as a whole. Because the natives were concentrated in different regions than the Irish, and because educational attainment varied by region, the reliance on national figures is less than optimal and probably favors the Irish.

28   The 1960 U.S. Census data, of course, cannot provide support for the argument that Irish patterns of behavior in 1880 were quite different from what they were later, because the data do not extend that far back in time; they provide support for only the second argument made in this

section: that by 1900 the Irish level of educational attainment was not low relative to that of other groups.

For one historical study that lends direct support to the idea of a change in Irish patterns of behavior during the decades of the late nineteenth century, see the discussion of child labor and school attendance in John Modell, "Patterns of Consumption, Acculturation and Family Income Strategies in Late Nineteenth Century America," in Tamara K. Hareven and Maris A. Vinovskis, eds., *Family and Population in Nineteenth Century America* (Princeton, 1978), 206–40. Modell's data cover several northeastern cities between 1874 and 1901. His main purpose is to show that by 1901, and probably by 1889, there were no differences between patterns of schooling among the children of Irish and natives when other demographic factors are taken into account. But in the present context, the critical point is the strong possibility that such differences did exist in 1874.

29 The sample includes children eleven to sixteen years old in 1880. Those eleven to twelve years old were traced to the directory of 1892, rather than to the directory for 1890, to increase the likelihood that they would be old enough to be listed.

30 We can also try to refine the controls for father's and son's education by restricting attention to homogeneous subgroups. Most who entered high school or graduated from grammar school can be identified and excluded from analysis; in this way, most of the effects of differences in schooling between Yankees and Irish can be eliminated. Nearly all those remaining received less than a grammar school education. Finally, those who had illiterate parents can be excluded. With all these exclusions, the magnitude of the Irish–Yankee gap in job levels remains large. It drops from 6.4 to 4.8 points in 1880, and from 7.2 to 6.8 points in 1900.

31 There is no reason to assume that sensitivity to the value of schooling was perfectly correlated with all other forms of familiarity with modern ways. It was especially tied to the diffusion of schooling and literacy in Ireland; these, in turn, were only imperfectly related to the diffusion of other forms of social transformation. Similarly, the Irish influence in the school system and that in the labor market probably grew at different rates.

These reasons for differences in timing may help explain why Irish school attainment appears to have changed by 1900, whereas occupational attainment changed only in 1915 (relative to that of Yankees). However, the difference in trends must be treated cautiously; it is based, after all, on only one of the four samples, the 1900 sample. That two measures might spread fairly far apart in one of four samples is not terribly improbable. Another reason to suspect that the 1900 gap between Irish educational and occupational attainments is due to sampling variability is that the gap is less pronounced for the third generation of Irish-Americans than for the second (see Tables 2.2, 2.4, and 2.7).

32 On the historiography of Catholic education in the United States, see James W. Sanders, "Roman Catholics and the School Question in New

York City: Some Suggestions for Research," in Diane Ravitch and Ronald J. Goodenow, eds., *Educating an Urban People: The New York City Experience* (New York, 1981), 116–40, especially 116–19; Marvin Lazerson, "Understanding American Catholic Educational History," *History of Education Quarterly*, vol. 17 (Fall 1977), 219–317. On the earlier period, see Jay P. Dolan, *The Immigrant Church: New York's Irish and German Catholics, 1815–1865* (Baltimore, 1975). Major studies of the contemporary American situation include Andrew M. Greeley, *The American Catholic: A Social Portrait* (New York, 1977); Andrew M. Greeley and Peter H. Rossi, *The Education of Catholic Americans* (Chicago, 1966); James S. Coleman, Thomas Hoffer, and Sally Kilgore, *High School Achievement: Public Catholic and Private Schools Compared* (New York, 1982).

33 See studies such as that of Michael B. Katz, "Who Went to School?" *History of Education Quarterly*, vol. 12 (Fall 1972), 432–54, and others cited by Maris Vinovskis, "Quantification and the Analysis of American Antebellum Education," *Journal of Interdisciplinary History*, vol. 12 (Spring 1983), 761–86. Little of this sort of work has focused on the Catholic schools, partly because census schedules, which most historians have mined, provide information on school attendance generally, but not on whether or not the school attended was Catholic.

34 Their social origins, unfortunately, cannot be studied fully with the sample data; Catholic elementary school records, as well as Catholic high school records prior to 1915, were too poorly preserved to permit that. Consequently, this section rests more heavily than others on published data.

35 Sanders, *The Education of an Urban Minority*; Sanders, "Roman Catholics and the School Question in New York City"; Sanders, "Boston Catholics and the School Question"; Sanders, "Catholics and the School Question in Boston: The Cardinal O'Connell Years."

36 See Sanders, "Roman Catholics and the School Question in New York City," 119, for the difference in the proportions of Catholics in Boston and Chicago; see Table 2.8 for the similarity between Boston and Providence.

37 From Table A.2 in the Appendix. Some Italians (and some French Canadians) no doubt enrolled in territorial parish schools rather than in the schools of national parishes, but their numbers can hardly have invalidated the conclusions from the figures in the text.

38 On the Irish–German contrast, see especially Sanders, "Roman Catholics and the School Question in New York City," 127, "Boston Catholics and the School Question," 56, and "Catholics and the School Question in Boston," 164–5.

39 Sanders, *The Education of an Urban Minority*, 45, indicates enrollment in national parish schools. The Immigration Commission, *The Children of Immigrants in Schools* (Washington, D.C., 1911), vol. 2, Chicago report, Table 2 (pp. 564–8), indicates the ethnic identity of public school pupils in attendance on a particular day in 1908. Although these figures relate to attendance and those cited by Sanders relate to enrollment, biases

should be similar for both groups. As for Italians, 702 enrolled in their national parish schools, and 9,258 in the elementary grades of the public schools. For the Poles, the figures were 21,310 in the parish schools and 6,915 in the public schools.

40 Dowling, "Diocese of Providence." For example (p. 383), during the mid-nineteenth century "the first cost of the churches made the building of schools impossible." It is, however, difficult to determine how much instruction preceded the construction of buildings.

41 Indeed, some 45–50% of the Providence school children were Catholics in 1880, 1900, and 1915, and by 1925 that proportion had risen to 55–60%. By comparing these proportions to the estimated proportions that pupils in the Catholic grade schools constituted among all pupils (Appendix Table A.2, line 9), it would appear that about 38% of the Catholic pupils were in parochial schools in 1880, about 32% in 1900 and 1915, and about 28% in 1925. If these estimates were compared with the proportion of Irish Catholics in the Catholic school system, it is clear that the two series bear little relationship. The reason is the changing ethnic composition of that Catholic population: In 1880, nearly all were Irish; by 1900, they included many Italians.

42 Even the formulation of the Third Plenary Council left room for exceptions when it was impractical to establish schools. James A. Burns, *The Grown and Development of the Catholic School System of the United States* (New York, 1912), 193.

43 Greeley, *The American Catholic*, 167.

44 Sanders, "Roman Catholics and the School Question in New York City," 130–1. See also Thernstrom, *The Other Bostonians*, 174, and especially Howard Ralph Weisz, *Irish-American and Italian-American Educational Views and Activities, 1870–1900: A Comparison* (New York, 1976), 47–96.

45 James A. Burns, who studied American Catholic schools in the first decade of this century, indicated that tuition generally ranged between fifty cents and a dollar per month. He also concluded that "the increasing tendency in the public school system of late years to eliminate every element of expense to the parent, has greatly accelerated the movement toward Catholic free schools. The change has been made quite generally in the larger cities, as well as in many of the towns. . . . In many parishes textbooks are also provided free." The only direct evidence from Providence itself is a comment made in 1893 by the Superintendent of the Providence public schools Horace Tarbell, in which he distinguished the parish schools from Catholic academies: "the academies charge tuition while the parochial schools are all free." But whether or not the burden of tuition and other school costs had really been removed from parents as fully as these observers suggest is unclear. Finally, Studs Lonigan's father paid a dollar per month in Chicago during the World War I years. Burns, *The Growth and Development of the Catholic School System*, 276–7; James T. Farrell, *Studs Lonigan* (New York, 1938), 13; Providence School Committee, *Report* for 1893, 35. On wages, see, for example, Thernstrom, *The Other Bostonians*, 298–300.

46 Providence School Committee, *Report* for 1893, 35–6.
47 In addition to the works already cited, Charles C. Carroll, *Rhode Island: Three Centuries of Democracy* (New York, 1932), and Rhode Island Commissioner of Public Schools, *Annual Report* for 1892–1921 (Providence), include useful information about the Catholic schools.
48 Joel Perlmann, "Curriculum and Tracking in the Transformation of the American High School: Providence, R.I., 1880–1930," *Journal of Social History*, vol. 19 (Fall 1985), 29–55.
49 Perlmann, "Curriculum and Tracking."
50 The academic program in which a student was enrolled was not indicated systematically in the Catholic high school records prior to that time.
51 Among the sons of the Irish, the trends are especially strong (Table 2.14), but their extreme nature may well owe something to sampling variability. Also, evidence from the 1915 sample suggests that the extreme differences in curriculum choice among the Irish sample members of 1925 did not hold among their predecessors of 1915. For the earlier year, curriculum information is not available at La Salle, but it is available at the comparable public high schools. In those schools, a larger proportion of the sons of Irish immigrants were in college preparatory programs than in 1925 (38% versus 24%).
52 The trends in the samples receive important confirmation from the reports of the Rhode Island Commissioner of Public Schools. These indicate the number of students enrolling in each high school and the number of graduates from each for the years 1891–1921. The proportion that graduates constituted among total number enrolled provides a rough measure of the graduation rates in Catholic schools compared with those in public schools. Prior to 1905, the proportion was greater in public high schools for both boys and girls in every year but two. In 1905 and after, it was larger in the Catholic schools for both boys and girls in twelve of the fifteen years, and larger by at least 50% in seven of these years. Even when compared only with the Classical High School pupils, the Catholic high school students were more likely to graduate.
53 In the 1915 regression analyses, all Catholic school pupils were compared with pupils in the public high school college preparatory programs. This procedure was used because curriculum-choice data for that year was unavailable in the Catholic schools.
54 Nearly all the sons of the Irish immigrants who chose a college preparatory program in 1925 chose one at La Salle; nearly all who chose a terminal program chose it at a public high school (Table 2.14). Consequently, the relevance of ethnicity and curriculum track cannot be fully distinguished. In 1915, however, many Irish-Americans in the public institutions were enrolled in college preparatory programs, so that comparisons between them and the Catholic school students permit us to distinguish the impacts of ethnicity and curriculum. See also the preceding note.
55 Coleman, Hoffer, and Kilgore, *High School Achievement*.
56 Richard J. Murnane, "A Comparison of Public and Private Schools: Les-

sons from the Uproar (Review Essay)," *Journal of Human Resources,* vol. 19 (Spring 1984), 263–77.

57 It is possible that the list identifies priests only, excluding other brothers. Still, it is probable that less than one-eighth of the entrants chose the school with the intent of entering the clergy. Moreover, some among the public high school students, particularly Protestants, were also considering a career in the clergy. Their behavior affected the public high school graduation rates.

58 Lapati, "A History of Catholic Education in Rhode Island," 160, 201.

59 The peer influence will not be captured by the regression analysis even when that analysis takes account of the social origins of each individual. This peer influence is an example of a contextual effect. Contextual effects are discussed more fully in Chapter 3.

60 An intriguing question raised by this material concerns the parochial schools: If the Catholic high schools were academically special in the ways indicated, was the same true for the parish schools? They shared many of the attributes of the Catholic high schools that might have mattered. In particular, by the twentieth century, the Irish parochial schools in Providence were serving a long-settled community. However, on this issue the Providence data shed no light.

Chapter 3

1 The magnitude of the Italian immigration can also be appreciated by noting that those from the northern, more economically developed, provinces of Italy (although but one-sixth of all Italian immigrants) would, if considered alone, have constituted the eighth largest immigrant group during the period, after the Irish, but before any Slavic group except the Poles.

See Thomas J. Archdeacon, *Becoming American: An Ethnic History* (New York, 1983), chap. V, and especially Table V-3, for a useful summary of the data on immigrant arrivals and departures. See Imre Ferenczi, comp., *International Migrations, Vol. I: Statistics* (New York, 1929), Table 10, for the figures distinguishing northern and southern Italians. For a discussion of remigration, see Dino Cinel, *From Italy to San Francisco: The Immigrant Experience* (Palo Alto, 1982), especially chap. 3–4. For comparisons of northerners and southerners, remigration, and intriguing international comparisons, see also Samuel L. Baily, "The Adjustment of Italian Immigrants in Buenos Aires and New York, 1870–1914," Herbert S. Klein, "The Integration of Italian Immigrants into the United States and Argentina: A Comparative Analysis," Jorge Balan, John D. Gould, and Tulio Halperin-Donghi, "Comments" (on Klein's paper), and Klein, "Reply," *American Historical Review,* vol. 88 (April 1983), 281–346.

2 Leonard Covello, *The Social Background of the Italo-American School Child* (Leiden, 1967; edited by Francesco Cordasco from Covello's New York University doctoral dissertation of 1944), especially chap. 8–10.

3 See, for example, citations to the work in Herbert J. Gans, *The Urban*

Villagers: Group and Class in the Life of Italian-Americans (New York, 1962), and in Nathan Glazer and Daniel Patrick Moynihan, *Beyond the Melting Pot: The Negroes, Puerto Ricans, Jews, Italians and Irish of New York City* (Cambridge, Mass., 1963), passim.

4 Covello, *Social Background*, 287.

5 Covello, *Social Background*, 403; he adds (403–4): "The most overt conflict between the American school and the Italian parental home seems to derive from the economic values of Italian family life. This does not necessarily mean that the poverty of the family *per se* – material deficiency, unemployment, etc. – are the real motives. The economic motives are subordinate to the total culture complex of the Italian family, but the conflict itself is most frequently rationalized by the Italian parent as one of economic validity. Thus the old-world tradition which demanded of the child a share in the economic upkeep of the family regardless of the child's age and capacity, was invoked in America. The American compulsory school attendance law which conflicted with the economic role of the child was bound to produce a negative attitude toward the American school and toward formal education." Further sources of conflict arose over the nature of social life and discipline in the schools (chap. 9).

6 Covello, *Social Background*, 401.

7 Alice Kessler Harris and Virginia Yans-McLaughlin, "European Immigrant Groups," in Thomas Sowell, ed., *American Ethnic Groups* (Washington, 1978), 119–20.

8 "Cultural factors have little independent effect on educational outcomes, but are influential only as they interact with class factors." Stephen Steinberg, *The Ethnic Myth: Race, Ethnicity, and Class in America* (Boston, 1981), 132–44. From the examples he provides, one can infer that Steinberg expects the differences between Italians and others to be greatly diminished when social class is controlled (pp. 141–5). See also Stephen Steinberg, *The Academic Melting Pot: Catholics and Jews in American Higher Education* (New York, 1974), chap. 4. Steinberg's views are also discussed in the Introduction and the Conclusion; see especially the Conclusion, note 17.

   Other authors who have stressed the cultural factors include Virginia Yans-McLaughlin, *Family and Community: Italian Immigrants in Buffalo, 1880–1930* (Ithaca, 1977), Thomas Sowell, *Ethnic America, A History* (New York, 1981), chap. 4, and Michael R. Olneck and Marvin F. Lazerson, "The School Achievement of Immigrant Children: 1900–1930," *History of Education Quarterly*, vol. 14 (Winter 1974), 453–82.

9 John W. Briggs, *An Italian Passage: Immigrants to Three American Cities 1890–1930* (New Haven, 1978), especially chap. 3, 9, and 10. This work is discussed further in the concluding section of this chapter. Another author who has treated the cultural theme with some skepticism is Miriam Cohen, "Changing Educational Strategies among Immigrant Generations: New York Italians in Comparative Perspectives," *Journal of Social History*, vol. 15 (Spring 1982), 443–66.

10 Michael J. Piore, *Birds of Passage: Migrant Labor and Industrial Societies* (New York, 1979).

11 On comparisons among particular groups, see Josef J. Barton, *Peasants and Strangers: Italians, Rumanians and Slovaks in an American City 1890–1950* (Cambridge, Mass., 1975), John Bodnar, Roger Simon, and Michael P. Weber, *Lives of their Own: Blacks, Italians and Poles in Pittsburgh, 1900–1960* (Urbana, Ill., 1982), Thomas Kessner, *The Golden Door: Italian and Jewish Immigrant Mobility in New York City 1880–1915* (New York, 1977), Judith E. Smith, *Family Connections: A History of Italian and Jewish Immigrant Lives in Providence, Rhode Island, 1900–1940* (Albany, N.Y., 1985).

12 Changes in the proportions of the foreign-born could also have been brought about if the sample had included more younger children of established families, or more children from families in which the parents began raising children at a later age. In fact, there were no consistent rises in the fathers' ages over time, which would have been expected had either of these explanations been correct.

13 More precisely, the data indicate little family dissolution among couples who were raising children.

14 See U.S. Immigration Commission, *Reports* (Washington, D.C., 1911), vols. 29–33: "The Children of Immigrants in Schools," Table 4 for each city. The rates are calculated from the numbers enrolled in school at ages twelve and fifteen. The assumption is that very few of either sex had dropped out by age twelve, so that the number enrolled at that age reflects the size of the cohort. Also, the figures are based on public school enrollments only. However, few Italians were enrolled in the parochial schools (see Chapter 2).

Covello, *Social Background*, 287, 292, stressed that for girls, in particular, extending schooling was regarded as both unnecessary and unattractive because it mingled adolescent boys and girls. See also Jerre Mangione, *Mount Allegro: A Memoir of Italian American Life* (New York, 1981; original edition Boston, 1943), 162, 218, 274–5, 308. For an interesting discussion of the changing roles of these cultural values, see Donna R. Gabaccia, *From Sicily to Elizabeth Street: Housing and Social Change Among Italian Immigrants, 1880–1930* (Albany, 1984), especially 111–15. Even Gabaccia's formulations, however, leave plenty of room for ethnic distinctiveness in the treatment of girls.

15 Restricting analysis to native-born children may also reduce the range of ethnic differences in economic standing. Those families whose adolescent children had been born in the United States had had a longer time to establish themselves. Although controlling for the father's occupation and for other aspects of family background is meant to capture the family's economic standing, it no doubt does so imperfectly.

16 The ethnic composition of the "other immigrant" group was as follows:

	1915 (%) (U.S.-born only)	1925 (%)
French Canadian	25.6	32.4
Other Canadian	11.6	
Scandinavian	16.1	8.2

Table (Cont.)

	1915 (%) (U.S.-born only)	1925 (%)
German	9.7	5.3
Austrian	6.0	4.7
Polish	10.9	19.4
Other eastern European	4.0	10.0
Portuguese	6.7	6.5
Turkish and Armenian	4.1	8.3
All other	5.3	5.2
Total	100	100

The 1925 Rhode Island Census did not distinguish French and English Canadians. The figures for the three earlier census years suggest that about three in ten Canadians were of English background. Obviously, the comparison with the Italians would be conceptually more satisfying if the English were excluded here (because the intention was to exclude English-language groups). However, in 1925, the distinction, as just indicated, could not be made. It seemed pointless to redefine the ethnic groups for 1915 that had been used throughout the study simply to isolate the small group of English Canadians. However, additional runs confirmed that their exclusion would have made little difference in the tables, and none in the conclusions.

The Russian-born were excluded on the assumption that they were Jews (see Chapter 4). Poles and others from eastern Europe were less likely than Russians to be Jews, but many of those in Providence were (as their names show).

These "other immigrants" are discussed further in Section 3.5.

17 Had the Italians been compared with all other immigrants, or with the Jews or Irish, instead of with the restricted subgroup used here, the differences in each of the following tables would have been greater than those presented.

18 The point is clear even in a comparison of high school entry rates among the sons of white-collar Italians and low-manual-worker "other immigrants": 24% versus 19% in 1915, 46% versus 51% in 1925.

19 The limitations of the GPA evidence are also less serious when the focus is not on the Irish (the group most concentrated in Catholic schools). The GPA data are discussed in the Appendix (Section 4B2); see also Joel Perlmann, "Who Stayed in School? Social Structure and Academic Achievement in the Determination of Enrollment Patterns, Providence, Rhode Island, 1880–1925," *Journal of American History*, vol. 72 (December 1985), 588–614.

20 The exception concerns the boys in 1915, who had the highest mean GPA of any ethnic group. The anomalous result probably is due to sampling variability. High school grade differences were more likely to have been due to sampling error than were those of sixth-graders (the t ratios comparing Italians and all others were all below 1.7 in the former case, and

all above 3.1 in the latter). To attribute the anomaly to the academic self-selection of the Italians choosing to go on to high school seems rash in the face of the low mean GPAs for ninth-grade girls in 1915 and boys in 1925. On the anomalous group, see also the figures in note 28.

21 U.S. Immigration Commission, *Report,* vol. 29, 64–5 (Tables 46 and 47). The tables refer to pupils eight years old or older.

22 The retardation figures based on the Immigration Commission data, of course, do not include controls for family background, but in the context of the rest of the evidence they strongly suggest that Italian grade retardation would have been much greater than that of other groups even if such controls had been imposed.

In the Providence data, the school patterns of boys, in particular, suggest the importance of the grade-retardation factor: Ethnic differences in child labor rates at age fourteen or fifteen are much smaller than ethnic differences in high school entry rates (under ten percentage points, compared with over twenty-five).

A third factor in determining who received extended schooling was, of course, the age at which children started school. If the Italians started much later than others, they could have reached high school less often even if they were as likely to remain enrolled through age fifteen or sixteen. The Immigration Commission data cited in the text, indicating that even among those starting school at age six there were great differences in rates of retardation, provide strong evidence that much more than entry age is involved in explaining low rates of extended schooling among the Italians.

23 Fewer of the foreign-born were found in Providence ten years later, a fact that might seem to suggest that more had returned to Italy. However, fewer of the Russian Jews born abroad were successfully traced across time than were Russian Jews born in the United States, and very few Russian Jews returned to their country of origin.

24 Stephen Thernstrom, *The Other Bostonians: Poverty and Progress in the American Metropolis, 1880–1970* (Cambridge, Mass., 1973), provides some data on the Italians that support the same conclusion. The Italians in his 1910 sample were more concentrated in lower-strata jobs, but their progress over time does not seem particularly different from the city norm (*The Other Bostonians,* 61, 136):

	High white-collar (%)	Low white-collar (%)	Skilled manual (%)	Low manual (%)	N (100%)
All sample members					
1910	5	26	27	42	(1,067)
1930	14	36	22	28	(278)
Italians only					
1910	2	10	23	65	(138)
Last job	10	25	27	38	(48)

Data pertain to 1930 for the entire group, and to the last known job for the Italians.

Discussions of Italian advancement do not typically argue that the Italian occupational mobility was particularly slow, only that the starting position was low, and that the particular positions taken by the second generation may have been affected by patterns of schooling. See also Kessler Harris and Yans-McLaughlin, "European Immigrant Groups," 107–38, especially 112–15, and Sowell, *Ethnic America: A History*, chap. 5, especially 123–4, 126–7.

25   There was some variation by level of schooling in the magnitude of the Italian disadvantage in occupational attainment (for the figures, see note 28). The variation is interesting here chiefly because it suggests that in 1915, the Italian disadvantage may have been somewhat larger than Table 3.5 implies for those who had not entered high school, four-fifths of the entire Italian cohort. Nevertheless, even among this group, the Italian occupational disadvantage amounted to only 3 points, and some part of it was surely due to years of elementary schooling completed (0.6 of a point controlling for differences indicated in the imperfect Providence elementary school data). Also, the relevant variation by educational level (the interaction term) was not statistically significant.

26   Admittedly, ambiguities arise in comparing ethnic differences in educational and occupational attainments. The difficulty is especially great when one has been measured in terms of categories (high school entry, high school graduation) and the other in terms of a continuous scale (the 100-point occupational scale). Nevertheless, the conclusion that Italians differed from others in schooling more than in jobs is strongly supported by several sorts of evidence.

First, differences in schooling between Italians and others were as large as any ethnic differences in schooling encountered in any period – comparable to those between Irish and Yankee in 1880, or those between Jews and others in 1915 and 1925. But the differences in occupational attainment between Italians and others were not large compared with those that stand out: the Irish–Yankee contrast in the first two periods, the position of the Jews in the later periods, or the position of the blacks in each of the four periods.

Second, differences on GPA were stated in terms of a continuous scale (Table 3.4). Because the standard deviation of sixth-grade GPA was about 0.76 in 1915 and 0.80 in 1925, the GPA difference between the Italians and others was between 0.29 and 0.37 of a standard deviation in each of the three samples. The difference between Italian men and others in occupational attainment, by contrast, was only 0.06 in 1915 and 0.13 in 1925 (see Table 3.5).

Efforts to estimate differences in mean years of schooling between groups on the basis of the Providence data (and with an eye to published census data as well) are more difficult and involve larger risks of errors in estimation, but they, too, suggest that ethnic differences in mean years of schooling completed were greater than ethnic differences in occupational attainment in both samples.

27   One can argue, in the terms of the economist, that the costs of eventual occupational attainment were partly, or fully, offset by the additional

income earned in the extra years of work made possible by entering the job market at an earlier age. The assumption here is that other groups were acting to maximize their returns in leaving school when they did. By deviating from the behavior of these other groups, the Italians were acting in a way that did not maximize those economic returns. See also note 28.

28 The large difference between Italian and other rates of entry into white-collar work noted earlier was analyzed in detail. At first sight it seems to hint at an important shift in the relationship between schooling and jobs among the Italians, for the white-collar jobs were surely the ones demanding extended formal schooling as a requirement. Moreover, an important part of the difference in white-collar employment rates (in contrast to mean occupational scores) remains even when family background and schooling have been controlled (the odds ratio for white-collar employment with no controls is 0.33, and with controls, 0.51, $t = 2.42$). Further controls for the curriculum in which high school students enrolled and the number of semesters high school dropouts had completed showed that these could not account for the ethnic difference in white-collar employment. The Depression may provide the broad context for the change since 1915, but the precise causes remain unclear.

Is it possible that the returns to schooling were lower among the Italians, at least by 1925? Such lower returns could help explain the lower school achievement of the Italians. The possibility of lower returns was examined by assessing the magnitude of the ethnic difference in occupational attainments within levels of educational attainment. Results for mean occupational scores are presented at the end of this note; those for rates of white-collar employment were similar. The 1925 ethnic differences, lower for the high-school-educated, are consistent with lower returns to schooling for the Italians, but they are not statistically significant. Moreover, lower returns in 1925 would still leave unexplained the origin, or early strength, of the Italian educational pattern, because no hint of lower returns was found in the 1915 sample. Indeed, if the earlier data reflect any more than sampling variability, they would seem to point to higher Italian returns to schooling. On the 1915 high school entrants, see also note 20.

Differences in mean occupational scores: Italians compared with all others (family background characteristics controlled)

	1915	1925
College entrants (1925 only)		+1.0 (0.25)*
High school graduates	−3.2 (0.03)*	−5.1 (0.97)*
High school entrants	+9.0 (2.41)*	−5.4 (1.30)*
Nonentrants	−3.0 (1.44)	−0.5 (0.25)
All (from Table 3.5)	−1.2 (0.64)	−2.2 (1.31)

*These t ratios refer to the contrast with the magnitude in the last row (i.e., to the statistical significance of the interaction term).

29   The occupational classification scheme routinely takes into account some sectoral differences (chiefly among semiskilled and unskilled workers) in assigning occupational scores (see discussion and references in Chapter 1 and the Appendix). However, the advantage of the analysis here is, first, that it does so for every occupation and, second, that the distinctions it recognizes are those that most sharply distinguished Italians from others.

30   On the argument that the employment status of the household head should matter greatly, see Michael B Katz, "Social Class in North American Urban History," *Journal of Interdisciplinary History*, vol. 11 (Spring 1981), 579–605, David J. Hogan, "Whither the History of Urban Education?" *History of Education Quarterly*, vol. 25 (Winter 1985), 531, and Joel Perlmann, "Who Stayed in School? Social Structure and Academic Achievement in the Determination of Enrollment Patterns, Providence, Rhode Island 1880–1925," *Journal of American History*, vol. 72 (December 1985), 603. The census-takers asked each gainfully employed individual whether he was an employee or an employer or was "working on his own account." On the coding of the industrial sectors, see the Appendix, Section 6.

31   Calculated from the number of Italian arrivals and departures and the proportions they constituted among all immigrants and departures, provided by Archdeacon, *Becoming American*, 118–19, 139. Note that the measure of the prevalence of remigration, the ratio of departures to arrivals, is very crude. It does not tell us, for example, if a small proportion of an immigrant group crossed the ocean many times or if a large proportion came to America only to return permanently to the old country.

32   See, for example, Klein, "Integration of Italian Immigrants," 328–9, and Briggs, *An Italian Passage*, 242–3, for a similar argument.

33   The return rates were calculated from Ferenczi, *International Migrations*, Tables 10 and 19. Numbers of arrivals are available for 1899–1924 (25 years), and departures for 1908–24 (16 years). The latter were multiplied by 25/16 and divided by the former. This method is identical with that used by Archdeacon, *Becoming American*, chap. 5, see especially 118–19, in calculating the return rates for males and females together.

34   Betty Boyd Caroli, *Italian Repatriation from the United States, 1900–1914* (New York, 1973), 12–13. Caroli cites the *Reports* of the U.S. Commissioner General of Immigration, 1908–13, and Robert F. Foerster, *The Italian Emigration in Our Time* (Cambridge, Mass., 1919). See also Cinel, *From Italy to San Francisco*, chap. 3–4.

35   In San Francisco, the typical Italian immigrant had arrived four to seven years before finding a spouse (Cinel, *From Italy to San Francisco*, 174). Even if a first child was born soon after marriage, the sample members were not necessarily firstborn children. The parents of most native-born, then, must have been resident substantially longer than twelve to fifteen years.

36   See Cinel, *From Italy to San Francisco*, chap. 3–4, on the reaction of American-born children to the return.

37 On the nature of citizenship hearings in this period, see Reed Ueda, "Naturalization and Citizenship," in Stephan Thernstrom, ed., *Harvard Encyclopedia of American Ethnic Groups* (Cambridge, Mass., 1980), 740–1.

38 The implied rate is calculated from the rate of others (converted to odds) and the odds ratio: $[0.396/(1-0.396)] \times (1/1.76) = 0.373$, the implied Italian odds of entry. Because odds are converted to a rate when divided by (1 + the odds), $0.373/(0.373 + 1.00) = 0.271$, the implied Italian rate of entry.

39 Conceivably, decisions about school enrollment versus work were more subject to plans for remigration than day-to-day behavior related to grades. Of course, the differences in the impact of citizenship by gender and across the two dependent variables (GPA and high school entry) may be due to no more than sampling variability. The logic of the argument in the text is to explore the strongest possible case for an association between citizenship rates and schooling. This is done by focusing on secondary schooling rather than on GPA, and on boys rather than on girls.

The differences in results across the dependent variables were not due to the fact that GPA regressions were OLS, whereas those for high school entry were logits. The differences remain even after expressing the dependent variable in standard-deviation units (the standard deviation of the former dependent variable is about 0.8, and that of the latter about 2.0).

Drop in ethnic coefficient due to including household head's citizenship status in the model (units are standard deviations)

	Boys	Girls
GPA	0.024	0.059
High school entry	0.141	0.122

40 Because the immigrants likely to remigrate were primarily low-skill workers, some correlation would be expected between the contextual effects related to the remigration rate and those related to the class composition of the group.

41 It is striking how little work has been done on this issue. Even in the work of Cinel (*From Italy to San Francisco*), whose treatment of remigration is the fullest, there is little discussion of how the lives of those Italians who remained in the United States were different as a result of being part of a group in which so many chose not to remain.

42 For discussions of contextual effects in the social science literature, see Appendix, note 35. Contextual effects, of course, might also have contributed to the Irish–Yankee differences in schooling and jobs found in the 1880 and 1900 samples. For a discussion, see Appendix, note 40.

43 Another sort of contextual effect of class composition can be conceived to operate on the later cohorts. It involves the class composition of earlier cohorts of sons of Italian immigrants. If the earlier cohorts received relatively low-level jobs, as a result of family origins and schooling, their ability to help the younger cohorts, with job offers or information or as role models, would have been reduced. Such an effect might show up in reduced returns to schooling for the later cohorts, because those Italians who received extended schooling would not have had as many options as other youths (see note 28 on the weak evidence for such a possibility). Lower returns, in turn, would help discourage extended schooling in the later cohorts.

44 On the use of the five strata, see the comments in Section 1.5. Another experiment with alternative occupational classification included using the mean wage reported for each occupation, based on a classification scheme kindly provided by Claudia Goldin, "Family Strategies and the Family Economy in the Late Nineteenth Century: The Role of Secondary Workers," in Theodore Hershberg, ed., *Philadelphia: Work, Space, Family and Group Experience in the 19th Century* (New York, 1981), 285. A third, involving Russian Jewish differences from others, is described in Chapter 4, note 57. Finally, each occupation including at least a minimal number of workers was entered separately as a dummy variable in a regression, and many categories for the miscellaneous occupations were included. This method of classification did not actually involve a great change in the number of occupational categories (after all, the occupational scale used throughout the study involves almost 100 categories), but it did not treat the categories as levels arranged along a linear scale.

45 Contemporary efforts to study the impact of measurement errors in fathers' occupations and in other economic and demographic variables suggest the same conclusion. See Christopher Jencks et al., *Who Gets Ahead? The Determinants of Economic Success in America* (New York, 1979), 34–6.

46 Also, the regressions may understate the influence of pre-migration cultural attributes by assigning some of it to the controlled family background characteristics. For example, Italians may have viewed both family limitation and American schooling in a negative light because each violated important cultural norms. Part of the association between large families and low levels of schooling would then have been due to the relation of both to the same complex of ideas. That part of the association could be interpreted as the result of pre-migration cultural attributes, yet be attributed to the family-size variable in the regression analysis.

47 Indeed, the same point may be made about parental education generally. If information on years of schooling completed by each parent had been available, and if controlling for these characteristics had reduced the difference between Italians and all others, parental education might well have "accounted for" the ethnic difference precisely because it would have reflected the sorts of cultural differences that Lopreato described. Controlling for parental literacy had relatively little impact on the Irish–Yankee differences, once other controls were imposed (see Table 2.4).

48 Nor could the pattern of residuals remaining be dismissed as random. Those discussed throughout this book are confirmed in multiple independent samples from different years and often across gender (a summary, including those found in later chapters, appears in Tables C.1 and C.2 in the Conclusion). The Irish residual changes dramatically over time, but the change over time is itself statistically significant.

49 The most influential formulation is that of Max Weber, *The Protestant Ethic and the Spirit of Capitalism* (New York, 1958). Further comments on its relevance to American immigration history will appear in later text. Joseph Lopreato, *Italian Americans* (New York, 1970), 149–61, and Steinberg, *The Academic Melting Pot*, chap. 3, offer unsympathetic but useful surveys of the research on personality differences among ethnic and religious groups in the United States. Herbert Gutman, "Work Culture and Society in Industrializing America, 1815–1919," *American Historical Review*, vol. 78 (1973), 531–88, can be read as suggesting that differences in pre-migration cultures created differences in immigrant work ethics, and the essay discusses explicitly presumed differences between the work ethics of natives to industrial societies and those migrating from a pre-industrial milieu (see also the discussion of Gutman in the Introduction). Thernstrom, *The Other Bostonians*, chap. 7, also speculates on the possible importance of the Protestant–Catholic distinction, as well as others that involve differences in work ethics between groups. See also note 24 and the discussion of his argument in Chapter 2. John Bodnar, "Materialism and Morality: Slavic American Immigrants and Education, 1890–1940," *Journal of Ethnic Studies*, vol. 3 (Winter 1976), 1–19, also discusses immigrant aspirations.

50 See, for example, Covello, *Social Background*, and Gabaccia, *From Sicily to Elizabeth Street*.

51 Covello, *Social Background*, 403 (cited in Lopreato, *Italian Americans*, 153–4).

52 Lopreato, *Italian Americans*, 153–4.

53 Lopreato, *Italian Americans*, 154. Lopreato's own conclusion is that "Italian immigrants were not always energetic in guiding their children through the formal educational channels" (p. 160). He argues, however, that the reasons are at least in part shared with all immigrants: The school held immigrant cultures in contempt, schools often trained students for manual jobs for which training was available on the job, and poor families needed income from children's work. In addition, he notes that "school and teachers were generally hostile to the family. The immigrants saw little or no value in the education provided by the American high school" (p. 160). Whether or not he means these to be features specific to Italian immigrants is unclear. In any case, the issue here is to explain the large degree of difference between Italian and other immigrant groups. Most of the factors Lopreato cites would be true for all of them, or, like degrees of poverty, were largely controlled in the regressions. These factors did not eliminate the substantial differences between Italians and others.

54 See Briggs, *An Italian Passage*, 242. Much of Briggs's interesting work actually sets a rich background for the question of a cultural heritage's

influence, instead of dealing with it directly. Descriptions of workers' organizations calling for more schooling in Italy, or ethnic leaders doing so in the United States (chap. 2, 3, and 9), are not evidence of popular patterns of behavior, nor even necessarily of representative attitudes. Indeed, reading those descriptions, one recalls Donna Gabaccia's comment: "Briggs's immigrants resemble artisans; Yans-McLaughlin's [*Family and Community*] peasants" (Gabaccia, *From Sicily to Elizabeth Street*, 142). In any case, both Covello and Cinel (*From Italy to San Francisco*, 88–9) interpret Italian attitudes on schooling in a different way than Briggs. Briggs's analysis of Italian regions shows that where there was little schooling, illiteracy was most prevalent, that the common people had little power to determine the availability of schools, and that many *contadini* attended where schools were available. These realities do not indicate what proportion actually attended where schools were available nor provide other credible measures of popular attitudes toward schooling. Briggs's discussion of schooling in southern Italy must be supplemented by that of Covello, *Social Background*, chap. 8, for Covello stresses just how rare schooling was in the countryside and how much rarer still extended schooling (beyond three years) or any schooling for girls was there.

55 Concerning conditions in the United States, Briggs offers an intriguing discussion of school performance (chap. 10). He matched each Italian child listed in school registers to the nearest non-Italian child listed. He then determined if the Italian had been less likely to have been promoted or had been a truant or overage. The Italians were indeed overage, but differed little from others in promotion or truancy rates. Briggs therefore argues that the critical issue is the age at which Italian children started school; it was later, he suggests, than the age of other children.

However, social differences within schools could well have been large, and Briggs could not control for them. Non-Italians in Italian neighborhoods may have been quite special populations, as Briggs himself notes (p. 232). So, too, in one of three cities (Rochester), he was obliged to choose Italians outside the areas of greatest Italian concentration (p. 230); they were very likely unrepresentative. In Providence, such individuals were much more likely than the rest to reach high school (even after controls for family background had been imposed). Also, Briggs does not indicate the grades from which his samples were drawn; yet by the higher elementary grades, many Italian children were retarded in grade or had dropped out of school. Both eventualities would affect an interpretation of comparable work in the grade. Finally, Italians may have started school at relatively late ages. However, as noted earlier in the text, the Immigration Commission *Reports* (vol. 5, Tables 46 and 47) show that among children who began school at age six or earlier (rather than overage), Italians were still far more likely to have been grade-retarded.

Briggs calls for better data (pp. 225, 274); those from Providence do not fit his views: (1) Italian GPAs obtained in the sixth grade were much lower than those of others, suggesting that more than merely a late start was at issue. (2) Working-class high school entry rates before 1920 were not so low that they must be ignored (as he suggests), and Italians reached high school much less than other working-class children. (3) There were great differences between boys and girls in patterns of schooling, suggesting cultural sources of behavior (at least concerning views of women and their relation to schooling) that he does not discuss.

56 Richard Easterlin, "Immigration: Economic and Social Characteristics," in Stephan Thernstrom, ed., *Harvard Encyclopedia of American Ethnic Groups* (Cambridge, Mass., 1980), 476–86, especially 482–3, and John Bodnar, *The Transplanted: A History of Immigrants in Urban America* (Bloomington, Ind., 1985), chap. 1, especially 20–2. See also Donna Gabbacia's comment cited in note 54.

57 Figures for ethnic groups are based on the proportions for the entire country. See U.S. Census Bureau, *Educational Attainment*, Table 2, and *Nativity and Parentage*, Table 12. The Immigration Commission *Reports* are less helpful on the issue of gender differences in schooling among Slavic groups, because in most cities relatively small numbers of most of these groups were found, and because the Poles, the largest of the Slavic groups, were heavily enrolled in Catholic schools (of which the commission's coverage was uneven).

58 On some related implications of membership in a large group, see Stanley Lieberson, *A Piece of the Pie: Blacks and White Immigrants Since 1880* (Berkeley, 1980), 379–82, as well as the discussion about the occupations of Russian Jewish fathers in the next chapter.

59 The Scandinavians, Germans and Austrians, Armenians, English Canadians, a few others from western Europe, and some Jews among the Poles and other eastern Europeans may well have amounted to a majority of the group. Indeed, even the Poles and other Slavs in Providence may have been atypical, for they settled where few others of their group did (see note 16).

Chapter 4

1 Thomas J. Archdeacon, *Becoming American: An Ethnic History* (New York, 1983), 116–19; Aryeh Goren, "Jews," in Stephan Thernstrom, ed., *Harvard Encyclopedia of American Ethnic Groups* (Cambridge, Mass., 1980), 571. Archdeacon estimates that the Italians constituted 16.9% of the permanent immigrants arriving between 1899 and 1924, and the Jews 14.3%. The next most numerous groups, the Germans and Poles, constituted 9.2% and 7.6%, respectively. See also Charles A. Price, "Methods of Estimating," in Thernstrom, ed., *Harvard Encyclopedia of American Ethnic Groups*, 1035–6.

2 There is an extensive literature on the schooling and economic advancement of eastern European Jews and their descendants in the United States, the subject of the next few paragraphs. See, for example, Nathan Glazer, "Social Characteristics of American Jews, 1654–1954," *American Jewish Year Book*, vol. 56 (1955), 3–41, David L. Featherman and Robert M. Hau-

ser, *Opportunity and Change* (New York, 1978), 448–61, Stanley Lieberson, *A Piece of the Pie: Blacks and White Immigrants Since 1880* (Berkeley, 1980), 162–5, 201–6, Stephan Thernstrom, *The Other Bostonians: Poverty and Progress in the American Metropolis, 1880–1970* (Cambridge, Mass., 1973), 130–75, Thomas Kessner, *Beyond the Golden Door: Italian and Jewish Immigrant Mobility in New York City, 1880–1915* (New York, 1977), Sidney Goldstein and Calvin Goldscheider, *Jewish Americans: Three Generations in a Jewish Community* (Englewood Cliffs, N.J., 1968), chap. 4, Michael R. Olneck and Marvin F. Lazerson, "The School Achievement of Immigrant Children: 1900–1930," *History of Education Quarterly*, vol. 4 (Winter 1974), 453–82, Selma Berrol, "Education and Economic Mobility: The Jewish Experience in New York City, 1880–1920," *American Jewish Historical Quarterly*, vol. 65 (1976), 257–71, Selma C. Berrol, "The Open City: Jews, Jobs and Schools, New York City, 1880–1915," in Diane Ravitch and Ronald K. Goodenow, eds., *Educating an Urban People* (New York, 1981), 101–15, Stephen Steinberg, *The Academic Melting Pot: Catholics and Jews in American Higher Education* (New York, 1974), Seymour Martin Lipset and Everett Carl Ladd, Jr., "Jewish Academics in the United States: Their Achievements, Culture and Politics," *American Jewish Year Book*, vol. 72 (1971), 89–128, George S. Counts, *The Selective Character of American Secondary Education* (Chicago, 1922), chap. 12, and Judith E. Smith, *Family Connections: A History of Italian and Jewish Immigrant Lives in Providence, Rhode Island, 1900–1940* (Albany, N.Y., 1985).

3   Berrol, "Education and Economic Mobility" and "The Open City"; Irving Howe, *World of Our Fathers* (New York, 1976), 277–8; Charles E. Silberman, *A Certain People: American Jews and Their Lives Today* (New York, 1985), 123–4.

4   U.S. Immigration Commission, *Reports* ("The Children of the Immigrants in School"), vol. 32 (Washington, D.C., 1911), 667, 692, 707. The figure is based on the ratio of the number in the fourth year of high school to the number twelve years of age.

5   The issue of an intellectual elite is considered very briefly in Section 4.3.

6   The relevant chapters in S. Ettinger, "The Modern Period," in H. H. Ben-Sasson, ed., *A History of the Jewish People* (Cambridge, Mass., 1976), 727–1095, offer one of the many overviews of the history of the Jews in eastern Europe. Calvin Goldscheider and Alan S. Zuckerman, *The Transformation of the Jews* (Chicago, 1984), offers a survey of much relevant information and a bibliography leading to much more. See also Simon Kuznets, "Immigration of Russian Jews to the United States: Background and Structure," *Perspectives in American History*, vol. 9 (1975), 35–124, and Glazer, "Social Characteristics of American Jews." Mark Zborowski and Elizabeth Herzog, *Life Is With People: The Jewish Little-Town of Eastern Europe* (New York, 1952), an effort at anthropological reconstruction of the life of the *Shtetl* (little town), is easy to criticize on methodological, substantive, and stylistic grounds, but it is useful here for its stress on the dual status hierarchies of wealth and intellect. There is also, of course, a vast imaginative literature that touches on Jewish life in eastern Europe:

for example, Abraham Cahan, *The Rise of David Levinsky* (New York, 1917), and I. J. Singer, *The Brothers Ashkenazi* (English edition, New York, 1936).

7 Kuznets, "Immigration of Russian Jews," 79–82.

8 How did the role of study differ from that in Christian Europe? To some extent, Judaism itself, as an intellectual system, may have stressed the value of study (or the value of relatively widespread study) more than Christianity. The fact that the system of laws and their interpretation was so central may have encouraged that difference. Perhaps, too, the more learned among the Christian clergy were more likely to be closed off from the population as a whole because of residence in monasteries. The critical difference, however, probably was that the social structural position of the Jews permitted more of them to be occupied with texts. Whether or not the scholarly life was, in the abstract, any less revered by the Christian peasantry seems moot. It was, for whatever combination of reasons, closer to the lives of the village Jews.

9 The discussion in the text stresses intellectual and social structural sources within eastern Europe for any distinctive pattern of educational behavior among their descendants. Other theories have also been offered regarding Jewish intellectuality generally. The theory of marginality argues that growing up between two cultures places marginal individuals in a cognitive and emotional position that contributes to their creativity. See, for example, Lipset and Ladd, "Jewish Academics." In Thorstein Veblen's original formulation of related views (although they do not involve the term "marginality"), the skeptical, critical stance acquired by those Jews who rebelled against the world view of traditional orthodoxy is emphasized: Thorstein Veblen, "The Intellectual Pre-Eminence of Jews in Modern Europe," in *Essays in Our Changing Order* (New York, 1934). The theory has generally been offered to explain intellectual achievement at the highest level, and it is doubtful that it makes much sense to invoke it in dealing, for example, with high school enrollment rates. But the theory involves a further difficulty. When formulated not in Veblen's narrow sense (the impact of breaking out of a rigid orthodox world view) but in the broader sense of occupying a marginal position between two groups, the theory includes nearly everyone. Blacks, Catholics, immigrants, rich men in a middle-class community – everyone can be considered marginal in some sense. Why some marginalities are conducive to intellectual achievement and others not is not explained by the theory. David Riesman argues a similar point in "Some Observations Concerning Marginality," in *Individualism Reconsidered and Other Essays* (Glencoe, Ill., 1954), 161.

Ernest Van den Haag, *The Jewish Mystique* (New York, 1971), argues for a higher intellectual capability among Ashkenazic Jews than among non-Jews or among Sephardic Jews. The culture of the former, Van Den Haag argues, rewarded the most intellectual with well-to-do wives and the economic position to sustain large families. Hence, the most intellectual produced more offspring. This argument does not consider how large a difference such factors might make (given the probabilistic nature of the inheritance of intelligence). It also conceives of intelligence in far too narrow a way. Many merchants, not to mention peasants, presumably had as much intelligence as many of the great rabbis, but not the interest or environmental support to engage in study; if they prospered, they, too, may have supported large families – and their descendants could one day engage in intellectual pursuits. Van den Haag also passes much too quickly over the cultural supports for rabbinic study in Sephardic Jewish culture (p. 19). It is true that Sephardic Jews do not exhibit the Ashkenazic pattern of high educational attainment in Israel. However, it is not at all clear that Sephardic scholars were not rewarded with well-to-do wives and large families.

10   The article was later reprinted or excerpted in at least two important collections: Louis Finkelstein, ed., *The Jews: Their History, Culture and Religion* (third edition, Philadelphia, 1960), and Marshal Sklare, ed., *The Jews: Social Patterns of an American Group* (Glencoe, Ill., 1958).

11   The following quotations are from Glazer, "Social Characteristics of American Jews," 1722–4.

12   See, to cite but one, Olneck and Lazerson, "School Achievement of Immigrant Children."

13   He has noted the impact of "studies of social and national character that had been pursued by Margaret Mead, Geoffrey Gorer, Abraham Kardiner and others" in Nathan Glazer, "*Beyond the Melting Pot* Twenty Years After," *Journal of American Ethnic History*, vol. 1 (Fall 1981), 43–55.

14   The following quotations are from Goldscheider and Zuckerman, *The Transformation of the Jews*, xi, 158, 168.

15   Goldscheider and Zuckerman do not say, of course, that long-held attitudes, habits, and values can never play a role, but as the preceding quotations make clear, they are emphatic, on methodological as well as substantive grounds, about the primacy of structural factors. Occasionally, however, they do allow a statement such as the following (p. 169): "The structural supports for educational attainment were strong. Opportunities were present and a relatively greater proportion of the Jews than other immigrant groups had the means to take advantage of them. *Jewish values stressing study and education supported their ability to attend school in relatively large numbers*" (emphasis added). Such statements seem quite undigested into the body of the book and leave the reader wondering on what basis a decision about the primacy of structural factors over values was made in this case.

16   Goldscheider and Zuckerman indicate the primacy of the occupational factor. After noting that the greater permanence of the Jewish migration had implications for the speed with which they learned English, these authors note that "the occupational links to education were more important." *The Transformation of the Jews*, 168.

17   Stephen Steinberg, *The Academic Melting Pot*, chap. 4, and *The Ethnic Myth: Race, Ethnicity, and Class in America* (New York, 1981), chap. 3 and 5. See also Colin Greer, *The Great School Legend: A Revisionist Interpretation of American Public Education* (New York, 1972), Miriam Cohen, "Changing

Education Strategies among Immigrant Generations: New York Italians in Comparative Perspective," *Journal of Social History*, vol. 15 (Spring 1982), 443–66, and Silberman, *A Certain People*, 131–48. A variant of these arguments suggests that educational attainments are adequately explained by the orientation to economic advancement, which brings about an interest in schooling to achieve that end. Mariam K. Slater, "My Son the Doctor: Aspects of Mobility among American Jews," *American Sociological Review*, vol. 34 (June 1969), 359–73.

18 A striking example is found in Glazer, "Social Characteristics of American Jews," which offers a wealth of detail about Jewish social patterns. However, it includes only one piece of evidence bearing on eastern European Jewish education before the Depression: "When the Immigration Commission surveyed seventy-seven colleges and institutions in 1908, no less than 8.5% of the male student body was composed of first- and second-generation Jews. (Jews at this time made up about 2% of the American population.)" (p. 1706). However, the Immigration Commission's survey was limited to institutions in the twenty cities it studied – cities in which the Jewish population was heavily concentrated and in which they constituted far more than 2% of the population (particularly among the young), such as New York, Chicago, Philadelphia, and Boston. In a survey covering the enormous number of collegiate institutions in existence throughout the country at that time, Jews would have been drastically less well represented. Moreover, of course, even if they had been 8.5% of the national student population, the figure ignores the issue of social background: For the sons of an urban group, unusually concentrated in middle-class occupations, was 8.5% high? Finally, the figure ignores the experiences of the overwhelming majority who did not reach college. The survey of colleges is described in U.S. Immigration Commission, *Reports* (Washington, D.C., 1911), vol. 33, 713. For similar considerations concerning European patterns, see Goldscheider and Zuckerman, *The Transformation of the Jews*, 86.

19 See Joel Perlmann, "Beyond New York: The Occupations of Russian Jewish Immigrants in Providence, R.I. and in Other Small Jewish Communities, 1900–1915," *American Jewish History*, vol. 72 (March 1983), 369–94. The figures in Table 4.1 are drawn from data presented in that paper. As a result, the groups compared are defined slightly differently than is the case for other comparisons in this book: The table is restricted to male family heads, and it counts the fathers of siblings in the sample only once. Also, it is based on the samples of all children and on the supplemental sample of Russian Jews, but excludes (from the comparison groups) the supplemental samples of the Irish, Italians, and blacks. The effect of these definitional differences on the rates shown is trivial, but the N's are considerably smaller than they would be if the omitted groups had been included.

20 Rhode Island Commissioner of Industrial Statistics, *Twentieth Report* ("The 1905 Rhode Island Census"), section on "Church Statistics and Religious Preference," 275.

21 In 1915, in any case, the mean number of children in a Russian Jewish family was the same (4.7) in families in which the sample member was born abroad as in those in which he was born here, although the second group of families must have been resident in the United States for a longer period.

22 Samuel Joseph, *Jewish Immigration to the United States: From 1881 to 1910* (Columbia University Studies in History, Economics and Public Law, No. 145) (New York, 1914), 192–4. Illiteracy data are also available on the parents of the 1900 sample members. The illiteracy rates in the sample are considerably above those reported in the text for all Russian Jewish immigrants. Of twenty-two fathers, seven were totally illiterate, and three were partly so. Two-thirds of the mothers were totally illiterate, and another one-fifth partly so. The differences between these and the figures of the immigration authorities could, of course, be due to the small sizes of the samples. Still, further work with the 1900 U.S. Census on Russian Jewish literacy would be interesting.

23 Under 3% of intact families included working mothers; 17% of the other families did.

24 The description of fathers' occupations in the 1915 sample, which follows in the next several pages, is based on Perlmann, "Beyond New York."

25 One might suppose that the underrepresentation of the Russian Jews in these industries was simply a reflection of the fact that so many were in trade. However, even among Russian Jewish low manual workers, the proportion in textile mills and metal and machine production were below the city norms. See Perlmann, "Beyond New York," 381.

26 Rhode Island Business Men's Association, *Manual* (Providence, 1912?), 49–50.

27 The mean occupational score also suggests the extent to which the socioeconomic position of the Russian Jewish fathers improved in Providence between 1900 and 1925. In 1900, the mean score was 16.4; in 1915 it was 28.0 (25.6 among the fathers of foreign-born sample members, 30.2 among the fathers of the native-born), and in 1925, 31.6.

     The occupational score for peddlers is 8; for laborer it is 6; for managers, officials, and proprietors it is 49. Thus, the scale treats the peddlers as roughly comparable to unskilled workers. The point is important in connection with the multivariate work discussed later. When the father's occupation is controlled, it is with the occupational scale. In terms of their ability to support children's extended schooling, the score for peddlers may be the most reasonable approximation. See also note 57.

28 Evidence from one point in time, 1915, also suggests that during the course of their careers, many who began as peddlers became petty proprietors and that many petty proprietors became major proprietors. Those whose sampled children were native-born were more likely than the rest to have been proprietors rather than peddlers, and more likely to have been major rather than petty proprietors.

29 Ida Cohen Selavan, "Jewish Wage Earners in Pittsburgh 1890–1930," *American Jewish Historical Quarterly*, vol. 65 (March 1976), 272–3; U.S.

Census Office, *Eleventh Census of the United States Taken in the Year 1890* (Washington, D.C., 1897), vol. 2, 714, and U.S. Census Bureau, *Thirteenth Census of the United States Taken in the Year 1910* (Washington, D.C., 1913), vol. 4, 593–4; W. M. MacDonald, "Population," in William Kirk, ed., *A Modern City: Providence R.I. and its Activities* (Chicago, 1909), 58.

30 Kessner, *Beyond the Golden Door*, 60. Kessner included many, but not all, self-employed individuals in the white-collar category (personal communication), whereas all were so classified in the Providence data. The difference in coding would give an upward bias to contrast between the concentration in white-collar occupations among the Jewish immigrants of the two cities.

31 A survey of thirty-six cities based on the 1900 U.S. Census revealed striking parallels and contrasts with the New York City situation. In the thirty-one smaller communities, as in Providence, the proportions occupied as peddlers or petty proprietors were higher than in the metropolises (Providence 42%, other small cities 34%, metropolises 19%). The proportion engaged in all "manufacturing and mechanical pursuits" was correspondingly lower (39%, 38%, and 57%, respectively). The proportion engaged as tailors reached 28% in New York City. It was somewhat lower in the other metropolises, but very much lower still in the small communities. For a detailed discussion of these intercity comparisons, see Perlmann, "Beyond New York," especially 385–94.

32 On the smaller communities, see also Oscar Handlin, *Adventure in Freedom: Three Hundred Years of Jewish Life in America* (New York, 1954), 106–7.

33 For some evidence supporting these arguments, see Perlmann, "Beyond New York," 385–93.

34 Kessner, *Beyond the Golden Door*, 52, 110. Kessner's comparison groups include 854 individuals who arrived within six years of the census, and 509 who arrived at least fifteen years before it, so that the results are very unlikely to be due to sampling error. Kessner also presents the proportion in white-collar work among the small number (twenty-eight) who had arrived at least twenty years before: 68%. We can, of course, have less confidence in that proportion, given the sample size, but it is entirely consistent with the figures cited in the text.

These figures also suggest a reconsideration of a central finding of Kuznets in "Immigration of Russian Jews to the United States: Background and Structure." Kuznets showed that the occupations listed by Russian Jewish immigrants arriving in the United States differed dramatically from those listed by Russian Jews in the census of 1897. Of the gainfully employed arriving in the United States, a mere 6% described themselves as engaged in commerce; of those in the Russian Empire, over 30% did. On the other hand, 64% of these immigrants and only 38% of the Jews in Russia listed themselves as engaged in manufacturing (including the needle trades). Was the migration from Russia, then, distinctly unrepresentative of the huge commercial element among the Jews? Before accepting this conclusion, consider the jobs at which the Russian immigrants actually worked after arriving in the United States. In large cities, a fifth of the Russians listed themselves as engaged in commerce in the 1900 U.S. Census, and a third of those surveyed eight years later by the U.S. Immigration Commission did so. Similarly, the data on New York men in 1905, as already indicated, show 35% in white-collar work, 54% among household heads. In short, one must conclude either that those involved in commerce were not as unlikely to immigrate as Kuznets thought or that despite an edge as skilled workers, the Jewish artisans fled that work at an astonishing rate to enter commerce. One possible explanation for Kuznets's finding could be the prevalence of "Columbus tailors," men who described themselves as tailors on arrival in America, perhaps because the description indicated their intentions, perhaps because they thought it would be a more acceptable description to immigration authorities than that of a businessman without resources.

35 The rate among the 1900 Russian Jewish sample members was greater than that among all 1900 sample members. These Russian Jewish rates are only suggestive; they are based on too few cases to be statistically meaningful.

36 Even among low manual workers, the Russian Jews were less likely than others to be found in the textile mills. Similarly, even among manual workers other than those in textile mills, the Russian Jews were more likely to be employed in skilled work.

37 The comparison with all others also exploits the larger sample sizes and thus produces more reliable estimates. This is particularly advantageous in observing the 1925 data, which do not involve any supplemental samples of ethnic groups. On the composition of the "other immigrants," see Chapter 3, note 16.

38 It is true that the remaining differences are not statistically significant in all cases. Nevertheless, many of the differences are statistically significant, and others are significant for graduation if not for entry; the uniform direction of differences adds additional confidence.

39 See, for example, Olneck and Lazerson, "School Achievement of Immigrant Children." For dissenting views, see Joseph Lopreato, *Italian Americans* (New York, 1970), 149–61, and John W. Briggs, *An Italian Passage: Immigrants to Three American Cities 1890–1930* (New Haven, 1978), chap. 3, 9, and 10.

40 1960 U.S. Census data on the age cohorts covered by the Providence data (forty-five to fifty-four and fifty-five to sixty-four in 1960) show about the same odds ratios as the sample data for high school completion among second-generation Irish and Russians in the Northeast (0.52 and 0.54, compared with 0.53 and 0.57 reported in Tables III and IV). U.S. Bureau of the Census, *U.S. Census of Population: 1960*, Final Report PC(2)-5B ("Educational Attainment"), Table 3, 45–6, and Final Report PC(2)-1A ("Nativity and Parentage"), Table 8, 16, and Table 12, 52, 63. On the other hand, the 1925 high school entry rates, in which the Irish slightly exceed the Russian Jews, probably are due to sampling error or are unrepresentative of other places (even in the Providence samples, the Irish lead disappeared by high school graduation; see Table 4.4).

In later years, the gap between the Russian Jews and the Irish may have widened. Estimates of differences in mean years of schooling based on the 1960 U.S. Census data show a difference of 0.6 of a year in favor of the Irish for the cohort born before 1885. Thereafter, it was in favor of the Russian Jews. For each succeeding ten-year cohort, the Russian Jewish advantage was 0.1, 0.6, 0.8, 0.5, and 1.0 year. See also David L. Featherman and Robert M. Hauser, *Opportunity and Change* (New York, 1978), 448–56.

41   The later Irish arrivals, of course, also entered a long-settled Irish-American community, as the earlier discussion of their schooling noted; but the Russian Jews followed the German Jews, who served at least a somewhat similar role.

42   Unfortunately, there is no way to be sure how complete the record-keeping was or what biases the process created, but records indicating collegiate education exist for a substantial proportion of the high school graduates, including those from Catholic schools.

43   The evidence on college enrollment from the small numbers in Providence is supported by census data on continuation rates: Whereas about half of the high school graduates continued to college, 64% of the sons of Russian immigrants did so between 1910 and 1930. The college continuation rates were calculated from the census tables described in note 40. For all males born in and living in the Northeast in 1960, the rates were 0.471 for those age forty-five to fifty-four, and 0.533 for those age fifty-five to sixty-four; for the sons of immigrants living in the Northeast, 0.498 and 0.552; for the sons of Irish immigrants there, 0.417 and 0.475; for the sons of Russian immigrants, 0.635 in both cohorts.

The census data, of course, do not offer controls for effects of family background, and the sample data cover too few members of each ethnic group to support a multivariate analysis. However, if the impact of controls were roughly the same as in Tables 4.3 and 4.4, that would still leave a considerable Russian Jewish advantage. For example, among Irish, the group most similar to the Russian Jews in those tables, the odds of continuation would have been no greater than 0.7 of those for the Russian Jews.

44   In my doctoral dissertation, I came to a different conclusion: that the Russian Jewish rate was indeed at the high end of the spectrum of length of schooling, but not uniquely high when family background was taken into account. See Ari Joel Perlmann, "Education and the Social Structure of an American City: Social Origins and Educational Attainments in Providence, R.I., 1880–1925" (Harvard University, 1980), 202–31. I focused almost exclusively on rates of high school entry and noted particularly the striking similarity between Russian Jewish and Irish odds of high school entry once social background had been controlled. The present discussion is based on controlling somewhat different variables (Duncan's occupational score was used for the father's occupation, instead of five occupational strata, and family-structure variables were controlled). However, the major difference in the analyses is the present emphasis on many different aspects of schooling: high school entry,

graduation, and college entry, as well as curriculum and GPA. The conclusion based on several indicators and comparisons with many groups must surely be that although not every group differed dramatically from the Russian Jews on every measure, the position of the latter was distinct even after controls had been imposed.

45 The college preparatory curricula included all enrollment at Classical High School and at the elite non-Catholic private schools. They also included enrollment in the classical track at Hope High School and in the classical and scientific tracks at the Catholic high schools.

46 The curriculum choices of the Irish-Americans in 1915 were based partly on estimation, because the Catholic high school did not provide that information for dropouts then. In 1925, 75% of the entrants were enrolled in a college preparatory program. Assuming that a comparable proportion were enrolled in such programs in 1915 produces the correction factor for 1915. See Section 4D in the Appendix.

47 In the sample, the boys were slightly more likely to enter, and the girls were slightly more likely to graduate, having entered; so graduation rates among all boys and all girls were nearly identical.

48 Sample data are useless on this point, college enrollment data being unavailable for the 1915 sample (the one that included the girls).

49 The figures for others pertain to those born between 1895 and 1904 in the Northeast (and residing there in 1960). The figures for the children of Russians pertain to the same age group (fifty-five to sixty-four in 1960) residing in the Northeast. In the 1960 U.S. Census data on educational attainment for children of Russians forty-five to fifty-four, fifty-five to sixty-four, and sixty-five to seventy-four years old, gender differences in the proportions receiving one to three years of high school were small (6 percentage points in the oldest cohort, 3 points or less thereafter). Differences in high school graduation rates were also small (3 points or less). By contrast, college continuation rates differed by very large amounts (the rates were 63.4–64.4% among the boys and 29.6–34.3% among the girls). For the references to the census data, see note 40.

50 The only comparable evidence of which I am aware is in Counts, *The Selective Character of American Secondary Education*, 110–12. It indicates that in Bridgewater, Connecticut, in 1920, (1) Russian Jewish boys were indeed far more likely to enter the "college" program than were Russian Jewish girls (and the difference was greater than among other groups), but (2) Russian Jewish girls were no less likely than other girls to do so.

51 Virtually all the Russian Jewish children who reached high school enrolled in the public high schools; the Catholic schools and the elite private schools were hardly serious options.

52 One could enroll in the normal school, and prepare for a career in teaching, with a degree from any of the city's high schools, so that aspirations to teach would not explain the choice of a high school. On the high school curricula, see Joel Perlmann, "Curriculum and Tracking in the Transformation of the American High School: Providence, R.I., 1880–1930," *Journal of Social History*, vol. 19 (Fall 1985), 29–55.

53 Was Russian Jewish behavior in the classroom less distinctive than their behavior in obtaining a long schooling? The available evidence is too inconclusive to support the view. The smaller Russian Jewish advantage in GPA compared with the advantage in length of schooling may be an artifact of the data limitations. Specifically, GPAs are available for only a part of the sample – for those who reached grammar school. Among these children, ethnic differences in high school entry rates were smaller than in the entire sample. Comparisons between the magnitudes of ethnic differences on the two dependent variables (entry and GPA) were made by standardizing both. In 1925, the entry-rate differences were larger. In 1915, the differences were only trivially different among girls; among boys, the results depended on the method of standardization. A standard deviation on GPA was about 0.8 of a grade.

54 Lipset and Ladd, "Jewish Academics in the United States"; Charles Kadushin, "Who Are the Elite Intellectuals?" *The Public Interest*, vol. 29 (Fall 1972), 109–25; Veblen, "The Intellectual Pre-Eminence of Jews."

55 Because they were more likely than most to enter high school, more likely to enroll in classical curricula, and more likely to graduate from high school, it is hardly surprising that this was the case. On the other hand, their rate of graduation from classical or other college preparatory programs was not greater than that of the Irish-American groups, who tended to enroll in the Catholic academies, which stressed these curricula and which had high graduation rates.

56 The GPA used was that based on the semester before the last of the student's career; in the case of graduates, this would have been the first semester of the senior year.

57 We can also confidently dismiss the possibility that the ethnic difference is due to an underestimate of the wealth and opportunities of the sons of peddlers. Even when all the peddlers were recoded to have the same occupational score as merchants (49 instead of 8!), the regression results changed little.

58 The interaction terms for Russian Jewish high school entrants, graduates, and college entrants were all trivial in magnitude and statistical significance in both 1915 and 1925. Thus, the Russian Jews did not derive a different occupational advantage from each specific increment in schooling than the rest of the population. Insofar as Russian Jewish occupational attainment was based on schooling, then, it was based on relatively greater proportions of boys reaching higher educational levels, not on special advantages derived from those levels. For more on this issue, see Section 1.6.

59 The availability of free colleges in New York may have had a similar impact. However, given the relatively low tuition charged by most colleges and the relatively limited sizes of the New York City colleges before 1930, the importance of this factor was probably limited. In 1908, for example, The College of the City of New York (CCNY) enrolled 676 students, of whom 493 were listed as Jews. If roughly 165 Jews per year entered CCNY, they would have constituted about 1.5% of the age co-

hort of 11,075 Jewish boys (assuming that the cohort size was approximately equal to the number of boys enrolling in school at age twelve, before many dropped out). See U.S. Immigration Commission, *Reports*, vol. 32 ("The Children of the Immigrants in School," vol. 4), 692, and vol. 33 ("School," vol. 5), 721.

60 Immigration Commission, *Reports*, vol. 32, 656, 665, 692. The estimates were made by dividing the number of first-year high school students and fourth-year high school students by the number who were twelve years of age (assuming the latter to represent the size of the age cohort).

61 As late as 1963–73, 34% of the Russian Jewish occupational advantage remained unexplained in one national survey, and 48% in a second, even after education and family background were controlled. In the Providence data, regressions that compared the Russian Jews with all others left 66% of their advantage unexplained in the 1915 sample and 54% in the 1925 sample, when controlling for many of the same variables as have the recent surveys. The recent surveys (1) are weighted heavily toward New York and the other large centers (where most Russian Jews lived), (2) pertain to a period in which more of the Russian Jews were preparing for the professions (possibly increasing the influence of schooling on their occupational advantage), and (3) impose more controls (more levels of schooling, and evidence on the father's education). Perhaps, then, the figures for 1963–73 may be regarded as a sort of lower bound for what results might look like if data comparable to those available for Providence were available for New York. See Featherman and Hauser, *Opportunity and Change*, 453.

62 On contextual effects, and on the use of the mean occupational score in particular, see the discussion in the Appendix, Section 9. In order to assess associations with educational or occupational attainment, the proportion of each group's concentration in commerce could be studied just as the mean occupational score of the group was (the procedure was discussed in the preceding chapter). Doing so illustrates the great risk of spurious correlation associated in measuring contextual effects directly. Such an exercise presents us with a strong independent association between the contextual factor and high school entry, but not between the contextual factor and later occupational attainment. This difference in outcomes is in itself improbable and certainly not predicted by the argument that the contextual effects of concentration in commerce were influential. Further evidence of spuriousness comes from analysis of the corresponding individual-level variable: whether or not one's father was engaged in commerce. As already noted in the text, it had a negligible independent impact on schooling and jobs.

63 The formulation of Simon Kuznets on this issue is also worth noting here. At the close of his long monograph on the demographic characteristics of the Russian Jewish migrants, he noted that the records "do not reflect directly the major features of the historical heritage of Russian Jewry that shaped the human capital transferred to the United States by immigration. It is this transfer of human capital that constitutes the es-

sential content of migration, internal or international; and while sex, age, occupational structure, and literacy tell us much about this human capital, they do not help us to distinguish the more fundamental characteristics of capacity for social organization and for adjustment to the challenges of a new environment. Nor do they describe the long-standing scale of priorities inherited from the past and likely to shape the goals of immigrants and their descendants for several generations after their arrival in the country of destination. . . . If one could establish the characteristics of this heritage of human capital other than the basic demographic and economic characteristics, one might be able to explain, in tracing their consequences in the history of the Jewish community in the United States, aspects of American social history that are otherwise obscure. But the tools needed for such a study of the historical heritage of Russian or East European Jewry are not those of economics and demography; and the account above, long as it is, must be left incomplete." Kuznets, "Immigration of Russian Jews," 123–4.

64 See, for example, Cahan, *The Rise of David Levinsky*, 61–2, Goldscheider and Zuckerman, *The Transformation of the Jews*, 164, Charles S. Liebman, "Religion, Class, and Culture in American Jewish History," *Jewish Journal of Sociology*, vol. 9 (1968), 230, and Aaron Rothkoff, "The American Sojourns of Ridbaz: Religious Problems within the Immigrant Community," *American Jewish Historical Quarterly*, vol. 57 (1968), 557–72.

65 Slater, "My Son the Doctor," argues that the differences in learning styles in eastern European Jewish culture and in American institutions suggest that the experience of the one would not be helpful in the other. The discussion in the text circumvents that issue in suggesting that the particulars learned, and the style of learning, may have been irrelevant to the transmission of a special prestige for education. See also Steinberg, *The Ethnic Myth*, 133–4.

Chapter 5

1 Robert Higgs, *Competition and Coercion: Blacks in the American Economy 1865–1914* (Chicago, 1980), 34. In Philadelphia, Pittsburgh, and Cincinnati, closer to the South, the black population reached 5%. For a social history of Providence blacks in earlier years, see Robert J. Cottrol, *The Afro-Yankees: Providence's Black Community in the Antebellum Era* (Westport, Conn., 1982).

2 This study of black family and school patterns follows some intriguing earlier work that lacked the data for an integrated exploration of all these school-related themes. Claudia Goldin, using an 1880 census sample, discussed child labor and, to a lesser extent, school attendance in the context of the family economy. Timothy Smith, using aggregate census figures from the first decades of the century, examined attendance rates. Stanley Lieberson, using later census publications, analyzed grade attainment. See Claudia Goldin, "Family Strategies and the Family Economy in the Late Nineteenth Century: The Role of Secondary Workers,"

in Theodore Hershberg, ed., *Philadelphia: Work, Space, Family and Group Experience in the 19th Century* (New York, 1981), 277–310, Timothy L. Smith, "Native Blacks and Foreign Whites: Varying Responses to Educational Opportunity in America, 1880–1950," *Perspectives in American History*, vol. 6 (1972), 309–35, and Stanley Lieberson, *A Piece of the Pie: Blacks and White Immigrants Since 1880* (Berkeley, 1980), 123–252. For a fuller discussion of Lieberson's conclusions than is provided in the text and notes, see Joel Perlmann, "A Piece of the Educational Pie: New Evidence and Some Reflections on Black and Immigrant Schooling since 1880," *Sociology of Education*, vol. 60 (January 1987), 54–51. Finally, for an analysis of school patterns in the South, see Robert A. Margo, "Accounting for Racial Differences in School Attendance in the American South, 1900: The Role of Separate-But-Equal," *Review of Economics and Statistics*, vol. 69 (November 1987), 661–6.

3 See, for example, Oscar Handlin, *The Newcomers: Negroes and Puerto Ricans in a Changing Metropolis* (Cambridge, Mass., 1959), Smith, "Native Blacks and Foreign Whites," Lieberson, *A Piece of the Pie*, and Stephan Thernstrom, *The Other Bostonians: Poverty and Progress in the American Metropolis, 1880–1970* (Cambridge, Mass., 1973).

4 Stanley Lieberson, "Generational Differences among Blacks in the North," *American Journal of Sociology*, vol. 79 (November 1973), 552. The 1915 Providence data, unfortunately, include no information on place of birth within the United States.

5 Elizabeth Hafkin Pleck, *Black Migration and Poverty, Boston 1865–1900* (New York, 1979), 50–5; Theodore Hershberg and Henry Williams, "Mulattoes and Blacks: Intragroup Color Differences and Social Stratification in Nineteenth-Century Philadelphia," in Hershberg, ed., *Philadelphia*, 407–8.

6 Edwin Leigh, "Illiteracy in the United States," *American Journal of Education*, vol. 19 (1870), 801–35; Lee Soltow and Edward Stevens, *The Rise of Literacy and the Common School in the United States: A Socioeconomic Analysis* (Chicago, 1981), 155–9.

7 Leigh, "Illiteracy"; U.S. Census Office, *Ninth Census*, vol. 1 (Washington, D.C., 1872), xxx, 4–7, 396–7, 618–19; U.S. Bureau of the Census, *Thirteenth Census*, vol. 1 (Washington, D.C., 1913), 1224–9, and *Negro Population 1790–1915* (Washington, D.C., 1918), 405–8.

8 The censuses of 1850 and 1860 suggest that about half of the free blacks were literate and that free blacks constituted about 6% of the southern black population. These individuals, then, may have constituted about 3% of all blacks in the South in 1870 (50% × 6%). Thus, 9% of southern black men in 1870 would have been literate former slaves (the 12% literate blacks less the 3% who had not been slaves). See the discussion of the 1870 census cited in the preceding note.

9 In 1880, even less than 22% of that southern cohort must have been literate. Some, after all, must have learned the skills of literacy after age thirty. Moreover, early death may well have been more common among

the illiterate. See Edward Meeker, "Mortality Trends of Southern Blacks, 1850–1910: Some Preliminary Findings," *Explorations in Economic History*, vol. 13 (January 1976), 30.

10 Ibid.

11 Lieberson concluded that in the decades after 1910, literate blacks were more likely than others to migrate (*A Piece of the Pie*, 220).

12 Higgs, *Competition and Coercion*, 32, 120. Pleck found that half of the Boston blacks of 1870 who had been born in Virginia had migrated from towns (*Black Migration and Poverty*, 51–2).

13 On the black family in the North, see, for example, Pleck, *Black Migration and Poverty*, 161–96. On contemporary trends, see Reynolds Farley, *Blacks and Whites: Narrowing the Gap?* (Cambridge, Mass., 1984), 133–42.

14 Goldin, "Family Strategies," 299, and "Female Labor Force Participation: The Origin of Black and White Differences, 1870 and 1880," *Journal of Economic History*, vol. 37 (March 1977), 87–108; Elizabeth H. Pleck, "A Mother's Wage: Income Earning among Married Italian and Black Women, 1896–1911," in Nancy F. Cott and Elizabeth H. Pleck, eds., *A Heritage of Her Own: Toward a New Social History of American Women* (New York, 1979), 381–8.

15 W. E. B. DuBois, *The Philadelphia Negro: A Social Study* (New York, 1967; original edition 1899), 111; U.S. Census Office, *Eleventh Census* (Washington, D.C., 1897), Table 118; U.S. Census Bureau, *Thirteenth Census*, vol 1, Table 8; Duane Clinker, Scott Molloy, and Paul Buhle, " 'We Want Integrity': An Interview with Al Sisti," *Radical History Review*, vol. 17 (Spring 1978), 184. Because the figures on black children come from the Providence sample data, and because each of the five supplemental "samples" of blacks actually includes the entire black population in the age range, no sampling error need be feared: No black of the sampled age worked in a mill. Also, there seems to have been a preponderance of those black children who did find work in Providence in menial service jobs – a pattern that suggests the difficulty of finding other work. Joel Perlmann, "After Leaving School: The Jobs of Young People in Providence R.I. 1880–1915," in Ronald K. Goodenow and Diane Ravitch, eds., *Schools in Cities: Consensus and Conflict in American Educational History* (New York, 1983), 3–43.

16 Goldin, "Female Labor Force Participation" and "Family Strategies," 299–301, 304–5.

17 The variables controlled in the regressions reported in Table 5.7, part B, were chosen in order to maximize the comparability to Goldin's work. The control for parental occupations, however, is based on the occupational score used throughout the study (see Chapter 1 for details). It should also be noted that the Philadelphia sample includes children in a wider age range, extending into the early twenties. However, the idea of a trade-off would seem to hold for the ages eleven to sixteen as well as for the later ones. Finally, it is precisely among boys in 1880 that the relationship between mother's work and child's work is most strongly posi-

tive in the Providence data; the evidence for Goldin's second hypothesis
was that the same relationship was positive in the Philadelphia data that
same year.

18 The proportion of low-manual-worker immigrant families that included
a working mother and a fourteen- to fifteen-year-old sample member
who did not work was 1.8% in 1880, 3.2% in 1900, and 7.0% in 1915.
Among low-manual-worker black families, the comparable figures were
22.2%, 21.8%, and 30.4%.

19 The 1925 census did not provide information on occupations; consequently, data from that year cannot be included here. Occupational data
were collected for fathers in that sample from the directories of the city,
but they did not indicate children's work.

20 Smith, "Native Blacks and Foreign Whites."

21 U.S. Immigration Commission, *The Children of Immigrants in Schools*, vols.
1–5 in *Reports of the Immigration Commission* (35 vols.) (Washington, D.C.,
1911). The figures used in Tables 5.9 and 5.10 were drawn from the "Public
School Pupils – General Investigation" section, Tables 3 and 4, for each
of the five cities indicated.

22 The ratio of the number of children enrolled in the public schools at fourteen or fifteen years of age to the number enrolled at age twelve (in each
ethnic group) was used to estimate the proportion attending school at
the higher ages (because few had dropped out by age twelve). The ratio
of the number in the ninth grade (at whatever age) to the number twelve
years of age provides the estimate of the proportion of the group entering high school.

23 Chicago Commission on Race Relations, *The Negro in Chicago: A Study of
Race Relations and a Race Riot* (Chicago, 1922; original edition 1922), 258.

24 For one group of cities, the commission reported the proportion of each
group's schoolchildren who were grade-retarded by two years or more.
The commission also reported these proportions in a separate table limited to the subgroup of children born in the same city in which they lived
in 1908. Although the comparison is a bit more restricted than would be
optimal, it does exclude southern-born blacks and foreign-born children
of immigrants. In this subgroup, the differences in proportions grade-
retarded are actually more unfavorable to blacks than in the whole group
(vol. 1, Table 32).

   If blacks started school later than others, their grade retardation at a
particular age could have been a result of that pattern rather than of
slower progression through the grades once enrolled. However, in connection with the comparisons noted in the preceding paragraph, the
commission also presented one limited to the subgroup who entered school
by age six. Once again, the limitation increases the black–white gap (vol.
1, Table 46). This evidence strongly suggests that the black retardation
was not due to those who started late, but rather to slow progress once
enrolled.

   One could, in fact, interpret the Immigration Commission data as suggesting a slightly higher black median age of entry (calculated from the

numbers enrolled at ages four to six on the assumption that the entire cohort at each age equaled the number enrolled at age twelve), but the differences could account for only a small part of the differences in grade attainments by age fourteen or fifteen. In any case, the U.S. Census tables on school attendance in 1920 (the earliest with the necessary information on young children) do not indicate late black school entry.

25 In the wake of the Great Migration, studies of black conditions in the North noted grade retardation and attributed it primarily to the presence of southern-born children, although the effects of poverty and family structure were noted as well. See the Chicago Commission on Race Relations, *The Negro in Chicago*, 256–67, and Louise Venable Kennedy, *The Negro Peasant Turns Cityward: Effects of Recent Migrations to Northern Centers* (New York, 1930), 196–200.

26 Computations comparable to those in Table 5.10 for Italians and Poles show levels of grade retardation at age twelve higher in some cases and lower in others than those of blacks, and generally quite similar. But in the Immigration Commission tables restricted to children born in the same city in which they lived in 1908, black–Polish and black–Italian differences in retardation rates are more unfavorable to blacks then without the restriction.

27 Lieberson, *A Piece of the Pie*, 162–7. Precise comparisons are not possible because the census data pertain to native-born children of immigrants and to northern-born blacks, whereas most of the Immigration Commission data presented pertain to all children of immigrants and all black children living in the North – quite apart from other differences between the two sets of data (median grade attainment in national, retrospective data compared with median grade retardation at a given age in data for several cities collected at the time). Lieberson called attention to the longer time blacks spent, on average, in each grade. However, his interest in that phenomenon was limited to whether or not the race difference in grade retardation changed enough to account for the relative drop in black median grade attainments later in the century (*A Piece of the Pie*, 229–33).

28 Therefore, notwithstanding the ambiguities involved in measures of black education based on length of schooling, the preceding does not challenge a central conclusion reached by both Smith and Lieberson about black educational levels relative to those of whites during the course of the century. Both concluded that there had been a relative decline (particularly after 1930). Lieberson, in particular, studied in detail the grade attainment of blacks compared with that of the new immigrant groups. He found that black grade attainment had been higher than that of some of these groups early in the twentieth century and declined later. The Providence data call attention to the conditions that helped produce the black grade attainments of the early decades.

29 There were a few sample members in each period for whom information on the father's occupation (or, more precisely, the occupation of the head of the family) was unavailable. Generally, these individuals constituted

a very small proportion of the entire sample and were simply excluded from the regression analyses. However, in the 1925 sample, there were more sample members for whom this information was lacking: The 1925 Rhode Island State Census did not provide occupational data, and hence the head of the sample member's family had to be traced in the city directory in order to obtain it; but the directory omitted many working women. This problem was significant for the study of blacks, because a higher proportion of blacks lived in families headed by women (see Table 5.4B). Consequently, in the relevant analyses discussed in Chapter 5 (and presented in Tables 5.11 and 5.13–5.15), the 1925 sample members whose family head's occupation was unknown were not excluded from the regressions. Instead, the family head was assigned the mean occupational score for their group (i.e., the mean score for native whites, foreign-born whites, or blacks). Also, in order to control for unobserved differences between these individuals and others, a dummy variable identifying these individuals was added to the regression model. However, the dummy variable was omitted from the regression analysis for Table 5.13, column 6, because the purpose there was to show the impact of controls for characteristics other than family structure. Also, this procedure was not used in analyses of 1925 patterns presented in other chapters (because the missing-data problem was far less common among the Irish, Italians, and Russian Jews). Because the cases with missing data were treated differently there, the N's, rates, and means presented for the native whites of 1925 in those other chapters (when the native whites are compared with the Irish and Russian Jews) differ slightly from those presented in Chapter 5. Lastly, because this procedure had not been used in two earlier papers (Joel Perlmann, "The Schooling of Blacks in a Northern City" and "A Piece of the Educational Pie"), results for 1925 differ here from those presented in those papers.

Because blacks received lower GPAs than others, and because there was a strong positive association between GPA and high school entry or graduation, we would expect that with GPA controlled, the likelihood of black high school or graduation would improve relative to that of others. It does. Put another way, controlling for GPA erases some of the discrepancy between school attendance and high school entry rates of blacks noted in the preceding section. On the association between GPA and high school entry, see Joel Perlmann, "Who Stayed in School? Academic Achievement and Social Structure in the Determination of Enrollment Patterns, Providence, R.I. 1880–1925," *Journal of American History*, vol. 72 (December 1985), 588–614.

30   See Cottrol, *The Afro-Yankees*, 91–101, and Providence School Committee, *Report* for 1899/1900 (Providence, 1900), 132.

31   The name of the last elementary school attended by each sample member was recorded. This was in most cases a grammar school. In the 1925 sample, blacks were less concentrated at particular schools, and in none did they reach 15% of the student body. The school name is unavailable for about a third of the 1915 and a quarter of the 1925 black sample mem-

bers. However, no matter what assumptions are made about the schools they attended, less than two-fifths of the black children could have attended a predominantly black grammar school in either year, or last attended a predominantly black school. The most reasonable assumptions about the missing data would reduce the estimated fraction considerably.

32 Joel Perlmann, "Curriculum and Tracking in the Transformation of the American High School: Providence, R.I. 1880–1930," *Journal of Social History*, vol. 19 (September 1985), 29–55.

33 Focusing on the lower economic strata is also worthwhile, because high school entry rates of black children from higher strata are perplexing. The children from these strata were not consistently more likely to enroll in high school than were blacks from lower strata. Indeed, when all periods are taken together (and the period itself is controlled), those in the higher strata actually reached high school significantly less often than those in the lower strata. Consequently, the race difference is much greater for the higher strata than for the lower strata. No such result occurs among other groups. The most probable explanation is that the occupations of blacks classified as skilled or as white-collar workers were atypical of those strata and that their economic well-being was not at all commensurate with that of others in the strata. In any event, it seems best not to base conclusions on the racial gaps in education among the children of the higher strata.

34 The specific occupation of the household head is controlled by using its score on the occupational scale (see Chapter 1 for details). See also note 29.

35 It is worth noting in passing that the patterns of high school graduation were similar to those of entry, at least in 1915 and in 1925, when the numbers of blacks enrolled were large enough to merit attention. Without controls, the proportion of black entrants to graduate from high school was the lowest, but when social background factors were taken into account, the size of the racial gap was reduced, so that it was within the white range; Joel Perlmann, "The Schooling of Blacks in a Northern City: Providence, R.I. 1880–1925," *Perspectives in American History*, N.S. 2 (1985), 125–82; see especially 157.

The only hint in the small samples of 1880 and 1900 that the earlier patterns within high school (patterns of GPAs achieved, tracking, or graduation) may have been different than later patterns concerns the graduation rate of the ten black students in the earliest sample who reached high school. None of them graduated. The 1900 rates resemble the later rates rather than the 1880 rate.

36 Lieberson, *A Piece of the Pie*, 1976; Chicago Commission on Race Relations, *The Negro in Chicago*, 262; Jacqueline Jones, *Labor of Love, Labor of Sorrow: Black Women, Work, and the Family from Slavery to the Present* (New York, 1985), 182–90; Goldin, "Family Strategies."

37 Stanley Lieberson reached the same conclusion about the relative strength of family and class based on an examination of some aggregate census

data from 1940–60 (*A Piece of the Pie*, 173–93, 220–6). For a full discussion, see Joel Perlmann, "A Piece of the Educational Pie: Reflections and New Evidence on Black and Immigrant Schooling Since 1880," *Sociology of Education*, vol. 60 (January 1987), 54–61. Race differences in school attendance rates, like those in high school entry, were more dependent on social class than on family structure.

38   The available data did not permit a direct analysis of grade retardation, controlling for family background. However, the contrast between high black school attendance rates and relatively lower black high school entry rates persists when family background is controlled.

39   Stanley L. Engerman, "Three Recent Essays of Ethnicity and Relative Economic Achievement: A Review Essay," *Historical Methods*, vol. 16 (Winter 1983), 30–5. Additional references to discussions of the cultural issues are cited later.

40   See, besides the earlier discussion of integration in Providence, David B. Tyack, *The One Best System: A History of American Urban Education* (Cambridge, Mass., 1974), 109–25, 217–29.

41   Higgs, *Competition and Coercion*, 129–33, offers a brief discussion of public- and private-sector discrimination.

42   Evidence of discriminatory attitudes and practices by administrators is not a clear guide to the impact of those practices. On a similar point, see Perlmann, "Who Stayed in School?"

43   Leon Litwack, *Been in the Storm So Long: The Aftermath of Slavery* (New York, 1979), chap. 9; Emmett J. Scott, comp., "Documents: Letters of Negro Migrants of 1916–18," *Journal of Negro History*, vol. 4 (July–October 1919), 290–340, 412–65; Lieberson, *A Piece of the Pie*, 139–40, 169; John Bodner, Roger Simon, and Michael P. Weber, *Lives of Their Own: Blacks, Italians, and Poles in Pittsburgh, 1900–1960* (Urbana, 1982), 35–9.

44   Thomas Sowell, *Ethnic America: A History* (New York, 1981), 199, 203, and *The Economics and Politics of Race: An International Perspective* (New York, 1983), 123, Higgs, *Competition and Coercion*, 128–9, Smith, "Native Blacks and Foreign Whites," and Lieberson, *A Piece of the Pie*, 169, 252, 354–9, discuss one or more of these arguments.

45   For a similar formulation, see Thernstrom, *The Other Bostonians*, 213–14.

46   Some examples: (1) Labor-market discrimination against black youth may have worked to keep them in school longer. (2) Discriminatory practices in school may have negatively affected black schooling (notably, grades, promotion, and tracking). (3) Blacks may have had a special commitment to schooling (for its own sake or as a hope of advancement) that was expressed in longer attendance, but, for various reasons, that commitment may not have extended to academic achievement, expressed in grades, promotion rates, and other measures. Alternatively, the commitment may have extended to academic achievement, but may have been masked by the effects of the second factor noted earlier (discriminatory practices in the schools). (4) Contrary to the third hypothesis, blacks may have had no special commitment to schooling; indeed, they may have been less committed than most other groups. However, measures related to blacks' length of schooling (school attendance and grade attain-

ment) may not reveal this because they may be driven up by the first factor (the indirect effects of labor-market discrimination). A related version of an argument about the dysfunctional nature of black culture would be that blacks had a commitment to schooling, but a less consistent work ethic than other groups (as a by-product of slavery, for example). (5) A greater acceptance of mother's work could have reduced child labor rates and increased school attendance. This factor could have operated in conjunction with any of the preceding dynamics.

47 However, black families may have had higher regard for the American public schools than did many immigrant groups (such as the Irish in 1880 and the Italians in later years) and may have been more willing than those immigrants to send mothers into the labor force instead of children.

48 If job discrimination led to the presence of more academically marginal black students, it did so only among children of an employable age. To the extent that grade retardation or low GPAs were more prevalent among blacks than among others at younger ages, ages seven to eleven, for example, the difference must be explained in other ways, for example, by discrimination in the schools or cultural patterns.

Perhaps an upper bound for an estimate of the effects of youth labor-market discrimination (combined with mother's work) can be found in the black lead over Yankees in adolescent school attendance rates. The ratio of the odds that Yankee children would attend school compared with those that black children would do so within low-manual-labor strata, and with other controls for family background, was 0.61 in 1880 ($t = 1.51$) and 0.57 in 1900 ($t = 1.18$); corresponding immigrant/black ratios were 0.24 ($t = 5.97$) and 0.27 ($t = 4.32$). Clearly, not all of the difference between blacks and immigrants can be attributed to the indirect impact of job discrimination in keeping blacks in school. After all, Yankees, too, remained longer than immigrants, and for other reasons (a greater commitment to schooling, for example, which may well also have held for blacks compared with immigrants).

Finally, a possible challenge to the theory that labor-market discrimination drove up black attendance, but drove down black GPA, is that other ethnic groups with high rates of school enrollment (Yankees, Irish in the later samples, Russian Jews) did not have low grammar school GPAs. Of course, the enrollments of these groups were not driven up by labor-market discrimination.

49 Jones, *Labor of Love*, 179–81. Also, academically marginal students, at least by 1925, may have been more likely to enroll in the Technical High School. Job discrimination, if it kept more marginal black students in the schools, could have contributed to the concentration of black students there. However, if that pattern were the predominant one, we would expect to find very small race differences in curriculum patterns once grades (as well as social background) were taken into account. Instead, the race differences for girls in 1915 and for boys in 1925 remain huge regardless of the controls.

50 Note also that labor-market discrimination itself could have had quite

different effects than those indicated here. For example, (1) the black handicap in the adult labor market could have served as a counterbalancing factor, encouraging whites to remain in school longer than blacks, and (2) family choices about the use of resources could have operated in a more complicated way than envisioned in the text. White families faced with the advantages of higher returns to child labor could have chosen to exploit those returns to keep some children in school longer. The discussion in the text is meant to call attention to one simple, plausible, and possibly very important source of black patterns of schooling (discrimination in the youth labor market, possibly supported by the effects of mother's work), some of the outcomes of which would have been quite subtle.

51 For examples of such beliefs in the schools, see the Chicago Commission on Race Relations, *The Negro in Chicago*, 438–40.

52 The differences in educational advantages by race are not statistically significant, but they are reasonably consistent, and the generalization in the text therefore seems warranted.

Advantages of	For whites	For blacks
1915		
High school entry	8.6 (6.31)	−3.9 (1.13)[a]
High school graduation	13.9 (7.34)	[b]
1925		
High school entry	7.5 (4.54)	1.3 (1.26)
High school graduation	12.7 (6.36)	−3.4 (2.09)
College entry	22.6 (8.75)	14.9 (0.90)

[a] These t ratios for the black advantage refer to the statistical significance of the difference from the comparable white advantage (to the significance of the interaction term).
[b] Only one black high school graduate of 1915 was successfully located in the directories ten years later.

53 Finis R. Welch, "Education and Racial Discrimination," in Orley Aschenfelter and Albert Rees, eds., *Discrimination in Labor Markets* (Princeton, 1974), 43–81; James P. Smith, "Race and Human Capital," *American Economic Review*, vol. 74 (September 1984), 685–98; Eric Hanushek, "Ethnic Income Variations: Magnitudes and Explanations," in Thomas Sowell, ed., *American Ethnic Groups* (Washington, D.C., 1978), especially 157–64. Finis R. Welch and James P. Smith, *Closing the Gap: Forty Years of Economic Progress for Blacks* (Santa Monica, Calif., 1986); Robert Margo, "Race, Educational Attainment, and the 1940 Census," *Journal of Economic History*, vol. 46 (March 1986), 189–98.

54 Smith, "Race and Human Capital," 695.

55 Joel Perlmann, "Who Stayed in School?" Sixth-grade GPA also correlated

reasonably strongly with ninth-grade GPA among those who stayed in school that long (0.45 in 1915, 0.25 in 1925).

56 Although the effect of GPA (via length of schooling) on occupational attainments in the population as a whole was noticeable, it is also true that virtually none of the black–white occupational differences are related to GPA, even if length of schooling is not controlled. This is because, as Table 5.14 shows, length of schooling itself had such trivial effects on the magnitude of that race difference.

57 A second test, in which the criterion for selection was the grade the boys had received for effort, rather than for academic subjects (B or above for blacks, C or below for whites), produced the same result. The proportions of black and white students with GPAs above or below 1.83 (cited in the text) refer to males successfully traced across time for whom GPA data were available. See Appendix, Sections 4 and 5, for details.

58 Even if contextual effects reduced the race differences in Table 5.14 by as much as family background did, they would barely affect the huge black–immigrant differences found there, except in the 1925 sample.

59 Higgs, *Competition and Coercion,* 80–9, 132.

60 For a recent formulation, see Sowell, *Ethnic America,* 187.

61 Assuming the sample member was about age fifteen and that his father and grandfather had each been in his early twenties when his child had been born.

62 As the coefficients suggest, the mean occupational scores of the young black men long resident in the North did not vary to a statistically significant extent (or in a consistent direction) from those of the descendants of more recent southern migrants.

On the school patterns of black children by parents' region of birth, see Perlmann, "The Schooling of Blacks in a Northern City," 179–81. That paper (and Perlmann, "A Piece of the Educational Pie") also compared black and Italian school performances and occupational attainments, showing that both blacks and Italians had low GPAs, but that the occupational-attainment difference between the groups was huge. It went on to acknowledge that the comparison was not a conclusive rejection of the cultural hypothesis, because the hypothesis could be reformulated to argue that Italians were especially uncommitted to schooling, but committed to work, whereas among blacks a weak work ethic operated on both. Subsequent work (presented in the chapter on the Italians) indeed suggests that their relative standings in school and occupational attainments differed, leaving the meaning of the comparison with blacks unclear. The more direct approach taken here, therefore, compares whites with low GPAs and blacks with higher GPAs. See also note 29.

63 Similarly, the other large residual difference in occupational attainments observed in the preceding chapters was the Russian Jewish advantage over all others: 8.7 points in 1915, and 5.4 points in 1925. But the black disadvantage regarding all others measured the same way amounted to nearly 14 points in 1915 and 10 points in 1925.

64 Lieberson and Smith mention the feedback hypothesis in connection with

the later years. Higgs raises the question of feedback without limiting the period in which it might have operated, and he notes that DuBois clearly thought that it operated when he wrote *The Philadelphia Negro,* published in 1899. See the references cited in note 44.

65 Eventually, a culture that developed out of such a mechanism could become self-sustaining, even in the face of reduced discrimination. Lieberson briefly notes such a possibility with regard to recent American social history (*A Piece of the Pie,* 237, 252; Perlmann, "A Piece of the Educational Pie"). However, such a process hardly describes the period 1880–1935.

Conclusion

1 Stephen Steinberg, *The Ethnic Myth: Race, Ethnicity, and Class in America* (Boston, 1981), 77–81; Robin M. Williams, Jr., "Structure and Process in Ethnic Relations: Increased Knowledge and Unanswered Questions," in Hubert M. Blalock, Jr., ed., *Sociological Theory and Research: A Critical Appraisal* (New York, 1980), 243–57, especially 243; W. Parker Frisbie and Frank D. Bean, "Some Issues in the Demographic Study of Racial and Ethnic Populations," in Bean and Parker, eds., *The Demography of Racial and Ethnic Groups* (New York, 1978), 1–14. See also Roger D. Waldinger, *Through the Eye of the Needle: Immigrants and Enterprise in New York's Garment Trades* (New York, 1986). The influence of these structural characteristics may be complex in nature. For example, social-class origins may have cultural as well as economic implications.

2 On the interactions of social structure and culture, and the tendency to minimize the independent role of the latter, see Steinberg, *The Ethnic Myth,* ix–x, 77–87, cf. 103, 127, 131–2, 137–8, 141–4; John Bodnar, *The Transplanted: A History of Immigrants in Urban America* (Bloomington, Ind., 1985), xvi–xxi, cf. 142. Steinberg's views are discussed in the Introduction and in Section 3.1, as well as later in note 17. Bodnar's earlier views seem to have stressed pre-migration culture more than these recent formulations. See, for example, Bodnar, "Materialism and Morality: Slavic American Immigrants and Education, 1890–1940," *Journal of Ethnic Studies,* vol. 3 (Winter 1976), 1–19. See also Calvin Goldscheider and Alan S. Zuckerman, *The Transformation of the Jews* (Chicago, 1984).

Some of the recent work on blacks has stressed the extent to which factors other than discrimination affected their advancement. Thomas Sowell's emphasis on their cultural heritage is described in the Introduction. Robert Higgs, *Competition and Coercion: Blacks in the American Economy, 1865–1914* (Chicago, 1980), stresses how the competitive position of blacks, in job skills, for example, as well as discrimination, determined their progress (see. e.g., "Preface to the Phoenix Edition").

3 Other important characteristics of a migrant group include, for example, the prevalence of males, of literate individuals, and of permanent migrants. Pre-migration cultural attributes (attitudes, beliefs, values) may have helped determine the migrants' position as well. If these attributes

did not affect the second generation directly, however, its behavior may be explicable entirely in terms of social structure.

4   See Section 5.5 and also Chapter 2, note 9.

5   Even if we were to find (and we do not) that the ethnic differences unexplained by family background could be explained by the contextual effects of structural location, ethnicity would still remain a critical part of the story, for the behavior of a group could not be sensibly discussed without recourse to ethnic origin: The ethnic bond, not merely the structural location of individual families, would have created the context. Italians (in this hypothetical example) differed from others not simply because so many were laborers, for example, but because those who were not were tied economically and culturally to those who were.

6   The latter classification scheme also exploits information on the value of family property holdings. See the Appendix. Note, too, in connection with Table C.1, that (1) the odds ratio associated with a 20-point difference in occupational score (roughly the standard deviation of the fathers' occupations) is the ratio associated with a 1-point difference raised to the 20th power, and (2) the odds ratio associated with a 28-point difference in occupational score (roughly the difference between the average white-collar and blue-collar occupations) is the ratio associated with a 1-point difference raised to the 28th power. These two ratios therefore differ by more than the ratio of 28 to 20.

7   The comparisons involving the Italians include controls for the household head's citizenship status, because it may reflect the commitment to return to Italy. However, it may also reflect pre-migration cultural attributes. See Section 3.4.

8   For this reason, as well as because of the ambiguity involved in assessing magnitudes that have been squared, the R^2 explained by ethnicity and social class is not a useful measure for interpreting the significance of membership in particular ethnic groups. The R^2 associated with ethnicity generally was much smaller than the R^2 associated with social class. However, this outcome tells us very little of use concerning the magnitude of particular ethnic differences in behavior.

9   In any case, even if unmeasured contextual effects were assumed to be as large as the total effects of measured family background factors – surely a risky assumption – several of the residuals in Tables C.1 and C.2 would still remain large. The point is especially noteworthy because some of the family background characteristics controlled were related to contextual variables of interest (father's occupational score, household head's citizenship status, and involvement in commerce). When the family background variables explained relatively little of the ethnic difference, it seems unlikely that the corresponding contextual variables could account for much of it. On contextual effects as explanations of Irish–Yankee differences, see Appendix, note 40.

10 Olivier Zunz, *The Changing Face of Inequality: Urbanization, Industrial Development, and Immigrants in Detroit, 1880–1920* (Chicago, 1982); Zunz,

"The Synthesis of Social Change: Reflections on American Social History," in *Reliving the Past: The Worlds of Social History* (Chapel Hill, 1985), 53–114; Zunz, "American History and the Changing Meaning of Assimilation," with "Comment" by John Bodnar and by Stephan Thernstrom, *Journal of American Ethnic History*, vol. 4 (Spring 1985), 53–84.

11   Moreover, it should be recalled that there is nothing novel about the method used here (it is the standard method used in studies of ethnic differences).

12   See the relevant references in the preceding chapters for some of these. Thomas Sowell, *Ethnic America, A History* (New York, 1981), provides something of a compendium.

13   The challenges of studying restricted qualitative evidence are large. For example, one typical kind of study involves examination of the statements of ethnic leaders, such as those appearing in the immigrant press. Do such statements by an ethnic elite reflect the attitudes of the majority? A similar issue must be faced, of course, even if the evidence comes not from an ethnic leader but from a follower – a reader of the press, for example. Moreover, the work using nonquantitative methods must be genuinely comparative. The Slavic press may indeed have written editorials against the gross materialism of America. But were such sentiments uncommon in the Yiddish press? Indeed, did not the organs of the Yankee urban elites decry an excessive concern with the things of this world? The statements in the Slavic press may be indicative of a more complete rejection of material values, but how can this be shown? Evaluating the impact of cultural attributes on behavior with qualitative data is harder still. What method is available in such studies for assessing the relative importance of cultural attributes as sources of action – relative, that is, to each other and to other sources of behavior? These issues may be well known, and they exist for many kinds of historical work. However, to recognize that fact is not to resolve the difficulty or the choice of methods.

14   Concerning the observation that not all Italians or Slavs were in fact former peasants, see Section 3.5. There are, no doubt, exceptions to the generalization that the origins of cultural attributes can usually be found in economic and social history. At the very least, for example, one would want to include the Jews' centuries of minority status, not merely social-class position, as part of the relevant social history. In addition, the particular role of learning in eastern European Jewish religious life, though supported by social and economic developments, had sources in religious history as well. The commitment to learning is difficult to assess as a distinct source of later behavior by Russian Jews in America, but it cannot be ruled out on the basis of available evidence.

Another hint that more than pre-migration economic developments and social-class position may have operated in creating pre-migration cultural attributes involves European educational institutions. Their prevalence presumably had sources in addition to economic development, such as religious, cultural, and political constellations unique to particular countries. The prevalence of those institutions, in turn, probably influenced responses to American schooling.

By contrast, in American ethnic history, evidence of a Protestant–Catholic difference in world view (i.e., a distinctive Protestant work ethic) is generally difficult to distinguish from other sources of difference that characterize the same people. Moreover, in the present study, a Protestant work ethic cannot explain the evidence: Yankee–Irish differences before, but not after, 1900, and distinctive Italian patterns of schooling, but not of jobs.

15 Steinberg, *The Ethnic Myth*, ix–x.

16 Sowell, *Ethnic America*, 194–200, 216–20. See references to Glazer's work in Section 4.1. Steinberg, *The Ethnic Myth*, ix–x.

17 On this question, Stephen Steinberg's important and generally clear analysis (*The Ethnic Myth*) does not provide a useful answer. His work was meant as a rebuttal to the "failure to consider class factors [that] has been characteristic of nearly half a century of social research" (p. 139), as well as to other alarming trends of thought that tended to obscure and romanticize the nature of ethnic differences (pp. ix–x). He discusses the interaction of culture and social structure, stressing issues such as those raised in the preceding paragraphs of the text. However, on the influence of pre-migration attributes in the American context, his formulations are vague and his evidence weak. He seems to assume not merely the dependence of culture on social structure in the long run, but its dependence and secondary nature even within the American social structure in the decades following immigration: "Where the class theory differs from the cultural theory is in its emphasis on the *primacy* of class factors. That is to say, it is held that cultural factors have little independent effect on educational outcomes, but are influential only as they interact with class factors" (p. 132). At the same time, he notes, for example, that "obviously, [Southern Italian] immigrants from peasant backgrounds were not likely to have the same outlook upon education as other immigrants, including Northern Italians, who came from more industrially advanced sectors of their countries of origin" (p. 141). However, he eventually concludes that "in short, if Italians and other Catholics have not excelled academically, this cannot be blamed on a value system that discouraged education, since these values themselves only reflect the operation of social class factors and the unfavorable structure of educational opportunity that confronts the lower classes generally" (p. 144). Leaving aside the issue of "other Catholics," the third passage seems to rule out the importance of the pre-migration cultural attributes recognized in the second, unless "the operation of social class factors" is meant to cover the pre-migration class structure as well. In either case, the question that emerges from the second passage (and is not answered clearly in the first or third) is the question stressed here, and, I believe, the question around which important debate has centered: Just how much did pre-migration cultural attributes (whatever their origin) determine patterns of behavior in America?

The evidence from the early part of the century on which Steinberg was obliged to rely is generally restricted to showing that the social compositions of ethnic groups differed and that these differences could reasonably be expected to have affected outcomes such as schooling and occupational attainments. The Providence data show that these factors did indeed influence the relevant outcomes, but not to a degree that would eliminate serious consideration of pre-migration cultural attributes.

18 Also, the nature of particular attributes may have been transformed. If, for example, the Jewish tradition of learning did have an important impact on the Jews' advancement in the New World, or in modern Europe, it was only because that tradition could be shifted to focus on secular learning rather than on religious study. That process may have been aided by the relative distance of most eastern European Jewish migrants from such study, while still accepting its status. See the concluding pages of Chapter 4.

For a discussion of the transformation of Italian views of women, see Donna R. Gabaccia, *From Sicily to Elizabeth Street: Housing and Social Change Among Italian Immigrants, 1890–1930* (Albany, 1984), 111–16.

19 Bodnar, "Schooling and the Slavic-American Family, 1900–1940," in Bernard J. Weiss, ed., *American Education and the European Immigrant, 1840–1940* (Urbana, 1982), 78–95, especially 85–6.

20 Interactions between the contextual effects of class composition and ethnic identity also may have had some effects; these we cannot measure. The techniques used to assess contextual effects cannot be extended to interactions with ethnicity, because the contextual and ethnicity variables cannot be entered in a regression model together. See Appendix, Section 9.

21 The pattern of the Irish in 1880 seems to point to the same conclusions as that of the Italians, but because discrimination leveled against the Irish may have been distinctly important, the Italians present the clearer case.

Perhaps the Jewish experience, as a minority engaged in commercial roles, is helpful in thinking about a few other groups, such as the Armenians.

Appendix

1 See Joel Perlmann, "Using Census Districts in Analysis, Record Linkage and Sampling" (a research note), *Journal of Interdisciplinary History*, vol. 10 (Autumn 1979), 279–89, Perlmann, "The Use of Student Records for the Study of American Educational History," *Historical Methods*, vol. 12 (Spring 1979), 66–75, the Appendices to Perlmann, "Who Stayed in School? Academic Achievement and Social Structure in the Determination of Enrollment Patterns, Providence, R.I. 1880–1925," *Journal of American History*, vol. 72 (December 1985), 588–614, and especially Perlmann, "Education and the Social Structure of an American City: Providence, R.I. 1880–1925: The Research Design and the Data Collection" (final report

submitted to the National Institute of Education, and document no. 170–220 in the E.R.I.C. [Educational Research Information Clearinghouse] microfiche collection), or the Appendix in Perlmann, "Education and the Social Structure of an American City: Social Origins and Educational Attainments in Providence, R.I. 1880–1925" (Ph.D. dissertation, Harvard University, 1980). An early, undistributed working paper, Perlmann, "The City Directory: The Quality of Its Coverage and Errors Resulting from Its Use, Providence, R.I. 1880–1935" (1977), also concerned methodological issues.

2   Women were also traced across time. They could not, however, be traced in the city directories, because those volumes regularly omitted large proportions of women and because even those included might not be found under their maiden names. Women were traced, instead, to marriage records, which also provided information on whom they married. The data on women's occupations, however, are not included in this study. Consequently, the use of the marriage records is not discussed here.

Male sample members were traced twenty years forward in time, as well as ten, but those data involved reductions in sample size that were not counterbalanced by the additional evidence about the rest (see Section 1.5). Similarly, the young adult males were also traced across time in tax books, but that evidence also was not used (see note 29).

3   Originally, the inclusion of those eleven to twelve years of age in 1880 was undertaken to permit comparisons between a randomly selected group of that age and a special sample (not used in this study) of those age eleven to twelve not attending school. Extending the age range by two years, however, was also advantageous because it increased sample size by half.

4   Statistical analyses were all based on the assumption of simple random sampling. The chief drawback of any sample not based on a purely random selection is that it may involve some unsuspected bias. The census pages are arranged by enumeration districts and, within district, by whatever route the census-takers chose to follow. It is difficult to see what socially important variables would not be accurately represented by selecting every nth page of the manuscript. Nevertheless, for a method of random selection using these records, see Joel Perlmann, "Using Census Districts in Analysis, Record Linkage and Sampling," 279–89.

When the handwriting in the census manuscripts was illegible, the case was skipped, and the first person in the age range listed on the following page(s) was selected instead. Replacements were rarely needed, except in the 1900 U.S. Census. The manuscript for that year had been through the smoke and water of a fire and also was difficult to read because a Census Bureau code had been written over many names.

5   The supplemental samples include all Jewish boys, three-quarters of the Jewish girls, half of the Italian and Irish boys and one-quarter of the girls. In each case, the proportions were obtained by sampling certain pages, in the manner described earlier.

6 "The 1905 Rhode Island Census," in *Twentieth Report of the Commissioner of Industrial Statistics* (Providence, 1907). On using the Russian-born as a surrogate for East European Jews, see Joel Perlmann, "Beyond New York: The Occupations of Russian Jewish Immigrants in Providence, R.I. and in Other Small Jewish Communities, 1900–1915," *American Jewish History*, vol. 72 (March 1983), 369–94.

7 Many runs were carried out with and without the high school sample members present, however, to be sure that, weighting notwithstanding, the results were not artifacts of the methods.

8 See my dissertation and final report to the NIE (cited in note 1).

9 In selecting the entrants, year of entry rather than age was the criterion. It seemed worth suffering a small loss of comparability to the samples drawn from the censuses in order to obtain profiles of entire classes.

10 For further details, see Perlmann, "Using Census Districts."

11 It might also be noted that the grade attainments, such as high school entry, reported in this study are generally lower than those reported in the 1940–70 U.S. Censuses for cohorts of comparable ages in the region. Some possible reasons for the differences include (1) the variation in educational attainment rates by place within the Northeast, (2) differential mortality by education in retrospective census data, (3) reporting errors by respondents or census-takers, particularly in converting years of school attendance into highest grade completed, and (4) missing data in the Providence samples. A rough perusal of published figures on enrollments and age cohorts indicates that the differences between the census data and the Providence data probably are due principally to the first factor, and in any case, not to the last.

    For example, according to the 1960 U.S. Census, 37.3% of the males sixty-five to seventy-four years of age who were born and resident in the Northeast had completed at least one year of high school. The comparable proportion among those fifty-five to sixty-four years of age was 47.0%. Among the Providence male sample members (twelve to sixteen years old in the census year), 17.1% had entered high school in 1900, and 33.6% in 1915. The Immigration Commission *Reports* (Washington, D.C., 1911, vols. 30–33) present figures for Providence that are roughly comparable to the sample data, with an estimated 28.1% of the age cohort reaching the first year of high school in 1908 (based on the ratio of first-year high school pupils to pupils twelve years of age in the public schools). The Immigration Commission data also show that the comparable figure varied widely, even within the larger urban areas. Among the fourteen large northeastern and north-central cities the commission studied, it was under 20% in two, 20–29% in six, 30–39% in three, 40–49% in two, and 68.7% in one (from Table 1, public school general investigation for each city; the median for the fourteen cities was 28.7%).

12 Some of the influences on age of school entry were the same as those on age of school leaving; others were not. These latter probably affected both the patterns of length of schooling and the patterns of high school entry in complicated and largely irrelevant ways. Age at school entry

would be important if many immigrant children entered the first grade at advanced ages. However, the analysis in the preceding chapters distinguishes native and foreign-born children of immigrants and concentrates on the former.

13 Curriculum coding for high school students was based in part on the designations found in the records. However, for many students, no curriculum was listed. This was the case for schools in which curricula did not entail enrollment in departments, but only completion of particular courses. In these schools, if the student did not graduate, the designation was not listed. However, extensive information on courses had been coded, as described later. Close study of the requirements for each curriculum and of course enrollment patterns permitted me to construct rules for assigning students to curricula based on the kinds of courses in which they were enrolled in their first year of high school.

14 No single course was chosen to reflect academic achievement, because the courses required (in all subjects) varied widely over time and across institutions. A maximum (six grades) was therefore selected from one term, the end of the first year of attendance at high school (before too many students had dropped out, but after an initial period of adjustment). For those who had already dropped out, semester or quarter grades were taken instead. If a student repeated a grade, the first set of marks was used. A similar procedure was used in recording grammar school grades: Those from the beginning of the sixth grade were taken; if the student had already dropped out, fifth-grade marks were substituted. Finally, for those remaining in high school at least five semesters, the penultimate semester's marks were taken for comparison with the first-year marks.

15 The proportion of children who had never reached grammar school was estimated from age–grade reports. These were published in the Providence School Committee's annual reports for 1917 and later years. By comparing the numbers attending public schools at ages thirteen and seven, one arrives at an estimate of the proportion still in school at age thirteen (about 90% in 1915, 95% in 1925). Among those enrolled at age thirteen, about 10% in both 1915 and 1925 were not then enrolled in grammar school. Therefore, one can estimate the proportion of those who had never reached grammar school among those who had dropped out of school before age thirteen (assume that that proportion is two to five times as high as it is among those thirteen years old who were still in school). By these calculations, 0.11–0.14 of the cohort did not reach grammar school in 1915 $[0.10 \times 0.90 + (0.20–0.40) \times 0.10 = 0.11–0.14]$, and 0.11–0.12 did not in 1925 $[0.10 \times 0.95 + (0.20–0.50) \times 0.05 = 0.11–0.12]$. Some other students (but not many) must have left grammar school before being graded. Perhaps, too, the attrition was slightly higher in 1912–16 than in 1917 and after (the years for which the age–grade reports are available). However, the estimate cited in the text, 11–20% (rather than the 11–14% range calculated here), allows for such possibilities.

The other source of bias was the unavailability of records from some grammar schools. Catholic grammar school records and the records for five public grammar schools covering at least part of the period relevant to the 1915 sample were unavailable. The proportion of children age eleven to thirteen in Catholic schools, according to the annual reports, was 17–18%. These figures suggest that perhaps 10–19% of the public grammar school records were missing in 1915 (of the 47% whose records were unavailable, between 11% and 20% had dropped out, and a further 17% were in Catholic schools, leaving 10–19% missing) and that virtually none were missing in 1925. On the relation of attrition to GPA, see Perlmann, "Who Stayed in School?"

16   Sample members were also traced in the catalogs of the Rhode Island School of Design and the Rhode Island Normal School (later the Rhode Island College of Education). These two institutions included post-secondary programs, and their records contributed to our knowledge of extended schooling among the sample members. The annual catalogs of both included lists of students. If other school records indicated that the sample member had earlier completed high school, enrollment at these institutions was treated as post-secondary. Otherwise, it was recorded as secondary.

17   The evolution of the laws pertaining to the working papers and school census are described in Charles C. Carroll, *Public Education in Rhode Island* (Providence, 1918), 200–2, passim.

18   On the commercial schools, see Edmund J. James, "Commercial Education," in Nicholas M. Butler, ed., *Education in the United States: A Series of Monographs* (Albany, 1906), 653–704.

19   Rules for tolerable differences in ages reported in school and census records were established. Few matches were ambiguous, but research assistants referred all those that were to me. For a fuller description, see the references in note 1.

20   Providence School Committee, *Reports* for 1875–1935, and its *Manual* for the same years (the latter has the title *Directory of the Public School* in some years). The author of the most detailed history of Rhode Island, Charles C. Carroll, came to his subject from studies of the educational history of the state. Several long chapters in his history, as well as his other work, provide a guide to the evolution of the schools. See Charles C. Carroll, *Public Education in Rhode Island* (Providence, 1918), and *Rhode Island: Three Centuries of Democracy* (New York, 1932). See also Sadlier's *Catholic Directory, Almanac and Ordo* (New York, published annually; title and publisher vary), Americao Lapati, "A History of Catholic Education in Rhode Island" (unpublished doctoral dissertation, Boston College, 1958), Mary C. Morgan, *Little Sketch of the Work of the Sisters of Mercy in Providence, R.I. from 1851 to 1893* (Providence, 1893), and Thomas B. Stockwell, *A History of Public Education in Rhode Island from 1636 to 1876* (Providence, 1876). The catalogs of the major private schools are available at the Rhode Island Historical Society Library and Brown University Library. Finally, invaluable records for the schools between 1893 and 1920 are found in tables published in Rhode Island Commissioner of Public Schools, *An-*

nual Report, for 1892–1921. They include enrollment by sex, number of graduates, number of students over age fifteen, and other information for every private school in the state and every public high school. When a school failed to report (a violation of state law), the school's name was still listed.

I also checked the records themselves in various ways to be sure they constituted complete collections. For example, I verified that they included both boys and girls, graduates and nongraduates, all parts of the alphabet and (in the case of high schools) all known curricula, and all relevant years of entry. Finally, for every public grammar school and high school in the 1915 and 1925 periods, numbers of graduates were selected from the newspaper lists and traced in the record cards.

21 Extensive efforts to test the resulting patterns of schooling against published data were described in my earlier discussions of the data-collection effort, and the findings were satisfactory. But, in fact, as stressed there, the tests are most important for determining the quality of the incomplete primary and grammar school data, rather than the much better high school data. Such tests involved constructing estimates of expected patterns from published school records, and all the estimates required many assumptions, each including some range for error. For example, the expected number of sample members entering Classical High School could be estimated from the school's total male enrollment, but only by assuming male dropout rates for each class over several years, as well as the distribution of entry ages. If such estimates were constructed from published sources, and were in fact found to be discrepant from the high school data, we would be well advised to attribute the discrepancy to errors in the crude assumptions required, not to the quality of the high school data.

22 For a critique of the school census procedures in Providence in the 1920s, see Division of Field Studies, Institute of Educational Research, Teacher's College, Columbia University, *Report of the Survey of Certain Aspects of the Public School System of Providence, Rhode Island, School Year 1923–1924* (New York, 1925). It would be naive to think that census procedures had been any better in earlier years.

23 Whereas all other male sample members were traced a decade across time, the eleven- and twelve-year-old boys selected from the 1880 census schedules were not traced in the directory of 1890, but in the directory for 1892 (comparability in age seemed more important than comparability in the year in which they were traced).

24 Stephan Thernstrom, *The Other Bostonians: Poverty and Progress in the American Metropolis, 1880–1970* (Cambridge, Mass., 1973), 270, urged such a strategy; his samples had been limited to individuals with uncommon names.

25 One might wonder if the presence of residential information meant that research assistants coded cases into the third category when they should have placed them in the fourth. That possibility is unlikely. Coding was done on the basis of commonness of name; if a sample member had a

name appearing but once in the directory, he was coded as found, and residential information was not consulted. If his name appeared more than once, the residential checks were made. Many months later, those found on the basis of name only were retraced in the directories in order to ascertain whether or not residential evidence also existed – permitting the analysis presented in Tables A.3 and A.4.

26 Sidney Goldstein and Kurt B. Meyer, *Metropolitanization and Population Change in Rhode Island* (Providence, 1962), 27–30. It should be noted that these towns are not all "suburbs." In some cases, notably much of Pawtucket and Central Falls, they are simply extensions of the same urban industrial area as Providence.

All the relevant directories were treated as one in determining if an individual had indeed been found: If the name appeared more than once in all out-of-town directories taken together, it was considered a common name. Few additional sample members, approximately 150 in all samples together, were found in these traces, perhaps because the Providence directory itself listed appreciable numbers living in surrounding towns.

27 This discussion is based on Alba Edwards, "A Social Economic Grouping of the Gainful Workers of the United States," *Journal of the American Statistical Association*, vol. 27 (1933), 377–87, and *Comparative Occupational Statistics for the United States, 1870–1940* (Washington, D.C., 1943), James Scoville, "The Development and Relevance of U.S. Occupational Data," *Industrial and Labor Relations Review*, vol. 19 (1965), 71–9, Gladys Palmer, "The Convertibility List of Occupations and the Problems of Developing It," *Journal of the American Statistical Association*, vol. 34 (1939), Otis Dudley Duncan, "A Socioeconomic Index for All Occupations," in Albert J. Reiss, *Occupations and Social Status* (New York, 1969), and Thernstrom, *The Other Bostonians*, Appendix B. On occupational classification generally, see also the discussion and references cited in Chapter 1.

28 Because both Duncan and Thernstrom relied on the alphabetical index of 1950, that seemed the logical one for me to use also. The only earlier one incorporating Edwards's work is the very similar 1940 index. Also, in 1940, a category of semiprofessional workers was used, and in 1950 all these workers were "promoted" to professionals. I retained the semiprofessional classification and followed Thernstrom in classifying those workers as low white-collar workers.

29 A few rare occupational titles, accounting for roughly 3% of all occupations coded, did not receive discrete codes. About half of the occupational descriptions included an industrial modification; 80% of these modifications were coded distinctly. Occupational titles and the industrial modifications not receiving a distinct code were nearly all coded at the level of detail retained by the Census Bureau. A tiny proportion (0.5%) not listed in the bureau's index were assigned to a broad stratum only. These cases were omitted from regression analyses because no occupational score had been assigned to them.

Thernstrom had distinguished between major and petty proprietors, designating as major those possessing real property assessed at $5,000 or more, or personal property assessed at $1,000. He assigned these to the high white-collar category. I used the same cutoff points, except in 1925, when they were raised to $7,500 and $1,500, respectively, because of a general rise in assessed property values. It probably would have been wiser to sacrifice comparability with Thernstrom's study and code assessed property values on a continuous scale. However, efforts to re-run some analyses controlling for a continuous property variable produced minuscule differences in the coefficients of interest.

Finally, the male sample members located in the directory were traced in tax books, but because so few were found with holdings, and because the data involved a problematic coding scheme, the tax evidence was not used. In the rare tables in which the young men were classified by strata, rather than by occupational score, the assignments to strata were also made without using tax data. Because these classifications involved only distinguishing which young men were white-collar workers (rather than distinguishing between high and low white-collar), the tax data would in any case have been of minimal use.

30 I was most compulsive about the forward traces in directories, checking approximately every tenth case throughout. For other operations, I generally checked one in fifteen or one in twenty-five, or even (for the simplest operations) one in forty.

31 The SAS programs CATMOD and REG were used for this work. Models studied with logit analyses generally were also run in OLS regression using the linear probability model for a second perspective.

32 On the common name problems involved in use of the property tax data, see Appendix, Section 5. Unless otherwise indicated, father's age was not included in the regression models. Its inclusion would not have affected the results in important ways. It should be recalled that the samples were restricted to children of certain ages or to high school entrants. Consequently, even assuming that important differences existed in the average age of members of ethnic groups, these differences would be reflected only in muted ways in the average ages of the fathers of young adolescents in these groups. The differences in means and standard deviations of fathers' ages were in fact small. In 1880, for example, the means (and standard deviations) of father's age were: Yankees, 45.6 (8.1); Irish, 46.6 (7.7); blacks 44.0 (8.8). In 1915 the relevant figures were: Yankees, 46.1 (6.2); Irish, 46.5 (6.0); blacks 44.8 (8.9); Italians, 45.5 (7.2); Russian Jews 43.8 (6.6). The trivial effect of omitting a control for father's age may be seen directly in two examples. When the logit regression model used in the first panel of Table 4.3 was rerun with a control for father's age, the t statistic for that control was 0.64; the odds ratios comparing the Russian Jews with the other five ethnic groups listed varied from those shown in the table by 0.02 or less. Similarly, when the OLS regression model used in the first panel of Table 4.10 was rerun with a control for father's age, the t statistic for that control was 0.25; the coefficients

comparing the Russian Jews with the other five ethnic groups listed varied from those shown in the table by 0.1 point on the occupational scale or less.

33 For examples, see Perlmann, "Who Stayed in School?" Appendix. Note that whereas the logit coefficients divided by the *t* statistics will give the standard errors, the errors are not symmetrical around the logit coefficients when the latter are in exponentiated form.

34 Weights were always added for members of the sample of high school entrants, even when controls for high school entry were included in the regression, because some high schools were not included in the high school samples, and sampling ratios differed by school (see Section 2B). It seemed preferable to weight them than to include high school of origin in the regressions, because that factor could have been related to other variables and could have complicated the analysis and exposition. For additional details on the treatment of missing data, see Chapter 5, note 29.

35 On contextual effects, see the useful review of the literature in sociology and social psychology by Hubert M. Blalock, Jr., "Contextual Effects Models: Theoretical and Methodological Issues," *Annual Review of Sociology*, vol. 10 (1984), 353–72, Blalock and Paul H. Wilken, *Intergroup Processes: a Micro-Macro Perspective* (New York, 1979), chap. 7, especially 288–300, and Robert M. Hauser, "Contextual Analysis Revisited," *Sociological Methods and Research*, vol. 2 (1974), 365–75.

36 Other measures tested included the proportions of the group in various categories: unskilled, low manual, blue-collar, white-collar, employers. Also, the proportion of males among migrants was studied, but as it correlated so highly with the proportion remigrating ($r = 0.69$), it was necessary to consider only one or the other. Because the proportions of males in several groups were not readily available, the remigration rate was used. See Thomas J. Archdeacon, *Becoming American: An Ethnic History* (New York, 1983), 139.

37 The remigration rates were derived from Archdeacon, *Becoming American*, 118–19. It might at first sight seem that the proportion of citizens in the group would be a good measure of remigration tendencies in Providence. However, that proportion would cover only those Italians living in families with a teenage child. The contextual effects of interest also concern the wider community, which included many other Italians. A similar argument could be made in connection with the contextual effects of the group's class composition (that the mean occupational score of all Italian workers, including young men, was much lower than that of sampled family heads, and that the difference was greater than in other ethnic groups). However, because remigration appears to have been more concentrated among the single men than were low-level occupations, the argument carries more force in connection with remigration than with class composition.

38 More precisely, in a logit regression analysis, high school entry was regressed on the variables indicated. The ethnic categories could not them-

selves be entered into the model because they correlated perfectly with the return rate (or mean occupational score), and a situation of perfect multicollinearity would have resulted. Rather, the procedure was to substitute a continuous variable, the return rate (or the mean occupational score), for the ethnic dummy variables. The procedure involved calculating

$$a - b \cdot c$$

where a is the logit coefficient for the ethnic term from the earlier regression in which family characteristics, household head's citizenship status, and ethnicity were controlled (the regression used for Table 3.9), b is the logit regression coefficient for the contextual effect (the rise in the log odds of high school entry associated with a unit increase in the contextual-effect variable), and c is the number of units by which the Italians differed from all others on the contextual-effect variable (percentage of return migrants, or points on the occupational scale). The result was exponentiated.

It will be recalled that the regressions compare native-born children of Italians with all other native-born children. The remigration rate for all native-born was determined by a weighted average for all the ethnic groups of the city. It made little difference whether the children of natives were included (and assigned a remigration rate of zero) or excluded. A second method was also used, producing parallel findings. The logit coefficients on ethnic dummy variables obtained when high school entry was regressed on family background factors were themselves regressed on the return rate for each ethnic group. Expected values for the ethnic differences in entry rates were obtained and compared with the actual values.

39 Obviously, an omitted variable could also act to suppress the true strength of an association. In the present context, in which several possible reasons for spurious correlations come to mind, spuriousness is the more serious concern.

40 In obtaining the coefficient for the mean occupational score's association with high school entry, the Italians were omitted from the regression analysis. This procedure was used when it became clear that their inclusion was dramatically inflating the coefficient (no other omission of a single group had a comparable effect on its magnitude). The assumption is that the increase in the association was spurious and was caused by factors other than the remigration rate. Rejecting that view, one would still be obliged to acknowledge that the association was strongly nonlinear, such that the Italians behaved in a different way than the association based on the other groups predicts.

For similar reasons, the contextual effects of the Irish social-class position were not assessed in Chapter 2. A regression of high school entry on the mean for fathers' occupational scores in each group in 1880, the critical year, would largely reflect the Yankee–Irish differences on both variables (because the city included fewer other groups in that year than in 1915, and these two composed three-quarters of the sample). Explorations of these effects in Chapters 3–5, however, strongly suggest that they did not create the change in Irish patterns observed over time (also, the mean for fathers' occupational scores for the Irish changed by only 3 points over those two decades).

41   The census data on medians are from U.S. Census Bureau, *Nativity and Parentage*, Table 12; the Commissioner of Immigration's figures for remigration are conveniently tabulated by Archdeacon, *Becoming American*, 118–19. Categories of immigrant origins differed between the two sets of figures. For the purposes of the association, Scandinavian was equated with Norway and Sweden; Bohemian and Moravian and Slovak with Czechoslovakia; Croatian, Slovenian, Dalmatian, Bosnian, Herzegovinian, Bulgarian, Serbian, and Montenegrin with Yugoslavia; Hebrew, Russian, and Ruthenian with the USSR. French and other Canadian were combined. The other groups included were British, Irish, German, Polish, Hungarian, Lithuanian, Finnish, and Italian. Mexicans, although included in both reports, were excluded from the calculation. Their pattern of school achievement differed dramatically from that for any of the European groups (the Italian median level of schooling among those fifty-five to sixty-four years old was 8.4 years; among the Mexicans, it was 4.3 years). Their inclusion would sharply skew the results, but would have much less relevance to the patterns of interest here.

42   These three reduced the odds that other boys would enroll in high school, compared with the odds that Italians would do so, from 3.17 to 1.76, a reduction ratio of 0.56 (1.76/3.17 = 0.56). The supposed contextual effects of remigration would imply a further reduction to 0.60, a reduction ratio of 0.34 (0.60/1.76 = 0.34). Among girls, the corresponding reduction ratios are 0.59 and 0.20.

Index